D0322384

AMERICAN ARCHIVES

THE MASQUERADE.

HOUSEWORTH, PHOTO.,   12 MONTGOMERY ST., SAN FRANCISCO

Thomas Houseworth and Company, *The Masquerade*, cabinet card advertisement.
Reproduced from the collection of Peter Palmquist.

AMERICAN ARCHIVES

GENDER, RACE, AND CLASS
IN VISUAL CULTURE

Shawn Michelle Smith

PRINCETON UNIVERSITY PRESS   PRINCETON, NEW JERSEY

The author gratefully acknowledges permission to reprint two chapters of this book that
were previously published elsewhere. Chapter 4 first appeared in *Yale Journal of Criticism* 11:1
(Spring 1998). Chapter 6 was published originally in *With Other Eyes: Looking at Race and
Gender in Visual Culture*, edited by Lisa Bloom (University of Minnesota Press, 1999).

Library of Congress Cataloging-in-Publication Data
Smith, Shawn Michelle, 1965–
American archives: gender, race, and class in visual culture/Shawn Michelle Smith.
p. cm.
Includes bibliographical references and index.
ISBN 0-691-00477-3 (cloth: alk. paper).— ISBN 0-691-00478-1 (pbk.: alk. paper)
1. Portrait photography—United States—History—19th century. 2. United States—Social
life and customs—19th century. 3. Social classes—United States—History—19th century.
I. Title.
TR680.S59 1999
306.4—dc21
99–20126

For Jay, Sandy, Shannon, and Joe

Contents

Illustrations

Acknowledgments

THIS BOOK is indebted to the efforts of many wise and kind people. I would like to thank Mary Ison and Jan Grenci for their generous help in the Prints and Photographs Division at the Library of Congress, Jennifer McClain for her assistance in the archives of the National Society of the Daughters of the American Revolution, and Lois Kettel for graciously offering me her home while I conducted research in Washington, D.C. My early work on this project was supported by a Predoctoral Humanities Dissertation Fellowship at the University of California, San Diego. A grant from the College of Liberal Arts at Washington State University helped me to secure many of the images for the book.

The members of my dissertation committee, Michael Davidson, Nicole Tonkovich, Wai Chee Dimock, Roddey Reid, Phel Steinmetz, and Stephanie McCurry, helped shape my first thoughts along these lines, and I am grateful for their many insights, which continue to inspire, and for the care with which they directed my research and writing. I am also indebted to Carolyn Haynes and Molly Rhodes for their critical commentary and good humor, and to Marsanne Brammer, Wendy Walters, Elise Hanley, Krista Lydia Roybal, Dave Harden, Mark Jenkins, and Linda Baker for their unwavering support. Lisa Bloom, Priscilla Wald, and Laura Wexler offered thoughtful and important suggestions that helped me to revise and expand the argument of this book, and I am thankful for their keen intellectual generosity. I have learned much from and felt sustained by conversations with Joan Burbick, Carol Siegel, and Maggie Sale, and I have come to depend especially upon the wisdom and cheer of T. V. Reed and Shelli Fowler. Deborah Malmud has been a wonderful editor, and I am grateful to her for guiding me through the final stages of this project. The constant encouragement of Jay, Sandy, and Shannon Smith has meant everything to me, and this book endeavors to live up to their examples of rigor and creativity. Finally, for Joe Masco, who cared for every word, let me count the ways.

AMERICAN ARCHIVES

American Archives

In "A Small History of Photography," Walter Benjamin proclaims, "Sudden shifts of power such as are now overdue in our society can make the ability to read facial types a matter of vital importance. Whether one is of the left or right, one will have to get used to being looked at in terms of one's provenance. And one will have to look at others the same way."[1] As he predicts radical social upheaval, Benjamin envisions a particular social use for the photographic portrait, one in the service of physiognomy. He celebrates photographer August Sander's catalogue of facial types (1930) as a precursor to a "scientific" archive that would function as antidote to the self-congratulatory, commercial use of the middle-class photographic portrait. Instead of displaying the signifiers of middle-class "taste"—curtains and pedestals, pillars and palm trees (247)—a scientific archive of photographic portraits, according to Benjamin, would enable a close reading of the face itself and a subsequent reevaluation of an individual's social worth. In Benjamin's "small history," the scientific photographic archive would help to establish a new social order in the midst of revolutionary chaos. Photographic technologies would enable recodifications of the body and reconfigurations of the social sphere.

This book proposes that photographic archives did indeed change the ways in which Americans viewed themselves and others throughout the century predating Benjamin's reflections, and it suggests that these nineteenth-century archives were anything but revolutionary (in Benjamin's sense of the term). In fact, *American Archives* studies the *convergence* of scientific and commercial photography in the constitution and transformation of middle-class identities in the nineteenth century. The "scientific" catalogue of facial types that Benjamin celebrates had ominous precursors in the nineteenth-century archives of criminologists, biological racialists, and eugenicists. By examining such archives, this study problematizes Benjamin's faith in physiognomy and demonstrates that the "types" on which Benjamin sought to ground a new social order were just as constructed as (and at least as pernicious as) the class structures he hoped to dismantle. *American Archives* argues that a catalogue of "essential" facial types was integral to the production of a *racialized* middle-class identity over the course of the nineteenth century.

The period of this study is inaugurated in 1839, by the introduction in the United States of daguerreotypy, the earliest form of photography. It spans the years 1839–1910, and thus traverses decades of tremendous social change in America, although certainly not the kind of anticapitalist transformation Benjamin would later anticipate. Indeed, the middle to late nineteenth century saw the consolidation of industrial capitalism and the ascendance of commodity capitalism in the United States. It saw the rise of the middle classes to social dominance, and with them new discourses of gender identity. And of course the period was not only one of class and gender transformation but also one of racial reinscription, marked by the Civil War and the legal and scientific reformulation of racialized American identities. Amid these social transformations, photographic archives grew in many different forms, particularly after the advent of reproducible photography in the 1850s. These archives, as Allan Sekula has argued, delineated the terrain both of the privileged white middle classes and of criminal and racial others.[2] The photographic archive generated and maintained essentialized discourses of interior character, and trained observers in how to read the body for the signs of a knowable interiority. Over the course of the nineteenth century, the photographic portrait inhabited archives as diverse as Mathew Brady's artistic Gallery of Illustrious Americans, Thomas Byrnes's criminological Rogues' Gallery, Francis Galton's scientific catalogues of racial "types," the "American Negro" exhibit at the 1900 Paris Exposition, and the middle-class family photograph album. Thus, it is not incongruous to introduce this study of nineteenth-century American visual culture with Benjamin's thoughts on photographic portraiture and physiognomy. For despite the categorical difference in the kind of social upheaval Benjamin awaited in the early twentieth century and that which occurred in late-nineteenth-century America, the period of this study was one in which Americans increasingly utilized new visual technologies to "read facial types" and to establish social hierarchies anchored in new visual "truths."

American Archives proposes that the processes whereby identity was envisioned in the nineteenth century produced a model of subjectivity in which exterior appearance was imagined to reflect interior essence. Bodies were mapped as the vehicles of gendered and racialized interior essences; that is, bodies were posed as the surface signs of interior depths. To "read" a body was to inscribe it with an imagined interiority, an essence that linked one to a specific position in a social hierarchy. As Judith Butler has suggested, "Interiority is an effect and function of a decidedly public and social discourse, the public regulation of fantasy through the surface politics of the body."[3] *American Archives* examines how nineteenth-century middle-class Americans utilized visual conceptions of identity to claim a gendered and racialized cultural privilege. The middle classes engaged "the surface politics of the body" in order to establish social boundaries founded in the name of discursively naturalized interior essences.

Photographic practitioners as diverse as artists, criminologists, and early race scientists utilized the photographic archive to inscribe the body's surface with an imagined depth—an ephemeral essence, a gendered and racialized character. Paradoxically, however, by throwing the body relentlessly into focus, photography highlighted the very constructed and contingent nature of the interiorities on which so much came to depend in nineteenth-century American self-conceptions. If interiority was the essence imagined to be stable as external signs fluctuated, it was stabilized only through the proliferation of surface signs, of representations of the body, called upon to make such essences readable, apparent, knowable. The photographic sign invited one to participate in a leap of faith whereby the body might serve as index to an imagined essence. And by this same leap of faith, by the same process of metonymy, individuals could imagine themselves linked to others similarly represented, and thereby mutually affirm an imagined essence. Photographic self-representation, then, enabled one to claim a visible, tangible, representable space in a community that could now be imagined in new ways, through new technologies of vision.

Inscriptions of "depth" (the depths whereby Benjamin's faces can be read as "types") were enabled by reference to a set of discourses the photographic archive in turn upheld. The photograph signaled an "essence" narrated for it by sentimental and scientific discourses. However, as the photograph literally gave middle-class discourses of gendered and racialized interiorities a face, it also circumscribed such discourses, framing and delimiting signifying possibilities. As photographs were called upon to signal what gender and race "look like," they generated patterns that would dictate future inscriptions of the body and challenges to that knowledge. As photographs enabled middle-class Americans to envision and to codify imagined discursive properties, they came to establish and to offer codes with distinct genealogies. In other words, photographs shaped and directed the discourses that gave them meaning.

Thus, *American Archives* suggests that visual culture not only reflects but also shapes the racialized formation of American identities. Archives of photographs with distinct visual genealogies function as sites through which narratives of national belonging and exclusion are produced. The nation itself, as "imagined community,"[4] is not simply the referent of photographic images but also the product. In the nineteenth century, state-sponsored institutional archives such as the Rogues' Gallery of criminal offenders and scientific archives of racial others created a normative space that delimited the bounds of "true" national belonging. Such archives marked the limits of white middle-class American identity and encouraged constant surveillance of the social body for "deviant" outsiders. At the same time, the family photograph album offered individuals a colloquial space in which to display practices of national belonging. Through repeated codes of dress, props, and poses, amateur photographers, much like Benedict Anderson's anonymous newspaper readers,[5] could link themselves to others whom they would never meet through the increasingly standardized rituals of photographic self-representation. Using the same photographic technologies and tropes, individuals could mutually affirm their places in an imagined community rooted in discursive fantasies of national character.

Over the course of the nineteenth century, shifting understandings of gender, race, and class circumscribed one's ability to observe and to self-represent in relation to such "official" archives. Certainly not everyone had equal access to the images of national character. But the limits of an imagined visual community were always contested, and I am interested in how dominant narratives were not only produced and reinscribed but also challenged and reconfigured in nineteenth-century popular self-understandings and representational practices. *American Archives* is thus not only a study of "official" representations and discourses but also a study of the practices whereby individuals reproduce, resist, and transform dominant images and conceptions.[6]

American Archives explores how visual technologies and visual paradigms enabled middle-class Americans to imagine bodies infused with interior essences. More specifically, I examine how the terms in which the middle classes invested these architectures of interiority were transformed over the course of the nineteenth century. I begin by demonstrating how the antebellum middle classes posed interior essence primarily in terms of gender, to trace how the postbellum middle classes reinscribed that essence with racialized significance. Over the course of the nineteenth century, the sciences of biological racialism reproduced gendered interiority in terms of blood and "race," transforming the body into the sign of racialized character. In conjunction with such shifts in science, the middle classes reenvisioned the heart of the middle-class family. The "private" "domestic sphere" of the "true" interiorized middle-class woman gave way to a genealogical architecture of bloodlines that transformed the sentimental bonds of the middle-class family into a web of racialized hereditary relations and converted the essence of the "true" middle-class woman into the stock of racialized character. However, while I argue that the dominant terms in which middle-class privilege was claimed shift from gender to race over the course of the nineteenth century, I do not mean to suggest that this transformation was unidirectional or absolute. The terms of gender and race are always interwoven, and as one representation becomes dominant, it never fully effaces the other. What is at issue in my study, then, is a matter of emphasis, of which terms are upheld most conspicuously by the shadow discourses with which they are bound. Thus, while I endeavor to demonstrate that the white nationalism of turn-of-the-century American visual culture has its roots in the gendered construction of the antebellum middle-class domestic sphere, my analysis suggests that turn-of-the-century racial paradigms remain haunted by their gendered origins.

The history of photography provides the impetus for much of my analysis, and yet this book is not a history of photography. Rather, it is an examination of visual paradigms that fundamentally influenced the conception and representation of American identities in the second half of the nineteenth century. Among such paradigms, photography is perhaps the most concrete example. However, I am as much interested in the popular, literary, artistic, and scientific discourses that called upon photographs to make claims upon identity as I am with photographs themselves. And ultimately, I am intrigued by a wider visual register that encompasses, but is not confined to, photography. Thus, the scope of my study expands the domain of visual culture to include literary representations that pose subjectivity and social power as mediated by various gazes, and cultural concepts implicitly informed by visual metaphors, such as the middle-class "private sphere."

Ultimately, *American Archives* is less concerned with visual practices per se than it is with the ways in which such practices produce subjectivities. As the prison architecture of the panopticon becomes the emblem of systems of state surveillance that produce a newly disciplined subject in Michel Foucault's important study of social control,[7] so the photographic portrait functions as the emblem (and not the end) of a new way of imagining subjectivity in my examination of nineteenth-century American culture. Building upon Jonathan Crary's study of "the observer" in the early nineteenth century, my book begins where Crary's investigation ends, with the reinvention of subjectivities through photography. Crary suggests that in the early nineteenth century the sciences of physiology blurred the distinctions between interior and exterior that had stabilized an eighteenth-century observer, collapsing a split subjectivity into a "single surface of affect."[8] This book examines how subjectivity is reinscribed with interiority through the surface effects of photographic texts (and the cultural discourses they inhabited and enabled) over the course of the nineteenth century. I argue not only that photographic archives stabilized a white middle-class subject in distinction to racial and criminal others, as Allan Sekula has suggested,[9] but also that such archives stabilized that middle-class subject by endowing it with a laudable interiority. Thus, the photographic archive both delimited the boundary between self and other and reaffirmed a distinction between interior and exterior, positing a split subjectivity that could be harnessed, in turn, to the larger delineations of self and other that determined national identities.

American Archives begins with a close examination of Nathaniel Hawthorne's *House of the Seven Gables*. These initial readings of Hawthorne's romance establish visual architectures of interiority in antebellum middle-class gender representations and point toward their transformation in the scientific discourses of race. *The House of the Seven Gables* itself is a site of convergence, tension, and transformation, a text that demonstrates how middle-class discourses of gender and race were intertwined through new visual paradigms in mid-nineteenth-century American culture. Chapter 1 examines how the middle classes consolidated claims to cultural privilege through gendered identities founded in visual paradigms and circulated through new visual media (daguerreotypes) in the mid–nineteenth century. I read *The House of the Seven Gables* against the cultural anxiety surrounding the mysterious daguerreotype to demonstrate how feminine interiority was construed and paradoxically displayed vis-à-vis a masculine gaze. Assessing Hawthorne's images of wizards mesmerizing young ladies with penetrating gazes, I suggest that such imagined threats to the sanctity of the female body and its private domestic haven necessitated a model of middle-class masculine protection to neutralize the potential menace of other masculine intruders.

I return to Hawthorne's romance in chapter 2, to demonstrate that the seeds of a racialized reformulation of middle-class interiority are already apparent in his gendered romance of middle-class ascension. The text envisions gendered middle-class identities as "healthy" antidotes to an aristocratic identity posed in terms of blood, and by treating blood solely as a class discourse, Hawthorne's romance would seem to efface the newly racialized discourses of blood that were becoming popular in the sciences of biological racialism by the mid–nineteenth century. Examining the text's discursive intersections with those emerging sciences, I draw out a racialized subtext of *white* middle-class privilege in *The House of the Seven Gables*. Together, the first two chapters point toward the whiteness that circumscribes the founding authority of a masculine gaze, and thereby provide the basis for my later analysis of the "white supremacist gaze" that comes to dominate American visual culture by the turn of the century.[10]

In the first two chapters I examine an emergent visual culture primarily through the lens of literature and daguerreotypy. In chapter 3 I explore the advent of negative/positive, reproducible photography, what Walter Benjamin has called "mechanical reproduction."[11] As mechanical reproduction generated images on an unprecedented scale, the photographic portrait enabled new forms of social surveillance even as it provided new venues for cultural contestation. To demonstrate how new forms of power were both established and challenged through new visual texts, I read the popularity of the middle-class portrait first in relation to criminological and eugenicist photographs, and second in relation to a remarkable selection of subversive self-portraits made by white women in the late nineteenth century. In the latter images, women play with the process of visually mapping identity, posing their bodies in picture frames and strange dresses covered with photographs. Through an analysis of these disparate archives, I theorize how the advent of the reproducible photographic portrait inaugurated new modes of visual self-perception and self-production.

The chapters at the center of *American Archives* investigate how antebellum images of middle-class gender were transformed into representations of *white* middle-class racial superiority over the course of the late nineteenth century. I fully examine here the processes of transfiguration toward which my analysis in chapter 2 points. I argue that the sciences of biological racialism, which culminate in Francis Galton's enormously influential eugenics, or "science of race," at the turn of the century, effected a racializing of middle-class privilege during a period of heightened racial tension in the postbellum and post-Reconstruction United States. Chapter 4 examines the striking similarities between "family photographs" promoted by eugenicists and those celebrated in popular white women's magazines such as the *Ladies' Home Journal*. The sentimental enthusiasm with which middle-class families cherished baby pictures resonates uncannily with the scientific fervor with which eugenicists stockpiled and studied child photographs as the turn of the century. Through an analysis of this disturbing discursive convergence, I suggest that one of America's most widespread cultural rituals, namely, photographing babies, has a startling correlation in the reproduction of white supremacy.

I explore the racializing of middle-class identity and privilege further in chapter 5 by assessing a transformation in the rhetoric of what Linda Kerber has called "Republican Motherhood" over the course of the late nineteenth century.[12] Looking specifically at the early eligibility debates of America's most prominent and enduring patriotic organization, namely, the Daughters of the American Revolution, I demonstrate how the imagined "moral suasion" of the antebellum middle-class mother was infused with racialized discourses of blood and heredity as the Daughters claimed an exclusive heritage of patriotic "blood," "bone," and "sinew." By assessing the image of white motherhood as a contested site in the early eligibility debates of the Daughters of the American Revolution, and by situating those debates in the context of eugenics and lynching in the 1890s, this chapter demonstrates how the white middle-class American woman, once heralded as the embodiment of middle-class moral virtue, increasingly was held up as the bearer of superior Anglo-Saxon racial stock by the turn of the century. In making this argument, I draw upon the work of Hazel Carby to demonstrate how African American feminists like Ida B. Wells and Anna Julia Cooper challenged efforts to construct a privileged white American identity around the figure of the white middle-class woman.[13]

Building upon an analysis of the ways in which popular photographic practices were founded in racial logics at the turn of the century, chapter 6 examines the photographs displayed in the "American Negro" exhibit at the

Paris Exposition of 1900. This chapter extends an investigation of racialized national identities and demonstrates the role that photography played in envisioning racially codified American identities at the turn of the century. I look specifically at the work of two contributors to the American Negro exhibit, namely, Frances Benjamin Johnston and W. E. B. Du Bois, and propose that both, to varying degrees, challenged the tenets of biological racialism and eugenics in their attempts to carve out a space for the "American Negro." Johnston's photographs of Hampton Institute visually document the transformation of "Africans" into "Americans," while Du Bois's albums of "Negro Types" subtly challenge the assimilationist assumption that African Americans are not always already Americans.

The final chapters of the book examine challenges to the authority of a white masculine gaze and a white middle-class patriarchy at the turn of the century. Chapters 7 and 8 explore resistance to and reconfigurations of gendered and racialized power relations represented and enacted in visual culture. Chapter 7 suggests that two of Pauline Hopkins's novels for the *Colored American Magazine* undermine the visual paradigms upon which eugenicist definitions of African American character and intellect were founded at the turn of the century. Through an analysis of Hopkins's *Hagar's Daughter* and *Of One Blood*, I demonstrate how Hopkins challenges the authority of a white supremacist gaze to delimit the terrain of racial others. Her biracial white characters problematize, with their very bodies, the visual evidence upon which eugenicists supported their categorization of racial types. Further, the clairvoyance and supernatural sight of Hopkins's biracial characters (particularly in *Of One Blood*) trouble the "objective" supremacy of a dominant scientific vision. Finally, Hopkins's narratives of incestuous romantic intrigue query the convergence of blood, race, and character that is fundamental to eugenicist definitions of racial difference.

Following an analysis of the ways in which Pauline Hopkins's fiction undermines the visual paradigms informing the racial science of eugenics, chapter 8 examines white patriarchal anxieties over such perceived threats to the supremacy of a white, masculine gaze. In this final chapter, I examine how representations of white femininity as spectacle reconfigured the position of the white male viewer at the turn of the century. Theodore Dreiser's *Sister Carrie* presents a masculine gaze no longer in control of, and increasingly dependent upon, the feminine objects under its view. Surprisingly, in Dreiser's text a woman's objectification under a male gaze lends her a kind of mobility, and self-commodification transports her out of patriarchal exchange.

American Archives concludes with a brief look at the striking and much-discussed cover image of *Time*'s 1993 special issue on multiculturalism. I discuss *Time*'s "new Eve" as a kind of afterimage, a representation that demonstrates the powerful legacy and contemporary currency of the nineteenth-century visual paradigms of gender and race this book studies.

CHAPTER ONE

Prying Eyes and Middle-Class Magic in
The House of the Seven Gables

IN NATHANIEL HAWTHORNE's *House of the Seven Gables*, Holgrave describes daguerreotypy as a process of making pictures "out of sunshine" and asserts, "There is a wonderful insight in heaven's broad and simple sunshine. While we give it credit only for depicting the merest surface, it actually brings out the secret character with a truth that no painter would ever venture upon, even could he detect it."[1] According to Holgrave, in its image of the body—that "merest surface"—the daguerreotype captures an elusive depth, a "secret character" hidden to unaided eyes. As a daguerreotypist who comes from a long line of wizards endowed with supernaturally powerful vision, Holgrave is posed as a particularly penetrating spectator in Hawthorne's romance. He sees through the facades people present to "the world's eye" (329), to the cores that constitute their characters. Holgrave's eyes pry beneath surface signs to see hidden recesses. Through his eyes one imagines innermost depths.

Images of interiority were central to American middle-class self-articulations in the nineteenth century. Imagined partly in relation to new visual technologies, such as daguerreotypy, interiority functioned as a complementary countersign to bodies brought increasingly into visual display. In the early to mid–nineteenth century, such visual discourses of depth converged with gendered middle-class narratives of interiority, namely, those of domestic "private spheres."[2] As Gillian Brown has argued, middle-class domesticity inflected American individualism with the "values of interiority, privacy, and psychology."[3] That domestic middle-class interiority was singularly gendered, anchored around the figure of the True Woman, heralded for her piety, purity, domesticity, and submissiveness.[4] Celebrated as an ethereal domestic angel defined by her spiritual character traits, the "true" middle-class woman emblematized interiority itself.

In *The House of the Seven Gables* feminine interiority is literally envisioned, as new visual technologies and discourses of domestic interiority merge through mesmerizing eyes. Hawthorne's tale of middle-class ascendance poses the sacrosanct feminine interiority that anchors a middle-class "private" sphere through a violating masculine gaze that supernaturally sees that essence.[5] In Hawthorne's romance, that which middle-class domesticity will protect, namely, feminine interiority, must first be pried.[6]

As Holgrave muses upon the penetrating power of the daguerreotype, he suggests that he would like to test the "wonderful insight in heaven's broad and simple sunshine" on a "perfectly amiable face" (328)—on Phoebe Pyncheon—intimating that he would like to probe Phoebe's interior essence. The gendered dynamic of this desire is repeated across generations in Hawthorne's text, as prying masculine eyes generate feminine interiorities in need of "private" protective spheres. Violation produces feminine interiorities that require protection in Hawthorne's romance, and thus, the penetrating masculine gaze that engenders feminine interiority must be transformed, finally, into a middle-class masculine gaze that will preserve feminine privacy.

In *The House of the Seven Gables* gendered interiorities provide the symbolic terrain on which class confrontation and transformation occur. Feminine interiority functions as the sign of class dominance or demise, and the very site of class conflict. Hawthorne's romance of middle-class ascendance legitimizes middle-class cultural dominance by posing virtuous middle-class essences against pseudo-aristocratic decay and artisanal destruction. In Hawthorne's tale, feminine interiority, magically envisioned, functions as the banner of middle-class virtue, the self-identifying gendered trope of an emergent class.[7]

"MAGNETIC" DAGUERREOTYPES AND THE MASCULINE GAZE

Hawthorne invests Holgrave and a long line of his Maule ancestors with enhanced visual powers in order to see (and to seize) interiorities in *The House of the Seven Gables*. In the short history of the Pyncheon family that introduces Hawthorne's tale, the narrator describes the "interior life" of the family's seven-gabled house in relation to a mirror, "a large, dim looking glass," that was said to have embellished one of the many rooms of the gloomy dwelling, once upon a time. According to popular legend, the mirror was believed "to contain within its depths all the shapes that had ever been reflected there—the old Colonel himself, and his many descendants, some in the garb of antique babyhood, and others in the bloom of feminine beauty or manly prime, or saddened with the wrinkles of frosty age" (266). Unlike most mirrors, the Pyncheon looking glass did not provide a simple indexical sign, a representation marking physical and temporal presence; instead, retaining and preserving its reflections, the Pyncheon mirror seemed to have a memory. The descendants of Matthew Maule maintained a mysterious connection with this looking glass, and only they could draw out of the mirror's depths, as if by "a sort of mesmeric process," its memories of Pyncheon posterity; only Maule's descendants could make the "inner region" of the magical mirror "all alive with the departed Pyn-

cheons" (266). The mirror's memory seems to have been singularly penetrating, revealing the Pyncheons "not as they had shown themselves to the
world nor in their better and happier hours, but as doing over again some
deed of sin, or in the crisis of life's bitterest sorrow" (266). In Hawthorne's
novel the looking glass "is always a kind of window or doorway into the
spiritual world" (490), and this particular mirror provided, for a Maule, a
view into the dark interiorities of the Pyncheon family.

In the narrative present of Hawthorne's novel, the mythical Pyncheon
mirror of old has been replaced by another "mirror with a memory"—the
daguerreotype.[8] The first photographic form, invented by Louis-Jacques-
Mandé Daguerre in 1839, the daguerreotype was deemed a "mirror with
a memory" by Oliver Wendell Holmes due to the image's shiny, reflective
metallic surface.[9] A monochromatic image produced on a highly polished,
chemically processed metal plate, the daguerreotype, unlike later forms of
photography, was a single, nonreproducible image. The first daguerreotypes required twenty-minute exposures, but by 1840, exposure times had
been reduced to thirty seconds. With the aid of braces the body could be
kept still for the duration of these newly shortened exposure times, and
thus the photographic portrait was inaugurated, a commodity wildly popular with Americans. In the 1840s and 1850s, "daguerreotypomania" swept
America.[10]

Over ninety percent of the daguerreotypes made in the mid–nineteenth
century were portraits, images with a particular importance as new class
signifiers. According to John Tagg, "To have one's portrait done was one
of the symbolic acts by which individuals from the rising social classes made
their ascent visible to themselves and others and classed themselves among
those who enjoyed social status."[11] Daguerreotypy opened up the elite domain of portraiture to members of the emerging middle classes. Once the
exclusive purview of pseudo-aristocrats with the time and means to sit for
paintings, portraiture became available to anyone with $1.50 and thirty
seconds to spare.[12] In one sense, then, the daguerreotype portrait functioned as a middle-class appropriation of aristocratic self-representation,
as a sign of emerging middle-class cultural power. In *The House of the Seven
Gables*, Holgrave's daguerreotypes signify in the shadow of Colonel Pyncheon's painted portrait; technologies of representation provide a metaphor for the cultural power of classes, and daguerreotypy makes visible the
economic and social heirs of a new cultural dominance.[13]

Despite the general enthusiasm with which middle-class Americans
greeted the daguerreotype, many also viewed these images with suspicion
and even fear. According to Alan Trachtenberg, the mysterious, mirrored
quality of the daguerreotype's polished surface produced misgivings and
anxieties surrounding this early form of photographic representation. As a
mirror functions indexically, reflecting one's image only when one is pres-

Portrait of an unidentified woman. Sixth-plate daguerreotype, circa 1840–60. Reproduced from the Collections of the Library of Congress.

ent, many early daguerreotype viewers felt that the person whose visage was
seemingly "reflected" in the daguerreotype was somehow magically present
in the photographic frame.[14] Daguerreotypy and mesmerism were often
linked in the mid-nineteenth-century popular imagination, many surmising
that one's image had to be tricked or seduced into giving itself up to the
daguerreotype's surface. T. S. Arthur, a popular nineteenth-century author,
described the process of daguerreotypy as follows: "The different impressions made upon sitters is curious enough. The most common is the illusion
that the instrument [the camera] exercises a kind of magnetic attraction,
and many good ladies actually feel their eyes 'drawn' towards the lens while

the operation is in progress!"[15] One can imagine that the gendered, eroti-cized nature of this process as described by Arthur—good ladies feeling their eyes drawn to the phallic camera lens—exacerbated further the anxie-ties of many early daguerreotype consumers. Given this cultural context, it comes as no surprise that Hawthorne's daguerreotypist is the descendant of wizards who control magic mirrors and who, as we shall see, exercise "magnetic attraction" and mesmeric power over "good ladies."[16]

Uncertain as to the means of the process, many early daguerreotype consumers were also nervous about the ends to which such images could be used. Ultimately, the daguerreotype provoked anxiety surrounding the exact relationship between one's image and one's self. A story contempo-rary to Hawthorne's *House of the Seven Gables*, "The Magnetic Daguerreo-types," published anonymously in the *Photographic Art-Journal* of June 1852, plays directly upon the misgivings associated with the uncanny da-guerreotype and demonstrates particularly the gendered nature of those anxieties. In this strange story, daguerreotypes literally provide a window onto the world of their subjects, and private feminine interiorities are imag-ined as they are pried by masculine gazes.[17]

"The Magnetic Daguerreotypes" tells the tale of an evil professor, Ario-vistus Dunkelheim, and his "curious improvements in the daguerreotype" (353). The narrator of the story is Ernest, a young man eager to secure portraits of himself and his lovely betrothed, Elora. Ernest seeks the ser-vices of Professor Dunkelheim, who creates "living portraits," representa-tions that move, as reflections, following the lead of their referents. By a mysterious kind of magnetic process, an "inexplicable sympathy," Dunkel-heim's polished sheets of steel act as mirrors of absent subjects (355). Like Hawthorne's mythical Pyncheon mirror, Dunkelheim's portraits function as magical indexical signs, marking presence even in absence, providing the viewer a permanent window onto another's every movement.

Ernest discovers the magical powers of the portraits while alone in his quarters, and he revels in the continuous communication the mirrors will enable the lovers to maintain: "Delicious thought! From the present mo-ment to the hour of our nuptials, our parting would be nominal and not real. Spiritually united, we could hardly be said to be materially separated; since the magic mirrors would, by the medium of the most noble of senses, render us forever present to one another. How superior to the cold, ghastly, shadowy immobility of the mere daguerreotypes, were these living por-traits of Dunkelheim's" (355). In Ernest's rapturous meditations, "the most noble of senses," the sense of sight, spiritually unites subjects and objects of view. The sense most commonly held to objectify the items under its perusal becomes in Ernest's imagination the sense most likely to join ephemeral spirits; the sense of sight intimately joins the spiritual interior-ities of bodies physically separated.

Ernest's joy is shattered as he remembers that he is not the only viewer empowered by the magic portraits: "*The Professor possessed copies*" (355). Ernest's face, index to his thoughts, would be open forever to the "critical and penetrating" gaze of Dunkelheim; more horrifying yet, Elora's charms would be vulnerable to the professor's scrutiny: "A loathsome and accursed fantasy! to live forever in the presence of such a man as Dunkelheim, to be forever subject to an excruciating moral espionage! to be denied for life, the security and luxury of privacy! to be haunted, in solitude, by an unseen tormentor!" (355). Privacy becomes a luxury "denied" at precisely the moment in which Ernest imagines his intimacy to be on display; privacy is established textually at the moment in which it is "pried" by an unseen tormentor. Ernest is distraught thinking that his own visage is accessible to Dunkelheim, but he is truly disturbed when he realizes that Elora's body is also on display for the professor. Further, although infuriated by the professor's encroachment upon his own delicate interactions, Ernest cannot help participating in the act of peeping which so enrages him to grant to another. Espying on the living image of Elora all night, Ernest proclaims: "An irresistible fascination withheld me, and I continued to gaze and gaze with an intense and burning ardor that threatened to disorder my intelligence" (355). Ernest is tortured by the "perpetual contemplation" of Elora's "exquisite charms in their careless and unconscious abandonment" (355). His power to look unseen on the unconscious moments of his idol sparks in him a "fever of impatient love" (355).

As he begins to experience voyeuristic pleasure, Ernest's first thrill in thinking of his spiritual union with Elora is transformed into a distinctly erotic desire for physical union with his beloved. The textual inscription of Elora's interiority is thus closely associated with a fantasy of sexual possession. The sexually charged dynamic that first establishes individual interiority also necessitates, according to the logic of heterosexual romance, a private sphere in which a woman's body will be protected from the trespasses of all men except the one to whom she is lawfully beholden. Thus the voyeuristic gaze sets in motion a narrative of heterosexual masculine desire aimed first at penetration and then at protection. As "prying eyes" focus upon the woman's body, a private sphere is necessitated in order to prohibit unsanctified sexual relations. In Ernest's struggle to establish his own masculine prerogative, privacy becomes the defensive apparatus that regulates access to Elora's body. Ultimately, privacy also functions to discipline woman's potentially promiscuous desire. Narratively construed through Ernest's thoughts, privacy becomes the architecture of a fantasy of masculine privilege and control, a prerogative upheld by the monogamous mandate of heterosexual marriage.

As the mystery of the magic mirrors is disclosed to her, Elora immediately understands her position as the object of desire in a masculine struggle to possess her, body and soul. Elora refuses to marry until the original portraits are returned, resisting a double threat to her purity on her wedding night. Especially disturbed by Ernest's abuse of power, Elora blushes crimson when she learns he has spied upon her, and she commands him to return her portrait. Asserting his masculine "rights" as Elora's suitor, Ernest cries, " 'What! would you deny your lover a privilege possessed by Ariovistus Dunkelheim?' " (356). In "The Magnetic Daguerreotypes" the power of the gaze presupposes ownership over the object of that gaze; the portrait provides a claim over Elora's body and soul that Ernest will not relinquish. For Ernest, marriage provides a similar sort of ownership of his beloved, and when the lovers decide to wed, Ernest begins to feel secure in his privilege, stating: "We were married. Elora was now mine" (358). Once claiming legal possession of Elora, Ernest is less troubled by the visual mastery another persists in wielding over his beloved. Elora, on the contrary, cannot forget her objectified relation to Dunkelheim: On her wedding night she falls into a faint, exclaiming, " '*The Portraits*!' in a tone of indescribable emotion" (358). According to his own account, Ernest's "sterner manhood" expels its fury in visions of revenge and fantasies of tormenting the professor with the images of his own joy. Answering Elora's despair, Ernest protests: " 'Let him see and envy!' " (358). Assuming a heterosexual, patriarchal privilege, Ernest would flaunt his trophy before the professor. Claiming through marriage legal access to Elora's body, the object of desire, Ernest perceives Elora with all his senses, not simply the desire-inspiring sense of sight.

Recognizing her own disempowered position as object in this jealousy play between men, Elora takes no pleasure in tormenting the professor, responding bitterly to Ernest, " 'Were I a *man*!' " (358). Implying both that she might be able to understand Ernest's pleasure in tormenting the unsatisfied voyeur if she shared Ernest's social prerogative, and also that she might handle the situation differently if she were thus empowered, Elora sends Ernest into a rage of challenged masculinity. Compelled to pursue the professor for a year, Ernest finally finds and kills him in Paris, returning only then to claim Elora without reserve. Elora celebrates with satisfaction, " 'Henceforward we are at least our own masters, and not puppets, acting for the amusement of a detestable old necromancer!' " (359). Of course, Elora is not now her own master but simply the object of a single man's claim. "The Magnetic Daguerreotypes" constructs the sanctity of privacy and of a woman's body, the central object of that newly created private sphere, first by posing the "threat" of unlawful claims to the female body and second by subverting that "threat" with a legally sanctioned,

"rightful" masculine prerogative. As the gaze inspires a fantasy of ownership and an imaginary proximity between viewer and viewed, the professor's voyeuristic gaze on Elora's body usurps the patriarchal privilege that
legally belongs to Ernest alone. As husband, Ernest acquires both gaze over
and ownership of Elora's body, claiming as his sole right mastery over her
sexualized interiority. Thus, "The Magnetic Daguerreotypes" generates
anxiety about woman's sexual vulnerability in order to establish the desire
for a protective private sphere, in which one man's social prerogative can
be claimed through public, "legitimate" display.

Imbued with first-person narrative authority, Ernest's legal, "romantic"
gaze is doubly prominent in "The Magnetic Daguerreotypes." First, Ernest
as narrator provides the reader's only access to the events told; the reader
sees things solely from Ernest's point of view. Second, Ernest's passionate
gaze upon the image of his beloved is emphasized throughout the story:
Ernest continues to "gaze and gaze" upon Elora (355, 357). The sadistic
and even "scientific" gaze of the professor is represented in the story as
penetrating (353), "piercing" (354), and "fiend-like" (357). Although never
actually witnessed in relation to the living portraits, the professor's terrifying gaze upon the magic mirrors is imagined obsessively by Ernest and
Elora, sending them into rages and fainting spells: " '*He* sees us' " (356).
While masculine gazes are represented prominently, Elora's gaze remains
almost entirely absent from the narrative. Beyond one "look of painful
reproach" (356), a reprimand for Ernest, Elora's gaze is effectively erased
from the story. Elora looks at her image of Ernest just once, in order to
test the power of the portraits. The experience fails to throw her into a fit
of delirious rapture; she responds only to say, " 'And you can watch me at
all times, when I am alone?' " (356). Elora is too conscious of her disempowered position as object of the gaze to enjoy her own voyeuristic powers.
Further, Elora exercises her gaze only in response to Ernest's request. As
Ernest grants Elora permission to watch him, she does not enjoy the voyeuristic pleasure of watching Ernest's unconscious movements. Contained
within the domain of patriarchal control, the woman's gaze is figured as
nearly unimaginable in "The Magnetic Daguerreotypes."

Elora exercises little power through her own gaze, but she does exert
influence as the object of a masculine gaze. Even though she agrees to
consummate her marriage with Ernest while the magic portraits remain
abroad, Elora suggests that their marriage will not be sanctified until Ernest destroys the fiend who compromises Ernest's singular privilege. Evoking an interiority that has been constructed precisely through the professor's penetrating gaze, Elora utilizes her vulnerability to discipline Ernest's
manhood. Elora forbids Ernest to approximate the professor's rival model
of masculinity. Elora's vulnerability, her very interiority, demands a com-

plementary protective masculinity that Ernest must now provide. For the two to be truly married under the sign of Elora's feminine interiority, Ernest's competitive masculinity must be replaced by a sheltering disposition, and his own gaze upon Elora's body must be transformed from a voyeuristic act into a legitimately claimed prerogative.

EVIL EYES AND FEMININE ESSENCE

Nathaniel Hawthorne narrates masculine voyeurism, feminine interiority, and masculine protection as key elements in a romance of middle-class ascendance in *The House of the Seven Gables*. In Hawthorne's text, the gaze functions as a weapon in battles of class prerogative, posed first as an aristocratic privilege usurped by artisanal challengers.[18] As Professor Dunkelheim disrupts gender privilege with his prying eyes in "The Magnetic Daguerreotypes," Matthew Maule challenges class prerogative with his "evil eye" in *The House of the Seven Gables*. Hawthorne's middle-class man emerges from the wake of these battles to figure feminine interiority with a penetrating eye that will revere that essence. Holgrave's prosthetic vision serves as a vehicle toward a middle-class "cure" for class antitheses in Hawthorne's text; however, as an heirloom inherited from Matthew Maule, Holgrave's supernatural vision is posed as a potentially dangerous power. According to the logic of Hawthorne's middle-class romance, Holgrave must utilize his gaze not only to disrupt class hierarchies (like Maule) but also to reconstitute them in gendered middle-class forms. Holgrave must dismantle aristocratic architectures to build middle-class homes.

Gender roles and class positions are negotiated primarily through vision in the strange tale with which Holgrave seduces Phoebe Pyncheon, a story about their ancestral forebears that foreshadows the erotic trial soon to develop between Holgrave and Phoebe themselves. Holgrave's story is one of a struggle between class and gender prerogative waged in the tragic meeting between Matthew Maule and Alice Pyncheon. At the request of her father, Maule mesmerizes Alice Pyncheon, using her as a kind of spiritual medium to search for a lost land deed that would secure the Pyncheon fortune. In the process, Maule uses his penetrating gaze to break Alice's haughty will, ferociously denying her the power of her own desiring gaze.

Alice Pyncheon, described as artistically refined, beautiful, and "naturally" elite, exemplifies the seventeenth-century aristocratic woman who functions as an object of display for the envious and admiring gaze of an entire community;[19] however, she can be met one-on-one, looked at face-to-face, only by those of a very elite class. Hawthorne demonstrates the privileged class status that sanctions social intimacy with aristocratic bodies by detailing Matthew Maule's "outrageous" breech of this social code. Hawthorne's Matthew Maule understands the intimate gaze upon the aristocratic lady's body to be an explicit class privilege, and it is this prerogative that Maule challenges by asserting the power of his masculine gaze. In this way, Maule represents the forerunner of a new social discourse that defies aristocratic entitlement in the name of gender. However, as Hawthorne makes clear in the narrative present of his text, through the union of Holgrave and Phoebe, Matthew Maule asserts the authority of the wrong gender. In Hawthorne's romance, Maule's destructive masculinity must be replaced by the transformative femininity of middle-class claims to social ascendance. Masculine penetration and domination must be transfigured into masculine reverence for and protection of a peculiarly feminine middle-class essence.

Throughout his story, Holgrave describes Maule's mesmeric power as a kind of supernatural vision: "There was a great deal of talk among the neighbors, particularly the petticoated ones, about what they called the witchcraft of Maule's eye. Some said that he could look into people's minds; others, that, by the marvelous power of this eye, he could draw people into his own mind, or send them, if he pleased, to do errands to his grandfather, in the spiritual world; others, again, that it was what is termed an Evil Eye, and possessed the valuable faculty of blighting corn, and drying children into mummies with the heartburn" (412). Despite the "witchcraft" of his eye, the mythical power of his vision, Matthew Maule's social caste denies him the power to look "up" at Alice Pyncheon, and it is this social privilege of intimate viewing that Maule blatantly trespasses. Upon entering the Pyncheon mansion through the front door, his initial affront to Pyncheon authority, Maule inquires after Alice Pyncheon. The African American servant Scipio, well aware of both their social castes, is appalled by Maule's request: " 'He talk of Mistress Alice!' cried Scipio, as he returned from his errand. 'The low carpenter man! He no business so much as to look at her a great way off!' " (411). Maule's "low" status denies him the advantage of masculine scrutiny; his class status effectively emasculates his gaze.

Alice's class position fashions her "unnaturally" bold in the middle-class terms of Hawthorne's romance. The aristocratic lady's class presumptions corrupt her "proper" gender role as defined according to middle-class mores—a system of class elitism blinds the elegant Alice to her "true," pure and submissive, gender "nature." As Alice meets Maule face-to-face, she fails to recognize his masculine prerogative and instead asserts her own class privilege by objectifying him as the erotic object of her aristocratic gaze; Alice's class privilege debases her submissive gender superiority.[20] Enraged by Alice's exercise of this class prerogative, Maule punishes her brutally, proclaiming the sadistic power of his gendered authority over her class entitlement.[21]

> As Alice came into the room, her eyes fell upon the carpenter, who was standing near its center, clad in a green woolen jacket, a pair of loose breeches, open at the knees, and with a long pocket for his rule, the end of which protruded;[22] it was as proper a mark of the artisan's calling as Mr. Pyncheon's full-dress sword of that gentleman's aristocratic pretensions. A glow of artistic approval brightened over Alice Pyncheon's face; she was struck with admiration—which she made no attempt to conceal—of the remarkable comeliness, strength, and energy of Maule's figure. But that admiring glance (which most other men, perhaps, would have cherished as a sweet recollection, all through life) the carpenter never forgave. It must have been the devil himself that made Maule so subtle in his perception.
>
> "Does the girl look at me as if I were a brute beast?" thought he, setting his teeth. "She shall know whether I have a human spirit; and the worse for her, if it prove stronger than her own!" (422)

Alice's admiring and objectifying gaze displays her presumed mastery over Matthew Maule, and for this assumption Maule retaliates viciously. He receives Alice's look and its implications as a challenging gauntlet, and a battle of the classes, waged as a war of the sexes, ensues, fought through the eyes. Maule says with bitter sarcasm, " 'Do me the favor (though altogether beyond a poor carpenter's desserts) to fix your eyes on mine!' " (423). Assenting to Maule's request, Alice invokes her own gender authority as her salvation—the "preservative force of womanhood"—and overestimates the "impenetrability" of her pure feminine sphere. Claiming that she does not believe " 'that a lady, while true to herself, can have aught to fear from whomsoever, or in any circumstances!' " (423), Alice puts "woman's might against man's might" (423). Responding to Maule's challenge in his own terms, those of gender, Alice sets aside her aristocratic claim to class power. Unfortunately, Alice has already forfeited her gender dominance by demonstrating her class prerogative; as an aristocratic "lady," Alice cannot be "true" to her (middle-class) womanly self. Attempting to resist Maule's mesmeric gaze, Alice yelps as she becomes aware of a "sinister or evil potency . . . striving to pass her barriers" (423). Alice's womanhood, her very soul, is penetrated by Maule's masculine mesmeric forces; Alice's "impenetrable sphere" is engendered even as it is violated by Maule's "evil eye."

"Threat" and "penetration" produce an interiority that corresponds to Alice's aristocratic body. In Holgrave's story, the "inviolable" self is constructed precisely through its vulnerability; interiority is posed against outside threats. Hawthorne offers a glimpse of Alice's "true" womanly nature in the moment her aristocratic ladyhood is overpowered; just as Alice's essential will is "seen," it is also seized by Matthew Maule: "Her spirit passed from beneath her own control, and bowed itself to Maule" (428–429). As Alice is mesmerized by Matthew Maule, her conscious will is over-taken by Maule's mind, leaving her a kind of puppet to his desires.[23] Haw-thorne himself was rather acutely attuned to the sexualized subtext of mes-merism and feared it even as practiced by medical doctors. When he learned that his betrothed, Sophia Peabody, was seeking mesmeric treat-ment to alleviate pain from headaches, he warned her that mesmerism "vio-lated" "the sacredness of the individual," a trespass particularly damaging to the purity of womanhood.[24]

If Alice's body once functioned to display her own aristocratic privilege, her will or soul, the essence of her interiority, becomes the site of Maule's performance of power. Through the supernatural force of his mesmerizing gaze, Maule inverts class privileges, asserting the entitlement of a control-ling masculinity. According to Gillian Brown, "It is the fact that Matthew Maule's rapelike possession of Alice Pyncheon must display itself—the re-enactment of the initial violation which publicity entails—that constitutes the horror of mesmerism in *The House of the Seven Gables*."[25] Maule masters (even as he invents) Alice's interiority with his mesmeric gaze and punishes her publicly by demonstrating the power of his "prying eye" to control her will and essence.

While an interiority, the site of a sanctified self (in Hawthorne's middle-class terms), is constructed for Alice precisely through Maule's violation of that domain, this realm is not redeemed until it has been permeated with humility. Alice is "saved" only as she repents the sin of her pride and comes to resemble Hawthorne's model of a "true," submissive middle-class woman. Alice achieves a feminine interiority steeped in humility only after she has been chastised for her aristocratic, and erotic, presumptions—for her "unnatural" gender comportment. While Maule's mesmerizing gaze and the control it grants him are marked in Hawthorne's text as evil, sadis-tic, and violating, an exaggerated punishment for Alice's slight offense, Alice's pride, as well as her sexual desire, exemplified by her unabashed ogling, is consistently marked as a transgression, for which she might have been castigated in the netherworld if not recovered in this one. In *The House of the Seven Gables*, the aristocratic woman is salvaged spiritually only as she adopts the signs of a nineteenth-century model of middle-class femi-ninity, only as she becomes pious, pure, and *submissive*, in short, as she becomes "true." However, according to the logic of Hawthorne's romance, there is no place for Alice, newly imbued with a "true," submissive interior-ity, in the world of the aristocracy. As a True Woman, Alice can no longer survive within her class, and so she dies.

The ancestral history of Holgrave and Phoebe foretells potential disasters lurking in their own nascent relationship. In order to fabricate the sanctity of their forthcoming middle-class future, Hawthorne first provides counterexamples via the gender roles of other classes: He critiques the aristocratic Alice Pyncheon's "perverse" gender comportment and the abuses of Matthew Maule's working-class masculinity; further, he condemns the compromised constitution of Gervayse Pyncheon's aristocratic paternity. Hawthorne demonstrates, through Holgrave's story, that the tragic demise of Alice Pyncheon would never have ensued had her father, Gervayse Pyncheon, performed a proper paternal role and protected his daughter against violation. Pyncheon's aristocratic ambitions lead him to martyr his daughter to Maule (428); his class obsession misdirects his "proper" gender role.

Holgrave's story clearly demonstrates that Alice's purity is not a sufficient safeguard for her holy self; a feminine interiority established through violation needs the subsequent reinforcement, and the reverence, of a protective masculinity. Thus, a benevolent (middle-class) patriarchy, which Alice Pyncheon's father fails to provide, is necessitated through threats to the unprotected sanctity of womanhood. Gervayse Pyncheon forsakes his daughter because he does not venerate and defend her essence. In his quest to secure an aristocratic entitlement in land, Gervayse only partially entrusts the fate of his future heirs to the purity of Alice's feminine essence; in Pyncheon's mind, land secured through a lost parchment remains the most secure means of providing for himself and his descendants. According to the logic of middle-class superiority forwarded by Hawthorne's text, the sanctity of feminine interiority must function as the very site, not the means to an end, of class entitlement. Further, as we have seen, as feminine interiority is transformed into the authorization of middle-class ascension, an "essence" that inspires masculine care, it must become a more glorified terrain than the aristocratic woman's "will." Finally, in Hawthorne's romance, the validity of social hierarchies is founded upon masculine protection of a sanctified feminine essence. Even after her haughtiness is transformed into humility, Alice is depicted as ultimately powerless as an aristocratic woman in a world of patriarchal exchange. Feminine interiority, the seat of middle-class virtue and the fount of middle-class domesticity, is not safe in aristocratic houses. In a cruel perversion of the aristocracy's "normal" traffic in women,[26] Alice Pyncheon is sacrificed to her father's class ambitions.

As Holgrave finishes narrating his tale of Pyncheon and Maule posterity, he finds Phoebe drooping in her chair, as if in a trance. Mirroring the overpowered Alice Pyncheon of his story, Phoebe leans slightly toward Holgrave, mesmerized by his narrative of transgression and possession: "A veil was beginning to be muffled about her, in which she could behold

only him, and live only in his thoughts and emotions" (431). As Phoebe's
conscious will slips away from her, Holgrave is tempted with the power
cruelly seized by his predecessor, but his "reverence for another's individuality" withholds him (432). Unlike his ancestor, Holgrave "is awakened into
sympathy" and chooses to guard the essence of a feminine spirit.[27] His self-
control and his "reverence" for Phoebe's "true" interiority demonstrate
Holgrave's superiority to both the ambitious aristocratic patriarch and the
challenging artisanal man. By tempering Maule's penetrating and domi-
nating vision, Holgrave alters a long tradition of gendered class dynamics
and becomes a "true" middle-class man. "Whatever his defects of nature
and education, and in spite of his scorn for creeds and institutions" (432),
Holgrave proves himself a man worthy to protect a delicate essence. While
Phoebe's humble nature commands a masculine reverence that the aristocratic lady's pride repels, it takes a "true" man to recognize that spiritual
purity. Ultimately, Phoebe is saved from a disaster akin to Alice Pyncheon's
not only by her own "true" essence but also by Holgrave's (middle-class)
masculine integrity (432).

MAKING THE HOUSE A HOME

In *The House of the Seven Gables*, domestic private space emblematizes the
interiorized essence of its inhabitants; domestic atmosphere "blooms" and
"grows out" from the spiritual fount of individual characters (320). Not
unlike Holgrave's daguerreotypes, Hawthorne's seven-gabled house reflects the interior essences of those it shelters, providing a kind of external
evidence for the purity or malady of individual souls. The home is also a
space of class conflict in *The House of the Seven Gables*, and its state registers
not only the essence of its inhabitants but also the "health" or "disease" of
their class-delimited gender roles.

Phoebe and Hepzibah Pyncheon, and the domestic realms they engen-
der, typify Hawthorne's distinction between "new Plebianism and old Gen-
tility" (319) in *The House of the Seven Gables*, an opposition that is finally
resolved in the inclusive middle-class sphere of idealized domesticity.
Phoebe and Hepzibah represent two stages in what Hawthorne depicts as
the "inevitable" progression from the lady to the True Woman. Representatives of a fading pseudo-aristocracy and an emergent middle class, respec-
tively, the elderly, scowling Hepzibah wanes[28] as Phoebe, with the blush of
youth in her face, comes into full bloom. Describing the two characters as
spring to fall, as May to November, Hawthorne naturalizes class transformation and normalizes the cultural dominance of the middle classes.

After securing the reluctant acceptance of Hepzibah, Phoebe crosses the
threshold of the seven-gabled house and enters an interior space remark-

able for its dark, dismal, and oppressively dreary atmosphere. The parlor, guarded by the portrait of the stern Puritan forefather, is a "low-studded room," "paneled with dark wood," and peopled with chairs "so straight and stiff, and so ingeniously contrived for the discomfort of the human person that they were irksome even to sight, and conveyed the ugliest possible idea of the state of society to which they could have been adapted" (277). The primary tenant of this inhospitable domain is depicted over and over again as a reclusive, elderly maiden with a perpetual scowl and a singular wardrobe of dusty black silks; indeed, Phoebe's aunt Hepzibah herself seems to be a relic of some uncomfortable past. Phoebe enters the "gloomy old mansion" (308) like a ray of sunshine, brightening the decaying aristocratic house with a new interior life. "As pleasant about the house as a gleam of sunshine falling on the floor through a shadow of twinkling leaves, or as a ray of firelight that dances on the wall while evening is drawing nigh" (319), Phoebe revitalizes Hepzibah's hereditary hermitage. Dispelling two centuries of gloom in a single night with the sweetness of her dreams and half an hour's seemingly laborless work, Phoebe purifies the former evil and sorrow of her bedchamber and infuses the ancient house with her sunny cheer (312). "Little Phoebe was one of those persons who possess, as their exclusive patrimony, the gift of practical arrangement. It is a kind of natural magic that enables these favored ones to bring out the hidden capabilities of things around them" (311). Not unlike Holgrave's daguerreotypes, Phoebe's "homely witchcraft" (311) harnesses sunshine to bring out the interior essence of things around her.

Phoebe's sunny charms are particularly feminine virtues, the emblems of a new gender dominance on the home front. The efficient country girl infuses a once-patriarchal edifice with her airy goodness. In its historic prime, as the prize of an aristocratic family fortune, the seven-gabled house was a perfectly patriarchal structure: "It was a substantial, jolly-looking mansion, and seemed fit to be the residence of a patriarch, who might establish his own headquarters in the front gable and assign one of the remainder to each of his six children, while the great chimney in the center should symbolize the old fellow's hospitable heart, which kept them all warm, and made a great whole of the seven smaller ones" (413–414). On the threshold of little Phoebe's reign, the decline of patriarchal Pyncheon prosperity is marked by the unpopulated state of disrepair in which Phoebe finds the house and its tenants. Dank, dark, moldy, and dusty, the once-grand patriarchal house is inhabited only by an elderly maiden, Hepzibah, her rather broken brother, Clifford, and their mysterious boarder, Holgrave. Further, the relic of the grand old master's heart is manifest only gothically and grotesquely in the blood that gurgles in the throats of Pyncheon men.

Phoebe transforms the once-patriarchal Pyncheon house into the feminine sphere of middle-class domesticity. Regenerating this decrepit domain of failed masculinity and misguided femininity with her productive feminine charms, Phoebe infuses the seven-gabled house with the "health, comfort, and natural life" (435) of her body, her presence, and her labor. "A ray of firelight" (319), Phoebe purifies the house of the seven gables with her glowing flame. "Look where she would, lay her hand on what she might, the object responded to her consciousness, as if a moist human heart were in it" (438). Replacing the patriarch's heart, and the bloodlines that connected him to the residents of the smaller gables, Phoebe reinvigorates the very seat of the patriarchal Pyncheon line with the spiritualized essence of "true" love.[29]

THE PUBLIC PRIVATE SPHERE

Phoebe's private, domestic domain is intertwined with a public market in *The House of the Seven Gables*. Indeed, Phoebe's home is infused with the "public sphere" of commerce through the penny shop that is tucked within the seven-gabled house. Phoebe's success in the little shop marks the congruence of middle-class domesticity with market capitalism in *The House of the Seven Gables*, highlighting the interdependence of spheres once generally represented as separate. With Phoebe's ventures into the terrain of buying and selling, Hawthorne extends the sphere of influence commanded by the "true" domestic woman. In this way, Hawthorne's romance reinforces contemporary scholarship that questions the once-dominant depiction of "true" middle-class women as the secluded mistresses of hidden domestic domains protected from the public world of a capitalist market.[30] The feminine angel who transforms Hawthorne's seven-gabled house into a home also turns a pathetic financial venture into a "pretty good business" (523). Phoebe's success in the cent shop serves as yet another marker of the middle-class woman's industrious virtue in contrast to the aristocratic lady's rather ridiculous ineptitude. While Hepzibah's encounters with a "mass" of "plebian" shoppers fundamentally reconfigure her waning aristocratic "ladyhood," Phoebe's forays in the little shop do not threaten her "true" middle-class womanhood.

Laboring for a living dismantles Hepzibah's aristocratic ambitions, and she takes pains to protect herself from the "filth" of earned money with dainty white gloves. However, the threat that Hepzibah feels most viscerally as she falls from her ladied status into a market economy is the scrutinizing gaze that enters her secluded space along with common cash. Clinging to the aristocratic ambitions of her ancestors, Hepzibah trembles and weeps as she prepares her shop to receive "the public eye" (283). She is tortured "with a sense of overwhelming shame that strange and unloving eyes should have the privilege of gazing" (290). Much to her horror, Hepzibah must invite into her secluded domain not a party of her imagined social equals but a mass public of common shoppers, "as if all were household friends" (284).[31] The familiar gaze terrifies Hepzibah Pyncheon, as it symbolically dismantles the privileges of class hierarchy. Thus, it is not only the fact that she must now earn her living but also her subjection to public scrutiny on intimate terms that transforms Hepzibah from a lady into a plebian woman (279, 282, 283).[32]

The invasion of the seven-gabled house by a prying public eye produces the potential aura of a middle-class "private sphere" for Hepzibah, but Hepzibah herself lacks the feminine skills necessary to domesticate this newly privatized space. Hepzibah's withdrawal functions as a sign of aristocratic inadequacy, of her inability to survive in a world of buying and selling; her reclusive habits mark a secretive, antiquated aristocratic nature. Only Hepzibah's cousin Phoebe, a "true" middle-class woman, can offer Hepzibah entrance into the realm of a domesticity founded in a market economy. Phoebe purifies the decaying aristocratic house and revitalizes the ancient cent shop, melding "public" and "private" spheres in the essence of her gendered middle-class virtue.

Hawthorne's True Woman is not only a domestic angel but also a shrewd little capitalist. Rescuing Hepzibah from the horror of her unraveling class status, Phoebe replaces her aunt in the meager public spotlight of the cent shop and in just one day proves herself to be "as nice a little saleswoman" as she is "a housewife" (317). Because she has "not been brought up a Pyncheon," Phoebe is prepared to earn her keep (and to support her elderly relatives), and she suffers no slight of pride at the thought of making a small profit. Strictly speaking, Phoebe is not a "lady": "Instead of discussing her claim to rank among ladies, it would be preferable to regard Phoebe as the example of feminine grace and availability combined, in a state of society, if there were any such, where ladies did not exist" (319). Phoebe is the exemplar of femininity, a True Woman, in a society in which the elitism of aristocratic "ladies" has seemingly been effaced. This industrious domestic angel claims the virtues not of "rank" but of "feminine grace." Even in the little cent shop, Phoebe "makes a home about her" (369).

Phoebe Pyncheon is perfectly happy as the admired object of a public gaze, and she occupies this spotlight without any of the class presumptions of her aristocratic ancestors. Phoebe functions as the emblem of middle-class virtue, the sign of a "natural" middle-class dominance, and access to her spheres of influence is not circumscribed by explicit class elitism. Anyone may enter Phoebe's cent shop and benefit from the sweetness of her practical charms, so long as they do not pry, for Phoebe's interior spaces will be protected by a middle-class man. Phoebe's interiority, her very essence, distinguishes her from the exterior display of the aristocratic woman, and her gendered submissiveness shields her from class pride. In *The House of the Seven Gables*, it is the magic of middle-class gender that enables the True Woman paradoxically to display her essence in a public "private" sphere.

Hawthorne figures the rise of the middle class not in gender division ("separate spheres") but in gender dominance. The "natural" prevalence of a newly gendered terrain, not class ambition, seemingly propels the ascension of the middle class in Hawthorne's romance. Phoebe represents gender interests over those of class, even as she becomes the emblem of middle-class dominance. As Stuart Blumin has argued, the nineteenth-century middle class came "to express awareness of its common attitudes and beliefs as a denial of the significance of class."[33] Hawthorne's narrative of middle-class ascendance denies the significance of class hierarchies by masking them in a culture of gender. As middle-class domesticity is enabled by the effortless labor of the True Woman, it is secured only through the consecration of marriage in *The House of the Seven Gables*. Holgrave's union with Phoebe transforms class conflicts into new gender relations.[34] As Phoebe and Holgrave turn to one another on the brink of love, Holgrave whispers, " 'Do you love me Phoebe?' " Phoebe responds shyly: " 'You look into my heart.' " Letting her eyes drop, she confesses, " 'You know I love you!' " (513). Casting her eyes down in maidenly modesty, Phoebe symbolically relinquishes her gaze and her very self to the man she loves. Although unbeknownst to Phoebe, Holgrave has already proven himself a fit protector for her delicate feminine essence. Having restrained himself from violently trespassing her inner sanctity, Holgrave is ultimately given permission, by Phoebe herself, to look into her heart and to claim it as his own. Phoebe's humility, the symbolic disavowal of her gaze, compensates for the historic sin of Alice Pyncheon's haughty look, the symbol of her class pride; Holgrave's protection and gentle pursuit of Phoebe's soul repairs Matthew Maule's demonic transgression of Alice's spirit. As Phoebe and Holgrave are united by mutual love, performed through a willing submission and a gentle domination according to the gender roles proscribed by middle-class domesticity, Alice's posies reach full bloom in a chapter entitled "The Flower of Eden." Through the union of Phoebe and Holgrave, a legacy of ancestral evil is overcome and a middle-class family is born, blessed with all the spiritual purity of a new Eden.[35] In the final scene of the novel, a wise neighbor believes he sees floating toward heaven the spirit of Alice Pyncheon, the beautiful young woman who willfully, and within the logic of Hawthorne's narrative, wrongfully asserted her class privilege by claiming an objectifying gaze over the male body. As if confined to purgatory in the seven-gabled house, trapped in the patriarchal parlor of her Puritan ancestor, Alice Pyncheon is not absolved of her own sin until Phoebe casts her eyes down in love and becomes "truly" middle-class.

CHAPTER TWO

The Properties of Blood

"To plant a family! This idea is at the bottom of most of the wrong and mischief which men do. The truth is, that, once in every half century at longest, a family should be merged into the great, obscure mass of humanity, and forget all about its ancestors. Human blood, in order to keep its freshness, should run in hidden streams, as the water of an aqueduct is conveyed in subterranean pipes (408)."[1] Thus proclaims Holgrave on the eve of his transformation into a middle-class man in Nathaniel Hawthorne's *House of the Seven Gables*. Holgrave condemns an obsession with blood purity and ancestral inheritance as the cornerstone of aristocratic malady, as the key to Pyncheon demise. In Hawthorne's romance, blood maps the circuit of aristocratic inheritance, predictably directing the flow of property from generation to generation and defining the "blue" branches of the Pyncheon family tree. However, the seven-gabled house is not the only gothic possession handed down from parent to child in *The House of the Seven Gables*. The blood itself also bequeaths a legacy of congenital disease and ancestral character. A long line of Pyncheon patriarchs choke on their own blood, the very sign of aristocratic inheritance, and several seem to inherit intact the corrupted character of the Pyncheon founding father.

Aristocratic obsession with blood and blood purity is the cloud that middle-class essence dispels in *The House of the Seven Gables*. As we have seen, gendered images of interiority announce middle-class virtue in Hawthorne's romance of middle-class ascendance. Those gendered constructs are upheld, in turn, by a "healthy" mixing of blood across class lines that repairs the ills of the Pyncheons' aristocratic obsessions. Phoebe and Holgrave meet on the middle ground between their high and low birthrights, to regenerate bloodlines that have grown stagnant and stale. Reinvigorating a fount that has reached a standstill in Hepzibah's singular devotion to her brother, Phoebe and Holgrave produce a "healthy" new middle-class family line.[2]

Hawthorne's middle-class critique of blood as an *aristocratic* class obsession is remarkable because, by the mid–nineteenth century, conceits of blood purity, heredity, and inherited character were rapidly becoming the categories of "race" that most fascinated white *middle-class* Americans. During the period in which Hawthorne wrote and published *The House of the*

Seven Gables, blood purity was reinscribed in a new register in the sciences of "biological racialism."[3] Biological racialists believed in innate, permanent, heritable differences in both the physical and the moral and intellectual capacities of races. For biological racialists, both physical "type" and character were heirlooms rooted in the blood. These scientists invented and rigorously reinforced a racial hierarchy that celebrated Anglo-Saxons as inherently superior to those of other races, and they condemned interracial reproduction as a threat to the supremacy of the white race. According to biological racialists, racial blood mixing hampered the process whereby Anglo-Saxon heirs inherited superior racial character.

Over the course of the late–nineteenth century, the sciences of biological racialism reinvested middle-class images of interiority with a newly racialized biological character. As I will begin to outline here and in subsequent chapters, the architectures of interiority produced by gendered middle-class visual paradigms and domestic discourses of privacy were remapped as racial essences in the sciences of biological racialism. The very aspects of aristocratic elitism that Hawthorne denigrated as antithetical to middle-class values were later adopted and reconfigured as racial attributes by the white middle classes themselves.

This surprising discursive reinvention of middle-class interiority is not entirely obscured in Hawthorne's romance of middle-class ascendance. For even as Hawthorne explicitly critiques an obsession with blood purity as an aristocratic disease that must be healed by middle-class gender dominance, he simultaneously upholds the new scientific paradigms that link blood to hereditary character in nineteenth-century race theory. In this chapter I would like to return, in part, to *The House of the Seven Gables* to tease out the ways in which this text, exemplary in its articulation of middle-class gender dominance, simultaneously represses and prefigures the return of the racial reconstruction of the American middle classes. When we read *The House of the Seven Gables* in the context of new nineteenth-century race sciences, we see that by forwarding gender, Hawthorne's romance simultaneously masks, even as it foreshadows, the racial reinscription of the American middle classes.

In *The House of the Seven Gables* Hawthorne traces a twisted and conflicted path through the minefields of nineteenth-century race theory. Despite his critique of blood purity, which would seem to distance his argument from the tenets of biological racialism, Hawthorne's faith in inherited character reinforces the claims of nineteenth-century race scientists. The proof by which Hawthorne discredits an aristocratic obsession with blood purity, namely, his inscription of hereditary character, aligns his text with the claims of biological racialists, which he initially would seem to reject. Ultimately, *The House of the Seven Gables* outlines the routes whereby the blood discourses that Hawthorne represses will return as racialized middle-class constructs. *The House of the Seven Gables* is thus emblematic of the intertwined discourses of gender and race that articulated and transformed both the middle-class body and the national body over the course of the late nineteenth century.

THE BLOOD THAT FLOWS IN SUBTERRANEAN PIPES

Holgrave's celebration of blood mixing in *The House of the Seven Gables* becomes particularly striking when read against the strident warnings against blood mixture authored by biological racialists in the mid–nineteenth century. During the period in which Hawthorne wrote and published *The House of the Seven Gables*, scientists infused discussions of blood mixture and blood purity with racial significance. Because new sciences of race profoundly influenced American culture over the course of the nineteenth century, and ultimately informed shifting middle-class articulations of identity and cultural prerogative, I would like to spend considerable time here outlining the advent, the import, and the cultural and political manifestations of the sciences of biological racialism.

In the early nineteenth century, biological racialists, including phrenologists, craniologists, physiognomists, anthropometrists, ethnologists, polygenesists and Egyptologists, worked to establish innate biological differences between the races. Contrary to the eighteenth-century race theorists who preceded them, and who generally attributed racial distinctions to environmental conditions, biological racialists argued that racial differences were innate, permanent, and biological. These scientists were particularly eager to establish inherent differences in the moral and intellectual potentials of different races, and they argued that Caucasians, and specifically Anglo-Saxons, constituted a superior race throughout all human history. According to historian Reginald Horsman, such theories permeated American popular thought at midcentury: "By the early 1850s the inherent inequality of races was simply accepted as a scientific fact in America,"[4] and "Americans eagerly read popular discussions of the new scientific theories."[5] Such "scientific theories" had profound political implications throughout the early nineteenth century; the tenets of biological racialism were evoked to justify Indian Removal as the "natural" advance of a superior race at the expense of an inferior race, and to explain slavery as a "natural" institution mirroring innate racial hierarchies.

Biological racialism challenged not only eighteenth-century scientific thought but also dominant Christian beliefs in monogenesis, or the common origin of all humans as descended from Adam. Most biological racialists advanced the theory of "polygenesis," or "the separate creation of the races as distinct *species*," to explain racial inequalities.[6] Polygenesis was a

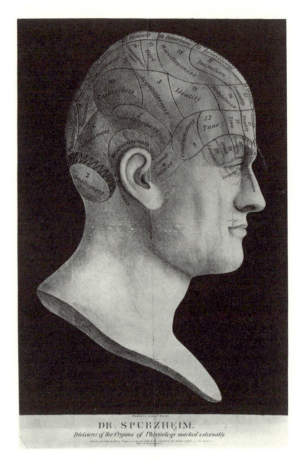

DR. SPURZHEIM.
Divisions of the Organs of Phrenology marked externally.

Dr. Spurzheim, Divisions of the Organs of Phrenology marked
externally. Lithograph by Pendletor, 1834. Reproduced from
the Collections of the Library of Congress.

central tenet of the influential new school of American ethnology founded
by the University of Chicago in the 1840s and led by scientists such as the
craniologist Samuel George Morton, the Egyptologist George Gliddon,
and the polygenesist and scholar of hybridity Josiah Nott.[7]

Polygenesists jealously guarded the imagined "superior stock" of Anglo-
Saxons, decrying racial blood mixture as a crippling contamination. Josiah
Nott did much to incite objections to interracial mixing in the early to mid–
nineteenth century, focusing his pseudoscientific studies on the product of
interracial mixing, the so-called mulatto.[8] Nott's famous studies of hybridity forwarded the notion that the races were distinct *species* in the genus
Homo. He argued that the interracial child was a true hybrid (the result of

an inter-*species* coupling) and therefore sterile. The obvious prolificacy of biracial slaves, raped and impregnated generation after generation, however, proved an obvious stumbling block in Nott's argument. Consequently, Nott nuanced his definitions of species and of hybridity, allowing for "remote, allied, and proximate species" which could interbreed with relative degrees of prolificacy or sterility.[9] He also extended the time frame generally used to measure true hybridity through sterility, arguing that "mulattoes," although not immediately sterile, were increasingly unprolific and had a tendency to die out after three or four generations. According to Nott, when "species the most widely separated, such as the Anglo-Saxon with the Negro, are crossed, . . . their mulatto offspring, if still prolific, are but partially so; and acquire an inherent tendency to run out, and become eventually extinct when kept apart from the parent stocks."[10] Nott eventually described four "degrees of hybridity"[11] and finally abandoned sterility as a test of interspecies coupling altogether. Ultimately, Nott defined the species simply as "a type, or organic form, that is permanent; or which has remained unchanged under opposite climatic influences for ages."[12]

Nott's theory of "types" enabled him to skirt the impossible proof of hybridity (sterility) and to maintain the propositions he held most dearly, namely, that "Negroes" were permanently, innately inferior to Caucasians both intellectually and morally, and that intermarriage between the two races was to be avoided because it resulted in weak, relatively unprolific offspring and "contaminated" the superior Caucasian stock. Nott proclaimed that "the superior race must inevitably become deteriorated by any intermixture with the inferior,"[13] and he proposed that "the superior races ought to be kept free from all adulterations, otherwise the world will retrograde, instead of advancing, in civilization."[14] Nott believed that it was only the "strictly-white races" that were "bearing onward the flambeau of civilization."[15] He proclaimed that "in the broad field and long duration of Negro life, not a single civilization, spontaneous or borrowed, has existed, to adorn its gloomy past."[16] Thus, according to Nott, any mixture between the "remote species" of Anglo-Saxons and "Negroes" would threaten the forward march of white Western "progress."

Nott's celebration of the white origins of all civilization provided scientific justification for Western colonialism, imperialism, racial extermination policies, and racial slavery. Indeed, Nott suggested that "the unintellectual races seem doomed to eventual disappearance in all those climates where the higher groups of fair-skinned families can permanently exist."[17] But Nott particularly celebrated the implications his theories held for proslavery advocates, unlike some earlier theorists of polygenesis such as Dr. Charles Caldwell. Indeed, during the years preceding the Civil War, Nott was a major pro-slavery apologist.[18] While Nott's scientific studies were not necessarily accessible to a wide reading audience, his views were popularized by writers and propagandists such as John H. Van Evrie, George S. Sawyer, and Samuel A. Cartwright.[19] In the 1840s, soon after Nott proposed that "Negroes" were a distinct species, inferior to Caucasians, his theories were heralded in the influential Southern journal *De Bow's Review*, and by the mid-1850s Nott's views had been accepted by the *Southern Quarterly Review*.[20] Thus, in Nott's work the connections between scientific race theory, popular race ideologies, and political race propaganda are made visible and explicit.

The issue of interracial reproduction became increasingly politicized before and after the Civil War, as racial identity, citizenship, property, and ownership were renegotiated in relation to bloodlines. New words were coined in popular arenas to encompass new conceptions of the races as distinct species and to emblematize the imagined dangers of racial blood mixing in political terms. In 1863 the term "miscegenation" was first used to connote inter-*species* reproduction in an anonymous political pamphlet produced by Democratic journalists David Goodman Croly and George Wakeman.[21] Written as if from the point of view of a radical abolitionist and designed to scandalize the Republican platform, the pamphlet advocated interracial mixing, proposing, contrary to the dominant claims of biological racialists, that mixed races were actually superior to pure races, and that such mixture would be the logical and beneficial result of Republican policies. In a similarly satirical political pamphlet, published in 1864 and entitled *What Miscegenation Is! and What We Are to Expect Now That Mr. Lincoln is Re-elected*, L. Seaman quips: "A man whose veins are coursed by a certain amount of dark blood, and whose skin is correspondingly dark, is believed to be a superior being."[22] The biting irony of both pamphlets demonstrates the degree to which the tenets of biological racialism had in fact been adopted by an American public that could be relied upon to recognize such inversions as "preposterous."

Throughout the elections of 1864, Southern Democrats harnessed the imagined "threat" of interracial mixing to the political agenda of Northern Republicans. Effacing the long-standing evidence that white masters raped black slaves generation after generation, reproducing their wealth in their own biracial children, Southern Democrats proposed that emancipation would increase amalgamation between the races. A political lithograph produced by Bromley and Company in 1864, entitled *The Miscegenation Ball*, caricatured a Republican campaign celebration, depicting "mystical and circling rites of languishing glance and mazy dance" at the "Lincoln Central Campaign Club." The lithograph depicts white men paired with black women, dancing, flirting, and fondling one another. Skirts are raised, heels are kicked back, and legs are spread. *The Miscegenation Ball* reenvisions a history of Southern white male aggression as the imagined lust of Northern white men for black women. The banner that hangs over a row

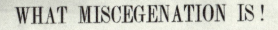

Cover, *What Miscegenation Is!* by L. Seaman, LL.D., 1864.

of interracial partners declares: "Universal Freedom: One Constitution, One Destiny, Abraham Lincoln President." The caricature implies that uniform representation under the Constitution will result in a literal unification of the races through amalgamation. In another sense, the lithograph also suggests that in a racially stratified culture, political equality is generally imagined only through an erasure of racial difference.

Another political lithograph produced by Bromley and Company in 1864, entitled *Miscegenation, or the Millennium of Abolitionism*, depicts then-dominant social relations inverted: White men are coupled with black women, black men are coupled with white women, and black families are driven by white coachmen. The lampoon imagines the social upheaval predicted by L. Seaman in his pamphlet "commemorating" the reelection of President Lincoln: "Things are changing. They are being reversed. It will be fashionable for colored 'genman' to have a white driver upon the same grounds that it has, heretofore, been fashionable for white men to have negro drivers."[23] The "humor" of this political caricature and the irony of its satire derive from the supposed disjunction between these "unnatural" pairings. In the lithograph the "real" inferiority of African Americans is represented through exaggerated physical features and unsophisticated language. Their failed attempts to mimic refinement demonstrate their physical inability to "properly" enjoy the fruits of freedom and of property ownership. Ultimately, this "joke" registers an even deeper social rift perpetuated by white supremacist biological racialists who believed that men and women of color were incapable of the self-governance necessitated by democracy. Josiah Nott explicitly argued that "dark" races were unfit for democracy, proclaiming, "*Dark*-skinned races, history attests, are only fit for military governments."[24] In Bromley's lithograph, only immigrant whites "correctly" criticize interracial coupling; however, the caricatured language that identifies them as recent immigrants marks their inferiority to Anglo-Saxon whites, who speak, even in their supposedly "ridiculous" positions, "proper" English. The image proposes that even ignorant immigrant whites have more pride in the integrity of whiteness than do Anglo-Saxon abolitionists, who should, according to the logics of biological racialism, assert their "natural" superiority over both African Americans and "ethnic" white Americans by maintaining the purity of their Anglo-Saxon racial stock.

The specter of racial mixing generated profound white anxiety on the eve of emancipation, for the liberation of slaves promised to break down the rigid racial boundaries whereby interracial rape had worked to reproduce white patriarchal privilege. In the racialized patriarchal economy of the antebellum South, interracial reproduction generally increased the economic power of white slaveholders. Because a biracial child born to a slave woman was always a slave, and therefore a form of capital, white slavehold-

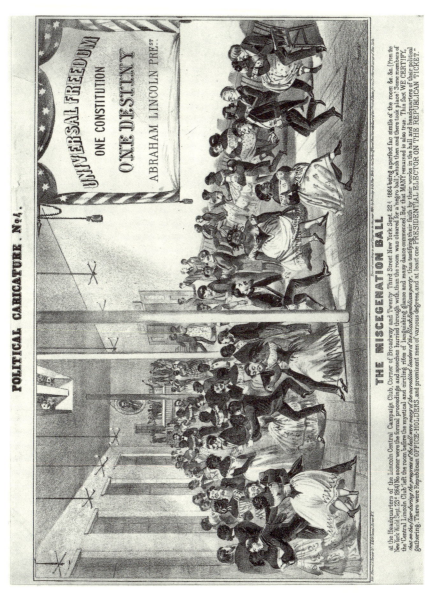

The Miscegenation Ball. Lithograph by Bromley and Company, 1864. Reproduced from the Collections of the Library of Congress.

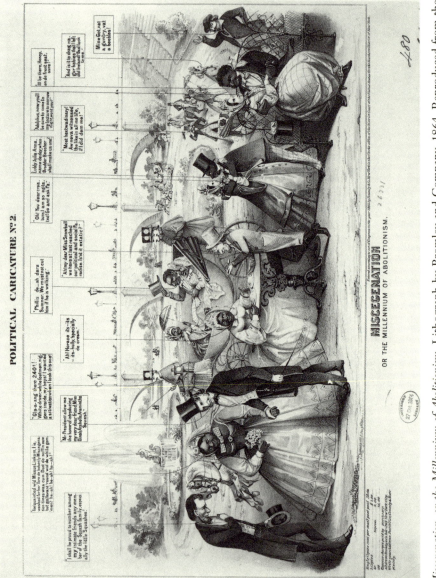

Miscegenation, or the Millennium of Abolitionism. Lithograph by Bromley and Company, 1864. Reproduced from the Collections of the Library of Congress.

ers could increase their property by raping and impregnating slave women. Thus, Southern law reinforced the institutionalized rape of slave women by maintaining that children would follow the "condition" of their mothers. According to Hazel Carby, the slave woman's "reproductive destiny was bound to capital accumulation; black women gave birth to property and, directly, to capital itself in the form of slaves, and all slaves inherited their status from their mothers."[25]

Under the "peculiar system" of Southern slavery, "miscegenation" was nearly always posed as the union of a free white man with an enslaved woman of color. In his "scientific" study of "the mulatto," Josiah Nott declares, "In the United States, the mulattoes and other grades are produced by the connection of the white *male* with the *Negress*; the mulattoes with each other; and the white male with the *mulattress*."[26] Nott utterly erases the unions of white women with black men, proclaiming, "It is so rare, in this country, to see the offspring of a Negro man and a white woman, that I have never personally encountered an example."[27] Nott's "scientific" theories reinforced sexualized racial stereotypes, perpetuating the intertwined racial and gender hierarchies that deemed the white woman "pure" and the woman of color "promiscuous."[28]

According to Hazel Carby, white supremacists ideologically circumscribed free white women in a discourse of "purity" because they depended on white women "as the means of the consolidation of property through the marriages of alliance between plantation families"; free white women "gave birth to the inheritors of that property."[29] A sexual, reproductive relationship between a male slave and a free white woman would threaten the racial boundaries of a white patriarchy, enabling biracial children theoretically to inherit white patriarchal property through the free white mother. Thus, as Karen Sanchez-Eppler has argued compellingly, the white woman's potential desire for a black man was exactly what had to be denied in order to maintain the white patriarchal Southern slave system.[30]

Within a white supremacist racial patriarchy, the white woman's sexual desire must be controlled because so much depends on her sexual reproduction. Within this system, white women must remain reliably "pure" in order to serve as the stable cornerstones of the white patriarchy, "properly" diverting the bloodlines that determine one's political status, material inheritance, and even one's imagined character and intelligence. Given this cultural context, L. Seaman's pamphlet is particularly inflammatory because it depicts the blind spot, or repressed point, in the discourses of female sexuality, race science, and miscegenation that helped to perpetuate the antebellum patriarchal slave system, namely, the possibility of an interracial relationship between a white woman and a black man. Indeed, in Seaman's lithograph we find the rigorously repressed power of the white woman's potentially uncontrollable sexuality awakened in the arms of a black man. Seaman's white woman clasps her arms affectionately around her African American partner, displaying her bosom proudly as the sign of her willing desire.

Seaman's lithograph tapped into the anxieties of pro-slavery advocates who proclaimed that the abolition of slavery would undermine the racial and gender relations that consolidated power for white patriarchs through carefully controlled interracial mixing. By inverting the claims of white slave owners over black female slaves, Seaman's "scandalous" cover page emblematizes the political equality emancipation would signal between white men and black men through the image of their newly equivalent relationship to sexualized white female property. And even more powerfully, Seaman's lithograph brings to light the relationship that would most dramatically redirect the flow of blood and property on which an antebellum racial patriarchy was maintained.[31]

Certainly Hawthorne's romance of middle-class ascendance does not promote an inversion in racial hierarchies or advocate *racial* blood mixing in any explicit manner. Indeed, the only evidence we have of a politically contested racial context in Hawthorne's romance is found in the cameo role of Scipio, an African American servant relegated to the Pyncheon past, the "Jim Crow" cookie in Hepzibah's shop, and the Free Soil debates noted in Judge Pyncheon's political campaign. However, even in these subtle signs we find that Hawthorne's celebration of blood mixing across class lines in *The House of the Seven Gables* is literally supported by white supremacist alliances. In her little shop, Hepzibah sells "Jim Crow" cookies as part of an exotic "natural history" to be consumed by little Ned Higgins. The sign of the happily segregated slave unites white aristocrats and white working-class consumers in Hawthorne's romance of middle-class economic development. Such alliances are made even more pronounced in the foundation on which Hawthorne literally establishes an ascendant middle class. For the estate to which Phoebe and Holgrave, Hepzibah, Clifford, and Uncle Venner retreat, namely, Jaffrey's country home, is an edifice built upon pro-slavery economic and political unions. We learn circuitously, through the strange, extended description of Jaffrey's death scene, that he has been politically allied with Southern pro-slavery politicians. And while Hawthorne does not explicitly celebrate such associations, casting Jaffrey off as the embodiment of inherited Pyncheon wickedness, nevertheless, he concludes his romance with the triumphant middle-class couple trotting off to claim Jaffrey's large country house. Even though Jaffrey is dismissed, Phoebe and Holgrave benefit from the property he has acquired by politically supporting the expansion of slavery, and thus Hawthorne builds the very foundations for his (white) middle class on pro-slavery sentiments. As property crosses class boundaries in Hawthorne's middle-class romance, it continues to follow and to reinforce the racialized bloodlines that divide free property owners from enslaved commodities. Indeed, we find that the blood that streams through Holgrave's "subterranean pipes" is also the repressed, racialized blood that flows under white middle-class homes.

BLOOD, CHARACTER, AND RACE

While Hawthorne's rejection of blood purity might seem at first to align his class critique with an implicitly antiracist agenda, we find that his fantasy of middle-class ascendance is ultimately enabled by the economic foundations established through Northern and Southern pro-slavery alliances. In more subtle terms, we also discover that Hawthorne's romance upholds the new scientific laws of inherited character that would come to dominate the sciences of biological racialism, and particularly the science of eugenics in the late nineteenth century. In order to challenge the aristocratic conceits of blood purity, Hawthorne calls upon the proof of inherited character upheld by biological racialists and eugenicists. Specifically, in the case of the Pyncheons, we find that blood purity is detrimental because it reproduces a corrupt congenital character.

In *The House of the Seven Gables*, Hawthorne portrays character as an ancestral legacy, a kind of familial property bequeathed from father to son, and he thereby situates his romance within the conceptual purview of nineteenth-century race sciences. In fact, I suggest that *The House of the Seven Gables* encompasses and prefigures an ideological domain that would not be articulated fully until half a century later, as eugenics came to dominate U.S. race theory. Reproducing connections between character and heredity, *The House of the Seven Gables* plants the seed of a theory of biological inheritance newly articulated by biological racialists in the first half of the nineteenth century (and heralded by pro-slavery advocates in the interracial debates of the 1860s), a theory that would finally support eugenicists' romance of Anglo-Saxon superiority at the turn of the century.

As Hawthorne's narrator describes the ancestral legacy of his central characters in the first chapter of *The House of the Seven Gables*, he offers a "weighty lesson": "the little-regarded truth that the act of the passing generation is the germ which may and must produce good or evil fruit in a far-distant time; that together with the seed of the merely temporary crop, which mortals term expediency, they inevitably sow the acorns of a more enduring growth, which may darkly overshadow their posterity" (254). Colonel Pyncheon's avarice generates two ancestral curses: His sin invites Maule to condemn Pyncheon progeny, and it corrupts the character he himself will bestow upon his biological heirs. Pyncheon's sin infects the fount of Pyncheon character, passing along a propensity for greed and dishonesty as a congenital flaw. As Pyncheon men inherit the physical malady that destroyed their forebear, the gurgling blood that chokes Colonel Pyncheon, they also inherit the degraded character engendered by their forebear's "expediency."[32]

Phoebe Pyncheon recognizes a startling resemblance between her uncle, Judge Jaffrey Pyncheon, and their distant relative, Colonel Pyncheon. In fact, Phoebe cannot even discern the difference between the two men when she first sees a daguerreotype portrait of Jaffrey Pyncheon. Later, when Phoebe meets Jaffrey in person, she again sees the scowl of the Colonel reflected in her uncle's face:

> Then, all at once, it struck Phoebe that this very Judge Pyncheon was the original of the miniature which the daguerreotypist had shown her in the garden, and that the hard, stern, relentless look now on his face was the same that the sun had so inflexibly persisted in bringing out. Was it, therefore, no momentary mood, but, however skillfully concealed, the settled temper of his life? And not merely so, but was it hereditary in him, and transmitted down, as a precious heirloom, from that bearded ancestor in whose picture both the expression, and, to a singular degree, the features of the modern Judge were shown as by a kind of prophecy? A deeper philosopher than Phoebe might have found something very terrible in this idea. It implied that the weaknesses and defects, the bad passions, the mean tendencies, and the moral diseases which lead to crime are handed down from one generation to another, by a far surer process of transmission than human law has been able to establish in respect to the riches and honors which it seeks to entail upon posterity. (351–352)

This passage brings together the (racialized) threads of blood, inheritance, and character that are woven throughout Hawthorne's romance. The narrator suggests, not unlike Francis Galton, the British founder of eugenics, that character is a kind of ancestral heirloom passed through the blood from one generation to the next. Not only corporeal diseases, such as the ominous "gurgle" that brings so many Pyncheon patriarchs to their demise, but also "moral diseases," such as greed and malice, are inherited from one's ancestors.

The congenital character that Hawthorne thematizes in *The House of the Seven Gables* was theorized as a racial attribute in the science of eugenics. Francis Galton, the cousin of Charles Darwin, began his studies in the "science of race" in 1865, finally calling his work "eugenics" in 1884.[33] Like the polygenists before him, Galton proclaimed that racial differences were biological and that they determined not only exterior physical features but also innate, inherent moral and intellectual characteristics. Galton reinforced the racial hierarchies founded by antebellum biological racialists, celebrating the Anglo-Saxons as a superior race. Like Josiah Nott,

Galton opposed racial mixing and was eager to apply his theories to political debates about colonialism and imperialism. While certainly growing out of a general trend toward biological racialism, Galton's eugenics placed a new emphasis on heredity as a determining factor in deciding one's moral character, intellectual potential, and physical health. Galton attempted to demonstrate that "a man's natural abilities are derived by inheritance."[34] Selecting many "great men" according to historical reputation, and tracing their ancestral lineage, Galton surmised that "genius," or intellectual ability, was hereditary. Consequently, he claimed that a race might be improved through regulated marriages and procreation. To that end, Galton advocated early marriages and prolific procreation for mentally and morally strong Anglo-Saxons, and he discouraged reproduction of the physically, morally, and racially "weak."[35] Ultimately, Galton offered a practical plan for improving racial character through controlled breeding.

Viewing it through the lens of eugenics, we might also come to understand Hawthorne's celebration of Holgrave's soon-to-be-middle-class character in a new light, as a celebration of the "property" that springs from a sturdy racial stock. Holgrave is both contemplative and endowed with "a springy alacrity and vigor," qualities that are "perceptible, physically, in his make and motions," and also apparent "immediately in his character" (287). The correspondence between Holgrave's physical qualities and his personal character resonates powerfully with the racialized connection linking body to mind that Francis Galton would proclaim and that Josiah Nott imagined decades earlier. In his introduction to *Types of Mankind*, Nott pronounces the "permanence of moral and intellectual peculiarities" consequent to and inseparable from permanent physical types or "races."[36] Holgrave's superior character is a permanent attribute—in Nott's terms, an innate racial characteristic—unaltered by the changing conditions of his life: "Homeless as he had been—continually changing his whereabout, and, therefore, responsible neither to public opinion nor to individuals; putting off one exterior, and snatching up another, to be soon shifted for a third—he had never violated the innermost man, but had carried his conscience along with him" (*The House of the Seven Gables* 401).[37] Holgrave's sturdy character holds steady in the face of temptations that corrupt others, including a long line of Pyncheon patriarchs. Read in relation to Nott's biological racialism, Holgrave's purportedly superior character signals his "rightful" ascendance to social power in terms not only of class but also of race.[38]

Now, while the Pyncheons are clearly "white" in Hawthorne's romance, they do not try to improve their hereditary character through eugenical marriages. The Pyncheons privilege material property gains, family names, and elite class standing in their unions. As Josiah Nott would say, the Pyncheons breed "in and in." Nott, like the eugenicists who would follow him, advocated blood mixing across class lines, as long as such unions remained within the racial bounds of Caucasian groups. Nott decried the obsession with blood purity upheld in pseudo-aristocratic families: "Cannot every one of us individually point to degenerate offspring which have arisen from family intermarriages for mere property-sake?"[39] Undermining the cultural authority of pseudo-aristocratic patriarchs, Nott proclaims, "It is not to children of the educated class alone that we look for ruling intellects, but nature's noblemen, on the contrary, more often spring from the families of the backwoodsman, or the sturdy mechanic."[40] Nott's "natural noblemen" are, of course, always Caucasian, and preferably Anglo-Saxon, but not necessarily to be found in the purported "best" (white) families. Indeed, Nott's racialized "natural nobleman" looks quite a bit like Holgrave, Hawthorne's soon-to-be-middle-class hero, who has worked as a country schoolmaster, a salesman in a country store, the political editor of a country newspaper, a peddler, a dentist, a mesmerist, and a daguerreotypist, among other things (401). Through Holgrave, Hawthorne's romance opens a space for a newly racialized measure of character, a new means of articulating middle-class claims to social privilege and cultural dominance. While decrying the class elitism of the Pyncheons, Hawthorne leaves room for the "true" superiority of the white middling man's character.

The convergence of racialist values with a narrative of middle-class ascendance that we find in *The House of the Seven Gables* is not surprising, for Francis Galton's eugenicist plan for racial improvement was a singularly middle-class fantasy, a romance of racialized middle-class superiority. Galton argued that the kind of civilization best suited to nurture the improvement of the Anglo-Saxon race was one in which "incomes were chiefly derived from professional sources, and not much through inheritance; where every lad had a chance of showing his abilities and, if highly gifted, was enabled to achieve a first-class education and entrance into professional life, by the liberal help of the exhibitions and scholarships which he had gained in his early youth."[41] Ultimately, Galton sought to redistribute wealth and social standing along bloodlines imagined to be more racially "well-deserving." Not unlike Hawthorne and Nott, Galton denaturalized a system of aristocratic inheritance to celebrate a racialized "natural" worth as the key to middle-class inheritance. Galton thus effectively shifted the terms in which inherited "properties" could be defined and valued, transforming intellectual ability and moral character into family heirlooms. Ultimately Galton proposed that the racialized ancestral qualities of "good blood," moral character, and intellectual capacity should be rewarded with the monetary properties once exclusively linked to pseudo-aristocratic bloodlines.

As David Green has argued, eugenics reinforced the ideological interests of the professional middle classes, which distinguished themselves by claiming exclusive access to recently accredited systems of knowledge, such as the new biological sciences of race.[42] According to Green, "Insofar as eugenics proposed the reordering of society in accordance with the distribution of mental abilities and cognitive skills amongst the population, it placed a high value on those whose contribution to society was based upon intellectual expertise rather than the ownership of capital or the supply of labour."[43] Eugenicists transformed an aristocratic system of inheritance, replacing a fascination for hereditary property with an emphasis on the imagined intellectual and moral "properties" of the blood itself. In this way, eugenics provided a racialized discourse of middle-class superiority.

Hawthorne's negotiation of implicitly racialized class logics in *The House of the Seven Gables* is truly complicated. For whereas Hawthorne argues against blood purity, he makes his case only by drawing upon the armature of biological racialism and eugenics. Blood purity is problematic in Hawthorne's eyes because for him blood does indeed carry congenital character traits, such as the Pyncheons' avaricious ambition. In Hawthorne's romance blood must be mixed, but it must be mixed with the "proper" (middle-class) sources. As we have seen, while Hawthorne condemns aristocratic Pyncheon character as an ancestral inheritance, he celebrates Holgrave's (middle-class) character in ways that conform to later middle-class celebrations of white racial stock. Hawthorne's middle-class romance lays out the eugenicist concepts that would transform the terms of middle-class discourses of rightful cultural dominance (from gender to race) over the course of the late nineteenth century.

The "properties of blood" eventually became the anchors of a white middle-class identity. The pseudo-aristocratic obsession with bloodlines that Hawthorne critiqued in his celebration of middle-class character would be taken up and rearticulated by the middle classes themselves, in terms of racial privilege. Indeed, as I will demonstrate in subsequent chapters, the very paradigm Hawthorne represents as the counterdiscourse to middle-class identity—the discourse of blood purity—would become one of the founding tenets of a racialized middle-class identity by the late nineteenth century.

THE SPECTACLE OF RACE

"Race" both informed and transformed the visual terrain through which Hawthorne articulated a dominant, gendered vision of normative middle-class ascendance. Mid-nineteenth-century racialized discourses of blood intersected with the visual paradigms of interiority and exteriority that were forwarded as the emblems of middle-class moral character in the antebellum period, and "race" determined the gendered scenes of threat and violation that enabled the construction of middle-class privacy. Indeed, if we read the vulnerability of the slave family through the lens of middle-class discourses of threatened violation, we see that Hawthorne's domestic sphere was not only a gendered but also a racialized middle-class realm.

Middle-class privacy was violently denied to slaves and slave families. Indeed, violence itself, not an imagined threat of violation, was integral to the formation of the slave's identity and community. In Northern middle-class terms, the horror of slavery was symbolized not only by the breakup of the slave family, as Harriet Beecher Stowe proclaimed,[44] but also by the terrifying exposure to a threatening gaze that preceded and begot violence upon the slave body. The sexualized display of the slave woman's vulnerability at the slave auction did not secure her rescue in the arms of a man of superior character; the slave pen trapped her in a public sphere where she was ever vulnerable to aggressive masculine gazes, to probing touches, and ultimately to purchase. Threats to the sanctity of the slave woman's body ended in violation, as she was relegated to the world of commodities and thereby denied the protection of middle-class domesticity. In one sense, then, the slave woman's body was the commodity displayed in the little shop windows of white domesticity. As she was forced to serve as sexual surrogate for the "pure" white woman, she was also forced to reproduce a flow of commodities through her own body.[45]

In her analysis of the ways in which public scenes of torture inform African American self-identifications, Elizabeth Alexander has argued compellingly that such scenes have served as sites in the formation of a black consciousness that bears witness to and identifies with the threat and experience of violence.[46] In assessing Frederick Douglass's 1845 *Narrative*, Alexander demonstrates how Douglass comes to recognize his own enslaved status by witnessing the torture of his aunt. Reading Douglass's narration of this brutal performance, Alexander suggests that Douglass "can scarcely articulate what it means for that visual narrative to become forever a part of his consciousness."[47] The spectacle of violence registers empathetically in Douglass's body; it becomes a kind of corporeal image for him, a sensorial experience that links him to a collective slave memory stored in slave bodies. Witnessing the scene of his aunt's torture—that "horrible exhibition," that "most terrible spectacle"—gives Douglass the terrifying sense that he is next, and in this way he comes to recognize his own disempowered status as equivalent to that of his aunt's. In bearing witness to the scene of his aunt's torture, Douglass realizes that his own body, which viscerally responds to the sight, is also "vulnerable and black."[48] Douglass comes to identify with the tortured slave body and to recognize it as his own.

In witnessing this spectacle of violence, Douglass is terrified further by the sense that he can do nothing to stop the torture, that he is unable to protect his aunt. He cannot deter the "threat" of violation that is enacted by the white master upon the black female body; he can only bear witness to the spectacle of black pain. In the gendered terms of free white middle-class discourses, Douglass, as a slave, is unable to enact "proper" masculine protection over the female body. In Douglass's narrative the slave woman's body becomes the site through which two racially differentiated masculinities are defined. White masculinity is posed as a destructive force unleashed upon the black body, and black masculinity is relegated to the position of all slaves vulnerable to white terrorism.

As such spectacles made the white male's capacity for violence abundantly clear to African American witnesses, they also suggested to white women that their claims to domestic sanctity were tenuous, constantly exposed to a volatile white male anger. The very men who brutally enacted violence upon black bodies were those who purported to protect white women from the threats of other masculine intruders. In this way, then, the display of torture from which the white woman was protected functioned to keep her carefully confined in a position whereby the flow of white patriarchal bloodlines could be regulated through her body. And when the white woman raised her own hand against the slave, she viciously reinforced the boundaries of her own fragile privilege.

A racialized paradigm of threat and violation produced the sanctity of a middle-class domestic sphere bound not only by gender oppositions but also by racial homogeneity. The spectacle of the tortured black body reinforced the *racialized* privilege of a *white* middle-class privacy produced by middle-class narratives of threat to the white female body. Such racialized displays of violence powerfully reinforced the distinction between protected white middle-class bodies and black bodies ritually tortured before a public gaze.

SEEING BLOODLINES

As racialized sight lines divided antebellum American culture into separate racial spheres, visual paradigms also informed the ways in which individual bodies were racially conceptualized and identities were racially articulated. It is through the visual medium of the daguerreotype, that early photographic form, that Judge Jaffrey Pyncheon's sinister ancestral character is first revealed in Hawthorne's romance. Indeed, as I have noted briefly, Phoebe mistakes Holgrave's daguerreotype of Judge Jaffrey Pyncheon for a modernized copy of Colonel Pyncheon's dark, painted portrait, telling Holgrave: "To be sure, you have found some way of copying the portrait without its black velvet cap and gray beard, and have given him a modern coat and satin cravat, instead of his cloak and band" (329). While Holgrave assures her that the daguerreotype is a modern portrait of a living man, he does marvel at the penetrating powers of his work with light and mirrors, proclaiming, as we saw in chapter 1: "There is a wonderful insight in heaven's broad and simple sunshine. While we give it credit only for depicting the merest surface, it actually brings out the secret character with a truth that no painter would ever venture upon, even could he detect it" (328). The secret character Holgrave's daguerreotype captures is the stern glower of Pyncheon posterity. In Hawthorne's romance of middle-class ascendance, a visual technology provides the mechanism whereby racialized logics of blood, heredity, and character are represented and established. The daguerreotype poses a visual map of interior essence. Thus, it is not only the evidence of gurgling blood but also the evidence of visually codified physiognomy that binds Pyncheon men to the common ancestral inheritance of a corrupted character.[49] Ultimately, then, both genealogies and visual technologies trace the bloodlines that direct the circulation of soon-to-be racialized ancestral "properties" in *The House of the Seven Gables*.

Hawthorne's treatment of daguerreotypy in *The House of the Seven Gables* looks both back to earlier studies of the relationship posited between exterior surface signs and interiorized character traits in the antebellum sciences of physiognomy and phrenology, and forward to Francis Galton's later use of photography to establish distinct social "types" in the late-nineteenth-century science of eugenics. The study of facial features as traces of interiorized character traits was intimately linked to racialized conceptions of innate character from its inception in physiognomy and phrenology. This desire to read physical signs as the markers of interior character originated in the United States with the work of Swiss-born minister Johann Kaspar Lavater, who in the late eighteenth century attempted to describe character through a detailed study of the head and face.[50] Lavater's work generated interest in anthropometry and physiognomy, projects that became racially inflected in the work of early phrenologists in the 1830s. Phrenology, the study of the bumps and angles of the skull as signs that indicate the "strength" of areas of the brain linked to specific intellectual, creative, and moral capacities, was a respected scientific endeavor in the 1830s, a project vitally linked to the new, biological conceptions of "race" developing in the early nineteenth century. Indeed, phrenologists like Dr. Charles Caldwell provided the first "scientific evidence" supporting the existence of superior and inferior races.[51] Later craniologists, such as Samuel George Morton, a colleague of Josiah Nott, utilized cranial measurements to reinforce a theory of permanent racial hierarchies. Morton's 1844 *Crania Aegyptica* drew upon data secured from the craniums of ancient Egyptian mummies in order to claim the earliest known civilization for the Caucasian race. Morton's findings were applauded by Josiah Nott and

George Gliddon, who used Morton's studies to argue for the "natural" racial hierarchy maintained by Southern slavery.[52]

Josiah Nott viewed the face as a crucial map of interiorized characteristics, believing, once again, that "the intellectual man is inseparable from the physical man."[53] In *Types of Mankind*, Nott proclaims: "However important anatomical characteristics may be, I doubt whether the *physiognomy* of races is not equally so. There exist minor differences of features, various minute combinations of details, certain palpable expressions of face and aspect, which language cannot describe: and yet, how indelible is the image of a *type* once impressed on the mind's eye! When, for example, the word 'Jew' is pronounced, a type is instantly brought up by memory, which could not be so described to another person as to present to his mind a faithful portrait. The image must be seen to be known and remembered; and so on with the faces of all men, past, present, or to come."[54] For Nott, the image crystallizes a racial "type," equating a multitude of people with a single, imaginary face, a face that apparently will haunt and circumscribe one's future conceptions of diverse individuals—when one hears the word "Jew," a single misrepresentation will appear to the mind's eye. As we shall see, Nott's enthusiasm for codified images of racial types was taken up later in the nineteenth century, as biological racialists and eugenicists harnessed new photographic technologies to their studies of "race."

Francis Galton believed that photography could provide visual evidence to support his theory of racialized character inheritance. According to Galton, the photograph could capture telltale physiognomical traces of an individual's inherited racial characteristics. In this light we might consider Holgrave's daguerreotypy in *The House of the Seven Gables* as a kind of precursor to eugenicist uses of photography.[55] Holgrave's death portrait of Judge Jaffrey Pyncheon provides visual evidence of biological heredity, demonstrating that Jaffrey fell victim to the same congenital blood disease that plagued a long line of Pyncheon patriarchs. The blood that flows out of Pyncheon mouths is the sign of that inheritance, and Holgrave's daguerreotype captures and reproduces that sign in the name of scientific and legal evidence. But Holgrave's daguerreotypes demonstrate not only the fact of physical inheritance but also the fact of a more ephemeral character inheritance indexed in the facial expressions of his subject. Holgrave's first daguerreotype portraits of Judge Pyncheon uncannily reproduce the sinister stare of the Puritan Pyncheon ancestor. Daguerreotypes serve as a kind of visual evidence that traces inherited moral characteristics in the curves and expressions of the face. In Holgrave's hands, as in Francis Galton's, the photograph becomes a tool with which one can read the signs of ancestral character in another's face.

I will leave a discussion of racialized scientific uses of photography for succeeding chapters and simply emphasize here, once again, the ways in which Hawthorne's *House of the Seven Gables* prefigures the means whereby the terms of middle-class cultural prerogative would be transformed from discourses of gender to discourses of race over the course of the late nineteenth century. Hawthorne's text provides an estimation of character that resonates powerfully with the racialized measure of character celebrated in the mid-nineteenth-century sciences of biological racialism. His focus on hereditary traits and his celebration of "healthy" marriages in *The House of the Seven Gables* prefigure the tenets of eugenics, the late-nineteenth-century professional middle-class discourse of white supremacy. Further, the visual medium that provides evidence of ancestral inheritance in Hawthorne's romance, the photographic portrait, was to be utilized by eugenicists, as we will see, in their attempts to link racialized character traits to distinct facial features, to join newly racialized interior essences to codified physical exteriors. Finally, then, the "secret truth" of Holgrave's daguerreotype magically prefigures the eugenicist conceits that were to dominate middle-class discourses of identity and cultural privilege in the late nineteenth century.

CHAPTER THREE

Superficial Depths

Somehow it gives me a desolate feeling to think
of having my faded picture trundled about some
hundred years hence as worthless lumber, or
being tolerated as a thing of habit, rather than
affection, in some out-of-the-way corner.
Perhaps saucy children will some day stick pins
through my eyes, and scratch my cheeks and
nobody will be grieved or angered by it.
(R.H.E., Godey's Lady's Book, *April 1867*)

AT THE MOST basic level, R.H.E.'s evocative statements express regret over the inevitable fate of her own passing and fading from memory. In grieving for her own death, R.H.E. also mourns the passing of her loved ones and the termination of the bonds of intimacy that have commanded respect and love. When the last of her relatives and friends are gone, all that will remain of R.H.E. is the trace of her face recorded in an old photograph. Those who gaze upon the image in years hence will not know if she was kind or clever, creative or strong; to them, perhaps, her image will mean nothing.

At another level R.H.E.'s comments express anxiety over her inability to control the reception of her photographic portrait as it circulates beyond the bounds of intimacy. Writing in the 1860s, R.H.E. attests to the exponential increase in and ever-widening distribution of photographic portraits enabled by what Walter Benjamin has definitively called the advent of "mechanical reproduction," or negative/positive photography. Mechanical reproduction proper began in the 1850s with the collodion/albumen process, a negative/positive photographic printing technique. With this new process, photographic imaging exploded into multiplicity. For the first time, photography was no longer limited to the production of discrete, unique objects, as in daguerreotypy; photographers could now make countless identical positive prints from a single negative. The proliferation of images enabled by mechanical reproduction gave rise to a host of new cultural forms, including the photographic calling card, or carte-de-visite, the

André Adolphe Eugene Disredi, Portrait of Princess Buonaparte, uncut carte-de-visite, circa 1862. Reproduced from the Gernsheim Collection, Harry Ransom Humanities Research Center, The University of Texas at Austin.

popular celebrity image, the cabinet card, the stereograph card collection, and the family photograph album.[1]

The advent of mechanical reproduction radically transformed the historical purview of art, according to Walter Benjamin. In his now famous essay on the invention of the reproducible photographic process, Benjamin explains that mechanical reproduction dismantled the "aura"[2] of the original work of art by enabling the production of exact copies. Indeed, with the negative/positive photographic process there is no original work of art distinct from a copy. The negative is not the work of art itself, and all positives made from it are potentially identical images. Benjamin celebrated this transformation in the production of art, believing the aura of the original to be linked problematically to the sacred estimation of religious objects in ancient times. For Benjamin such reverence detracted from the work of art's capacity to render the historical evidence necessary for political liberation and revolution.

While celebrating the dissolution of aura surrounding the work of photographic art, Benjamin also suggests that aura makes its final appearance in the photographic portrait, clinging to the representation of the human countenance, before it is finally abolished by the unsentimental standards of evidence. Locating the aura that surrounds the early photographic portrait in a "cult of remembrance," a privatized worship of missing loved ones, Benjamin defines this particular (and he thought ultimate) aura as an associative link relating representation to referent, a bond of love tying a material signifier to an absent signified.[3] In this way, the photographic portrait can be said to function in much the same way as the religious icon, the crucifix or image of the Madonna, as a physical marker of an invisible being (because absent or spiritual) for a devoted worshiper.

In colloquial terms R.H.E. describes her relationship to a photographic portrait as decidedly auratic: "It becomes alive to me through sentiment. I weave a little history for it. . . ."[4] In her own understanding, R.H.E., as viewer, brings the portrait to life, breathing the soul of her affections into the image, spinning a history for the mute object. However, in recognizing the function of the photograph as "a link between you and the memory of its owner,"[5] R.H.E. also expresses horror at the possible loss of this auratic connection around her own portraits, as noted earlier. R.H.E. implicitly discerns that the aura of the "cult of remembrance" depends on the sentimental labor of portrait viewers and owners. In shifting her imaginary role from viewer to sitter, from observer to represented, R.H.E. once again reveals a certain anxiety about the circulation of her image: "It becomes a sort of vitalized thing to you, an emanation from your own being, and you rebel at making it a common gazing stock, as you shrink from the gregariousness of a common crowd."[6] The dissolution of aura, the disintegration of that nearly spiritual bond that joins a portrait to a beloved through sentiment, the transformation that Benjamin celebrated, is a rather terrifying prospect for R.H.E.

As photographic images proliferated, so did the anxieties concerning them. If the exact copy, a reproducible positive, obliterated the notion of the original in mechanical reproduction, what happened to the self whose semblance was reproduced in photographic portraits? While daguerreotypy suggested new relations between subjects and objects of view, and troubled the very essence of what could be seen, photography in the age of mechanical reproduction multiplied the questions surrounding the cultural prerogative of the look and its connection to identity. As more and more images could be had, identity, and corresponding social hierarchies, were imagined increasingly to be mutable. Indeed, R.H.E. ultimately worried that unknown viewers would not be able to "see" her, that they would not be able to read and to evaluate the worth of her character as rendered in the reflection of her image.

Perhaps intimating threats to middle-class cultural dominance unleashed by mechanical reproduction, the nineteenth-century American middle classes did not herald the dissolution of aura as Walter Benjamin did, but instead attempted to preserve this ephemeral attribute as an exclusive characteristic of middle-class portraits and middle-class identities. One's inability to control the readings of one's portrait, and the uses it may be put to if circulated outside the bounds of intimacy, fueled new visual discourses that aimed to delineate sanctified middle-class identities in opposition to cultural others. Such discourses endeavored to imbed aura within the portrait itself, as a recognizable, undeniable quality not dependent upon the attention of loved ones. In the late-nineteenth-century debates that attempted to differentiate the artistic (middle-class) photographic portrait from the "mere" photographic likeness, one finds a continued investment in interiority as the (auratic) sign of middle-class rights to cultural dominance, an estimation of self-worth anchored in the variously named "essence," "character," and even "soul" of the middle-class individual. Like the feminine interiority that must be seen in Hawthorne's romance of middle-class ascendance, this interiorized essence had to be made visible in middle-class self-articulations. The middle classes produced an exteriorized discourse of interiority as an emblem that demonstrated middle-class superiority.

Middle-class discourses of photographic portraiture proposed that if one's character could be said to shine through her portrait, then one's representation would certainly command a loving gaze, and even the sauciest of children would hesitate to poke out the eyes of the image. Further, if the soul could be captured within the portrait itself, the person represented would reciprocally be imbued with sacred qualities, recognizable on the body and in the photograph. One's essence could once again be claimed as "essential," and the sentimental labor of intimate admirers would no longer be required in order to establish the presence of a sanctified interiority. In late-nineteenth-century discussions of the mechanically reproduced photographic portrait, a middle-class interiority was posed that did not depend upon the protective, reverent gaze of intimacy.

The revelation of interiority that permeated middle-class discourses of photographic portraiture required a codification of the body as a map of interior essences. As Walter Benjamin himself notes, the aura of the early photographic portrait was constructed not only in a "cult of remembrance" but also around "the fleeting expression of a human face."[7] It was through this "fleeting expression" that the middle classes hoped to stake indelible claims to a superior interiority through their photographic portraits. Exterior "expressions," namely, the physical contortions of the face, were said to register or reflect in the body's surface the "character," "emotion," "mind," "disposition," or "soul" imagined to reside within the body's depths. Such articulations of aura proposed that skilled observers could perceive this interiorized essence on or through the body, and that professional artists could capture the transitory physical manifestations of essence in photographs of the body. Ultimately, such discourses both reinforced Christian notions of a split between the body and the soul, and forwarded scientific attempts to codify and control such split identities through mechanical means.

In the age of mechanical reproduction, the middle classes policed the borders between inner and outer in the performance and control of identity.[8] As this chapter will demonstrate, the anxieties produced by the proliferation of self as sign in the age of mechanical reproduction propelled new visual discourses that aimed to differentiate sanctified, auratic middle-class interiorities from the purported deviant, deceptive masquerades of imagined usurpers. Over the course of the late nineteenth century, looking was conceived as a more and more important regulatory practice, and American culture became more surveillant as photographic images were catalogued in police archives and circulated in popular Rogues' Galleries. However, while surveillance enforced state systems of social control, it paradoxically also suggested the potential for a kind of freedom from identification. As surveillance reproduced split selves, posing the body as auratic index to an interiorized essence, the very split between body and soul was harnessed to the disruptive discourses of passing, performance, and play. Minutely scrutinized and rigidly codified in middle-class discourses of identity, the body was variously inscribed both as the index of interiority and as an unreliable terrain on which to establish self and by which to identify others.

THE PORTRAIT AND THE LIKENESS:
PHOTOGRAPHING THE SOUL

In an 1859 column entitled "How I Don't Like Pictures," Fanny Fern begins a short tirade with the following exclamation: "Do you want to be amused? Go to our daguerreotype, halliotype, ambrotype, photograph and similar establishments, and see how human nature comes out in frames."[9] According to Fern, when framed by photographers, cameras, and finally photographs, human nature generally comes out stuffy, stiff, fake, overdressed and overcoiffed. Responding to the new craze for self-representation introduced by mechanical reproduction in the 1850s and 1860s, Fern satirizes the desire for standardized representations and scolds the photographers who make such images: "Oh, for goodness' sake, give us a bit of nature, kind sirs, or shut up shop."[10]

Fern's estimation of mass-produced photographic portraits is steeped in middle-class discourses of both art and identity, discourses that converged in discussions of the photographic portrait in the late nineteenth century. Fern complains that a portrait of a friend stuffed into Sunday clothes, instructed to stare at a spot on the wall, and informed when and how to smile, is " 'not a *bit* like him' "; "And yet it *is* like, after all."[11] Although at first seemingly contradictory, Fern's simultaneous assertions that a photographic portrait is "not a bit like" her friend, although it is "like" him, correspond to nineteenth-century art debates that sought to distinguish the photographic "portrait" from the photographic "likeness." The debate itself was rather confusing, since both "portrait" and "likeness" technically denoted the same kind of image, namely, a small photograph mechanically reproduced in a studio and generally mounted on a cardboard backing. However, despite the formal and ontological similarities between the photographic portrait and the photographic likeness, artists and art critics fervently sought to differentiate the two *discursively* in the name of both photographic art and auratic identity.

In such discussions, a photographic "likeness" was deemed an image that simply and perfunctorily enabled the viewer to recognize the subject represented in the photograph. Called "a topographic chart of the countenance,"[12] the likeness was associated almost entirely with physical attributes. In middle-class discourses of "high art," the likeness was considered a second-rate, superficial photograph, an image that represented only the body. For Fern the likeness is unsatisfactory because it represents merely how one looks, failing to capture the "real" person hidden behind excessive exterior trappings. In middle-class terms, the likeness lacks the "imprint" of the subject's personality. The "true" (auratic, middle-class) portrait requires an "inner likeness" as well as exterior representation.[13]

The photographic likeness was trotted out systematically as a point of departure from which to distinguish the "true" middle-class portrait as an auratic work of art. The debate over what exactly constituted a photographic portrait began with the very inception of photography, as a subset of the debate over whether or not photography could be considered an art form,[14] and it was far from resolved by the turn of the century, despite over fifty years of discussion. Indeed, given the length of the debate, its general consistency over several decades, and its seemingly straightforward oppositional elements (between the "artistic" portrait and the "mechanical" likeness), I would like to suggest that the debate itself served a cultural function beyond the bounds of its seemingly limited artistic contexts in the nineteenth-century United States. In an expanded, discursive sense, what was at stake in this debate that framed photographic production in the latter half of the nineteenth century was the construction of identity itself.

Artists and art critics representing the canons of middle-class taste argued that the "mere" photographic likeness failed to depict the fleeting glimpses of an individual's interiorized essence, while the auratic photographic portrait rendered visible the very soul of the (middle-class) subject by capturing a decisive expression. While both portraits and likenesses were mechanically reproduced photographic images, the likeness was said to lack the (discursively constructed) aura that the middle classes hoped would sanctify their images. Indeed, it was through discourses of the auratic work of art that the middle classes sought to demonstrate claims to a superior interiorized essence.

From 1897 to 1902, during its original tenure under the management and editorship of Alfred Stieglitz, *Camera Notes*, "the official organ of the Camera Club, New York,"[15] functioned as one of the most prominent forums for professional discussions regarding the distinctions between photographic portraits and photographic likenesses. In the essay "A Portrait and a Likeness," printed in the January 1899 edition of *Camera Notes*, Arthur Hoeber explains that the portrait is first of all a likeness; however, if such a representation remains a "mere superficial exterior resemblance of the human features," the image has little artistic value, and cannot be considered a portrait. Labeling popular photographs "still-life performances," careful arrangements, and displays, Hoeber relegates them to the realm of "mere likenesses," claiming that they lack the "human note," the "character"—the "soul"—of the subject. For Hoeber, as for Fanny Fern, such likenesses are about silks, satins, and poses, not people. According to Hoeber, all of this display, although very cleverly done, distracts the viewer from the "human side" of the sitter and keeps the image maker out of the high realm of artists. Again in accordance with Fanny Fern, Hoeber encourages photographers to "get the natural aspect of the sitter," avoiding "uncomfortable finery" and "unfamiliar objects." If photographic portraitists want to be artists, they must shoot for the essence, not the appearance, of their subjects.[16]

The true portraitist captures the essence of an individual with "sincerity" and "honesty," claims Hoeber. "Most real likenesses [i.e., artistic portraits] speak for themselves, for their sincerity is unmistakable."[17] Evoking a strangely circuitous logic, Hoeber proclaims: "As a matter of fact, it is by no means always necessary to see the original of a portrait to be impressed with its fidelity."[18] With these statements, Hoeber effectively imbeds aura within the photographic portrait itself, assuaging the anxieties expressed thirty years earlier by R.H.E. The "true" portrait, which represents one's essence with sincerity, will demonstrate its own value and the worth of its subject, and thereby remain impervious to the wiles of naughty children.

Definitions of the photographic portrait as auratic artwork were intricately tied to the question of whether the photographer could be consid-

Portrait of Sara Payson Parton (Willis) (Fanny Fern), carte-de-visite, 1869. Reproduced from the Collections of the Library of Congress.

Portrait of Sara Payson Parton (Willis) (Fanny Fern), carte-de-visite, 1864. Reproduced from the Collections of the Library of Congress.

ered an artist. Unlike the portrait painter, who had to undergo extensive training and acquire sophisticated skill in order to create a painted likeness, in order to produce an image that did indeed resemble its subject, the photographer outfitted with a camera and a tripod need learn only where to aim the camera and how to open the shutter to produce an easily identifiable likeness. Most turn-of-the-century critics found it difficult to call the process of setting up a camera, pushing a button, and perhaps mixing some chemicals an artistic production, and they consequently deemed the photographic portraitist's art to be something else, namely, his or her ability to depict the inner soul of an individual in a representation of external countenance.[19] The true photographic artist had to be, like Hawthorne's Holgrave, part technician and part sorcerer, one who could capture, as Alan Trachtenberg has suggested, the "bodily expression of characteristic inward feeling" and realize "a knowable inscription of manifest inwardness across the body and face."[20]

In order to capture the "inward feeling" of another, the photographer, as artist, had to manifest his or her own interiorized creative essence as well. However, the imagined demonstration of the artist's interiority further complicated the definition of the photographic portrait. While one critic proclaimed that the artist's individuality must be visible in the photographic portrait in order "to mark the fact that it owes its existence to a man and not to a machine,"[21] others argued that the artist must suppress his or her self to represent the essence of another.[22] One turn-of-the-century critic went so far as to claim that artists have too much individuality to be good portraitists: "Individuality makes an artist . . . unfit for getting a [true] likeness."[23] However, that same critic simultaneously held "that art without individuality is no longer art."[24] Apparently, if the "true" photographic portrait was deemed a work of art that represented both body and soul, it was not always clear whose soul the image was meant to represent.

In late-nineteenth-century discussions of artistic photographic portraiture, we find a moment in which it appears that the subject's soul is paramount in defining the work of art. But such definitions create problems for determining authorship and ownership. If the expression of the subject's essence determines the status of the photographic portrait as art, is the subject, then, the author of the portrait, and therefore its rightful owner? While arguments were made for the latter case, ultimately copyright law determined that the artist's "imprint of personality" surpassed the subject's manifestation of interiority as the decisive factor in determining not only the artistic status of the photographic portrait but also the artist as author of the representation, and therefore as owner of the image.[25]

In middle-class discourses of photographic art, the portrait came to emblematize not only the interiority of the middle-class subject it represented, and the artist who authored the work, but also the viewer who "appreciated" the image. According to William M. Murray, a frequent contributor to *Camera Notes*, while a likeness appeals to the eye alone, a "true portrait" appeals by suggestion and abstraction to the imagination of the viewer, to his or her own interiorized essence. While the proliferation of details in the likeness anchors the representation firmly in exterior appearance, the abstraction and suggestion of the "true" portrait, the very lack of minute details, allow the viewer to employ his or her own creative essence to ponder depths beyond the exterior, surface qualities seen by the eye alone.[26] Ultimately, then, the artist and the subject of the artistic photographic portrait, as well as professional art critics and middle-class viewers, were posed on the same side of a divide that distinguished middle-class Americans, imbued with "superior" interiority, from their cultural others.

The debate over photographic portraits and likenesses in the late nineteenth century reinforced a split model of middle-class subjectivity, an identity imbued with an interior essence closely associated with the middle-class domestic realm. As we saw in chapter 1, the conceptual ties between interiorized middle-class essences and "private" middle-class domestic spheres were often intricately interwoven in the antebellum period. Such connections remained important to some later photography critics; indeed, Arthur Hoeber links these two interiorized realms much as Hawthorne intertwines them in *The House of the Seven Gables*. Hoeber suggests that photographers should attempt to portray subjects in homey atmospheres because "we are accustomed to seeing our friends in the quiet refinement of private houses."[27] Hoeber invokes an earlier discourse of middle-class domesticity to suggest that the middle-class "private" sphere is the realm in which the interior "essence" of a middle-class individual is most likely to be discovered.

As physical appearance was readily represented and circulated in the age of mechanical reproduction, interior essence was posed as an elite, sacred realm only accessible to (and perhaps only possessed by) members of the privileged middle classes. The "true" middle-class photographic portrait, produced by the intuitive artist, appealed not only to the eye but also to the imagination and the intellect. The photographic portrait both captured the interiorized essence of the person imaged and interpellated an interiorized viewer. Indeed, all players in the production of photographic meaning were imbued with interiority as the process of mechanical reproduction was invested with aura in turn-of-the-century middle-class discourses of art. Ultimately, then, debates about the artistic quality of photographic portraits also addressed the "sacred character" of middle-class identity and the "essential nature" of cultural exclusivity.

CLASS ACTS: REAL THINGS AND TRUE PERFORMANCES

Henry James engages cultural debates over the nature of photographic portraiture, identity, and class standing in a short story of 1893, entitled "The Real Thing."[28] "The Real Thing" is a tale of class mobility told through the story of an artist's encounters with several different models. The story is narrated by the artist and set entirely within the walls of his studio in England. Superficially, the plot revolves around four models who compete for roles in black-and-white sketches the artist is making for the first volume of a new series of illustrated novels. The artist must choose two of the four models, those who best suit his needs and inspire his creative expression. The decision is important because the artist's success with the first set of illustrations will determine whether he will be hired to illustrate the entire series of novels.[29]

At another level, "The Real Thing" provides an allegory about the nature of art and the nature of identity in a changing social landscape. Set in the context of shifting class structures, "The Real Thing" outlines new criteria for the evaluation of social worth. The story affirms a middle-class conception of identity established in the imagined manifestation of interiority. But as it does so, the story also suggests one's ability to control and to alter exterior appearance, to seem, to appear, to perform. "The Real Thing" celebrates expression, but not an essential correspondence between interiority manifest in exteriority. "The Real Thing" makes way for the multiplicity of expression, for the possibilities of passing, performance, and deception. James's story subtly demonstrates the ways in which the very anchor of middle-class identity, its split configuration, might be used by others to undermine the boundaries of middle-class exclusivity. And yet, as we shall see, as the story suggests such possibilities, it also contains them, reassuring middle-class readers that middle-class social structures remain in place.

The story begins as an elderly aristocratic couple, the Monarchs, enter the artist's studio. Pleased by the promise of wealthy patrons, the artist is shocked to find that the Monarchs have not come to him seeking a portrait, but instead, seeking employment. The Monarchs have fallen on bad times and hope to work as models, indeed, as model aristocrats. The Monarchs introduce themselves to the artist as "the real thing," claiming to be superb models for dukes and duchesses, kings and queens, because they need not merely pretend to be blue bloods. Major Monarch queries, " 'Wouldn't it be rather a pull sometimes to have—a—to have—? . . . The *real* thing; a gentleman, you know, or a lady' "(51).

Recovering from his surprise and disappointment, the artist inquires about the Monarchs' modeling experience, and they tell him they have been " 'photographed, *immensely*' " (48). The Monarchs explain that they have never had to pay for their photographic portraits, and the artist understands that photographers have sought them out as model customers. Displayed for advertising purposes in photographers' studios, the Monarchs' photographic portraits suggest that other customers might associate symbolically with aristocrats like the Monarchs by paying for the same kinds of representations.[30] The artist recognizes a future for the Monarchs in advertising: "I could imagine 'We always use it' pinned on their bosoms with the greatest effect" (47). The Monarchs could easily sell their identity as a commodity for the promotion of other products. Once again, the logic of commodity capitalism and advertising would allow consumers to mingle symbolically with the blue-blooded Monarchs through the consumption of the same (mechanically reproduced) objects.

Such advertising would be effective only if potential consumers were able to recognize the Monarchs as "real" aristocrats, as the Monarchs themselves. But if it were known that the Monarchs were accepting remuneration for their endorsements, if they were actually to commodify their aristocratic identities, their very ontological status as aristocrats would be threatened. Such considerations inform the negotiations between the Monarchs and James's artist, and the fading aristocrats are careful to steer clear of the face, the locus of public identity, in discussing their possible work as models. Understanding the source of the Monarchs' timidity and embarrassment, the narrator muses: "They would also perhaps wish our relations to be kept secret: this was why it was 'for the figure'—the reproduction of the face would betray them" (49). The Monarchs must subvert their own ontological status as aristocrats, their "selling" point—the fact that they are "the real thing"—in the act of working.[31] By attempting to model their aristocratic appearance, the Monarchs necessarily undermine their aristocratic being.

The Monarchs' chief competitors in the artist's studio are Miss Churm, an experienced professional model described as a freckled cockney, and Oronte, a novice, described as a five-foot-seven-inch Italian immigrant. Although uncultivated, Oronte's talent is apparent almost immediately; the artist sees a picture in his every gesture. Miss Churm's gift is her penchant for imitation, performance, and make-believe, and her genius never fails to surprise the artist: "How odd it was that, being so little in herself, she should yet be so much in others" (52). Convincing in the guise of a shepherdess or a Russian princess, Miss Churm's changeling ability is invaluable to the artist and indiscernible to the Monarchs. Mrs. Monarch, sure of her own success in securing lead roles for herself and her husband, remarks to the artist, " 'Now the drawings you make from us, they look exactly like us' " (61). The artist reflects in response: "I recognized that this was indeed just their defect. When I drew the Monarchs I couldn't, somehow, get away

from them—get into the character I wanted to represent; and I had not
the least desire my model should be discoverable in my picture. Miss
Churm never was, and Mrs. Monarch thought I hid her, very properly
because she was vulgar; whereas if she was lost it was only as the dead who
go to heaven are lost—in the gain of an angel the more" (61). In "The Real
Thing," the "ideal thing" for an artist is a model who can, through his or
her performance, evoke a character in the artist's mind, a being that tran-
scends the model's identity (like an angel), sparking the creative alchemy
of the artist.[32] Unlike Miss Churm and Oronte, the Monarchs have no
labor, but only themselves, to sell. The Monarchs cannot perform; they
can only be.[33]

Mrs. Monarch's failure as a model is precisely her undisguisable identity,
her "definitive stamp." The artist finds he can make portraits of her that
represent her alone; she is always the referent of any representation she
sits for. Sketches of Mrs. Monarch resemble photographs, and the artist
despairs: "I could see she had been photographed often, but somehow the
very habit that made her good for that purpose unfitted her for mine. . . .
Do what I would with it my drawing looked like a photograph or a copy
of a photograph. Her figure had no variety of expression—she herself had
no sense of variety. . . . I placed her in every conceivable position, but she
managed to obliterate their differences. She was always a lady certainly,
and into the bargain was always the same lady. She was the real thing,
but always the same thing" (55–56). The detailed precision of the single
photograph, that which makes it ideal for the reproduction of individual
likenesses, makes it less useful for the production of either generalized or
idealized illustrative "types." Here James's narrator echoes the concerns of
William M. Murray, who exclaims, "I hear it urged, a portrait is intended
to be the likeness of a person, and can it, then, be too like life? Most as-
suredly it can."[34] The artistic portrait must exceed "the mere purpose of
identification."[35] And for James's narrator, the artist must capture not simply an individual's interiorized essence but an idealized type reminiscent
of Platonic forms recodified in terms of social class. According to James's
artist, in order to really understand something, in order to really see it,
one must look not to individual manifestations but to ideal "types." And,
paradoxically, one's ability to express such types is not dependent on one's
ontological or social claim to the category one represents.

James proposes that the photograph's tenacious grip on the detailed referents of the physical, its tie to the "real" body, hinders it from reproducing
representative, fictional types. Further, as the photograph is tied to physical
referents, so is the identity of Mrs. Monarch stamped directly on her
body—in her figure, on her face, and in her attire. Mrs. Monarch's "essence," her being, cannot be separated from her appearance; she is exactly
what she seems. "She was singularly like a bad illustration" (46).[36] In an

age of interiorized identities, Mrs. Monarch continues to emblematize the seventeenth-century aristocratic woman, described by Nancy Armstrong as a body on display, "representing the [aristocratic] family's place in an intricately precise set of kinship relations determined by the metaphysics of blood."[37] Mrs. Monarch can be only who she was born to be, and can represent only what she was born to represent. Her virtues are dictated by inheritance, her beauty by blood. Unlike the middle-class True Woman, epitomized by Nathaniel Hawthorne's Phoebe Pyncheon, Mrs. Monarch can claim nothing on the basis of her own "pure" essence. As a remnant of the aristocracy, Mrs. Monarch is sheer exteriority—she apparently lacks the interior life that "blooms forth" from the middle-class woman. In short, Mrs. Monarch cannot approximate the "split," interiorized model of middle-class identity that secures the social ascendance of the middle classes throughout the nineteenth century. Further, although Mrs. Monarch is certainly more beautiful than Hawthorne's latter-day "lady," she is, like Hawthorne's Hepzibah, utterly inept at self-commodification. Mrs. Monarch presents a fine display, but she lacks practical skills, intuitive efficiency, and the ability to mark herself as interiorized. Therefore, despite, or perhaps because of, her aristocratic elegance, Mrs. Monarch cannot transform herself into other guises; finally, she cannot transform herself into a "true" middle-class woman.

While Hawthorne sends Phoebe to provide for Hepzibah in *The House of the Seven Gables*, James offers no middle-class angel to save Mrs. Monarch in "The Real Thing." James refuses to resolve the class tensions that arise between his artist's hired help, between his working-class models and aristocratic relics. While Hawthorne's characters meet in the inclusive realm of feminine middle-class domesticity, James's protagonists interact only in a bachelor's art studio. Contrary to Hawthorne's depiction of class antagonisms delineated according to ancestry and recuperable through a restructuring of family unions, James portrays class relationships as purely business. In "The Real Thing," no sentimental feminine sympathy will save the Monarchs; either they will learn to replace aristocratic display with commodified performance, or they will perish. James transforms the split identity construct Hawthorne depicted as delicate, domestic, and in need of protection at midcentury into a commodified, individualized identity that must be enacted at the turn of the century.[38]

There is no place for fallen aristocrats in James's depiction of the late nineteenth century. The story reconfigures class roles at the symbolic level, substituting working-class models for the "real thing," as well as at the practical level. Toward the end of the story, in a fit of creative reverie that he cannot interrupt, the artist asks Mrs. Monarch to prepare tea, "a request which, for an instant, brought all the blood to her face" (65), and which reverses an earlier scene in which the artist has Miss Churm, to her embarrassment and annoyance, prepare tea for the Monarchs. Returning a few days after this symbolic event, finally resolved to the fact that they have been bettered by Miss Churm and Oronte, the Monarchs attempt to act the part of servants, the only role that seems to be left to them: "They had accepted their failure, but they couldn't accept their fate. They had bowed their heads in bewilderment to the perverse and cruel law in virtue of which the real thing could be so much less precious than the unreal; but they didn't want to starve. If my servants were my models, my models might be my servants. They would reverse the parts" (68). The artist endures the Monarchs as servants for one week and then dismisses them, explaining, "It was dreadful to see them emptying my slops" (69). The Monarchs' service is "dreadful" because it is so "unnatural": They are not only awkward at performing such tasks but also unfit for them. Serving goes against their "nature"; it contradicts their ontological status as aristocrats, the only thing they have, their "being." It would appear that the Monarchs' fate must be to fade out of existence. The artist finally gives them a small sum of money and turns them away from the studio, never to see them again.

In a story about identity, representation, essence, appearance, performance, and social class, it is odd that the artist, the central figure who connects all the other characters, is never named, is never identified other than as a type, an artist, in "The Real Thing." The reader discerns that the narrator is a man and also discovers that he is single and childless, but in addition to this one learns only his profession, the project he is working on to maintain a living, and the project to which he aspires. The artist is left unannounced as the narrating "I" throughout the story. Despite several direct references to his name, this personal title is never actually uttered. In describing Oronte, the narrator says: He was "an Italian acquainted with no English word but my name, which he uttered in a way that made it seem to include all others" (59). Refusing to illustrate how the name is pronounced by representing this utterance as it occurs, the narrator teases the reader, emphasizing his name without disclosing it. The name, as a signifier, would tie the artist/narrator to a discrete identity, to a singular being, to a "real" (within the imaginary confines of the story) body. The physical appearance of the narrator is never described; he is represented as sheer interiority—the reader is permitted to "see" only his memories, thoughts, musings, reflections, intimations, insights, and nagging fears. Further, he is presented only within the realm of his private, interiorized space, his home and studio. If the Monarchs, as aristocrats, represent sheer exteriority, the narrator, as artist, represents sheer interiority. Ultimately, "The Real Thing" presents a self-portrait of its narrating "I," situating the essence of identity strictly within an interior sphere.

Framed within the artist's studio and literally contained within his own thoughts and feelings, "The Real Thing" is a story utterly saturated with interiority, the sign of middle-class virtue. Indeed, "The Real Thing" marks the continued dominance of a middle-class conception of the self as centered in an interior sphere,[39] even as it recontextualizes that identity outside the bounds of a feminine domestic intimacy. Further, as the future consumers of the artist's illustrations, the middle classes implicitly determine the cultural values that predominate in James's story. The artist's illustrations are to be used in an *edition de luxe* for a contemporary writer recognized late in life as a "great writer" by a "higher criticism." The special edition is posed as a work of art, presented almost as an apology for the neglect of the "vulgar" masses, as a tribute not only to the author but also to an educated, elite middle-class taste.[40]

The artist participates in the construction of an elite literary canon distinguished by "higher" critics from the work that appealed to the "multitudinous vulgar" (50), but he does not consider his illustrations for these texts, which he makes to sustain himself, his true art. He would prefer to be known as a great portraitist: "I couldn't get the honours, to say nothing of the emoluments, of a great painter of portraits out of my head. My 'illustrations' were my pot-boilers; I looked to a different branch of art (far and away the most interesting it had always seemed to me), to perpetuate my fame" (45). The artist himself is caught somewhere between the falling aristocracy and the shifting middle and working classes, and his work must take its place in the midst of mass circulation and mechanical reproduction. As the aristocratic classes fall into decline, the market for expensive painted portraits also diminishes, as well as the tradition of patronage. In the age of mechanical reproduction, James's artist must make his living through sales. And while the mechanical reproduction of printed media enables James's artist to sustain himself, providing a market for his illustrations, his "pot-boilers," it also decreases his chances of establishing himself as a "great painter of portraits." As early as the mid-nineteenth century, an elite market for painted portraits diminished as the "real portrait" was replaced by the mechanically reproduced portrait. Ultimately, James's artist must adapt to the taste of a middle-class consumer market.

The relative survival and mobility of working-class, immigrant, middle-class, and aristocratic figures in James's story is determined by their ability to manipulate a middle-class model of subjectivity in which the self is conceptualized as split into separate spheres of interiority and exteriority. In one sense, James depicts a split middle-class identity as a construct that has been appropriated and successfully manipulated by members of the working classes by the turn of the century. Unlike those art critics who sought to essentialize middle-class interiority, making it readable in the image of a transparent, virtuous middle-class body, James seems to celebrate imitation and performance, not aura and sincerity, as fundamental to art. Although they are not represented as possessing the idealized interiority of the middle classes, Miss Churm and Oronte are capable of shifting exterior appearance in order to pass in various guises, in order to perform multiple identities. If the middle classes hoped to make interiorized essence readable, transparent, undeniably auratic, James seems to herald the *inessential* characteristics of appearance, performance, and seeming. James's artist expresses a "perverse" preference for performance over being: "I liked things that appeared; then one was sure. Whether they *were* or not was a subordinate and almost always a profitless question" (50).

The artist's "innate preference for the represented subject over the real one" (50) suggests a radical reconfiguration of middle-class models of split identity. However, even as it seems to celebrate passing and performance, "The Real Thing" contains the social flux such practices theoretically enable by reaffirming class boundaries. In an era in which performance posed perceived "threats" to middle-class social dominance, James portrays such adaptive abilities as harnessed to middle-class ends. In "The Real Thing," Miss Churm enacts alternate identities for payment only; her performances never threaten to elevate her "real" class status. Miss Churm may temporarily adopt the role of a Russian princess while posing for one of the artist's sketches, but entering and exiting his studio she remains a "freckled cockney." Ultimately, James's story consolidates a new social hierarchy around a "real" middle-class "thing." In the story, appearance can be imitated, but interiority is essential and unchanging. Miss Churm can *look* many parts, but she can only *be* a working-class laborer.

Miss Churm's role is to inspire the artist's creativity, and it is the expression of his imagination that will ultimately give his illustrations the status of art. While both must sell their labor and experience alienation in relation to the products of their work, the artist will claim authorship of and ownership over the work of art because the object will be defined by the mark of his inspired imagination. In a sense, then, Miss Churm's labor will be reified in the aura of the artist's (middle-class) commodity. Thus, "The Real Thing" both contains the implied "threat" of working-class social mobility and assuages anxiety over middle-class alienation. While even middle-class artists must sell their labor, they can still claim to see their marks, to see themselves, in the aura of the commodified artwork.

THE CRIMINAL BODY AND THE PORTRAIT OF A TYPE

The desire to contain the power of passing and performance, as demonstrated in "The Real Thing," powerfully informed the practices and discourses that consolidated middle-class identity in late-nineteenth-century American culture. While a subject conceived as split into two spheres, an interior and an exterior, enabled one to imagine a pure, virtuous essence, character, or soul residing within a physical shell, it also enabled one to imagine sinister interior essences lurking within the bodies of others. Paradoxically, the body, expressive vehicle for an auratic middle-class interiority, might also serve as a masking shield, hiding a disruptive, duplicitous will. The desire to control interpretations of photographic representations that led members of the middle classes to deem their own photographic portraits auratic led them to categorize and to classify—to monitor—the representations of others. Studies of the criminal body, in particular, answered to middle-class concerns about the essences some bodies might mask and hide, and attempted to make those bodies transparent to the technologically aided, professional middle-class eye. As Alan Trachtenberg has argued, "What was needed was confidence that the eye could reliably discern inner character from outer appearance."[41]

As we have seen, in the aesthetic debates that aimed to distinguish the (middle-class) photographic portrait from the photographic likeness, the likeness was generally associated with the body, not the soul. In many discussions, the likeness was linked particularly to the criminal body. William Murray proposed that the highly detailed likeness was suitable for identifying criminals, and R.H.E. similarly claimed that inexpensive, mass-reproduced card photographs, "mere" likenesses, were good for catching thieves: "A card photograph must always be untrue to an inspired face, for it gives no room for the artist to engraft high toning of your inner life upon the harsh truthfulness of your mortal features. They are chiefly valuable, therefore, as the currency of common friendship and common life, and they have a broad mission in this working, everyday world. Thieves are caught by them."[42]

As members of the middle classes constructed their own identities as auratic, discursively pinning inner essences to exterior likenesses, they also developed huge archives for identifying others. As Allan Sekula and John Tagg have observed, even as the photographic portrait became the site of middle-class self-recognition, the Rogues' Gallery came to signify the boundary of respectable middle-class inclusion. The police archive functioned as a public counterexample to the middle-class portrait gallery, and the criminal body served as a point of distinction against which middle-class citizens could identify themselves. According to Allan Sekula, "To the extent that bourgeois order depends upon the systematic defense of social relations based on private property, to the extent that the legal basis of the self lies in the model of property rights, in what has been termed 'possessive individualism,' every proper portrait has its lurking, objectifying inverse in the files of the police."[43]

The photographic mug shot, the preeminent photographic likeness, was introduced into police archives in the nineteenth century by Alphonse Bertillon, the director of the Identification Bureau of the Paris Prefecture of

Police. Bertillon employed the photographic mug shot as one of the central and most important documents in his intricate system of individual identification, which he called the "signaletic notice," or "Bertillonage." By the turn of the century, Bertillonage had been adopted enthusiastically by the U.S. penal system and was utilized by almost every police station in the country. Corresponding to middle-class anxieties, Bertillonage endeavored to stop the professional criminal from passing, from assuming false disguises and identities. Bertillonage aimed to enable trained observers to "see through" the performance of the passing criminal and to identify his or her one "true" (criminal) self.[44]

Bertillon's signaletic notice, which codified a system of documentation designed to measure and record the criminal body, was based entirely on the documentation of salient physical features. In addition to photographs of an offender's "mug," practitioners of Bertillonage also made fingerprints and recorded the size of an offender's hands, head, feet, arm span, height, and even ears.[45] In order to catch the professional, passing criminal, trained observers would compare one offender's measurements to records already collected in the Bertillon file. If they found that an offender's measurements corresponded to an occupied place in the grid of the police archive, the police would be able to prove that the previous and present offender were one and the same individual; a single represented body would conflate various performed disguises into a particular, authorized identity.

Bertillonage promulgated the myth of a successful surveillant society in U.S. culture at the turn of the century. Indeed, the system of Bertillonage introduced institutionalized practices of social surveillance to the United States on an unprecedented scale. The photographic mug shot, deemed the most important of all Bertillonage measurements, was also the one "signaletic" document that permeated U.S. popular culture in the nineteenth century.[46] It was the mug shot that extended the domain of criminal observation outside the limits of expertise to a broader range of viewers. As I have noted, a criminal archive of photographic "likenesses" grew alongside a middle-class archive of photographic "portraits" in the latter part of the nineteenth century. As one nineteenth-century writer commented, " 'As soon as a rascal becomes dangerous to the public, he is taken to the Rogues' Gallery, and is compelled to leave his likeness there, and from that time on he may be known to any one.' "[47] However, in order for a Rogues' Gallery to be effective, in order for a "rascal" to be recognized, a likeness had to be reproduced prolifically and distributed widely. In 1886 Detective Chief Thomas Byrnes of New York City published *Professional Criminals of America*, a showcase of his criminal archive.[48] But even with this aid, this archive designed for home viewing, a surveillant method of popular social control could function only if individuals *studied* the criminal archive, if they scrutinized the facial features documented in a police mug shot, committed them to memory, and were able to recall them accurately at some point in the future. The message implicitly addressed to viewers of a published Rogues' Gallery was that they needed to discipline their gazes in order to protect themselves, their loved ones, their property, and the state. Ultimately, the circulation of the mug shot in the Rogues' Gallery trained the larger social body to scrutinize itself in search of deviant behavior, and one can imagine that this self-surveillance reinforced popular identification with normative social codes.[49]

Assessing Bertillon's criminal catalogue in his influential essay "The Body and the Archive," Allan Sekula has proposed that the archive was the mechanism through which individuals came to have identities in the nineteenth century. The photographic archive enabled an extensive categorizing and cataloguing of the body on an unprecedented scale, as images of individual bodies were placed in relation to one another.[50] Further, drawing upon the comparative process constitutive of Bertillonage, Sekula suggests that an individual body (and its correlative "self") could be discerned as unique only as positioned in relation to other bodies: "The individual only existed as an individual by being identified. Individuality as such had no meaning. Viewed 'objectively,' the self occupied a position that was wholly relative."[51] According to Sekula, the photographic archive served not only as the principal regulatory metaphor for controlling (deviant) bodies in the late nineteenth century but also as one of the principal mechanisms for establishing identity in the United States. However, as I have argued, middle-class aesthetic discourses sought emphatically to differentiate middle-class identities from their cultural others. And as we shall see, scientific discourses of absolute biological difference also sought to claim a space for "real things" determined by biology and blood, not by an arbitrary, relative grid.

While Bertillonage focused entirely on recording the physical features of individuals, making them identifiable precisely as individual *bodies*, the practice of Bertillonage coexisted with theoretical studies of criminology that studied the body not as a unique marker of individual identity but as the clue to a more general biological "type." Studies in criminology such as those inaugurated by Cesare Lombroso, father of the Modern Penal School, which was enormously influential in the United States in the late nineteenth century, shifted the object of criminological study from crime in the abstract to the criminal him- or herself.[52] Lombroso read the body as the map of a *congenital* self that could be classified within a "natural" hierarchy of groups, making individuals, and more important, *types* of individuals, readable to professional experts.[53] The criminal, as a type, could be identified, claimed Lombroso, according to certain physical characteristics: "The criminal was knowable, measurable and predictable, largely on the basis of cranial, facial and bodily measurements."[54] Utilizing many of the

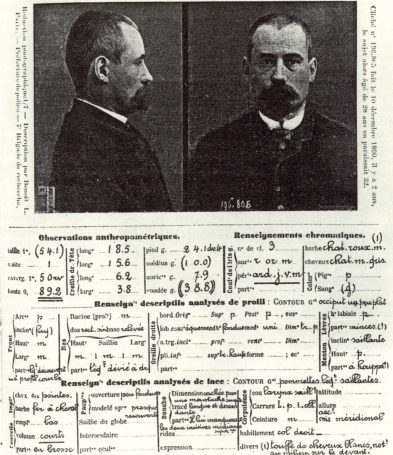

Reproduction Par la Photogravure, Alphonse Bertillon, *Identification Anthropométrique*, *Instructions Signalétiques*, Nouvelle Édition (Melum: Imprimerie Administrative, 1893). Reproduced from Manuscripts, Archives and Special Collections, Washington State University Libraries.

Verso D'une Notice Signalétique, Alphonse Bertillon, *Identification Anthropométrique, Instructions Signalétiques*, Nouvelle Édition (Melum: Imprimerie Administrative, 1893). Reproduced from Manuscripts, Archives and Special Collections, Washington State University Libraries.

anthropological devices and indices of physical anthropology invented by Paul Broca,[55] Lombroso made anthropometric measurements of criminal bodies, especially of skulls, and also collected physiognomic data to document the appearance of criminals, using photography extensively to document heads and facial features (his photographs of Russian "female offenders" and "fallen women" are particularly famous).[56]

While Lombroso's emphasis on physical measurements ties his work on the congenital, biological criminal type closely to Bertillon's signaletic notice, Lombroso sought to connect physical features to innate, *interior* criminal characteristics. In Lombroso's "criminal anthropology"[57] the body served as an index to an interiorized criminal essence.[58] Lombroso claimed that the criminal was a born type, a congenital anomaly, and even a distinct species—"homo delinquens."[59] He deemed the congenital criminal a kind

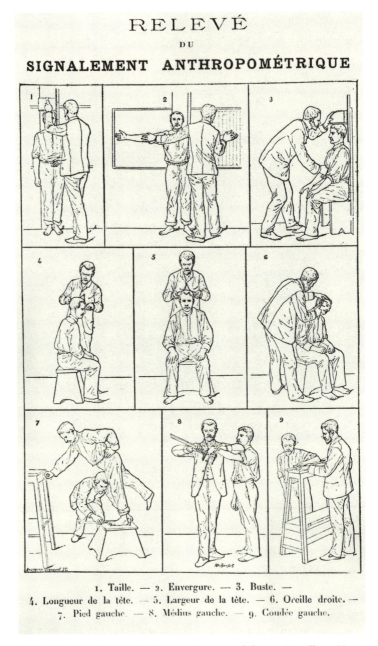

Relevé du Signalement Anthropométrique, Alphonse Bertillon, *Identification Anthropométrique, Instructions Signalétiques*, Nouvelle Édition (Melum: Imprimerie Administrative, 1893). Reproduced from Manuscripts, Archives and Special Collections, Washington State University Libraries.

Taking Bertillon measurements for identifying prisoners, New York City Police Headquarters, circa 1888–1902. Reproduced from the George G. Bain Collection, Library of Congress.

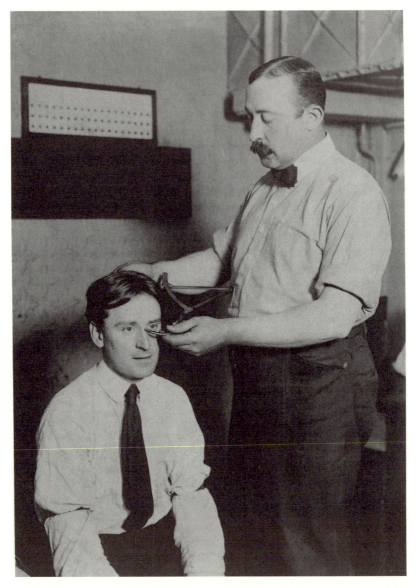

Taking Bertillon measurements for identifying prisoners, New York City Police Headquarters, circa 1888–1902. Reproduced from the George G. Bain Collection, Library of Congress.

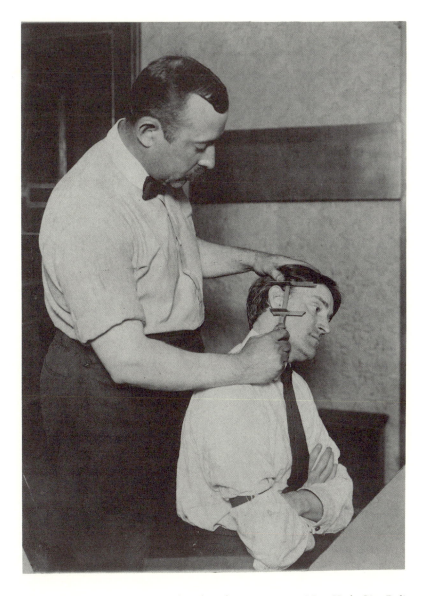

Taking Bertillon measurements for identifying prisoners, New York City Police Headquarters, circa 1888–1902. Reproduced from the George G. Bain Collection, Library of Congress.

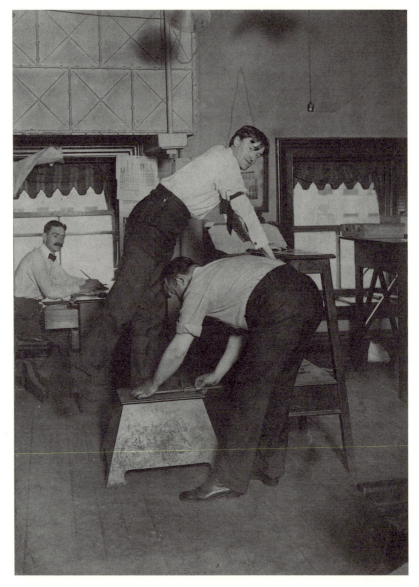

Taking Bertillon measurements for identifying prisoners, New York City Police Headquarters, circa 1888–1902. Reproduced from the George G. Bain Collection, Library of Congress.

Taking Bertillon measurements for identifying prisoners, New York City Police Headquarters, circa 1888–1902. Reproduced from the George G. Bain Collection, Library of Congress.

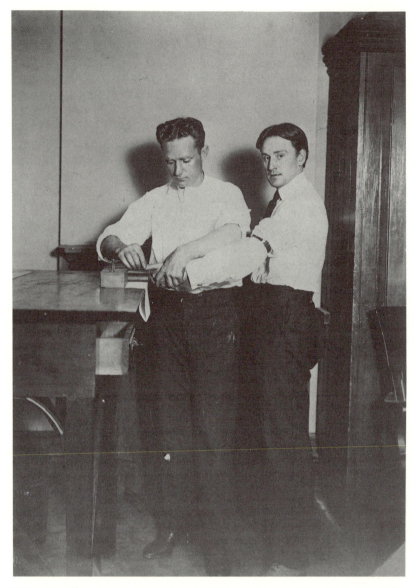

Taking Bertillon measurements for identifying prisoners, New York City Police Headquarters, circa 1888–1902. Reproduced from the George G. Bain Collection, Library of Congress.

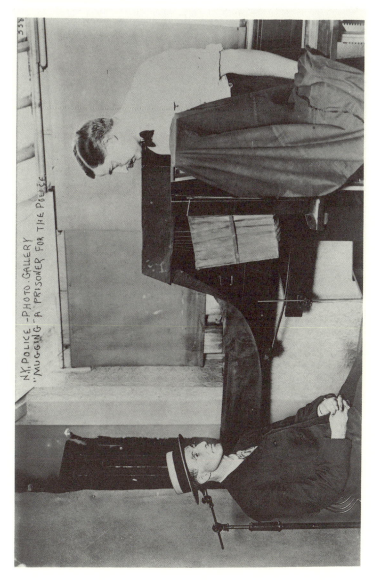

New York Police Photo Gallery, "Mugging" a Prisoner for the Police, July 2, 1909. Reproduced from the George G. Bain Collection, Library of Congress.

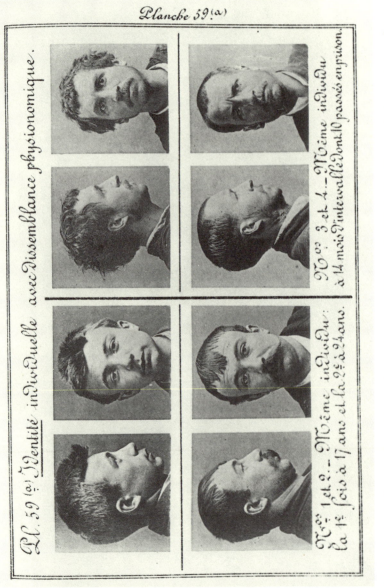

Identité individuelle avec dissemblance physiognomique, Alphonse Bertillon, *Identification Anthropométrique, Instructions Signalétiques*, Nouvelle Édition (Melun: Imprimerie Administrative, 1893). Reproduced from Manuscripts, Archives and Special Collections, Washington State University Libraries.

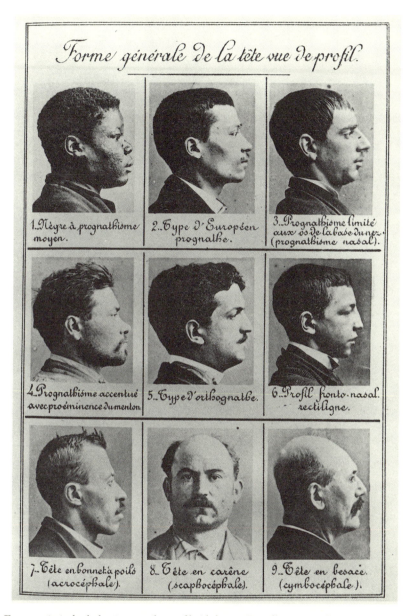

Forme générale de la tête vue de profil, Alphonse Bertillon, *Identification Anthropo-métrique, Instructions Signalétiques*, Nouvelle Édition (Melun: Imprimerie Adminis-trative, 1893). Reproduced from Manuscripts, Archives and Special Collections, Washington State University Libraries.

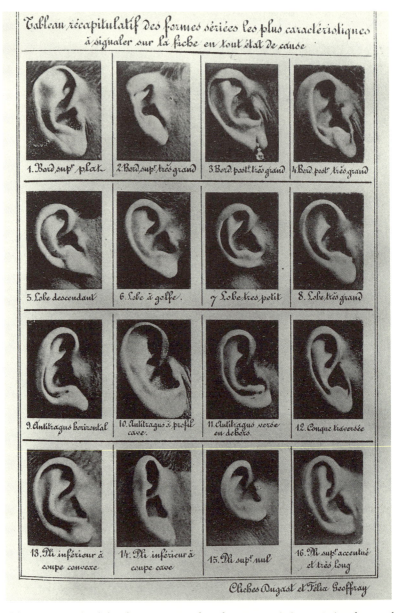

Tableau récapitulatif des formes sériées les plus caractéristiques á signaler sur la fiche en tout état de cause, Alphonse Bertillon, *Identification Anthropométrique, Instructions Signalétiques*, Nouvelle Édition (Melun: Imprimerie Administrative, 1893). Reproduced from Manuscripts, Archives and Special Collections, Washington State University Libraries.

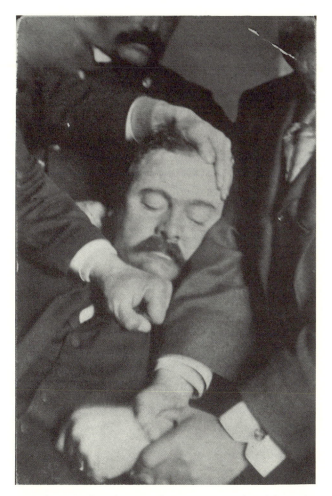

Mug shot of Edward McCarthy, 1896. Reproduced from the
George G. Bain Collection, Library of Congress.

of physiological throwback, a being similar to children and to "primitive
races,"[60] conflating the terms of race and criminal behavior into the same
position along an imagined biological time line.

Abstracting from and generalizing individual Bertillonage texts, criminologists following Lombroso sought to map the social body, to make the
innate character of any given individual readable according to his or her
physical "type." Thus, at least theoretically, Lombroso's criminology
sought to make social surveillance a more readily efficient system, in which
one need not recognize every individual body but merely differentiate be-

tween several types of individuals. Indeed, while emphasis was placed on
the body across a wide range of classificatory endeavors, there was also a
sense in which the "criminal body" had to be tied even more emphatically
to a specific interior than the middle-class body in order to appease middle-
class anxieties. As the populations of U.S. cities grew and diversified
through immigration and interior migration in the nineteenth century,
many feared that cities would become havens for criminals who could hide
their identities in the anonymous crowd. Lombroso himself claimed: "The
agglomeration of population produced by immigration is a strong incentive
to crime, especially that of an associated nature,—due to increased want,
lessened supervision and the consequent ease with which offenders avoid
detection."[61] Various ways to identify and classify a population via codified
representations were construed in large industrial cities in the nineteenth
century. In addition to the Rogues' Gallery, literary forms such as the
"physiologies," popular in Paris in the 1840s, depicted social types endemic
to modern culture, including the street vendor and the dandy.[62] Thin,
pocket-size, paperbound volumes sold on the streets, the physiologies "as-
sured people that everyone was, unencumbered by any factual knowledge,
able to make out the profession, the character, the background, and the life-
style of passers-by."[63] The physiologies served as guidebooks, as elementary
readers for "respectable citizens" of city life.[64]

By attempting to define a biological type, Lombroso's criminology coincided with the sciences of biological racialism developed in the middle to
late nineteenth century. For example, Francis Galton defined and studied
both criminal and racial "types" as biological categories in his science of
eugenics. Galton also utilized photographic technologies in his scientific
endeavors, and his composite photographic portraits stand out as unusual
cases in the range of representations encompassed by the photographic
portrait and likeness debates. With his composite photographic portraits,
Galton presumed to capture the essence not of an individual but of an
entire (always previously defined) biological type.[65] Describing the composites as "generalised images," "blended images," "generic portraits,"
"pictorial statistics," and "pictorial averages,"[66] Galton claimed that composite photographic portraiture "enables us to obtain with mechanical precision a generalised picture; one that represents no man in particular, but
portrays an imaginary figure possessing the average features of any given
group of men. These ideal faces have a surprising air of reality. Nobody
who glanced at one of them for the first time would doubt its being the
likeness of a living person, yet, as I have said, it is no such thing; it is
the portrait of a type and not an individual."[67] Galton's "typical" portraits
represent only imaginary beings, mathematical averages of actual people.
They are not likenesses, material referents for individual bodies, but portraits of an abstract type, representations that supposedly reveal the "es-

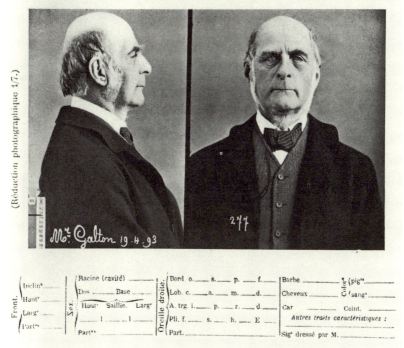

Francis Galton, aged 71, photographed as a criminal on his visit to Bertillon's
Criminal Identification Laboratory in Paris, 1893.

Francis Galton, aged seventy-one, photographed as a criminal on his visit to Bertillon's Criminal Identification Laboratory in Paris, 1893. Reproduced from Karl Pearson, *The Life, Letters and Labours of Francis Galton*, vol. 2, *Researches of Middle Life* (Cambridge: Cambridge University Press, 1924).

sence" of a biologically determined group. In short, they are the scientific counterparts of Henry James's aesthetic types.[68]

Galton made his eerie composite portraits by overlaying a series of standardized frontal and profile mug shots. He would layer multiple individual images on top of one another, exposing each of the individual photographs for an equally proportionate time. For example, to make a composite portrait using eight individual portraits, he would expose each of the individual images for one-eighth of the proper exposure time, laying these fractions

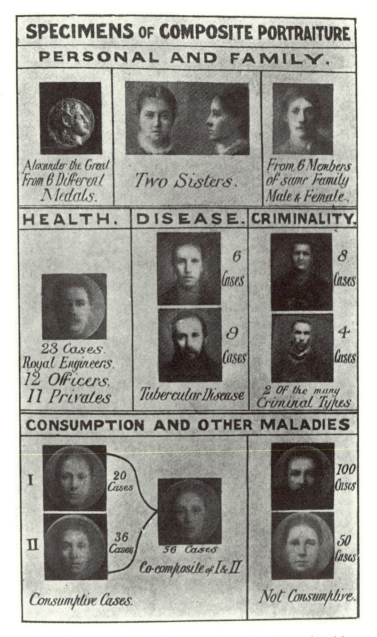

Francis Galton, Specimens of Composite Portraiture. Reproduced from *Inquiries into Human Faculty and Its Development*, 2d ed. (London: J. M. Dent and Co., 1907).

of images on top of one another, to compose a whole made up of eight equal parts. Any individual image would be incorporated into the composite as an even fraction, each component constituting one-eighth of the "ideal" image. By combining individual portraits in even percentages, Galton hoped to ensure that no single portrait would dominate the composite whole, and that only those features common to all would be readable in the final image. All "irregularities" would be visible only, if at all, as ghosts in the composite image.

Galton claimed he could capture "the central physiognomical type of any race or group" with his composite photographic portraits.[69] Unlike Bertillon's signaletic notice, Galton's composite photography sought and privileged the common characteristics of a previously defined group, attempting to erase precisely the unique features of an individual body that Bertillon documented with such care.[70] "Individual peculiarities are all irregularities, and the composite is always regular."[71] In the composite portrait, "all that is common remains, all that is individual tends to disappear."[72] Galton saw his composites both as ideal and as *truly* average images. He proclaimed: "All composites are better looking than their components, because the averaged portrait of many persons is free from the irregularities that variously blemish the looks of each of them."[73] For Galton the ideal was also normative, and he believed his composite portraits represented not simply the "average man" but the mathematically "averaged" man: "Composite pictures, are, however, much more than averages; they are rather the equivalents of those large statistical tables whose totals, divided by the number of cases, and entered in the bottom line, are the averages. They are real generalisations, because they include the whole of the material under consideration. The blur of their outlines, which is never great in truly generic composites, except in unimportant details, measures the tendency of individuals to deviate from the central type."[74] While Galton blends the individual body into a composite type, he simultaneously throws other individual bodies into relief by constructing an abstract norm against which the deviance of individual physical "peculiarities" can be measured.

Galton applied the process of composite portraiture somewhat paradoxically to the visual representation of individuals, as well as groups. He claimed that by combining images of the same individual, it was possible "to obtain a truer likeness of a man than in any other way."[75] In the same way that a composite portrait of a group would erase individual "irregularities," leaving only the typical features common to the group, Galton believed that a composite portrait consisting of multiple images of the same individual would do away with the momentary whims of expression performed by the individual or created by various artists, leaving a truer representation of a person's essential features and expressions. However, Galton's "ideal" composite portrait would represent only the averaged

Composites, made from Portraits of Criminals convicted of Murder, Manslaughter or Crimes of Violence.

Francis Galton, Composites, made from Portraits of Criminals convicted of Murder, Manslaughter or Crimes of Violence. Reproduced from Karl Pearson, *The Life, Letters and Labours of Francis Galton*, vol. 2, *Researches of Middle Life* (Cambridge: Cambridge University Press, 1924).

COMPOSITES

5 COMPONENTS 7 COMPONENTS 4 COMPONENTS 2 COMPONENTS

PREVALENT TYPES OF FEATURES AMONG MEN CONVICTED OF LARCENY (WITHOUT VIOLENCE)

5 OFFICERS 12 OFFICERS 11 PRIVATES 30 PRIVATES

NORMAL POPULATION. OFFICERS & MEN OF ROYAL ENGINEERS

Comparison of Criminal and Normal Populations.

Francis Galton, Composites, Comparison of Criminal and Normal Populations. Reproduced from Karl Pearson, *The Life, Letters and Labours of Francis Galton*, vol. 2, *Researches of Middle Life* (Cambridge: Cambridge University Press, 1924).

body, not the soul of its subject. In his attempt to erase all individual peculiarities, potential "imprints" of the unique personalities of the sitter and the
artist alike, Galton effectively denied his composite subjects a soul as defined by nineteenth-century discourses of photographic portraiture. The
soul, said to be perceived precisely in the fleeting expressions of the sitter,
skillfully discerned and caught by the artist (according to nineteenth-century popular and professional artistic discourses), was effaced in Galton's
composite portraits.

While Galton aimed to erase the traces of individual personalities in his
mathematically averaged composite photographic portraits, he did not
want to do away with the idea of interiorized essences altogether. As noted
in the previous chapter, Galton believed that each race, each physical, biological "type," had its own innate mental and moral character, its own inherent biological essence. For Galton, who began his study of race by investigating "genius," that essence, that moral and intellectual character,
defined a racial group. Because he believed such essences to be biological
and immutable, corresponding reliably to physical appearance (or type),
Galton believed he could make his racial hierarchy visible with his composite images. Indeed, we can think of Galton's composites as answering Josiah
Nott's earlier call for images of racial types. Thus, while clearly referencing
a different signifying register from the auratic middle-class portrait, recalling a scientific rather than an aesthetic paradigm, Galton's composites also
function as signs of interiority, as portraits of an imagined character. However, with his composites Galton aimed to provide visual evidence not of a
spiritual but of a *biological* essence, representing the racialized character
construed in the discourses of biological racialism.

While recalling a different discursive map of interiority, Galton's composites, like Bertillon's mug shots, reinforced middle-class discourses of
sacred, exclusive interiority by providing and containing a "threatening"
counterexample. As discussions of criminal passing dovetailed with discourses of racial passing in the work of criminologists and eugenicists,
white anxiety over the perceived "threat" of racial passing worked to encourage white surveillance over a racialized social body. Indeed, racial surveillance increased even as legally defined racial difference became indeter-
minate. As the legacy of rape in slavery combined with heightened racial
segregation at the turn of the century, several states adopted laws that posited "blackness" in one-thirty-second part African ancestry, and consequently, "blackness" and "whiteness" became paradoxically invisible social
categories. While African Americans utilized the indeterminacy of racial
signs to challenge racist social stratification, as I will discuss further in
chapter 7, whites invented intricate myths about the "telltale" signs of
blackness. In the midst of these ambiguities and clouded visions, the composite portrait and the mug shot reassured members of the middle classes

that they could read the bodies of others accurately, discerning "true" essences according to physical type. Criminals and individuals of other races might attempt to pass into the domain of white middle-class dominance, but professional middle-class observers would be able to see through their masquerades. Ultimately, then, such visual technologies enabled the middle classes to imagine a stable, knowable social sphere in which their own positions and those of others would remain quite literally apparent.

CONSUMING COMMODITIES:
GENDER IN THE AGE OF MECHANICAL REPRODUCTION

With their scientific, institutionalized photographs, eugenicists and criminologists aimed to control the perceived threat of performance that enabled social passing. And yet, the mechanically reproduced photograph also encouraged such performances in many ways. While the photograph was used to monitor and to control identity, it was also used to create new images and to posit new identities, proliferating the possibilities for representing and circulating the self. Indeed, the excess of identities photography enabled dialectically inverted the paradigms of surveillance whereby authorized observers attempted to harness multiple images to a single identity.

The proliferation of variously performed identities was intricately linked to the status of the photographic portrait as a commodity. And like so many other commodities in late-nineteenth-century U.S. culture, the mechanically reproduced photographic portrait was often conceived in decidedly gendered terms. The sexualized relationships imagined between consumer and commodity, and between viewer and viewed, were heightened and epitomized by anxious responses to the photographic portraits of women. Fanny Fern was troubled by the craze for photographic portraits, and she decried the publicity of these commodities on display in strangely gendered terms. First Fern exclaims: "There *was* a time when the presentation of one's 'likeness' meant something. It was a sacred thing, exchanged only between lovers or married people, kept carefully from unsympathizing eyes, gazed at in private as a treasure apart."[76] Fern hates the thought of a cherished face being treated like "a specimen of sea-weed, or a stuck insect, for the gaze of the curious,"[77] and her statements reveal the actual equivalence between the middle-class portrait and the institutionalized likeness effaced in the discourses of auratic art. But ultimately, Fern expresses her concerns about mechanical reproduction in gendered terms. In Fern's eyes, the mass circulation of the photographic portrait enabled by mechanical reproduction represents a kind of prostitution of the self: "People like their faces to hang out at street doors."[78] For Fern, the auratic middle-class photographic portrait is desecrated as it is "hawked about promiscuously and vulgarly," and, most important, Fern suggests that "public show-cases" have grave implications for women: "I have actually heard women express *pleasure* at being paraded in these public show-cases. Fancy an *old-fashioned* lover endorsing such desecration of his Laura's sacred picture!"[79] In Fern's estimation, the imagined loss of photographic aura is tantamount to a loss of sexual respectability; it represents a "desecration" of woman's sacred (sexual) essence. Fern implies that by circulating their images, women symbolically give themselves to any number of anonymous onlookers.

Fern's gendered response to the mass-reproduced, publicly displayed photographic portrait is not surprising given the cultural context in which she writes. Once again, as I have discussed in chapter 1, the relationship between photography and women, and between the camera and women, was sexualized in the earliest popular discourses of photography.[80] Readers will recall that T. S. Arthur describes the daguerrean process in an 1849 issue of *Godey's Lady's Book* as one of enchantment and seduction, claiming that some women feel their eyes drawn mysteriously to the camera lens while they are being photographed.[81] The "attraction" of women to the camera and to photographic self-representation recalls the mesmerizing power of Nathaniel Hawthorne's daguerreotypist. But, as we shall see, the public display of a feminized middle-class private realm so central to early middle-class self-representations, as in *The House of the Seven Gables*, is made both explicit and precarious in later discourses.

While antebellum depictions of middle-class domesticity elevated femininity, they also harnessed the performance of feminine virtues to a specific set of normative practices. Invested in feminine interiority as the sign of its claims to a virtuous, "natural" dominance, the middle classes demanded not only the circulation and display of that feminine "essence" but also the surveillance of that "private" domain. Such surveillance was never totalizing and complete, however, and statements such as Fern's demonstrate that some were anxious about the circulation of feminine interiority, and of the female body, outside the bounds of the middle-class patriarchal family. While such display was important to middle-class claims to cultural dominance in the antebellum period, as representations of middle-class women circulated beyond the bounds of intimacy, the middle classes could not depend upon these images to reinforce a particular, gendered class structure. In responses such as Fern's we see, once again, middle-class fears over one's ultimate inability to control the readings of photographic images.

By the turn of the century, the middle-class discourses epitomized by Phoebe Pyncheon's feminine interiority, and brought to light by the mesmerizing daguerreotypist, had accelerated and transformed dramatically. Holgrave's daguerreotype had been overtaken by the mechanically reproduced photograph, and Phoebe's little cent shop had been replaced by the department store. The mechanically reproduced image inhabited a new "consumer culture" at the turn of the century, a culture that informed and shifted the possible meanings and uses of photographic portraits.

"Consumer culture," which I will discuss extensively in the final chapter of this book, began as a new cultural configuration at the end of the nineteenth century in Western industrialized countries. The department store best represented this cultural moment, emerging out of various kinds of display introduced in the nineteenth century, including the arcades in Paris and the world expositions. With its vast variety of commodities for sale, related to one another only by their mass-reproduced, commodity status, the department store, with the help of advertisers, introduced shopping into capitalist societies as an activity no longer tied to necessity. Subjects of this society were addressed in terms of newly fabricated desires; an array of new lacks were produced and reproduced by the fashion industry and advertising, creating hitherto unknown needs.[82]

As consumer culture created new desires, it also posed new identities. A "citizen of consumer society," as theorized by Rachel Bowlby, is identifiable by the consumption of "appropriate" commodities, commodities which in turn advertise one's class standing.[83] As Bowlby explains: "What is by definition one's own, one's very identity or individuality, is at the same time something which has to be put on, acted or worn as an external appendage, owned as a property nominally apart from the bodily self."[84] In consumer culture, owners are represented, identified, and identifiable by the objects they possess. Thus, Bowlby's consumer is an individual defined in terms dramatically different from the self-ownership assumed by theories of possessive individualism, according to which the objects that one creates are his or her possessions because they are part of his or her self, the products of his or her conception.[85] In consumer culture, the products that one *buys*, not produces, are his or her possessions; more important, these products establish and secure one's identity, objectifying identity itself, turning it into the *product* of commodities. Thus, the relationship of owner to object is easily reversed in consumer culture: "There is thus a clear sense in which the consumer citizen is not so much possessor of as possessed by the commodities which one must have to be made or make oneself in the form objectively guaranteed as that of a social individual."[86]

Photographs and especially photographic portraits function as particularly problematic objects in this paradigm of cultural consumption, collapsing the already tenuous oppositional distance between subject and object, identity and commodity, owner and owned. With a portrait one can procure a commodified image of one's own self. And if, as Bowlby argues, commodities possess their owners, then portraits become the keepers of their consumers, body and soul. Through the process of photographic portraiture, the body becomes a kind of commodity, and further, as Alan

Trachtenberg has suggested, "That body, with its pose acting as its expressive vehicle, is assumed to belong to the 'self,' and is as much its external and material possession as the objects which define the fictive space."[87] Thus, while the interiorized self is posited as the owner of the body (and of the photograph), the converse is also true in consumer culture: the self wholly belongs to the body, its expressive organ, and the photograph that records this expression. And if this is true, then identity might be located neither in one's body nor in one's soul but in the *representation* of one's body and soul.

This role reversal, in which the owner of a commodity becomes a possession of the object that identifies him or her socially, affected women profoundly at the turn of the century. According to Rachel Bowlby, in consumer culture women are not simply owned by their commodities; through consumption they are further transformed into commodities to be possessed by others. Bowlby contends that the dominant European and American ideologies of feminine subjectivity in the late nineteenth century constructed Woman as a subject ready to receive passively the seductively advertised commodities that promised to heighten her femininity: "Seducer and seduced, possessor and possessed of one another, women and commodities flaunt their images at one another in an amorous regard which both extends and reinforces the classical picture of the young girl gazing into the mirror in love with herself."[88] Bowlby has also described Fashion itself as a mirror in which women come to recognize themselves as images.[89] We might think of this recognition of self as perfected image as an endless repetition of Lacan's mirror stage, as an image of unity always desired but never quite achieved, a process supported by the cultural logic that asks women to perceive themselves as images, as objects of desire for another's (masculine) gaze.[90] When looking into the mirror of Fashion, a woman sees not only how she might see herself but also how she might be seen by others. As Mary Ann Doane has summarized succinctly, "The process underlines the tautological nature of woman's role as consumer: she is the subject of a transaction in which her own commodification is ultimately the object."[91]

While Bowlby's analysis of consumer culture is truly compelling, her assessment of "woman staring in the mirror in love with herself" as a passive and even a pathological act remains slightly troubling. For in reinforcing the place laid out for women in consumer culture, and then deploring that position as one devoid of agency, Bowlby's analysis of gendered consumption reproduces the containment of women's self-determination encouraged by consumer culture. I would like to suggest that while narcissism might signal a woman's profoundly interpellated understanding of commodity logics, it might also signal her rejection of the gendered relationships (with men) assumed for her. In other words, a woman might embrace commodification even as she rejects hetero-normalcy. Through a reading of "deviant" portraits and self-portraits of women in the late nineteenth century, I would like to ask: If women can and do represent themselves as commodities in consumer culture, must they necessarily reproduce themselves as the objects of dominant cultural discourses and desires? Must a woman's desire to own her image be the doubly narcissistic seduction of consumer/commodity consuming itself as consumer/commodity? Can women represent themselves only by internalizing a masculine gaze? If women commodify themselves, do they necessarily go to market? Might they maintain another kind of commerce, among themselves?[92] Or, on the other hand, might such commodities go to market with a vengeance?

We might draw upon Rachel Bowlby's important theory of consumer culture to tell a different story about gendered consumption, production, performance, and play. We might find a disruptive potential in the conjunction of commodification, mechanical reproduction, and feminized consumption. In circulation and display we might see women claiming self-authorship and self-ownership.

In order to explore these issues, I would like to diverge briefly from the predominantly Americanist focus of this book, to examine a remarkable collection of nineteenth-century photographic portraits of the Countess de Castiglione, made by the Second Empire photographic firm of Mayer and Pierson in the late 1850s. The images of the countess are notable for their sheer number. The over four hundred photographs disrupt, in their very multiplicity, the process whereby a singular self is constructed around a definitive sign, as in Bertillonage. Instead of attempting to identify herself as a unique being in an archive of others, the Countess de Castiglione generated an archive of multiple identities from her "singular" self. Indeed, the countess's prolific self-representation reminds us of the question posed by cultural critic Jane Gaines: "At the same time that the photographic portrait appears as the fundamental confirmation of self-possession (the proud banner and badge of property in the self), do the multiple selves we have via the photographic image destroy the old self-containment of the (humanist) self we thought we had?"[93] We can read the hundreds of photographic portraits of the countess as a collection of multiple possible selves. The countess passes in many different guises; her "one self" is multiply reproducible.

Abigail Solomon-Godeau offers a fascinating analysis of the images of the Countess de Castiglione in their historical context in her important essay "The Legs of the Countess."[94] In my own assessment of the images of the countess, I will not attempt such a detailed reading but instead will examine the lens through which Solomon-Godeau has viewed these photographs. Ultimately, I hope to read Solomon-Godeau's essay as an important feminist analysis of photographic representation and gender,

Pierre-Louis Pierson, Countess Castiglione, circa 1860s. The Metropolitan Museum of Art, Gift of George Davis, 1948. (48.189)

and to shift some of her assumptions and conclusions in order to offer an alternative critical feminist strategy for discussing photographic representations of women. Part of what I see as troubling in Solomon-Godeau's sophisticated analysis of the portraits of the countess is the way she uses the metaphor of authorship to describe the countess's production. In stating that the countess is "less an author than a scribe" due to the cultural context in which she constructs her images,[95] Solomon-Godeau implies that there are "authors" whose possible representations are not predeter-

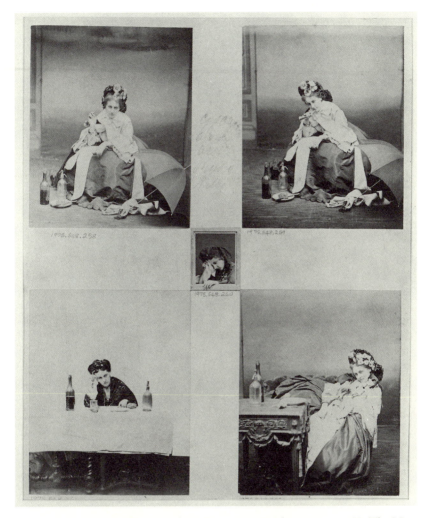

Pierre-Louis Pierson, Album, leaf 22, Countess Castiglione, circa 1900. The Metropolitan Museum of Art, David Hunter McAlpin Fund, 1975. (1975.248.258–262)

mined, real creators who do not imitate. And just as Rachel Bowlby decries the consumer, whom she deems passive in relation to producers, Solomon-Godeau seems to devalue the scribe as a "mere copier" in relation to authors who "produce." In both cases a traditionally feminized role is refeminized and simultaneously discredited.

In querying the countess's authorship we might recall Jane Gaines's analysis of the history of authorship as defined by copyright law cases. Once again, according to Gaines, the photographer was granted the title of artist/

Pierre-Louis Pierson, Les jambes, circa 1860s. The Metropolitan Museum of Art, David Hunter McAlpin Fund, 1975.
(1975.548.128–130)

author, and thereby given sole right to copy an image, because he or she could be said to have orchestrated a photograph, "imprinting" it with the marks of his or her individuality. Therefore, if the Countess de Castiglione herself conceived of the poses and plays for her photographic sessions, as Solomon-Godeau posits in her essay, one can propose that at least within the context of nineteenth-century law, the countess might be considered the author of her portraits. Of course this is a conveniently pat response, and it answers Solomon-Godeau's claims only superficially. For what is really in question in the portraits of the countess, and in Solomon-Godeau's and my own reading of them, is the authorship of womanhood itself. Who authors the representations of Woman? And, more important, who owns them?

In "The Legs of the Countess," Abigail Solomon-Godeau reads the images of the countess within what we might call, adapting Allan Sekula's term, a gendered archive registered by commodity capitalism and patriarchy. Having argued against the countess's ability to author her own representations, Solomon-Godeau begins her concluding remarks with the following statements: "The masks, the disguises, the postures, the poses, the ballgowns, the display of the body—what is the countess but a tabula rasa on whom is reflected a predetermined and delimited range of representations? And of what does her subjectivity consist if not her total absorption of them, her obedience to a scopic regime which inevitably undercuts her pretended authority as orchestrator of the look? It is in this sense that the photographs of the Countess de Castiglione are finally so troubling."[96] While I do not want to claim an explicitly subversive agenda for the countess, I do think we can read her portraits in a different light. What if we were to push through the binary Solomon-Godeau constructs, dividing the body from representations that can be mapped onto it, and reverse the order by which recognizable bodies are constructed? Certainly gender is mapped onto the body, but the body does not necessarily predate the mappings of gender. The body is an object of knowledge produced at the locus of gender performances, gendered discourses, and discourses of gender; the body is what Judith Butler has called "a signifying practice within a cultural field of gender hierarchy and compulsory heterosexuality."[97] We might ask ourselves: When was the body anything other than a tabula rasa?

Working back from Judith Butler's analysis of the disruptive strategies of drag as a gender performance which mocks the notion that gender is a product of anatomical sex,[98] we might read the images of the Countess de Castiglione as gender performances that are not contained by, even though they play within, the boundaries of patriarchy. While Solomon-Godeau reads the countess's imitation of gender tropes as evidence of her "obedience" to a patriarchal scopic regime, I think we can read these repetitions as the very site of the countess's agency within patriarchy.[99] The countess

Pierre-Louis Pierson, Countess Castiglione, circa 1860s. The Metropolitan
Museum of Art, Gift of George Davis, 1948. (48.188)

Pierre-Louis Pierson, detail, Album, leaf 22, Countess Castiglione "in despair," circa 1900. The Metropolitan Museum of Art,
David Hunter McAlpin Fund, 1975. (1975.248.260)

does indeed "invest in herself as image," as Solomon-Godeau suggests,[100]
but instead of reading this as an act of falsification, one might read it as an
act of self-construction. The countess locates identity in shifting representations, adopting multiple available visible positions, claiming the right
to mark herself visually. The portraits of the countess highlight the constructed status of signs mapped on the body (gender here) and of the body
as sign, and finally point to the constructed status of portraiture itself.
The countess frames herself within the photographic frame, marking the
process by which she is being constructed as a self photographically, denaturalizing the process of portraiture and self-representation, the feminine
and the female body. Finally, if the portraits of the countess do not question
the authorship of specific cultural tropes, perhaps they can be said to
question their ownership. If the countess presumes to copy cultural norms,
does she not also claim to own those poses?

Despite the multiple selves constructed by the Countess de Castiglione, we read all these representations as manifestations of the same woman— we recognize them all as photographs of a single subject. Trusting in the iconic properties of the photograph, the viewer traces all of these doubles back to the same source. How, then, is this process of identification any different from that of Bertillonage? While in Bertillon's archive of signaletic notice the body plays the role of ultimate arbiter of difference, in the countess's personal archive the body functions as the lowest common denominator registering the same. To make sense of the photographs as the representations of one woman, the viewer must construct a kind of composite portrait in her mind's eye, searching for similarities, not differences, between the photographs. When we read the disparate images of the countess, the body emerges as the locus of identity, as the unifying characteristic by which one can connect these images to the same individual. However, if one were to begin with the opposite assumption, that identity is not fixed in the body but in representation itself, heeding Chantal Mouffe's claim that "no center of subjectivity precedes the subject's identifications,"[101] and Judith Butler's assertion that identity is a "strategic provisionality," [102] then one might begin to think of the body as a product, not a producer, of identity. If the self is not fixed, but mutable, and this agent adopts signs from which to speak or to show (but never reveal) herself, the countess becomes an unending string of doubles.

As theorized by Mary Ann Doane, the act of doubling, of imitating, of copying, can become a feminist strategy: "Mimicry as a political textual strategy makes it possible for the female spectator to understand that recognition is buttressed by misrecognition. From this perspective, fantasy becomes the site of a crucial intervention, and what is at issue is the woman's ability to map herself in the terrain of fantasy."[103] Solomon-Godeau points to Doane's theory (a version similar to, if slightly predating, that quoted here) in her essay, but she does not, finally, take it on. After acknowledging the "subversive, or at least disruptive charge" of feminine masquerade, and femininity itself as masquerade, Solomon-Godeau refutes Doane: "But taking the case of the Countess as a (once) living instance of the mechanisms of feminine masquerade, one perceives less a refusal of patriarchal positioning than a total capitulation to its terms."[104] While accurately demonstrating the subtlety of Doane's "masquerade" (a play that might easily slip into a theoretical terrain necessitating the disclosure of intentionality), Solomon-Godeau's response to it might be tempered by reconsidering Doane's theory itself. In short, Doane's masquerade constructs agency for women in gender performances *through* the terms of patriarchy. Masquerade and double mimesis are neither "refusals" nor "capitulations" of the terms of patriarchy, but subversions of their claims to truth.[105] Double mimesis is a process whereby gender is performed to the negation of its power to make claims on the real. Double mimesis reveals mimesis, and even gender itself, to be fabrications, and allows a subject to claim her right to copy those constructions, to represent what is already represented. Finally, then, by claiming the right to copy through double mimesis, the subject usurps ownership.

Masquerade and double mimesis deflect the masculine viewer's presumption to see, to know, to penetrate an essentialized feminine interiority. The body that reflects an unending string of images will not be overpowered by a mesmerizing masculine gaze. With this insight garnered from the Countess de Castiglione's photographs, I would like to return to the nineteenth-century United States to read a range of otherwise enigmatic images of women in new ways. Examined through this altered lens, a turn-of-the-century photographer's advertisement depicting a woman cloaked in a dress of photographic portraits becomes more than just a quirky anomaly. The photograph presents us with a strangely literal image of the body as tabula rasa, representing the body itself as a kind of archive. The figure of the woman in this cabinet card becomes a living display case, a physical frame for the images of others. Posed in front of a typical studio background, complete with pillar and picturesque backdrop, the model's portrait becomes secondary to those she exhibits on her dress. Indeed, her exterior is mapped almost entirely by other personages; her face exists as one among many. The woman's body becomes a backdrop on which the photographic process and its results are displayed, as she inhabits both the studio and the products of the studio advertised. Denied an interior due to the emphasis placed on her exterior (it is almost impossible to imagine anything beyond the dress), the woman becomes a manikin draped in the identities of others. The photograph presents to the viewer/consumer not a likeness but an embodied archive onto which the viewer can project his or her own portrait. And yet, while an individual identity seems to be erased in this photograph of a woman's body as archive, one might also imagine that an individual identity has been protected from "the gaze of the curious" here, hidden by the almost unnerving effects of reflection.

This strange embodiment of the photographic process resembles another image, an engraving of yet another woman dressed in photographs. In this image, Fashion herself has "taken on" photography: The figure is a detail of a fashion plate from *Godey's Lady's Book* (1866). This fashion preview performs the same function as the department store window, and the mirror at the ball, offering an image onto which woman can project herself, in which she can see herself as both subject and object. Fashion reflects here an image in which woman sees herself embodying the whole of the photographic process, symbolically occupying at once all of the positions engendered by photography: photographer, photographed, and viewer. The model, draped in a dress displaying the photographic portraits of oth-

T. A. Ley, artist and gallery advertisement. Reproduced from the collection of Peter Palmquist.

ers, at first looks similar to, if more glamorous than, the woman represented in the photographer's advertising card. However, several features distinguish this damsel of photography. This model holds just beneath her chin an opened fan, revealing a miniature photographic portrait on each of its spines. As the fan is held up just beneath the face of the model, the image invites the viewer (the *Godey's* reader) to imagine the fan raised slightly higher, covering the face of the model, reflecting symmetrically the arc of photographs that trims the model's bodice and reveals her neck. Such a gesture of masquerade would draw the viewer's attention to the camera on the model's head, reversing the relation posed between viewer (magazine reader) and viewed (fashion model and her image) by transforming the viewer into the object of the camera's gaze. Thus, while the model's identity might be effaced in this act of masquerade, her vision would remain unimpaired, bettered in fact, by her photographic prosthesis. Indeed, the model, in her slightly alarming visage as cyclops, might unnerve the viewer with her usurpation of the gaze. Shifting the dynamics of looking and looking back at whim, Fashion as photographer might overwhelm a masculine observer presuming to watch unnoticed.

Photographer Alice Austen's "Trude and I Masked, Short Skirts 11 p.m., August 6, 1891," similarly refuses to engage a masculine gaze. Indeed, we might read this image as a representation of commodities that reject the market of male desire, as Luce Irigaray defines that market.[106] If women are typically commodified as the objects of heterosexual male desire and a masculine gaze, this image represents feminine commodities that will not perform for the market of male desire. An exaggerated exhibition of transgression, staged in the theatrical space constructed by half-drawn flowered curtains, this photograph presents itself as an act produced for the camera and the viewer, but it does not engage an anonymous viewer's desire to see. These derobed beauties do not stare back at the viewer; they do not display their bodies for the gaze and the imagination of others. Instead, they stare at each other, as mirror images on stage, performing a masquerade, refusing the culturally normative identity play. Their identities are hidden not only behind masks but also behind reflection, imitation, and reproduction. It is impossible to decipher who acts the part of original individual and who "merely reflects" identity in this photograph. In other words, it is an image that is difficult to read according to the terms of either straight male desire or middle-class auratic portraiture.

Alice Austen's "Trude and I" represents Woman creating and entranced by one "in her own image," but it depicts no hapless Narcissus drowning in her own reflection. Perhaps too self-consciously constructed to be considered an example of double mimesis, this photograph might be considered a demonstration of *mirrored mimesis*. As I conceptualize it, mirrored mimesis enacts neither reproduction nor imitation, mimesis, but instead,

Detail, *Godey's Lady's Book* fashion plate, October 1866. Reproduced from the collection of Peter Palmquist.

the reflection of mimesis. Like double mimesis, mirrored mimesis challenges the naturalized categories of gender, but it does not address the viewer as a knowing accomplice. Mirrored mimesis refuses to engage the viewer as a privileged subject of the gaze in relation to a viewed object. While double mimesis might be said to enact a knowing wink, mirrored mimesis performs an about-face. The image of mirrored mimesis repre-

Alice Austen, "Trude and I Masked, Short Skirts 11 p.m., August 6, 1891." Courtesy of the Staten Island Historical Society, Historic Richmond Town, Staten Island, N.Y. 10306.

sents an enfolded, self-reflected, enclosed space in which the represented subject presents herself viewing herself. The subject of mirrored mimesis refuses to move beyond the "mirror stage" described by Lacan; she will not enter the phallic terrain of the viewer's linguistic knowledge.[107]

Returning briefly to the portraits of the Countess de Castiglione, we see that they signify somewhere between double mimesis and mirrored mimesis. They engage the gaze of the viewer, but often only through reflected eyes: In several of her self-portraits, the countess utilizes literal mirrors to throw her gaze back to the viewer. Although certainly part of an eroticized tradition in which the viewer's gaze is given access to both the front and the back of a model's body, the countess's reflected gaze also emphasizes her essential absence. The countess herself, her essence or "being," is not "revealed"; instead, one sees a mediated reflection which the countess herself constructs and controls. She dismantles that composite portrait called womanhood, an abstract map that refers to no actual being or body, into hundreds of constituent parts, denaturalizing gender's claims on the "real." The countess copies, but she refuses to mark origins. According to nineteenth-century discursive categories, the photographs of the Countess de Castiglione would probably not qualify as portraits, for they would question the very assumptions on which such evaluations are made. The countess's brilliance is her ability to mark, but never reveal, a "true essence" in her archive of images. She imprints her personality as author of the conception of these images, but not through an imagined revelation of interiority. The countess authors the tabula rasa that is her body, locating herself not as expressed in or through that body but as the orchestrator of images. The countess's self is visible only in the traces of repeated production, in reproduction. Located across and between the countess's works of art in the age of mechanical reproduction, the self emerges only as an archive.

In producing their bodies as commodities through photographic portraiture, women also produced themselves as the owners of those bodies. The conjunction of commodity capitalism with the mechanically reproduced photograph enabled some women to pursue "deviant," disruptive identity performances founded in self-ownership at the turn of the century. Performative images of women subverted the surveillant authority of a masculine gaze by proclaiming the inessential nature of a feminine gender identity. Inverting the dynamic by which exteriors were said to reflect interiors, the images of the Countess de Castiglione reproduce the signs of femininity and de-center the supposed correspondence between exterior appearance and interior essence. While such images play to surveillance, they trouble the surveyor's claims to see and to control. These photographs embrace masquerade, celebrating the ultimate indeterminacy of photographic meaning and its potentially disruptive uses. Demonstrating the in-

Pierre-Louis Pierson, Les Yeux Miroir, circa 1860s. The Metropolitan Museum of Art, David Hunter McAlpin Fund, 1975. (1975.548.77)

essential nature of femininity and feminine interiority through perfor-mance, these images undermine the authority of a masculine gaze to enact what Judith Butler has described as "the gender border control that differ-entiates inner from outer, and so institutes the 'integrity' of the subject."[108]

By troubling the nature of womanhood itself, such performative por-traits also disrupted middle-class claims to a stable social position consoli-dated around the controlled display of interiorized feminine essence. As we shall see in the next chapter, however, the middle classes continued to invest in womanhood as a sign of cultural dominance by infusing that representation with the newly essentialized terms of race. The discourses and technologies of racial essence, such as those employed by nineteenth-century eugenicists, would come to dominate depictions of feminine interiority. By the turn of the century, a newly articulated white womanhood would function as a banner of middle-class cultural exclusivity. And as we shall see, popular discourses would harness women's capacities as image makers to their imagined role in racial reproduction.

"Baby's Picture Is Always Treasured": Eugenics and the Reproduction of Whiteness in the Family Photograph Album

*A baby's photograph, to all save doting parents and
relations, is a stupid thing.*
(*R.H.E.*, Godey's Lady's Book, *April 1867*)

To TWENTIETH-CENTURY readers accustomed to the now ubiquitous nature of "baby's photograph," R.H.E.'s observation about the stupidity of these images seems either shocking or wonderfully perverse.[1] Despite the fact that such photographs typically depict fleshy, wrinkled creatures, with eyes not quite focused, and expressions rather startled, baby pictures remain highly valued commodities in contemporary culture. Today the family photograph albums that protect these images are nearly sacred records. Indeed, it is almost impossible to imagine dismissing the importance of those documents which twentieth-century Americans consistently herald as the most important things to save from the imagined disasters of proverbial floods and fires.

Considered in its own historical moment, R.H.E.'s proclamation continues to surprise. Where is the nineteenth-century rhetoric of maternal love and pride? Wasn't R.H.E. addressing, in *Godey's*, a reading audience of white middle-class women raised on the rhetoric of True Womanhood?[2] The sentimental response to baby's photograph that one might expect to find here surfaces only thirty years later in an 1898 advertisement for the Cyclone camera in the *Ladies' Home Journal*. This advertisement, which encourages white middle-class women to buy newly manufactured hand-held pocket cameras, proclaims: "Baby's picture is always treasured."[3]

This utter reversal in the estimation of baby's picture does not settle the question of how or why the transformation itself occurred. Surely baby's photograph did not change dramatically over the course of thirty years. Perhaps focus was improved with shorter exposure times, but was there really anything more to see in a sharp rendering of baby's corpulence? What, then, *did* transform white middle-class evaluations of baby's picture over the course of the late nineteenth century?

In the period that separates R.H.E.'s disdain for these photographs from later exuberance over such images, "baby's photograph" came to emblema-

BABY'S PICTURE

is always treasured; more of them might be had by investing in a camera. A picture made with home surroundings is certainly more attractive than one obtained in a strange studio. With our

Cyclone Cameras

and outfits ANY ONE can make and finish good pictures. We manufacture cameras selling from $3.50 to $50.00. Our $6.00 CYCLONE, SR., makes pictures 4 x 5 inches.

Our MAGAZINE CYCLONE CAMERAS make TWELVE PICTURES WITHOUT RELOADING, and are without doubt the only up-to-date cameras on the market. YOU DO NOT OPEN CAMERA TO CHANGE PLATES—ONE TURN OF A BUTTON DOES IT. The shutter automatically sets itself.

Send for our 1898 catalogue. CYCLONE POSTER in five colors mailed on receipt of ten cents.

WESTERN CAMERA MFG. CO.
New York Office: 79 Nassau St.   Silversmith Bldg., Chicago

Advertisement, "Baby's Picture Is Always Treasured," Cyclone Cameras, *Ladies' Home Journal*, July 1898.

tize a racial fantasy as eugenicists claimed it for scientific evidence. The family album was a particularly important record for Francis Galton, the founder of eugenics, who defined "race" as an essential, biological characteristic rooted in heritable physical, moral, and intellectual capacities.[4] In eugenics the family became central to the discursive production of race and of racial hierarchies, as the family album became one of the social documents through which heredity was charted. Within this eugenicist context, photographs of children became powerful familial records through which racial hierarchies could be reproduced and maintained.[5] In this way, the "science" of eugenics transformed the signifying context for baby's "private" picture. What I propose to consider here is whether or not eugenicist appropriations of baby's picture in turn informed the shifting evaluation of these representations in popular white middle-class venues. How can we make sense of the uncanny formal consonance and temporal congruence of popular and eugenicist family albums? To what degree do these parallel representational practices share ideological contingencies?

In asking these questions, this chapter interrogates the genealogies that informed the seemingly innocuous practice of photographing baby in the late nineteenth century, and suggests that this sentimentalized middle-class ritual was also a racially inflected act. Such a perspective compels us to query the history of white normalcy and eugenicist desire, and to participate in efforts made by Deborah Willis and others to rethink the family photograph album as a site of cultural contestation, as a place in which competing American identities are posed and projected.[6] Today the family photograph album provides an important genealogical archive for Americans of color, as evidenced by the contemporary work of artists such as Clarissa Sligh, Carrie Mae Weems, Deborah Willis, and Julie Dash, and scholars such as Deborah Willis (again), bell hooks, and Christian Walker.[7] At the turn of the century, however, the same medium that enabled African Americans, according to bell hooks, to "disprove representations of us created by white folks,"[8] might also have allowed white Americans to reinforce dominant misrepresentations of themselves as good, healthy, natural, powerful, elite. What exactly *did* white middle-class parents learn from the popular articles that taught them how to photograph children "correctly"? Did they learn how to transform disparate experiences into normative eugenicist fantasies? Did they learn how to transform "stupid" images into racialized "treasures"?

MECHANICALLY REPRODUCING BABY

From the moment of its 1839 inception in daguerreotypy, the first photographic process,[9] the photographic image has been conceptualized as a means of preserving family history and of documenting family genealogy.

As we saw in chapter 1, for many members of the middle classes, daguerre-otypy provided the first affordable means of recording their own images and of collecting representations of their loved ones.[10] Parents frequently had their daguerreotype portraits made in order to give them to their children as heirlooms and keepsakes.[11] The daguerreotype enabled members of the middle classes to mimic the practices of their wealthier neighbors, displaying proudly the representatives of their family lines, after pseudo-aristocrats who enjoyed a longer tradition of decorating parlours and halls with the more costly, time-consuming painted portraits of their forebears. This early function of the photograph as heirloom is important because it connects the photograph, through inheritance, both materially to the circulation of goods and the preservation of likenesses, and ideologically to the continuation of the family blood line. As my later discussion of eugenics will demonstrate, the relationship between family photographs and (racialized) bloodlines became particularly problematic as the photograph began to play a role in the definition of heredity that provided the foundation for Francis Galton's racial theory of eugenics.[12]

Attesting indirectly to the cultural use of the daguerreotype as heirloom, T. S. Arthur, a popular nineteenth-century writer for *Godey's Lady's Book* proclaimed: "If our children and children's children to the third and fourth generation are not in possession of portraits of their ancestors it will be no fault of the Daguerreotypists of the present day; for, verily, they are limning faces at a rate that promises soon to make every man's house a Daguerrean Gallery."[13] Describing family photograph collections as "Daguerrean Galleries," Arthur subtly links the early practice of family photography to Mathew Brady's famous "Daguerrean Gallery," a national archive of "Illustrious Americans" devoted primarily to exalting the images of American political leaders.[14] As Brady's Daguerrean Gallery reproduced the "fathers" of the nation, presenting a national patriotic ideal, the family archives Arthur describes might be said to reproduce the "children" of the nation. The association of photography with the reproduction of national identities continued throughout the nineteenth century, but by the turn of the century, the "nation" itself was posed as a racial construct. Indeed, it is between the two terms of the family and the nation that Francis Galton located the site of racial reproduction. For Galton, the nation was simply a congregation of racialized families.

An understanding of this discursive context, in which the photographic portrait was posed as a signifier of both national and racial identity, enables one to begin to make sense of the postmortem images of babies that abound in the nineteenth century, images of dead babies that strike twentieth-century viewers as truly uncanny. While the proliferation of postmortem portraits of children might be attributed, on a superficial level, to high infant mortality rates and even to the technological difficulties of making images of squirming babies under long exposures, the possible cultural import of such images is more compelling. Throughout the mid–nineteenth century, daguerreotypists advertised their services to bereaved mothers, and they traveled with angelic figures and bouquets of flowers, the accessories and props of nineteenth-century mourning.[15] Thus, nineteenth-century Americans apparently assumed not only that children could and would die but also that images of dead bodies should be preserved for posterity. Given late-twentieth century understandings of the political nature of images of dead babies, most notable today in antiabortion propaganda materials, one can begin to ask what cultural and ideological function the photograph of a dead child might have served in the nineteenth century. In a period of eugenicist anxiety about the "death" of the Anglo-Saxon race, images of dead white babies may have served not only as memorials, highlighting the importance of every member of the race, but also as reminders to white adults of the "need" to continue procreating. Thus, nineteenth-century postmortem infant portraits may have functioned in much the same way as Theodore Roosevelt's early twentieth-century warnings about the threat of "race suicide," which encouraged "native" Anglo-Americans to reproduce prolifically, in order to combat the cultural influence of "less desirable" immigrants.[16] In other words, individual images of dead babies may have generated anxiety about white racial death, transforming private grief into a public mandate to reproduce.[17] In this way, the photograph as sentimental family memento may have also performed a racial function, in much the same way that photographs of live babies came to signify in racial terms in a culture permeated by eugenicist thought, as my discussion in this chapter will suggest.

The documentation of the family, and of individual members within the family, grew and was practiced with increasing enthusiasm as the invention of new photographic technologies dramatically expanded the potential for photographic consumption. As we saw in chapter 3, as early as the 1850s, with the invention of the negative/positive, collodion/albumen process, exposure times were shortened significantly, and photographic images became mechanically reproducible.[18] Unlike the daguerreotype, which, once again, was a single, unique, nonreproducible image, the negative/positive process enabled unlimited copying of any given image; consequently, photographs became both easier to obtain and easier to circulate. As a result of such innovations, photographic reproduction began to expand exponentially. In this era of mechanical reproduction, technological advances that shortened exposure times, combined with new business ventures, served to instigate popular new fads; by the 1860s, people began to collect mass-reproduced carte-de-visite and cabinet card portraits of famous actors and actresses, of politicians, of one's own friends, and of family members. To assist collectors in organizing, preserving, and cataloguing all these images, the photograph album became a popular cultural form.[19]

The family photo album remains the most enduring colloquial register developed during the period of photographic expansion. Over the course of the nineteenth century, the album came to function as a visual family archive, a record of ancestral legacies—the site where individuals were positioned within a family history.[20] By the turn of the century, according to Philip Stokes, "photography had thoroughly permeated family life."[21] With the invention of paper roll film and the handheld Kodak camera in 1888, photography pervaded the family as one of its self-identifying mechanisms. George Eastman aggressively targeted middle-class consumers with his popular advertising campaigns, and by the turn of the century the camera had become an accessible source of home entertainment. The photographic portrait, once the sole domain of professional photographers who could both afford and manage cumbersome cameras, became a product of family life itself.

By the 1890s, the family became a social unit increasingly imagined through the process of photographic representation. The advertisement for Kodaks in the *Ladies' Home Journal* of December 1897 reads: "The annual family gathering at the Thanksgiving table, the children's Christmas tree, groups of friends gathered to pass a winter evening—all make delightful indoor subjects for winter Kodaking. . . . Put a Kodak on your Christmas list."[22] Situated as both the subject and the object of the verb "to Kodak," the family becomes one holiday package among others. Things central to holidays regarded as particularly familial, objects around which the family is constructed—the Thanksgiving table, the children's Christmas tree—become ideal subjects to photograph: "Holidays are Kodak Days."[23] And, of course, holidays were not the only camera days: As we have already seen, by the end of the nineteenth century, anytime was the right time to photograph children—"Baby's picture is always treasured."

As the family was posed as a photographic reproduction at the turn of the century, the photographic industry situated white middle-class women at the cornerstone of this technological process. As previously noted, the Cyclone camera ad of 1898 appeals to mothers as the producers of infant photographic treasures. More directly, in 1898, the *Ladies' Home Journal* featured two articles instructing white middle-class mothers in how to photograph children successfully. In "Getting Good Pictures of Children," E. B. Core gives "a few suggestions to the mother," acknowledging her role as orchestrator of the photographic documentation of children, and offers eleven photographs of children as "models of their kind for the guidance of parents."[24] While "Getting Good Pictures of Children" assumes that parents will want to employ a professional photographer to enact their instructions, an article published ten months later, entitled "Photographing

The Family Photograph Tree. Lithograph by Currier and Ives, 1871. Reproduced from the Collections of the Library of Congress.

Children at Home," addresses parents themselves as photographers.[25] Isaac Porter, Jr., author of "Photographing Children at Home," offers parents "at home" photography tips in how to "preserve little records of their [children's] life, such as nothing but a good photograph can do."[26] Again, sample photographs are reproduced to spark the reader's imagination, and extensive preparation is emphasized: "Having all the details in readiness before the child is called upon to take its part in the process of taking the photograph makes success almost sure of attainment."[27] Porter's detailed instructions, and the emphasis he places on "proper" preparation, suggest that "family life" was not only technologically mediated but also construed with rather serious intent.

The "charm" of the sample photographs Porter offers as models for the production of middle-class family life is created through references to the adult world, representing children as mini-adults: young boys and girls are shown reading, holding their babies, and staring at their reflections in the mirror. "Photographing Children at Home" becomes a guide in how to perpetuate middle-class "family values": photographs of children project them into the educated, heterosexual, reproductive future of their parents' world, tracing the imaginary trajectory of the middle-class family line.[28] By mapping their aspirations onto their children, middle-class parents not only normalize but also naturalize their own adult activities, making them part of the imagined process of growing up white and middle-class. Commenting on the staged rigidity of turn-of-the-century amateur photographs made of children at play, Philip Stokes remarks that parents (the probable photographers) may have felt "an unwillingness to record the disorder and untidy behavior of the children, who were, after all, the family's centre and its future."[29] In Stokes's description, family photography becomes a technology that enables parents to monitor and reproduce middle-class aspirations. In this new context, "baby's photograph" ceases to be a stupid thing as it becomes the document through which the middle-class family's future is imagined and mechanically replicated.

Increasingly, at the advent of the twentieth century, photographing baby became essential to the social reproduction of the middle-class family, and the practice itself was most frequently represented as a maternal act. In addition to the Cyclone camera advertisement that depicts a white woman photographing a small girl, and the *Ladies' Home Journal* articles that target white middle-class mothers as photographers, some of George Eastman's famous "You press the button we do the rest" advertisements for the Kodak camera also depict white women photographing their children. And as the art of photographing baby is enacted by mothers upon daughters, it is also bequeathed from mother to child. A 1902 stereograph card produced by H. C. White Company further demonstrates how the act of photographing baby was becoming a normative performance, a kind of family heirloom

PHOTOGRAPHING CHILDREN AT HOME

By Isaac Porter, Jr.

PERHAPS it may be that your little assistant will tell you when the goldfish are still, so that they may be photographed. A little patience will generally result in a negative which will amply repay the time and care given to its production. If the

ONE of the most interesting undertakings of amateur photographers is the attempt to secure good pictures of the children at home, and perhaps more disappointments result from such attempts than from their work in any other field. To get good pictures indoors, in the homes of the children.

SOME excellent portraits of children were shown in the JOURNAL of February last, and the suggestions given by the writer of the article must have led many amateur photographers to try to obtain pictures of little ones in their own homes. It is with a desire to aid such that these photographs and suggestions are offered. It is well to bear in mind the fact that a child's

surrounded by familiar objects; to catch them while at play, and to preserve little records of their life such as nothing but a good photograph can do, is not so difficult as many imagine, but it requires considerable thought and any amount of patience.

HAVING in mind a clear idea of what is desired, arrange the accessories, and make sure of all the light it is possible to get; then place your camera, and by that time

interest may be very easily awakened, but not easily held for any great length of time, making it necessary to get everything ready except the subject before attention is turned to the child.

Too much stress cannot be laid upon this point, as the pursuing of a different course is almost certain to defeat the desired result, while having all the details in readiness before the child is called upon to take its part in the process of taking the photograph makes success almost sure of attainment.

children are to be caught out-of-doors, as shown on the first column of this page, the foregoing suggestions hold good, and, as the light is so quick, it may at first prove easier than getting pictures indoors.

THERE are many opportunities of interesting children if one will only consider their ways. It may be that their sympathy is

moved, as in the case of the pet dog whose foot is injured. It was not difficult to get the children very much interested and full of pity for the little sufferer, and they were then anxiously "Waiting for the Doctor."

The interest of a child is very easily aroused, and once enlisted in the getting of a picture the rest is comparatively easy, but there must be no impatience on the part of the photographer, and no commands and no reprimands if the most satisfactory pictures are to be secured.

perhaps your subject has become interested or is ready to be easily interested. The next step is to get the child to help you. It may be a little girl who will hold her dollies so that you may get a picture of them, as in the photograph of the "Happy Little Mother."

Again, it may be that the little one may be induced to give some time to "Reading Mother Goose," or, after a visit to the "Zoo," be easily led to trund her dollies to take "A Ride on the Elephant."

The pictures which are sure to be most valued, and which will prove most pleasing to all concerned, are those which show the little ones occupied as they are found to be when left to their own devices, so one has but to learn what the children like to play, how they amuse themselves, or what interests them, in order to choose a subject. It may be that "The New Bonnet" is to be admired, or that "Cutting Paper Dolls" is fun.

Isaac Porter, Jr., "Photographing Children at Home," *Ladies' Home Journal*, December 1898.

or ancestral legacy in and of itself. White's stereo card depicts a young white girl photographing her own "baby," and the text reads: "Now smile a little dolly, while I take your picture." By the turn of the century, family photography had permeated white middle-class culture so thoroughly that photographing baby had itself become a self-reproducing act.

REPRODUCING RACIAL INHERITANCE

As popular women's magazines targeted white middle-class women as the engineers of the mechanical reproduction of the white middle-class family, scientific discourses posed these women as the biological reproducers of whiteness. As the New Woman of the late nineteenth and early twentieth centuries began to challenge the reproductive destiny of the antebellum True Woman, physicians and sociologists condemned her freedom and independence as damaging to the future of the white middle and upper-middle classes.[30] By choosing education, professional work, and homosocial bonds over marriage, motherhood, and domesticity, the New Woman supposedly threatened the livelihood of her elite white social class by refusing to procreate.[31] In arguments aimed at containing middle-class and upper-middle-class women within the home, the white woman emerged as the foundation of racialized class and national discourses.[32]

Writing in the early 1920s, Albert Edward Wiggam, journalist, author, speaker, and prominent popularizer of eugenics in America, encouraged white middle- and upper-class women to use their newly acquired political power to advance the cause of eugenical marriages and motherhood. In Wiggam's vision, voting rights need not unsex white women; such power could make them better mothers for the race. Wiggam declared: "Woman's new Promised Land, the objective of her exodus from political bondage, science has at last discovered for her, and, through her, for the race. Its name is Eugenics. It is the land of the well-born. It is for woman to determine whether or not the race shall enter it."[33] Acquiring rhetorical speed, Wiggam proclaims, "Eugenics means that *the production of a great race* shall become the sum and meaning of all politics, the one living purpose of the state."[34] And Wiggam emphasizes women's role in this fantasy of white perfection: "It is peculiarly to woman that America looks for the realization of this ideal. She is the natural conservator of the race, the guardian of its blood."[35]

As "healthy" white middle- and upper-class women were heralded as the physical vessels through which a "great race" of white Americans was to be born, these women also played an important role in gathering the data that reinforced their positions as guardians of good blood. According to Marouf Arif Hasian, Jr., thousands of women became fieldworkers collect-

North Bennington, Vt., U. S. A.

H. C. White Co., "Now smile a little dolly, while I take your picture," stereograph card, 1902. Reproduced from the Collections of the Library of Congress.

ing family data for American eugenicists such as Charles Davenport, founder of the Eugenics Record Office in 1910 and first president of the New York Galton Society in 1918, and Henry Goddard, director of a New Jersey institute for the feebleminded and author of the famous study *The Kallikak Family*.[36] Among this small army of eugenics workers, Gertrude C. Davenport, author of "Hereditary Crime," and Elizabeth S. Kite, author of "Two Brothers" and "The 'Pineys,' " were perhaps the most influential. Both of these researchers promoted "the idea that mothers are more responsible than fathers in generating bad offspring,"[37] a sentiment shared by many eugenicists, and one that helped to shape racist anti-immigration sentiments among Anglo-Americans in the early twentieth century.[38]

By the turn of the century, white women were situated at the center of a new kind of "moral order," posed as the foundation of white propagation. If the rhetoric of motherhood in the antebellum period construed white middle-class mothers as the moral educators of their children, racialized discourses in the postbellum era situated white middle-class mothers at the locus of biological inheritance. While a child's character was deemed the result of the True Woman's training in the antebellum period, it was seen as the gift of the white woman's biological heritage in the latter half of the nineteenth century. In the context of eugenics, white womanhood came to represent not the moral but the biological superiority of white middle-class character.

The role of the middle-class white woman as both the mechanical reproducer of "baby's picture" and the biological reproducer of whiteness (in baby's body) converged in the nineteenth-century science of eugenics. It is within eugenicist research that "baby's picture" came to function most directly as a sign of racial inheritance. Situated within this cultural context, R.H.E.'s cantankerous rejection of the sentimentalized image of baby begins to take on new meaning. Indeed, a closer look at R.H.E.'s essay uncovers a new signifying register in which baby's picture might be treasured, ultimately, as the emblem of racial reproduction.

The image of a baby holds no great value for R.H.E. because one cannot read in the "features of obese babyhood" the "resemblances to those who have worthily wrought out their own lineaments of face and character."[39] In other words, a baby's pudgy body does not yet resemble that of its progenitors; family resemblances are not yet visible in an infant's rolls and folds—one cannot trace familial heritage in the baby's face. R.H.E. explains further in a particularly morbid passage that decisively situates the author beyond the pale of maternal affection: "Death will give you a more worthy picture of your baby's face than any mortal artist can do. Sharpened by disease, its little rigid features shall stand out to you with a storied distinctness, so that you may read, as from an open page, your child's possible and probable character and bearing."[40] For R.H.E., baby's face (and any representation of that face) does not become interesting until it has been "sharpened," either slowly by age or more rapidly by disease and death, into a gaunt, adult face. Baby's physique holds no intrigue for R.H.E. until it becomes like "an open page," on which one can read baby's inherited character. Thus, for R.H.E., the "worth" of a baby's picture (indeed the worth of the child's little body) is its ability to illustrate the character the child will assume in maturity, a character inherited from "worthy" parents. In these terms, baby's photograph is valued as the documentation of an ancestral trace, the visible continuation of the hereditary line. The baby's pudgy body does not signify sufficiently the "origins" of its physical features, it does not yet serve as an index of ancestral character, and therefore, according to R.H.E., there is no good reason to record the corpulent physique.

In social practice, the child's photograph eventually did serve as a testament to ancestry, inheritance, and continuity in family genealogies. By the late nineteenth century, family photography entered new cultural terrain as the images of loved ones were harnessed to science. If the photographic portrait was first circulated *as* a family heirloom, it was later exchanged as a document that *recorded* an ancestral heirloom, namely the "inherited character" heralded by R.H.E. Over the course of the nineteenth century, "baby's picture," the "treasure" of the family photograph album, became the evidence of the eugenicist album, the record of ancestral physical features and their supposed analogues, namely, racialized character traits.[41] In 1884, Francis Galton designed two eugenicist "family albums": the *Record of Family Faculties* and *The Life History Album*.[42] Aiming to acquire practical data to support and expand his theoretical descriptions of racial improvement through planned procreation, Galton promoted the albums to "those who care to forecast the mental and bodily faculties of their children, and to further the science of heredity."[43] Galton hoped that by encouraging a standardized method of accumulating and documenting "biological histories,"[44] a vast colloquial resource could be tapped for scientific purposes. As an incentive, Galton opened a national (British) competition and offered five hundred pounds in prize money to those who could supply him with the best family records by May 15, 1884.[45] Similar contests were held at midwestern fairs in the United States in the early twentieth century; however, in the United States such competitions evaluated not the quality of genealogical documentation but the eugenic fitness of the family itself.[46]

Galton's *Record of Family Faculties* aimed to help parents predict the development of their children by tracing their physical and mental attributes back through their ancestral heritage. In the *Record*, an entire page is devoted to each ancestor, going back at least as far as the child's great-grandparents, and seventeen questions are asked about each relative. In addition to information generally recorded by the state, such as date of birth, birthplace, residences, occupation, age at marriage, and date and age at death, the record also requires information about the physical attributes and character of each individual, including adult height, color of hair and eyes, general appearance, bodily strength, ability or imperfection of senses, mental powers, character, temperament, favorite pursuits, and artistic aptitudes. A separate section is left for ailments and illnesses, which Galton describes as "the most important of all in statistical investigations into the rise and fall of families,"[47] and, consequently, the rise and fall of races. In his description of the tables, Galton suggests that category number 8, for "general appearance," would be augmented by "a list of the best extant photographs or portraits of the person at various ages," which could be inserted as an extra page.[48]

Designed under the guidance of Galton by a committee of the British Medical Association in 1884, *The Life History Album* served as a companion to the *Record of Family Faculties* and encouraged parents to document the physical and mental growth of a child by following a standardized schedule of measurements and observations, and by collecting a continuous photographic record of the child's growth. If the *Record* allowed parents to place children (and themselves) within a history of inheritance, locating individuals in relation to a familial past, *The Life History Album* aided parents in projecting their bloodlines into the future, tracing their own features in the development of their immediate progeny.

The Life History Album begins with a condensed, one-page chart on which to record the child's family history, followed by a page on which to document the family's medical history. Subsequent pages are devoted to the child's individual history, which begins with a detailed description of the child at birth, including both physical and temperamental characteristics. First the mother's labor is described, and then the child's tiny body is documented in terms of "physical peculiarities," weight, length, girth, color of eyes and hair, general health, and comportment. From this point the album divides into five-year periods, from birth to age twenty-five, with less detailed segments devoted to the years twenty-five to fifty and fifty to seventy-five. Each five-year period provides a graph on which to record the child's annual stature and weight, and two blank pages on which to date and annotate important events in the child's life. Anthropometric observations are made at the end of the fifth year, and every five years thereafter, including color of eyes and hair, chest girth, strength of pull, acuteness of vision and color vision, and hearing in each ear. Descriptions of acuteness or dullness in the other senses, of trials of physical strength and endurance, of hard intellectual work, of artistic ability, and of physical or mental attributes that resemble those of other relatives are also requested. Each period ends with a page for photographs. Parents are called to make two photographic portraits of a child every five years, "an exact full-face and a profile,"[49] to be used along with other documentation to measure the child's physical and mental growth. Galton emphasizes uniformity in this photographic recording, stating that the images should be consistent in size to enable accurate comparisons. It is here, then, in *The Life History Album*, that the photograph becomes an important historical and scientific document.

Galton imagined that these standardized "family albums" would further enable his study of eugenics, which he deemed both a "science of heredity" and a "science of race." Initially a study of the reproduction of individual genius, Galton's study of heredity rapidly expanded to include the intellectual capacity of "races" and the "character" of races in general. Indeed, Galton's first major study, *Hereditary Genius*, published in England in 1869, was conceived as Galton was studying "the mental peculiarities of different races,"[50] and this first study of "hereditary genius" concludes with a comparative evaluation of the supposed intellectual capacities of different races. Further, as noted briefly in chapter 2, Galton devised his theory of eugenics with a practical purpose in mind; he suggested that "the improvement of the natural gifts of future generations of the human race is largely, though indirectly, under our control."[51] Ultimately, what Galton proposed with the science of heredity he later named "eugenics" was a system of racial improvement through breeding.[52]

As I began to outline in chapter 2, Galton argued that nine biologically distinct races populated the planet, and that each race had its own distinguishing physical characteristics and its own innate intellectual capacity and moral character. He organized these races along a hierarchical scale, placing Anglo-Saxons at the modern pinnacle and African Americans two (innate) grades below.[53] Mourning the ancient Greeks, whom he believed once claimed a now unreachable apex of racial genius, Galton warned that the fate of living Anglo-Saxons might become that of the historical Greeks if steps were not taken to stabilize and improve Anglo-Saxon breeding patterns. Galton's warning was aimed subtly at white upper-middle-class women; it argued explicitly against interracial mixing, correlating with contemporary American social opposition to the New (nonreproducing) Woman and to imagined sexual unions of white women with African American men. In an era in which middle-class white women were prolonging marriage dates, and even forgoing them, Galton feared that Anglo-Saxons simply were not reproducing enough—enough, that is, to compete with the reproduction of other races.[54] Second, Galton warned against interracial reproduction, arguing that the progeny of such unions were biologically "weak," and that they diluted the potency of sacred ancestral "stock." For Galton, the "mulatto" was a "tragic" figure not because he or she was born into a biracist culture that offered no stable position but because he or she "contaminated" the hereditary pool of (white) racial genius.[55] While

Description of Child at Birth.

Name ....

Date of Birth ....

Previous health of Mother * ....

Birth at full time, or premature ....

Labour natural, or instrumental ....

Physical peculiarities, if any (including " Mother's marks ") ....

Weight at birth (naked) ....

Length ....

Girth round nipples ....

Colour of eyes † ....

Colour of hair, if any ....

Child healthy, or ailing ....

„   quiet, or active ....

„   feeble, or vigorous ....

„   good-tempered, or fretful ....

* Any strong mental impression, fright, shock, or fancy, occurring to the mother previous to the birth of the child, should be recorded if possible *before* the birth.

† The eyes of infants at birth are always dark blue ; but it should be observed at what period after birth their colour begins to change. This generally occurs within a few days.

Francis Galton, "Description of Child at Birth," *The Life History Album.* (London: Macmillan, 1994)

Galton argued that interracial reproduction weakened both parent "stocks," he was concerned primarily to protect the purity of what he considered to be the "superior" stock, namely, that of the Anglo-Saxons. Thus, Galton's vision of racial improvement through controlled breeding was one that reinforced the color line in terms of biological survival.

Galton's *Hereditary Genius*, first published in Britain in 1869, was reprinted in 1892, in the period that his work first became popular in the United States.[56] Eugenics enthralled biological racialists at the turn of the century and became a very popular social movement in the United States over the course of the early twentieth century.[57] According to Marouf Arif Hasian, Jr., "In the first several decades of the twentieth century, 'eugenics' was a term that Anglo-Americans heard about from the time of their infancy."[58] In fact, "Growing up in the Anglo-American world in the first few decades of the twentieth century meant being constantly bombarded with lectures on eugenics from ethical, debating, and philosophical societies; health, women's and medical associations—sometimes even the YMCA. Hardly a year passed without new books coming to print written by both scientists and laypersons imbued with the zeal of the new faith. Much of this rhetoric followed a familiar format, beginning with the birth of the movement founded by Galton and ending with a call that the world take up the eugenics creed."[59]

For many white Americans, eugenics resonated powerfully, and in practical terms, with Josiah Nott's midcentury study of races as distinct biological species; it coincided with a gradual ideological shift away from Christian views of monogenesis, or ultimate racial equality, toward racialist views of polygenesis, or absolute racial difference.[60] Throughout the Progressive Era, eugenics played a central role in U.S. movements toward social reform and social control: The Eugenics Committee of America was an influential force in lobbying for the Immigration Restriction Act of 1924,[61] sterilization was practiced on patients and inmates in U.S. mental asylums and prison wards,[62] and laws prohibiting interracial marriages were established and upheld in most states. In a more general sense, Galton's studies of inherent racial difference provided many white Americans with a seeming scientific justification for cultural imperialism and social segregation. Galton's work ideologically fortified the status quo, naturalizing systems of oppression as the inevitable results of distinct biological gifts or capabilities.[63]

Through his theory of eugenics, Galton proposed that the foundation of "race" ultimately lay in the social locus of biological reproduction, namely, the family.[64] Galton proclaimed that intellectual and moral capabilities, as well as physical characteristics, were, first, ancestral heirlooms, and second, race specific. As Galton viewed race as a genealogical construct, he posed "character" as a central artifact in the articulation of race.

Eugenicist understandings of character in biological and racialized terms offer a means of comprehending R.H.E.'s strange estimation of familial character in 1867. When read through Galton's work, R.H.E.'s statements ring both ideologically pregnant and racially charged, providing the foundation for a new kind of racial identity. Once again, the antebellum discourse of moral maternal influence in the formation of a child's character is transformed into a discourse of biological maternal inheritance in the scientific register of eugenics and in R.H.E.'s essay itself.

R.H.E. suggests that one's inherited character, the heirloom of "worthy" parents, eventually will be legible in the outward indices of one's body; similarly, Francis Galton believed that ancestral character (a racialized construct) was visible in one's physical features, as his family records and albums demonstrate.[65] While it is difficult to discern the extent to which Galton's *Record of Family Faculties* and *Life History Album* were adopted by American parents, similar records were promoted enthusiastically in the United States in the early twentieth century. According to Hasian, "In the first decades of the twentieth century, thousands of families eagerly filled out their 'Record of Family Traits' and rushed to mail them to eugenicists for analysis by Davenport or other experts stationed at the Cold Spring Harbor Research Laboratory on Long Island."[66] Albert Wiggam distributed family-record forms to the audiences he addressed on his Chautauqua speaking tours, to be filled out and mailed to the American Eugenics Society,[67] and, as noted earlier, eugenicists sponsored "fitter family contests" at midwestern fairs, in addition to sponsoring eugenics displays and shows at such events.[68] In the United States, eugenicists augmented famous "negative" family studies with photographs of "degenerates," often doctoring the images to make subjects appear strange and even diabolical. Such works include Henry Herbert Goddard's *The Kallikak Family* (1912), Frank W. Blackmar's "The Smoky Pilgrims" (1897), Elizabeth S. Kite's "The 'Pineys'" (1913), Mina A. Sessions's *The Feeble-Minded in a Rural County of Ohio* (1918), and A. C. Rogers and Maud A. Merrill's *Dwellers in the Vale of Siddem* (1919).[69]

An investigation of early-twentieth-century U.S. "baby books" also suggests that the construction of genealogical identity, in terms uncannily similar to those outlined by Galton, permeated early-twentieth-century U.S. culture. Indeed, it appears that Galton's attempt to harness popular family albums to science was quite effective, for over the course of the early twentieth century, American baby books adopted many eugenicist terms and structures, even mirroring Galton's *Record* and *Life History Album*. As Galton appropriated and aimed to standardize the popular form of the family album, that very popular venue itself was transformed, adopting the terms of standardized data in *The Modern Baby Book*. It would seem that the popular and scientific forms of the family album mutually influenced one another in the early years of the twentieth century.

In *The Modern Baby Book and Child Development Record*, published by *The Parents' Magazine* (in connection with W. W. Norton) in 1929, John E. Anderson and Florence L. Goodenough attest to the popularity of baby books in the early twentieth-century United States: "For years parents have been attempting to keep records of the early development and behavior of their children. Pink and blue baby books abound."[70] Framed in contrast to "the old-fashioned Baby Books, containing merely a heterogeneous collection of snapshots, 'cute sayings,' locks of hair and what-not,"[71] *The Modern Baby Book* was designed to standardize family records and serve the purposes of both science and practical parenting, much as Galton had devised *The Life History Album*. Similar to Galton's *Life History Album* (which, once again, begins with a condensed, one-page chart on which to record the child's family history), *The Modern Baby Book* begins with a short family history, in which parents are called upon to record the "interests and accomplishments" of the child's ancestors. In this section, photographs of the parents and all the grandparents are to be collected at the time of the baby's birth, establishing a portrait of the family line at the time in which the baby enters that ancestral lineage. Following this section in *The Modern Baby Book*, the baby's birth and initial stature are described in much the same terms outlined by Galton: As Galton requested a detailed description of the child's physical characteristics at birth, including an extensive record of the child's tiny body—its "physical peculiarities," weight, length, girth, color of eyes and hair, general health, and comportment—*The Modern Baby Book* calls for a record of the baby's weight, length, and circumference. Subsequent measurements of height and weight are made every week for the first year and once a year thereafter to age sixteen. What Goodenough and Anderson add to the "scientific" terms of the baby book are explicit markers of class status—they ask parents not only to record the child's anthropometric measurements each year but also to describe the child's birthday party and to list the presents he or she received.

Both Galton's *Life History Album* and Goodenough and Anderson's *Modern Baby Book* are future-oriented, self-reproducing projects. While Galton imagines that the child will take over the process of self-documentation in adulthood, Goodenough and Anderson predict that when the child becomes an adult, the baby book will become especially significant, allowing him or her to compare "his [or her] own early development with that of his [or her] children and grandchildren."[72] Anderson and Goodenough imagine that the familial bloodline will reproduce itself long into future generations.

Francis Galton attempted to bridge scientific and popular uses of family photography through the *Record of Family Faculties* and *The Life History*

Album, hoping that by encouraging standardized procedures he could open family archives to scientific research. The popularity of modern "baby books" throughout the Progressive Era suggests that his mission was quite successful in the United States, as many eugenicist categories appear to be central to the production of familial documentation in modern baby books. It is within this ideological context, against the scientific backdrop of eugenics and an increasing cultural interest in heredity, that the popular form of "family photography" developed as a middle-class institution. Thus, we can begin to read the growing interest in "baby's picture" not only as a commercial fad or a sentimental ritual but also as a desire to delineate the future of racial bloodlines through photographic artifacts. In this expanded cultural context, "baby's picture" signifies not only as a sentimental memento but also as the scientific "evidence" of the family's racial reproduction.

SENTIMENTAL AURA AND THE EVIDENCE OF RACE

Reexamining the advent of the popular family photograph album from the cultural position established by Galton's "family albums," one can begin to see how the "treasured" image of baby secured by white middle-class mothers with pocket cameras may obscure a very troubling cornerstone of racial reproduction. The slippage between the seemingly innocuous evaluation of baby's picture in the family photograph album and the explicitly racialized measure of baby's photograph in Francis Galton's albums may be clarified by thinking about these two photographic practices in relation to Walter Benjamin's theories of photographic meaning. When addressing the popular form of family photography that developed contiguously with Galton's eugenicist records, the famous distinctions Walter Benjamin draws between the auratic and the evidential image become significant precisely as they are effaced.[73]

As I've discussed in chapter 3, according to Walter Benjamin, the technological shift from daguerreotypy to mechanical reproduction (which enabled both the popular form of family photography and Galton's eugenicist family records) fundamentally altered the character of photographic meaning. In Benjamin's estimation, the dissolution of "aura" surrounding the work of art begins with the invention of mechanical reproduction, or the negative/positive photographic printing process, and heralds a revolutionary moment in art history, one that frees the work of art from its "parasitic dependence on ritual."[74] Benjamin argues that the modern painting, in its singular originality, trapped within the museum, remains intricately tied to a tradition of religious ritual; the artist is analogue to the creator, and the modern painting, marked as an original creation, retains the aura of a pseudospiritual glow. According to Benjamin, mechanical reproduction frees the work of art from the tyranny of originality, destroying the unique in multiplicity, enabling the work of art to be harnessed to the work of politics. Negative/positive photography, with its capacity for endless reproduction, is, for Benjamin, the first revolutionary art form.

Yet even as he describes mechanical reproduction, or the negative/positive photographic process, as a gestalt, Benjamin also notes that aura maintains a lingering stronghold in the most popular of early photographic forms—the portrait.[75] According to Benjamin, aura or "cult value" haunts the photographic portrait, hovering around the photographed face, before it is finally dispelled by evidential standards. Once again, Benjamin describes the aura of the photographic portrait as the viewer's nearly sacred devotion to a loved one, which is analogous to the worship of the religious devotee before a cherished icon.[76] Here we have in Benjamin's analysis the one function of the photograph that satisfies that cantankerous critic of "baby's picture," R.H.E.—the image serves as "a link between you [the viewer] and the memory of its owner."[77] For Benjamin and for R.H.E., then, the aura of the photographic portrait is the beholder's investment of the image with sentiment.

While sentimental bonds rhetorically dominated photographic meaning in the family photograph album, what Benjamin has described as the "evidentiary" quality of nonauratic images was privileged at least partially in the evaluation of baby's picture in Francis Galton's *Life History Album*, in *The Modern Baby Book*, and in R.H.E.'s essay. I would like to suggest, therefore, that the photographs Francis Galton aimed to procure with his *Record of Family Faculties* and his *Life History Album* signified at the convergence of Benjamin's auratic portraits and evidentiary documents. Benjamin distinguishes the "evidential" photographic record from the "auratic" photographic portrait by its relative "emptiness." For Benjamin it is only the "deserted" image that can replace cult ritual with "hidden political significance," that can provide revolutionary evidence of "historical occurrences" like the "scenes of crime."[78] It is only when "man withdraws from the photographic image" that ritual value is superseded by exhibition value, the "revolutionary" estimation of historical events.[79] Finally, even such "deserted" images require captions in order to maintain their radical import, in order to harness photographic meaning to revolutionary objects.[80]

Providing detailed instructions regarding the size, format, and style of images to be collected, and situating those images within an extensive narrative "caption" of detailed documentation, Galton also attempted to demystify the once-sentimental meaning of the individual portrait, reclaiming it for science. While certainly not "deserted," Galton's images, drained of sentiment, would have been valued not simply as keepsakes but as testaments to the family bloodline. Transforming the portrait into a scientific record, Galton reinscribed the photographic likeness as the evidence of family character, and thus, in the terms of eugenics, as the sign of racial identity. While clearly evidential, Galton's use of the photograph was certainly not the counterhegemonic force that Benjamin envisioned. On the contrary, while Galton's "family portraits" are divested of a specifically sentimentalized aura, they are reinvested with what we might call a pernicious ritualistic aura of racism, which not only establishes racial distinction but also reinforces racial superiority. In Galton's albums the evidential quality of the image is reinvested with an aura that links the viewer, through baby's picture, to a racialized family bloodline. To summarize bluntly, in Galton's albums baby's picture is treasured as the measure of white supremacy.

How does this conversion of evidence and racialized aura in Galton's albums help us to understand the sentimentalized investment of white middle-class Americans in "baby's picture" at the turn of the century? If Galton's albums infuse the sentimental image with the fantasized "evidence" of racial superiority, do popular family photograph albums perform the inverse function? Does "baby's picture" become a kind of racial document invested with sentimental aura in the family photograph album? Surely many will protest such a suggestion, proclaiming that they do not think about the future, health, or dominance of their race when they photograph their children. But then how can we understand contemporary birth announcements that include baby's first photograph and document the weight and length of the newborn? And what does it mean when those same photographs are placed in baby books that reproduce so closely the terms of Galton's eugenicist albums?

We have already seen that popular and scientific baby albums were not static forms but exchanged and reappropriated terms and structures from one another throughout the late nineteenth and early twentieth centuries. R.H.E.'s desire to read ancestral character in 1867 is illuminated later by Francis Galton's theory of eugenics. Galton's desire to utilize family albums for scientific study in turn appears to inform the later production of those popular albums, as in *The Modern Baby Book*. When we find scientific and popular forms mirroring one another, what do we make of the ideological investments that inform those converging practices? Does R.H.E.'s strange essay announce the forthcoming ideological influence of eugenics? By the 1890s, R.H.E.'s parents need no longer wait for age or death in order to take measure of their child's future character—the discourse of eugenics provides this register for them. In this same period, does the family photograph album take on the ideological underpinnings of eugenics? And to what extent do the later pink and blue covers of modern baby books mask their true colors?

Photographing baby has endured as a self-defining mechanism for the white middle classes. Indeed, parents produce, reproduce, and circulate these photographs among friends and family and collect them in albums at an ever-accelerated rate. The images mark our love for and interest in the babies they depict, but they also represent adult desires, parental pride, and genealogical affiliation, perhaps reaffirming parents' own sense of their reproductive fitness. Can sentiment, then, fully account for the nature of our desire for baby's picture? As Michel Foucault reminds us, power secures its stronghold precisely in those practices that are held to be normal and natural,[81] and given the present object of analysis, we might also add "cute." While it is easy to say that white middle-class investment in the health and growth of babies is only natural, and that photographs of babies function simply as sentimental mementos, what might be the price of separating such practices from their historical and discursive counterparts? Much of the insidious power of eugenicist discourse in the early twentieth century was founded in its seemingly laudable proclamations to improve "health." Indeed, what could be wrong with monitoring and promoting the health of a family line? We know, of course, that Galton's desire to promote the procreation of the "strong," and conversely to deter the reproduction of the "weak," was informed by a racial ideology in which Anglo-Saxons were always the "strongest," always morally and intellectually superior to men and women of color. Given the transmutation of the baby book in eugenicist and sentimental terms, can we really understand photographing baby as a sentimental act utterly distinct from its performance in explicitly racialized venues? And what does it mean if we very urgently desire to do so?

Richard Dyer has argued persuasively that whiteness secures its cultural power by seeming to be nothing at all, by being invisible.[82] Does it not make sense, then, that the practices and rituals of white desire would also be invisible, remaining racially unmarked, perhaps masked by other terms, such as those of gender, class, or even sentiment? Today baby's picture is certainly not a stupid thing; but then again, a lot may depend on what it is we "always treasure."

CHAPTER FIVE

America Coursing through Her Veins

On April 30, 1890, the Sons of the American Revolution voted to bar women from their society, thereby laying the foundation on which a group of indignant white women would establish what was to endure as one of the most prominent patriotic organizations in U.S. history, namely, the Daughters of the American Revolution (DAR). On October 11, 1890, the Daughters convened for their first official meeting, with no more than a handful of women present but all claiming to have "the blood of Revolutionary heroes in their veins."[1] Their stated purpose was "to perpetuate the memory and spirit of the women and men of the Revolutionary period,"[2] and they limited their membership to those who could prove descent from an ancestor who had rendered "material aid to the cause of Independence" in the Revolutionary War. In just five years the Daughters boasted a membership of 10,300 women, as many as the combined memberships of both societies of the patriotic Sons.[3]

The DAR was one among many newly inaugurated genealogical societies dedicated to delineating "American" identities through a maze of bloodlines at the turn of the century. The 1890s alone saw the emergence of such groups as the Society of Colonial Dames, the National Society of New England Women, the Order of Descendants of Colonial Governors, and the Society of Mayflower Descendants.[4] Reading this rather concentrated interest in celebrating an aristocratically inflected image of American exclusivity within the context of racial segregation, a dramatic rise in the incidence of lynching, and the growing influence of the science of eugenics in the United States, I would like to suggest that such genealogical organizations enabled the consolidation of a *seemingly* stable, embodied, and racialized national identity, one that conflated American borders with Anglo-Saxon bloodlines. At stake in the membership debates of such patriotic societies were the definitions of "America" and "American," the racial and ethnic identities that would or would not be conflated under those signs, and the gendered nature of the body politic.

Notwithstanding the Sons of the American Revolution's decision to exclude women from their organization, many efforts to racialize American identity were posed through representations of white womanhood at the turn of the century. As we have seen in the previous chapter, white women were increasingly situated at the center of eugenicist discourses, and representations of white womanhood were being inflected with racial import in middle-class narratives of cultural dominance. Specifically, the "true" white woman's moral suasion was being recodified as the character of a racialized ancestral stock. While the middle classes still heralded the white mother as a central force in determining the character her children would adopt, they increasingly attributed her powers less to moral influence and more to racialized inheritance. In this chapter I would like to emphasize the ways in which eugenicist logics reinforced discourses of racialized *nationhood* through the figure of the white woman at the turn of the century. By examining the DAR's early eligibility debates, we can see how an investment of American identity in the white female body was enabled by a shift in the rhetoric of what Linda Kerber has called "Republican Motherhood"[5] over the course of the nineteenth century, a shift that was propelled by the growing popularity of the science of eugenics late in the century. While the DAR upheld the ideal of motherhood they inherited from their Republican forebears, they proposed that white American mothers "made Americans" by different means. In short, the Daughters racialized the sentimental force of American maternal influence.[6] By situating the early eligibility debates of the DAR in their historical contexts, we can see that much more than inclusion in an elite club was negotiated in such conversations, for representations of white American womanhood infused the very logics that legitimized American racial violence at the turn of the century. Consequently, as we will see, the Daughters' version of American identity, of American history, and of American womanhood did not remain uncontested.

FROM THE BONDS OF LOVE TO BLOODLINES

The DAR was first and foremost a genealogical society that posited American identity as an ancestral heirloom founded in a legacy of blood. Indeed, the Daughters of the American Revolution described American character as a kind of embodied possession. One nineteenth-century DAR historian declared: "The blood which flowed in the Revolutionary hero, whether man or woman, is still coursing in us; and this bone and sinew and nerve and muscle are but the outcome of our Revolutionary hero; this legacy of blood is ours by direct inheritance, and we cannot share it with another."[7] As direct descendants of revolutionary heroes, the members of the DAR claimed to reproduce in their bodies—in their very "bone and sinew and nerve and muscle"—a revolutionary American spirit. And further, as this "legacy" was bequeathed through "direct inheritance," it was available only to an exclusive minority. Thus, by anchoring their patriotic possessions in the blood and in the body, through direct ancestral inheritance spanning over one hundred years, the Daughters were able to pose a "true"

American identity seemingly inaccessible to more recent immigrants to the United States.

The Daughters also excluded Americans of color and those of mixed racial heritage from their patriotic society, even those women of color who claimed African American, Native American, and Anglo-Saxon American ancestors who rendered "material aid to the cause of Independence" in the Revolutionary War. In 1894, four years after the society was founded, the DAR officially banned women of color from the organization. Upon receiving a letter "asking about the meaning of the word 'acceptable' in the Constitution, and if colored people could be admitted to the Society," the DAR responded unequivocally—"no."[8] A white body was the origin point from which the Daughters began to trace American bloodlines imagined to be both Anglo-Saxon and "pure."

Inspired in part by the initial rejection of the Sons of the American Revolution, the Daughters hoped to celebrate especially the efforts of patriotic white women in the Revolutionary War. Miss Desha, one of the founding members of the organization, stated repeatedly, "All the patriotic societies honor men. . . . I want this Society to be the one Society to honor women."[9] However, recognizing women turned out to be more difficult than many had at first imagined, as official records of service and devotion were kept for soldiers and civil officers, but not for the women who made sacrifices at home to aid the cause of the Revolution. Seeking to honor the women for whom no records could be obtained except through their sons and brothers, the Daughters added a phrase to their eligibility statements in 1890, recognizing the descendants of the "mother of a patriot."[10]

In arguing for the "mother of a patriot" clause, Daughters evoked an antebellum discourse of maternal influence in the domestic sphere. By drawing upon the figure of the mother as the moral educator of her children, the Daughters claimed that the patriotic character of a child was shaped by his or her mother's example and influence. Therefore, some Daughters suggested that if one could prove that a child was patriotic, one might assume that his or her mother had also been patriotic; consequently, according to the discourse of maternal influence, one could conclude that all of the mother's children had been patriotic, even those whose actions could not be documented. The DAR's "mother of a patriot" clause thus enabled the "undocumented" descendants of brothers and sisters of known patriots to claim eligibility to the society through the common maternal figure. As the embodiment of the central force influencing the character development of her children, the "mother of a proven patriot" was deemed a "true" American.[11]

Although the "mother of a patriot" proposal acquired initial approval, not all Daughters concurred on the power of maternal influence. Dissenting Daughters claimed both that one's character was not necessarily the result of maternal suasion and also that maternal love could not be relied upon to affect all children equally. Skeptical Daughters sought to close what they saw as a loophole of love, with the documented evidence of patriotic performance, transferred to descendants through direct bloodlines. These women challenged an antebellum model of maternal influence with a racialized discourse of blood.

The counterarguments posed by dissenting Daughters in the "mother of a patriot" debates resonated powerfully with the scientific logics of eugenics then gaining credence in the United States. As one nineteenth-century commentator summarized their position, they believed that "sentiment is one thing, blood is another."[12] As we have seen, blood had increasingly become central to definitions of race and delineations of racial difference in the sciences of biological racialism over the course of the nineteenth century, culminating in the science of eugenics at the turn of the century. Once again, eugenics posed innate, heritable differences in moral character and intellectual capacity between the races, and imagined a modern racial hierarchy culminating in Anglo-Saxon superiority. Specific to eugenics, among the sciences of biological racialism, was its emphasis on heredity and on racial improvement through breeding. In this way, then, as a genealogical society the DAR shared with eugenicists at least a superficial interest in both blood and heredity.

As I have discussed in previous chapters, Francis Galton's first eugenicist study, *Hereditary Genius*, is a text permeated with anxiety over relative racial fertility and with explicit calls for increased breeding among upper-middle-class Anglo-Saxons. Implicitly it calls upon Anglo-Saxon women to heed the future of the race, to marry early, and to reproduce prolifically. Galton's interest in the Anglo-Saxon woman as racial or national "mother" is strictly biological, not sentimental. As the fount of a "superior" moral and intellectual character, according to Galton, the Anglo-Saxon woman must fulfill a reproductive duty for her race, passing on the gifts of her biological stock to numerous progeny.[13] Indeed, in the science of eugenics, the antebellum rhetoric of "maternal influence" is transformed into a scientific discourse of "biological inheritance." A child's character is no longer seen as the result of maternal direction and shaping but as a kind of ancestral heirloom, transmitted across generations through the blood. Thus, maternal influence is no longer imagined to be rooted in the heart, but in the blood—and bone, and sinew.

The Daughters eventually followed eugenicists in their adherence to the primacy of biological heredity and blood when they decided, in June 1894 (with a vote of 138 to 13), to oust "the mother of a patriot" phrase from their eligibility statements. Once again, they proposed, "sentiment is one thing, blood is another."[14] In praising this revision, one Daughter declared, "The new amendment restricts eligibility to *loyal* sources; it simply says we must descend from parent to child, and must prove that the blood which flowed in the Revolutionary hero is still coursing in us."[15] After four years of deliberation, the DAR decided that maternal influence could not be relied on as the loyal source of a patriotic bloodline. By rejecting the eligibility of the descendants of the "mother of a patriot," and by refuting arguments for their inclusion, the Daughters disowned the importance of maternal influence in the development of national character. Thus, in 1894, the moral suasion of the True Woman in the domestic sphere was discarded definitively by the DAR in favor of the documentation of "true" bloodlines. Effectively, the DAR transformed the rhetoric of Republican Motherhood that trumpeted the (white, middle-class) American woman's moral power into a celebration of her biological stock.

In deciding for blood, and against sentiment, the Daughters were still left with the problem of where to locate the fount of the patriotic bloodlines they claimed to embody, where to situate "loyal sources." Rejecting the maternal heart, they anchored their bloodlines in the imagined evidence of public documents garnered from the traditionally masculine spheres (in the eighteenth and nineteenth centuries) of politics, commerce, the law, the military, and men. Not unlike Francis Galton, whose initial study of "hereditary genius" focused on the ancestral inheritance of famous men, the Daughters reinforced the value of a historically masculinized realm of documented public action as the fount from which their racially inflected patriotic bloodlines would flow. While the undocumented, immaterial aid of "heart, soul and strength,"[16] of maternal influence, was, according to the DAR, all very nice, "true" American identity would have to be proven through the material evidence of public records. Then and only then, this privileged patriotism could be said to pass down direct bloodlines to proud Daughters.

Ultimately, the effects and implications of the motions taken by the early Daughters of the American Revolution in their initial eligibility debates undermined the DAR's purported intentions. The images of embodiment that permeate the rhetoric of these debates *did* serve to stabilize an exclusive, white American identity, but *not* the white *female* American identity the DAR hoped to celebrate. By posing their bodies as the privileged sites of American identity only vis-à-vis a record of official white male performance, the Daughters ultimately reinscribed a masculine white sphere of national political privilege. Thus, they ultimately staked their claims to American identity in the very political structures that effaced their bodies from the realm of political action—from the vote and from political office. In attempting to naturalize a politics of exclusion in their own organization, the Daughters of the American Revolution actually reproduced their own absence from the public record of patriotic performance. Further, in reinforcing a domain of white male prerogative in their attempts to celebrate white female privilege, the Daughters also substantiated the bonds of disfranchisement that linked them, paradoxically, to those bodies from which they most sought to dissociate themselves, namely, the bodies of men and women of color. Ultimately, then, the Daughters augmented what they aimed to deny and repress, namely, the fact that their own blood and bone and muscle and sinew were not categorically so very different from the blood and bone and muscle and sinew of American men and women of color. Finally, in legitimizing their white women's bodies via the domain of white men's history and politics, the Daughters of the American Revolution reinscribed the primacy of the white Sons who sought to exclude them.

AMERICA'S WHITE ARISTOCRACY

As a national organization, the DAR enabled a kind of social reunification of the North and South in the post-Reconstruction era. Tracing bloodlines back to ancestors who fought for a mutual cause, Daughters from the North and South could imagine themselves as part of the same community, as members of the same "family." A shared patriotic paternity allowed Daughters "to forget the disunion of a generation ago in the common glory of the Revolution."[17] By tracing white bloodlines back over a hundred years of racial, regional, and familial conflict in seamless strokes, the Daughters could forget not only violent meetings between Northern and Southern whites in the mid–nineteenth century but also the central cause of that conflict, namely, slavery. The symbolic reunification of Northern and Southern white sisters in the "glory of the Revolution" constructed a historical continuity that erased slavery as a national problem and reestablished a unified American utopia through the dream of an era in which slavery existed, and was embraced by many Revolutionary heroes. Further, by suturing over the conflict of the Civil War in celebration of the Revolutionary War, the Daughters also diverted their attention away from the radical social changes engendered by the Civil War. In forgetting "the disunion of a generation ago," the Daughters could also forget the social consequences of abolition in favor of a dream of white racial aristocracy. Finally, with intricate genealogical maps that carefully avoided the unnamed branches of interracial family lines engendered by rape during slavery, the Daughters could inscribe a fantasy of white Americanness over a long history of interracial mixing.

The Daughters' investment in the "purity" of patriotic white bloodlines, in patrimony and in genealogy, posed a kind of racial aristocracy at the center of American nationhood. As we have seen, the Daughters, not unlike biological racialists and eugenicists, construed national character as a property inherited from one's ancestors. Reinscribing an antebellum middle-class familial discourse founded on a mother's moral suasion with the racially codified terms of blood and genealogy at the turn of the century, the Daughters announced "democratic" middle-class ideals, even as they circumscribed a seemingly inclusive sphere with exclusive white bloodlines. The Daughters effectively transformed an aristocratic class paradigm into a racial and national discourse, a discourse the middle classes themselves could embrace. The very logics of blood purity from which Nathaniel Hawthorne was so at pains to dissociate an ascendant middle class eventually became the means whereby the middle classes would reinforce class privilege under the banner of racial exclusivity in a changing social sphere at the turn of the century.

While the Daughters embraced aristocratic logics in restricting their membership to narrow requirements based upon genealogies of direct lineal descent, and in arbitrarily excluding women of color from the organization, they vehemently refuted accusations that the organization was elitist. Devoted as they were to celebrating the foundations of democracy, preserving revolutionary history, and perpetuating revolutionary blood, the Daughters balked at being associated with anything as "un-American" as an aristocracy, and they were at great pains to emphasize that descendants of rankless soldiers entered the society on equal footing with the descendants of commanding officers. Honoring the progeny of "the best and most honored names" with that of "thousands of humbler heroes," the DAR made claims to antiaristocratic, democratic principles in terms of class inclusion.[18] But once again, while celebrating an apparently democratic impulse in terms of class, the Daughters simultaneously heralded the exclusivity of racialized bloodlines. Thus, even as they argued against the notion of a class aristocracy, they reinforced a vision of (middle-class) racial aristocracy.

Recognizing the implicit intent of white women's patriotic societies to establish an aristocracy of race reminiscent of the white patriarchal structures of the antebellum South, Anna Julia Cooper, an African American scholar, feminist, and contemporary of the first Daughters, argued that white Northern women's obsession with blood implicitly participated in and reinforced the racist caste system of the South. The reunification of white Northern and Southern Daughters established a national network of white supremacy. In *A Voice from the South*, 1892, Cooper explains that "the South represented blood—not red blood, but blue blood": "The South had neither silver nor gold, but she had blood; and she paraded it with so much gusto that the substantial little Puritan maidens of the North, who had been making bread and canning currants and not thinking of blood the least bit, began to hunt up the records of the Mayflower."[19] With wonderfully biting sarcasm, Cooper describes Northern interest in genealogy as a competitive response to the Southern white aristocracy's claim to social privilege. Northern mania over blood marked Northern white women's attempt to assert an aristocratic equality with their white Southern "sisters," a parity that would demonstrate the white woman's longed-for interregional superiority to those of other castes.[20]

Following Anna Julia Cooper, we can begin to read white women's obsession with blood as a reactionary response to a changing national landscape in the post–Civil War period. The abolition of slavery shifted the social positions not only of African Americans but also of white men and women, both North and South, quite dramatically. As African American men gained a status recognized by the ideologies of white individualism, claiming property in self as well as commodities, a new order of African American family was engendered. The very fact of a stable, self-regulated African American familial structure, the purported goal of white Northern sentimental abolitionists like Harriet Beecher Stowe, altered the conception of the white family across the nation, and most dramatically in the South. In the antebellum South, the caste system of slavery, which denied the legal and spiritual sanctity of the African American slave family, had maintained white women and children in a legally superior rank to African American slaves, even as free whites and enslaved blacks were classified alike as the "dependents" of "independent" white men in the discourses of Southern pro-slavery individualism.[21] The abolition of slavery reconfigured the landscape of Southern social hierarchies, posing white and black women similarly as the dependents of independent white and black men. Without the caste system of slavery, nothing secured the white dependents' elevated status in relation to other dependents. Realizing their new positions below independent black men, and on a par with dependent black women, white Southern women clung to the bloodlines that had regulated the caste system legally institutionalized by slavery. As white women of the North began to see their stations transforming within a changing national terrain, many joined with white Southern sisters in a quest to secure an "essential" superiority anchored in blood. In this way, the cultural authority of a once legally circumscribed domestic sphere was superseded by the racialized family bloodline.

The DAR's social reunification of Northern and Southern white women under the banner of an exclusive American identity also worked to fortify an old Anglo-Saxon American identity against the "threat" of new immigration at the turn of the century. Historically, the DAR sought both to speed the "Americanization" of new citizens and to decrease the numbers of immigrants permitted to enter the United States.[22] Not unlike the eugenicists who fought for the 1924 Immigration Restriction Act, the DAR policed both the racialized boundaries of the national body and the geographic borders of the nation. Critiquing such efforts, Anna Julia Cooper proclaimed: "America for Americans! This is the white man's country! The

Chinese must go, shrieks the exclusionist. Exclude the Italians! Colonize the blacks in Mexico or deport them to Africa. Lynch, suppress, drive out, kill out! America for Americans! Who are Americans? comes rolling back from ten million throats. . . . Who are the homefolks and who are the strangers? Who are the absolute and original tenants in fee-simple?"[23] Describing xenophobic nationalists as hysterics, Cooper both undermines the imagined stability of the white body and emphasizes the absurdity of white Northerners' claims to a "native" American identity through ancestry. Further, while first implying that the occupants of the *Mayflower* were themselves immigrants, Cooper then suggests that if the first foreign boat to arrive in America is to be marked as the site of original American identity, perhaps this privileged status should be given to African Americans whose ancestors landed on the shores of New England in 1619, one year before the *Mayflower* hit the "new" land.[24]

Anna Julia Cooper challenged not only the effacement of slavery and immigration under a banner of white Americanness but also the implicit degradation of black women's bodies embedded in white women's pursuit of "pure" American white blood.[25] By excluding African American women from the patriotic societies that engendered "true" Americans, white women denigrated black women's bodies, posing the blood that African American women passed to their children as a contaminating force, as not truly American. While many white women argued for segregation in the post-Reconstruction period, protesting what they deemed a "forced" (and "contaminating") society with the people "who were once our slaves,"[26] Cooper countered: "The overtures for forced association in the past history of these two races were not made by the manacled black man, nor by *the silent and suffering black woman*!"[27] Contrasting the "threat" posed to white womanhood by social integration to the rape of black women by white men in slavery, Cooper radically undermines the indignation of white supremacists with their own practices.[28] Cooper's critique also suggests that as the white master "sowed his blood broadcast" among his slaves,[29] he violently bequeathed the privileged patriotic property claimed exclusively by white women to a host of other family members. As Adrian Piper has argued, four hundred years of interracial mixing in the Americas heralds "bad news for the Daughters of the American Revolution."[30]

IN THE NAME OF WHITE WOMANHOOD

Anna Julia Cooper was not alone in critiquing the DAR's version of American identity and national history. In 1894 Frederick Douglass declared: "The native land of the American Negro is America. His bones, his muscles, his sinews, are all American. His ancestors for two hundred and seventy years have lived and laboured and died, on American soil, and millions of his posterity have inherited Caucasian blood."[31] The striking repetition of DAR terms that we find in Douglass's statements, his attention to "bones," and "muscles," and "sinews," underlines the centrality of the body in struggles over American identity at the turn of the century.[32] In these articulations, both Douglass and the Daughters figuratively dissect the body, investing its component parts with patriotic essence. But such dissections bear added resonance in Douglass's text, for Douglass symbolically dismembers the black male body in an essay that treats the literal mutilation of that body in lynching.

In "Why Is the Negro Lynched?" Douglass invests the black body with an American character gleaned from the land, from history, from labor, and from blood. Douglass claims the blood of both African ancestors and of Caucasians, suggesting that the "Revolutionary" blood jealously guarded by white Daughters also courses in the veins of Americans of color, proposing that the Daughters do indeed "share" their "legacy of blood" with others. While Douglass does not privilege "white" blood as the source of American character, in calling upon it he emphasizes the history of interracial mixing the Daughters sought fervently to deny. And further, by highlighting a legacy of interracial mixing, Douglass also evokes the specter that haunts the lynching mythology of the 1890s, as we shall see.

In the 1890s, the decade in which the Daughters convened for their first meetings, lynching was at an all-time high in the United States.[33] Defined as a murder committed by a mob of three or more persons, lynching has always borne heavy racial and sexual accents in this country, generally referring to the ritualized mutilation and murder of a black man by a mob of white men. Such acts of violence were legitimized most frequently with a cry of rape and were committed in the name of protecting white womanhood. In torturing and murdering a black man, white lynch mobs claimed to be avenging the virtue of a white woman allegedly raped by their victim.[34]

Identifying the cry of rape (of a white woman) as the fire that fueled white lynch mobs and protected them from public outcry and legal retribution, Ida B. Wells, a prominent African American journalist, began to investigate the purported reality of this rhetoric in 1892.[35] Wells understood how the cry of rape evoked a brutal crime that seemed to call forth an equally brutal retaliation, and as she states in her autobiography, she herself was appeased by such rhetoric for a time. But in 1892 three prominent businessmen, including one of Wells's close friends, were lynched in Memphis, Tennessee, for the "crime" of operating a successful grocery store that competed with white grocers for a predominantly black market. After this act of terrorism, Wells increasingly began to see lynching as a means of controlling and curtailing African American economic success.[36] Recognizing how the rhetoric of rape deflected the economic anxieties that generated lynching, Wells set about dismantling the banner of virtuous white womanhood under which lynching crimes were performed. Through careful research Wells demonstrated first that many lynchings were performed without accusations of sexual assault and, second, that many cries of rape were raised to cover up what were actually consensual romantic relationships between white women and black men.[37]

How or why, then, did the rhetoric of rape function so effectively to assuage public outcry over the crime of lynching in late-nineteenth-century U.S. culture? A screen of racialized sexual violence deterred white outrage over the murder of black men by playing both to anxieties over the legal and political position of white men in the post-Reconstruction period and to anxieties over the imagined threat of interracial reproduction fostered by the sciences of biological racialism and eugenics.

In the simplest terms, the abolition of slavery dismantled the absolute political power and social authority of the white patriarch. In the antebellum period, the white male's political power was defined by his "independent" status in relation to "dependent" white women and children, and all black slaves.[38] After the Civil War, the white Southern patriarch lost a great number of the dependents that had formerly demonstrated his own freedom, and he found himself sharing his independent status with African American men. Despite institutionalized racism, legal segregation, and systematic disfranchisement, the emancipated male slave, empowered as the head of his own household, met his former master on symbolically level terrain. Given this shift in relative power, lynching can be understood as an attempt on the part of white men to reclaim their former command over the black male body. As Hazel Carby has argued: "The emancipation of the slaves represented the loss of the vested interests of white men in the body of the Negro, . . . and lynching should be understood as an attempt to regain and exercise that control."[39]

White women also found themselves occupying new positions within a reconfigured social sphere in the post–Civil War period. Posed in subordinate positions to both white and black men, white women were situated as dependents no longer categorically distinct from women of color. And once again, while institutionalized racism, legal segregation, and the systematic disfranchisement of African American men in the post-Reconstruction era continued to privilege white women and men in practical terms, we might still examine the rise in white supremacist discourses of white womanhood as a psychological response to the "threat" of racial equality simultaneous with gendered enfranchisement. As manhood was posed as the common denominator of political power, white men and women called upon a racial hierarchy to reclaim a gendered hierarchy for whites only. Within this cultural context, we might begin to understand the lynch mob's cry of rape as an attempt to elevate the white woman who had fallen, literally in legal terms, to the black man. By celebrating his dependents over those of other men, the white patriarch attempted to raise his own relative social status. Rhetorically transforming the African American man's political advance into a sexual violation, the lynch mob produced an image of threatened white womanly virtue to reinforce the power of a white patriarchy over a black patriarchy.

The intersection of racial and gender discourses that informed the rhetoric of lynching also played out in the ritualized torture of the black male body in the act of lynching. Before killing a victim, lynch mobs often castrated him. Referencing the alleged rape for which the black man was to be punished, castration also symbolically feminized the black male body, removing the physical sign that posed him as equal to white men in the realm of masculine political power. As Robyn Wiegman has argued, "In the context of white supremacy, we must understand the threat of masculine sameness as so terrifying that only the reassertion of a gendered difference can provide the necessary disavowal. It is this that lynching and castration offer in their ritualized deployment, functioning as both a refusal and a negation of the possibility of extending the privileges of patriarchy to the black man."[40] By feminizing the black male body, the white male could once again claim his power and superiority over that body, effectively categorizing it alongside the female bodies, both black and white, over which he continued to wield political and social control.

By removing the black man's penis, white lynch mobs also symbolically excised the "threat" of interracial mixing at the hands of the emancipated black man. By castrating the black male body, white men defied the return of their own repressed rape of black women, denying the image of L. Seaman's lithograph that so haunted a white patriarchy, namely, the image of a passionate union between a black man and a white woman. The white lynch mob's cry of rape functioned to incite outrage not only at the violation of "innocent" white womanhood but also at the "contamination" of the white bloodline. As we have seen, the sciences of biological racialism and eugenics transformed an antebellum pseudo-aristocratic obsession with blood into a racialized middle-class discourse in the late nineteenth century, and called upon white womanhood to signify the embodiment of the white bloodline and its potential reproduction. In the post-Reconstruction nation, white womanhood came to represent not the moral but the biological superiority of the white middle and upper-middle classes. For white supremacists, then, "miscegenation" functioned as a discursive threat that necessitated the protection and the control of white women in turn-of-the-century U.S. culture.

White supremacist "miscegenation" anxiety was rooted in the essentialized hierarchies of biological racialism that it simultaneously fostered.

Drawing upon and reinforcing a racial hierarchy inscribed by the sciences
of biological racialism and eugenics, lynching mythology posed white
women as the bearers of a racialized civilization threatened by the unleashed brutality of the "natural" "Negro."[41] White supremacist discourses
suggested that the emancipated African American male, no longer disciplined by the "guidance" of white masters, would revert to a primitive state
of essential bestiality. Calling up the image of the "new negro crime" of
raping white women, one writer for *Harper's Weekly* proclaimed: "Such
outrages are sporadic indications of a lapse of the Southern negro into a
state of barbarism or savagery, in which the gratification of the brutish
instincts is no longer subjected to the restraints of civilization."[42] By evoking the mythic rape of a white woman over and over again as a legitimate
cause for violence upon the black male body, white lynch mobs posed the
white woman's body as a pure vessel of civilization violated by the attack
of a bestial black man.

The white supremacist discourses that legitimized lynching depended
on the stable white female body they construed.[43] And yet in medical discourses of the day, the white middle-class woman's body was often posed
as uncontrollable, tending dangerously toward hysteria. We need only
think of Charlotte Perkins Gilman's "creeping" young mother in "The
Yellow Wall-Paper" to evoke the flip side to eugenicist discourses of
healthy white motherhood. We might also take Cesare Lombroso's photographs of prostitutes as instructive here.[44] As the criminal body was being
scientifically essentialized, women's sexuality itself was demonized as a potentially criminal essence. Thus, while her racial identity was essentialized
at the top of a biological hierarchy, the white woman's sexuality was posed
as a force that threatened to destabilize not only her own social position
but also the racial hierarchy she was expected to reproduce.

A white patriarchy depended on the purity of white women as bearers
of bloodlines and distributors of property and racial character. As Ida B.
Wells's research into consensual romantic relationships between white
women and black men makes clear, however, white women's desires very
often exceeded and transgressed the racialized reproductive destinies dictated for them. As Adrian Piper has noted, by coupling solely with men of
color, white women could effectively erase racial differences in a single
generation. Indeed, the ever-present "threat" to the white patriarchy har-
bored in the uncontrollable bodies of white women is precisely what
Ida B. Wells evoked in her famous antilynching editorial of 1892: "Nobody
in this section believes the old thread-bare lie that Negroes assault white
women. If Southern white men are not careful they will over-reach themselves and a conclusion will be reached which will be very damaging to the
moral reputation of their women."[45] We can measure the degree to which
Wells spoke to the heart of white patriarchal anxieties in the response this

editorial provoked. Days after the editorial was published, a white mob destroyed the offices of Wells's newspaper, the *Free Speech*, and went looking for Wells with the intent to lynch her. Fortunately, Wells was in Philadelphia at the time, but the threat of violence kept her out of the South for decades. Wells evoked white rage not only because her editorial tarnished the reputation of white women but also because it challenged the power of white men to control "their" women. Wells named the nameless—white women might desire black men—and antimiscegenation laws might not hinder the fulfillment of those desires.[46] Ultimately, then, Wells intimated that the very foundation of white patriarchal privilege might easily be undermined by the wiles of white women.

Thus, we might think about the ways in which lynching expresses the white patriarch's fear of and desire to contain not only black male and female sexuality but also white female sexuality. As a gendered act of racial violence, lynching powerfully demonstrated the risks white women ran in defying a white patriarchy. This is not to suggest, of course, that white women were the victims of lynching; indeed, it is important to remember that white women's "crimes" against a white patriarchy were inevitably played out upon African American bodies. But by emphasizing how lynching functioned to harness white women's sexuality to a racialized reproductive destiny, we can begin to see exactly what white women embraced when they claimed racial privilege under the banner of the lynch mob's "white womanhood." Once again, by heightening their racial privilege through the revered image of white womanhood, white women ultimately affirmed white patriarchal power.

As lynching demonstrated the fears of a white patriarchy, such acts also catalyzed fear to reinforce that racialized patriarchy. As Elizabeth Alexander has argued, lynching, like slave whippings, functioned as an example of "violence made spectacular in order to let black people know who was in control."[47] White lynch mobs left burned and mutilated bodies hanging in trees as signs that foretold African American viewers of the reign of white terror. The "strange fruit" abandoned at roadsides powerfully evoked for black viewers the white surveillance that ever threatened to break into violence upon the black body.

For the predominantly white crowds that witnessed lynching, these violent spectacles offered a sense of control over racial signification. As "whiteness" and "blackness" ceased to signal clear social positions after emancipation and black male suffrage, the signs of "race" were reinvested with the absolute differences conjured by the scientific discourses and illegal practices of white supremacists. Like biological racialism, lynching situated racial difference definitively within the body itself, as an innate set of characteristics embedded in the bone and blood and sinew. Lynching encouraged white viewers to imagine that they possessed an indisputably embodied power. Lynching transformed "whiteness" into something visible and terribly tangible, into something "real." In the gruesome act of dissecting the body of an African American man, white men and women convinced themselves of their own physical superiority. Investing in the embodied nature of a racial hierarchy, the members of the white lynch mob proclaimed their superiority over the black body, bone for bone, muscle for muscle, sinew for sinew.

"A HERITAGE UNIQUE IN THE AGES"

As pure white womanhood became the battle cry of the white lynch mob, black women remained vulnerable to the aggressions of white men. As Ida B. Wells documented in *Southern Horrors*, the ire of Southern white chivalry was not raised by the rape of black women and girls. Lynch mobs were not rallied to protect the sanctity of black womanhood.[48] Bound by discourses dating from slavery that denigrated her as promiscuous, the black woman was posed as the impure twin to her white "sister" in late-nineteenth-century America.[49] As white supremacists deemed the black woman's body a carrier of second-class blood, they posited that body as always already contaminated.

Recognizing the image of black female impurity as fundamental to the reproduction of a white patriarchy under the banner of pure white womanhood, Anna Julia Cooper sought to dismantle racial hierarchies by reconfiguring the dominant image of black womanhood. Cooper argued that African Americans would be accepted as full Americans only when African American women were celebrated alongside white women. In short, Cooper proclaimed that racial equality could be achieved only by elevating the social position of the African American woman: "Only the Black Woman can say 'when and where I enter, in the quiet, undisputed dignity of my womanhood, without violence and without suing or special patronage, then and there the whole *Negro race enters with me.*' "[50] Transforming the degraded "condition" of the slave mother into a dignified sign of racial inheritance, Cooper poses black women as the key to racial uplift. Cooper's African American mother will bequeath a racial inheritance to her children, and those children will measure their own social standing according to the status of their "race mothers."[51]

Adopting an antebellum rhetoric of True Womanhood, Cooper seizes upon a cultural discourse that had been fundamentally denied to slave women who could neither protect their purity nor control their reproductive destinies. The slave mother, bought and sold away from children and spouse at the whim of white masters, could not protect a stable domestic sphere of her own. The slave woman's "domesticity" was always bound to fortify another's sphere.[52] In the postbellum period, Anna Julia Cooper reclaims the image of black womanhood for an American domesticity founded on "true" moral suasion. First invoking a discourse of bloodlines by heralding the African American woman as "the source from which the life-blood of the race is to flow," Cooper then infuses the sanctity of blood with the gendered moral "essence" of an earlier era: "The atmosphere of homes is no rarer and purer and sweeter than are the mothers in those homes. A race is but a total of families. The nation is the aggregate of its homes."[53] Reinvesting bloodlines with the rhetoric of Republican Motherhood, Cooper counters the popular and scientific discourses that revered white women at the expense of black women in the name of biological superiority. Challenging the racialized national genealogies celebrated by the Daughters of the American Revolution, Cooper situates African American women at the center of a nation composed of "true" families and homes.

The convergence of nation, race, and family in Anna Julia Cooper's work plays against the white national borders delineated by eugenicists and exclusive white Daughters. While clearly contesting this radical racism, Cooper's work also challenges the whitewash of a turn-of-the-century assimilationist platform, an agenda one finds emblematized in a series of "family records" produced for newly emancipated African American consumers in the postbellum era. The Strobridge and Company lithograph of 1873, entitled *Freedman's National and Family Record*, recalls Francis Galton's *Record of Family Faculties* even as it sutures over the violence of biological racialism to fold a free African American family into a national American community. The lithograph provides a kind of condensed family album, reduced to a single page, and an even further condensed national history, contained within seven small images. The African American family is set at the center of a national history, framed by three scenes meant to depict slavery on the left, and three scenes meant to depict life after emancipation on the right. The six panels tell a shorthand national history, beginning with the first slave ships, moving through African American citizenship, and ending in a pastoral middle-class family scene. The photographs to be placed in the center of this narrative will signify at the convergence of familial, racial, and national histories. Effectively, the Strobridge lithograph collapses personal history into a carefully scripted national history, calling upon contemporary photographs to serve as testaments to the truth and success of that national history. The center space to be populated with photographs of an African American family is supported by two Greek columns, which in turn frame a small congregation of white men grouped around President Lincoln. Lincoln holds a scroll very likely meant to represent the Emancipation Proclamation, and this little scene is presided over by a portrait of George Washington. Thus, the Strobridge lithograph both

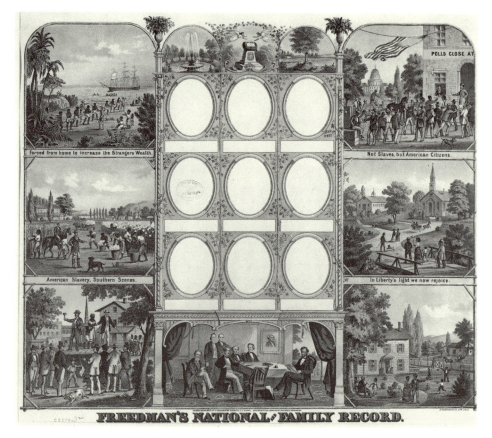

Freedman's National and Family Record. Lithograph by Strobridge and Company, 1873. Reproduced from the Collections of the Library of Congress.

formally and symbolically offers a reinvented national foundation for the African American family, a foundation that poses the middle-class African American family as the product of a national history determined by white patriarchs. The lithograph remaps the free African American family as part of a national community, but it encourages consumers to desire inclusion as grateful recipients within the narrow confines of a narrative of white patriarchal benevolence.

A second lithograph produced for African American consumers by Krebs in 1880 provides another idealized conflation of familial, racial, and national histories. The Krebs lithograph, entitled *Family Record,* calls for a very condensed life history of twelve family members, asking only for date of birth, marriage, and death. In this lithograph, portraits of individual family members have been replaced by a simple collection of written data, and these names and dates surround an idealized image of middle-class African American family life. The lithograph encourages viewers to imagine that the individuals named on its periphery participate in the state of familial wealth and bliss represented by the center image. In this way, the particularity and individuality of the actual members of a family can be subsumed under a sign of African American middle-class domestic perfection, complete with mother, father, children, and a black baby doll. The idealized family represented in the upper portion of the Krebs lithograph is upheld by a two-panel history of African American life in the nation. The bottom left panel depicts slavery, "before the war," and the bottom right depicts freedom—a country picnic with a dancing baby—"since the war." As represented by Krebs, enslaved African American men plowed the land by hand, under the command of a white man. In the days following emancipation, African Americans enjoy leisure time, and when they work it is with the aid of modern equipment, and in the service of well-to-do African American landowners. Read against one another, the two panels suggest a new economic status for African Americans after emancipation. The center scene that these two images support is infused with the markers of middle-class "taste," including heavy draperies, patterned wallpaper and carpet, bedraped table and urnlike vase. George Washington watches over the happy domestic scene, marking this family as unmistakably American as it is middle-class.

While popular "family records" evoked an image of idealized domesticity in order to harness the African American family to a white national history, Anna Julia Cooper calls upon a discourse of maternal influence in order to situate "sweet homes" at the core of a racial history that will determine a national future. Anna Julia Cooper's home is not the middle-class parlor that magically rises out of emancipation, nor the whitewashed cabin of the freedman's guide.[54] Cooper's work challenges the erasure of an assimilationist rhetoric that would repaint a history of African American struggle as a narrative of white benevolence. By reincarnating the rhetoric of True Womanhood, Cooper does not invest in the nostalgia of an earlier period but instead reclaims black womanhood from the erasure of white supremacist discourses. Further, in calling upon the "true" black woman's moral suasion, Cooper situates blackness in the heart of the nation.[55]

Writing in the 1890s, Cooper heralds the dawn of what Frances Ellen Watkins Harper deemed "Woman's Era."[56] According to Cooper's visionary version of American history, a new era of reflection and ideas will follow the periods of settlement and capitalist accumulation, and in this third epoch women will reign supreme through the strength of their moral force. "To be alive at such an epoch is a privilege, to be a woman then is sublime."[57] However, as Cooper seizes upon moral suasion as the key to woman's social power, she also significantly expands the purview of that

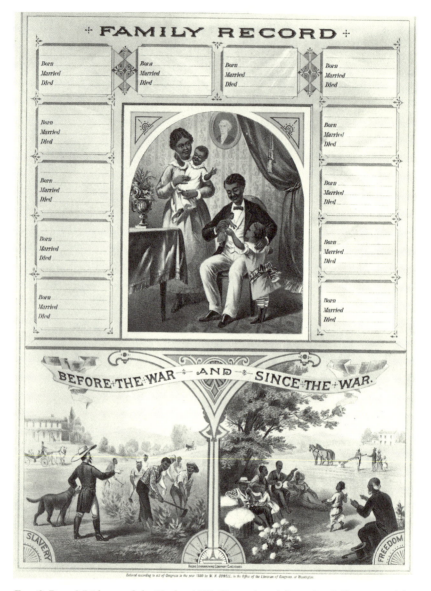

Family Record. Lithograph by Krebs, 1880. Reproduced from the Collections of the Library of Congress.

earlier trope: "Fifty years ago woman's activity according to orthodox definitions was on a pretty clearly cut 'sphere,' including primarily the kitchen and the nursery, and rescued from the barrenness of prison bars by the womanly mania for adorning every discoverable bit of china or canvass with forlorn looking cranes balanced idiotically on one foot."[58] Not particularly impressed with the "homely witchcraft" that announced an emerging middle class in the antebellum period, Cooper explains that moral "essence" must function not as the lock that bars Woman within a restricted sphere but as the key that makes her voice heard in all social, political, and economic arenas. "Not one of the issues of this plodding, toiling, sinning, repenting, falling, aspiring humanity can afford to shut her out, or can deny the reality of her influence. No plan for renovating society, no scheme for purifying politics, no reform in church or in state, no moral, social, or economic question, no movement upward or downward in the human plane is lost on her. . . . All departments in the new era are to be hers."[59] For Cooper, True Womanhood must not circulate merely as a banner under which class, race, or gender privileges are evoked and reinforced. Maternal influence must not reproduce hierarchies of race and class, or yet again reaffirm a white patriarchy while keeping women trapped within a prisonlike "protected" sphere.

In Cooper's history of America, "Woman's Era" converges with the rise of the "Negro" race, and therefore African American women are posed at the forefront of two historical epochs. "To be a woman in such an age carries with it a privilege and an opportunity never implied before. But to be a woman of the Negro race in America, and to be able to grasp the deep significance of the possibilities of the crisis, is to have a heritage, it seems to me, unique in the ages."[60] According to Cooper, the African American woman must shape an infant "Negro" race, a race "full of the elasticity and hopefulness of youth," and help that race to develop its "distinctive genius."[61] First drawing upon the eugenicist paradigm that each race has its own set of moral and intellectual characteristics, Cooper then transforms the hierarchical estimation of difference that attends such distinctions in eugenicist thought. Playing to the images of "civilization" cherished by white supremacists and eugenicists, Cooper cedes the height of nineteenth-century civilization to European and Caucasian races. But in Cooper's history, civilization will continue to advance, and it will be carried to new heights by a new race. According to Cooper, the "Negro" race "does not look on the masterly triumphs of nineteenth century civilization with that *blasé* world-weary look which characterizes the old washed out and worn out races which have already, so to speak, seen their best days."[62] In Cooper's history of the future, "white supremacism" will truly be a thing of the past.

Situated at the center of two great social movements, Anna Julia Cooper's "true" African American woman, unlike Nathaniel Hawthorne's "little Phoebe," will not be pried and penetrated, revered only via threat of violation. Cooper's True Woman will not be the object of a masculine gaze but an image maker herself. Describing African Americans as an emergent race "sensitive to impressions"—"Not the photographer's sensitized plate is more delicately impressionable to outer influences than is this high strung people here on the threshold of a career"[63]—Cooper suggests that African American women will shape and determine the image of this nascent race. Not unlike Nathaniel Hawthorne, who as author claims to manage the "atmospheric medium" of his middle-class romance "to bring out or mellow the lights and deepen and enrich the shadows of the picture,"[64] Cooper's "true" African American woman will be a kind of photographer for the race, taking "sole management of the primal lights and shadows" that will define an African American future.[65]

Photographing the "American Negro": Nation, Race, and Photography at the Paris Exposition of 1900

IN "The Conservation of Races," published in 1897, W. E. B. Du Bois asks, "What, after all, am I? Am I an American or am I a Negro? Can I be both? Or is it my duty to cease to be a Negro as soon as possible and be an American?"[1] As Du Bois attempts to plot a course through the "doubleness" of racial and national identities facing African Americans at the turn of the century, he asserts that distinct racial cultures must be maintained, even as different groups come to coexist as citizens of the same nation.[2] His essay is entitled, after all, "The *Conservation* of Races," and Du Bois asserts that African Americans must resist the ethnic erasure that assimilation into a dominant white culture would entail, while simultaneously fighting for political, economic, and social equality in Jim Crow America.

Du Bois affirms that the African American must struggle to be both an "American" and a "Negro" in his essay of 1897, and he helps to define the position of the African American further with his prominent participation in the "American Negro" exhibit at the Paris Exposition of 1900. Du Bois assisted in preparing many of the displays for the American Negro exhibit, and he also assembled hundreds of photographs of African Americans into a series of three albums (four volumes) for the presentation. Frances Benjamin Johnston, a professional white woman photographer, provided another collection of photographs for the exhibit, a series of images of the Hampton Institute commissioned expressly for the Paris Exposition. Reading Du Bois's photograph albums against Johnston's images of the Hampton Institute, this chapter investigates how racial and national identities were posed and negotiated in the terrain of visual culture at the Paris Exposition of 1900. Proposing that the American Negro exhibit itself was deeply invested in defining the place of the "Negro" in the United States, I examine how such positions were established in the visual codes of turn-of-the-century photography.

While most studies of the nation and of national identity have focused on the printed word as the medium through which a national community could be imagined in the nineteenth century, I demonstrate the role photography, another medium of mass reproduction, played in envisioning a racially codified American identity.[3] In order to understand fully the ways in which the photographs displayed in the American Negro exhibit participated in the formulation of visual codes of national belonging, one must locate the images within the historical legacy of representations which they both draw upon and significantly challenge. Johnston's and Du Bois's photographs of the "American Negro" entered a visual terrain already mapped in terms of both "race" and "nation" over the course of the nineteenth century. The American Negro exhibit itself, the frame in which Johnston's and Du Bois's photographs were presented, signified at the nexus of scientific discourses defining both race and national character at the turn of the century. Further, the images Johnston produced and those that Du Bois assembled circulated within a redefined field of photographic representation. Situating Johnston's and Du Bois's images within a changing historical context, I examine photographs not simply as signs that represent "real-world" referents but as signs with distinct visual genealogies—signs that enter into conversation and contest with other photographs. My argument proposes that visual culture is not a mere reflection of a national community but one of the sites through which narratives of national belonging are imagined. In other words, I suggest that photographic images not only represent but also produce the nation.[4]

Johnston's photographs and Du Bois's photograph albums initiated new visual strategies for representing both race and national character at the turn of the century. Both sets of images challenged the essentialized discourses of race and national identity dominant during this period, although they did so to varying degrees. While Johnston's photographs forwarded the American identity of Hampton students over their racial identities, Du Bois's albums suggested that the African American could indeed be both an "American" and a "Negro." This chapter illustrates how the photographs displayed in the American Negro exhibit marked a new and internally contested moment in the history of American visual culture.

RACIALIZED BODIES, NATIONAL CHARACTER, AND PHOTOGRAPHIC DOCUMENTATION

The American Negro exhibit itself participated in a new era in the history of race representation, both for the United States and for international expositions in general. Following a trend initiated with the "Negro Building" at the Cotton States and International Exposition of Atlanta in 1895,[5] Paris Exposition organizers invited African Americans to present their history, cultural achievements, and social advances to the world in their "own terms" at the Paris Exposition of 1900. A very few years after African Americans were denied official participation in the Columbian World Exposition of 1893,[6] they were invited to contribute as self-defining agents to the Atlanta Exposition of 1895, the Nashville Centennial Exposition of 1897, and the Paris Exposition of 1900. As W. E. B. Du Bois describes the American Negro exhibit at the Paris Exposition, it was "planned and executed by Negroes, and collected and installed under the direction of a Negro special agent, Mr. Thomas J. Calloway."[7] Unlike the exoticized displays of African villages that reinforced white European estimations of their own "civilized" superiority in relation to "Negro savages," the American Negro exhibit of the Paris Exposition represented African Americans as thoroughly modern members of the Western world. Through a series of maps, charts, models, photographs, and detailed descriptions of work in African American education, as well as hundreds of examples of African American literary production, the American Negro exhibit presented the progress made by African Americans in the terms of white Western culture. The exhibit was considered one of the most impressive in the Palace of Social Economy, and was honored with an exposition grand prize.[8]

While it is important to underscore the unique nature of the American Negro exhibit, it is also important to note that this was by no means a utopian moment. Housed in the United States section of the Palace of Social Economy, the American Negro exhibit was framed by international notions of social progress. According to Du Bois, the exhibits in the Palace of Social Economy did not portray sociology, the " 'science of society' " per se, but instead various systems of social reform. Included in national exhibits were the "mutual aid societies of France," "the state insurance of Germany," as well as "the Red Cross Society."[9] The United States section presented models of tenement houses, maps of industrial plants, and the work of factory inspectors. Within the Palace of Social Economy, amid displays expounding treatments for social ailments, the American Negro exhibit provided a social success story, but it was compelled to deliver that story within the implicit context of solutions to national problems, in this case, no doubt, the ubiquitous white-coined American "Negro problem." Thus, while the American Negro exhibit provided an opportunity for African Americans to visualize complex racial and national identifications, it remained confined within a white-dominated system of social surveillance.

The very term "American Negro" would have registered as a kind of oxymoron to particularly strident Anglo-Saxon American nationalists at the turn of the century. As I argued in chapter 5, by the turn of the century, many whites attempted to define "American" as an exclusively Anglo-Saxon purview, and their white supremacist nationalism was backed by the scientific discourse of eugenics.[10] Eugenicists and biological racialists in the United States were intent on establishing much less permeable national borders than those configured through the reading practices enabled by the expansion of print capitalism, and they sought to delineate the borders of an "imagined community"[11] through discourses of essentialized racial characteristics. As we have seen, Francis Galton claimed that national character was an effect of race, a kind of racial attribute. Further, Galton believed that the racialized properties of national character could be enhanced and controlled through monitored breeding. Conversely, Galton claimed that national character might be enfeebled both through unmonitored procreation of the "weak" and through interracial reproduction. In Galton's universe races were measured according to a hierarchical scale, in which the ancient Greeks represented a lost ideal, nineteenth-century Anglo-Saxons claimed the modern pinnacle, and "Negroes" occupied the lowest link. According to Galton, improvement might be bred within a race, but crossbreeding between the races would always result in tragically weakened stock. Further, while Galton argued explicitly against amalgamation, his work also implicitly buttressed antiassimilationist policies. Cultural equality among the races—a sharing of "essential" national character—was inconceivable according to Galton's notion of biological difference. In Galton's terms, nations of races were by definition separate and not equal.[12]

Galton's eugenics provided a scientific basis for the arrangement of racialized "others" commonly presented at international expositions by the turn of the century. Even as African Americans were represented as successful participants in white Western "progress" in the American Negro exhibit at the Paris Exposition, other "Negroes" were hired to people the living displays that represented an exoticized "sliding scale of humanity" popular at international expositions since their introduction at the 1889 Paris fair.[13] As Thomas J. Schlereth describes the racialized spatial logics of such exhibits on the Midway Plaisance at Chicago's Columbian Exposition of 1893, "ethnic" displays were arranged along the periphery of the fairgrounds, around the center of the exposition, which celebrated western European triumphs in science, industry, and art. At the Chicago Columbian Exposition, the imagined Western whiteness of the exposition center was dramatically represented by architect Frederick Law Olmsted's literally white stuccoed buildings, modeled after ancient Greek and Roman architecture. Outside this Greek- and Roman-inspired Anglo-Saxon "White City," ethnic displays in the Midway Plaisance were arranged according to their imagined proximity to Anglo-Saxon culture. The Teutonic and Celtic races, represented by German and Irish exhibits, occupied the Midway territory closest to the "White City" center of the exposition, while the Muhammadan and Asian worlds stood farther away, and the "savage races," including Africans and North American Indians, remained at the farthest reaches of the Midway.[14] A similar structure, in which a city center celebrating Western industrial, social, and artistic achievements, replete with educational exhibits, was surrounded by a relatively "chaotic" zone filled with new forms of entertainment and "exotic" displays of non-Western peoples, many the "trophies" of Western imperialism, dominated international expositions throughout the early twentieth century. It is within this context that one notes the most radical, and indeed perhaps the most contained, critique of turn-of-the-century notions of race and culture forwarded by the American Negro exhibit at the Paris Exposition of 1900. Contesting the colonialist and imperialist logics forwarded by living racial and ethnic displays, the American Negro exhibit disrupted the essentialized narratives that depicted people of color as the uncivilized infants of human evolution. The American Negro exhibit dissociated "race" from a single set of cultural practices and progressive potentialities.

While the space in which Johnston's photographs and Du Bois's albums were presented was the already unique and contested domain of the American Negro exhibit, the photographs themselves were also imbedded in changing conceptions of photographic documentation. Unlike Mathew Brady's daguerreotype portraits of "Illustrious Americans," which received the most prestigious awards at the London Crystal Palace Exposition of 1851,[15] Johnston's and Du Bois's photographs were not presented as art objects in a separate photographic salon. Instead, the images were meant to *document* and *illustrate* the "progress and present conditions" of the "American Negro." Johnston's and Du Bois's photographs signified in photographic registers developed outside the auratic domains of both the sentimental portrait keepsake and the photographic work of art.[16] Displayed in the Palace of Social Economy, alongside model tenement houses and the reports of factory inspectors, the photographs included in the American Negro exhibit functioned as evidence, just as the many charts and graphs included in exhibits served as scientific documentations of progress. Unlike the photographic portraits that dominated popular and professional photography in the United States throughout the nineteenth century, Johnston's photographs aimed not to emulate an individual but to capture the imagined essence of an entire group, namely, the "American Negro." Johnston rarely photographed solitary individuals, and the majority of her Hampton photographs depict entire classes concentrating on lessons staged for the camera. The students in Johnston's photographs are not named, nor in any other way identified as individuals. They are not memorialized as relatives, lovers, or glamorous stars; in short, they are not sentimentalized. In Johnston's images, Hampton students become examples, samples of the disciplined, successful "American Negro." Even Du Bois's photographs, the large majority of which are portraits, do not name or identify individuals but instead present portrait photographs as the unnamed evidence of African American individuality.

Presented within the context of both sociology and reform, Johnston's and Du Bois's images may have resonated with the contemporary sensa-

tionalist images Jacob Riis produced of the "other half," even as they fore-
shadowed the social documentary photography of Lewis Hine.[17] However,
unlike Riis's dramatic images of tenement squalor and Hine's detailed images of child laborers, the photographs Johnston and Du Bois brought to
the American Negro exhibit aimed not to document social problems but to
record the progress made by African Americans at the turn of the century.
Johnston's photographs, in particular, do not attempt to illustrate a need
for social reform but, instead, to demonstrate the success of a social reform
already in place, namely, the Hampton Institute's program of manual training.[18] Rather than attempting to incite public furor at social ills, the American Negro exhibit, as a whole, proclaimed to present the work of "a small
nation of people, picturing their life and development without apology or
gloss."[19] While the celebratory tone of the exhibit certainly marked a well-
deserved source of African American pride, it also may have communicated
a much more problematic message to Anglo-American viewers. The con-
gratulatory nature of the exhibit may have demonstrated to white viewers
that they no longer needed "to be afraid of black people or [to feel] guilty
at what had happened to them after Reconstruction."[20] To white American
viewers schooled in the rhetoric of the "Negro problem," the American
Negro exhibit may have indicated that segregation, disfranchisement, and
poverty were not debilitating social forces, and that in fact, the "Negro
problem" itself could be socially segregated.

Functioning as a kind of visual testimony or evidence, Johnston's and
Du Bois's images dovetailed not only with the photographs of social science
but also with the photographs that circulated in the registers of biological
science. By the turn of the century, photographs were being used in the
United States to map "deviant" bodies in prisons, medical treatises, and
scientific explorations into the nature of both gender and race.[21] Within
eugenics itself, photographs were used to illustrate the biological roots of
social structures. As we have seen in previous chapters, Francis Galton
devised two photographic techniques for recording what he believed to
be the physical indices of essential biological difference, both "composite
portraiture" and a standardized system of family photography. I would like
briefly to review both of these photographic forms here because they exem-
plify the scientific representations of racialized bodies that Johnston's and
Du Bois's photographs implicitly contest.

Readers will recall that Galton believed his system of composite photographic portraiture would enable one to document the common physical
features of a predetermined group. Further, as Galton maintained that
physical features indexed the intellectual and creative potential of races, he
felt corporeal signs could legitimately be said to demarcate an individual's
appropriate position in a hierarchical society. Faithful to the purported
objectivity of the photographic image, Galton held that the abstract, "per-

fected" signs of common physical characteristics could be determined by overlaying a series of standardized frontal and profile "mug shots" of any given group. Galton imagined his composite photographic records would serve as a kind of key for (presumably white) viewers, as a map of the racialized body, allowing one to study abstract, "pure" racial characteristics, and later to discern the racial identity of individuals according to that model, to assess their corresponding intellectual attributes and to situate them "appropriately" along a sliding social scale stratified by biological difference.

While Galton aimed to identify the salient characteristics of predetermined biological groups with his composite portraiture, he hoped to monitor the reproduction of racial attributes with his scientific "family albums." Once again, in 1884 Galton designed both the *Record of Family Faculties* and *The Life History Album*.[22] The *Record* served as a chronicle of one's ancestry (a kind of detailed family tree) and was intended to aid individuals in predicting their own, and their children's, future abilities and ailments. Galton suggested that photographic portraits would provide important illustrations of family members in the *Record*, enhancing verbal descriptions and medical histories. The photograph played a more central role in *The Life History Album*, as Galton proposed a system of thorough, standardized photographic documentation for that album. *The Life History Album* was designed to record the growth and maturation of an individual child (functioning as a precursor to the modern "baby book"), and Galton called upon parent contributors to make a standardized set of photographs of the child, "an exact full-face and a profile,"[23] every five years. In each of his records, Galton treated the photograph as a transparent document of the body, which was in turn regarded as the physical record of an essential racial character transmitted through the blood. By standardizing family photograph albums, Galton hoped to open the sentimental family archive to scientific scrutiny.

While systems of photographic documentation were being designed to record and codify the body as the ultimate sign of racial essence at the turn of the century, representing the more elusive national character that supposedly corresponded to racialized physical features (the very core of racial identity in Galton's terms) proved a more difficult task. It is at this juncture, between the photographic documentation of "race" and of "nation," that Johnston's and Du Bois's photographs for the American Negro exhibit enter public visual culture. While the photographic work of Frances Benjamin Johnston and W. E. B. Du Bois represents an important moment in the history of building national photographic archives, Johnston and Du Bois themselves were not the first to attempt to portray "American character" in photographs. Mathew Brady, a famous forerunner in the history of visualizing American identity, sought to emblematize

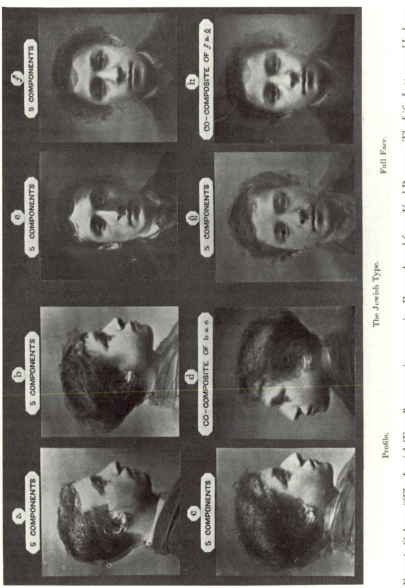

Profile.

The Jewish Type.

Full Face.

Francis Galton, "The Jewish Type," composite portraits. Reproduced from Karl Pearson, *The Life, Letters and Labours of Francis Galton*, vol. 2, *Researches of Middle Life* (Cambridge: Cambridge University Press, 1924).

national character in his portraits of "Illustrious Americans," which he made throughout the 1850s and 1860s.[24] Brady was one of the first, and one of the most famous photographers in the nineteenth-century United States, making a name for himself and his portraits in the early days of daguerreotypy, the first photographic process. Adhering to a long-standing aesthetic tradition that positioned the eminent individual of the formal portrait after the larger-than-life posture of Roman busts, in three-quarter profile, looking loftily up and away from viewers, Brady photographed an extraordinary number of famous American politicians, artists, and authors.[25] Brady showcased his portraits of "Illustrious Americans" in his popular New York galleries, intending, no doubt, to heighten his own public renown and also, as he himself explicitly contended, to provide salient examples of the American character for the praise and emulation of others. Hoping to increase the circulation of his portraits, in order to provide both a national historical record and an exemplary model of national character for Americans at large, Brady selected twelve of his many portraits to be reproduced and circulated in a printed *Gallery of Illustrious Americans*. Each of Brady's daguerreotype portraits, reproduced as a lithograph for printed form, was accompanied by a written biographical text that expounded the particularly American character of each representative individual. Brady's "Illustrious Americans" were not "typical," but model Americans, the embodiment of abstract ideals, and their biographies attested to the specific achievements that could not be read in their faces. Unlike Galton, who attempted to represent in abstract form the "typical" physical features of a "national race" with his composite photographs, Brady aimed to depict the equally abstract spiritual and moral characteristics of individuals who emblematized "national ideals" in his daguerreotype portraits. While Galton looked to the lowest common physical denominator as the definitive sign of a racialized national identity, Brady heralded the highest spiritual denominator as the signal of "true" American character.

While his aim was quite distinct from Francis Galton's later "scientific" attempts to document a racialized national identity, Mathew Brady's portraits of "Illustrious Americans" also, if only implicitly, forwarded a distinctly racialized notion of national character. As Alan Trachtenberg has argued, Mathew Brady's printed *Gallery of Illustrious Americans*, produced in 1850, placed "national heroes" from opposing sides of a dissolving nation upon the same patriotic landscape.[26] A portrait of Zachary Taylor, the Whig president, joins a portrait of John Calhoun, outspoken Democrat, on the patriotic horizon of Brady's *Gallery*.[27] In this way, Brady's images of "Illustrious Americans" extricate national character from the tense political conflicts developing over slavery and racial difference in the pre–Civil War era, reproducing (white, male) Americanness as an exalted quality removed from and unmarred by divisive politics rooted in racial conflicts. Half a

Mathew Brady, Portrait of Franklin Pierce, whole-plate daguerreotype, gold-toned, circa 1851–60. Reproduced from the Collections of the Library of Congress.

century later, Johnston's and Du Bois's photographs delineate national character after the Civil War, and decades after Reconstruction, in a period of heightened racial tension, continuing debate over the so-called Negro question, Jim Crow segregation, African American disfranchisement, and increased lynching. By representing the American character of people excluded from many levels of legal and cultural American privilege, namely, African and Native Americans at the turn of the century, Johnston and Du Bois situate national identity within the terrain of racial identity and racial conflict. In this later period, as evidenced by Galton's eugenics, racial divisions actually fueled the definition of national character, as this once-ephemeral, interiorized quality was harnessed to a racially inflected biology. Indeed, reading Brady's earlier images of "Illustrious Americans" from this turn-of-the-century vantage point, the implicit, albeit unmarked, signs of a racialized white national identity become (if not already) apparent in Brady's portraits.

While not the first photographs to attempt to portray "American character," Johnston's and Du Bois's images represent new visual strategies for representing an explicitly racialized version of national identity (unlike Brady's implicitly racialized "Illustrious Americans"). Responding to new notions of national and racial identities, Johnston and Du Bois present new means of visually codifying American identity. At the time of the Paris Exposition, Galton's theories of racial difference were gaining wide acceptance among physical and social scientists in the United States, and it is against an increasingly dominant discourse of racialized national essentialism that one must read Johnston's and Du Bois's efforts to visualize competing versions of the "American Negro" at the turn of the century. As I will demonstrate, Frances Benjamin Johnston's Hampton photographs and W. E. B. Du Bois's photograph albums both contest the racialist biological determinism of Galton's particular national paradigm, even as the two projects work toward different ends.

MAKING AMERICANS

Frances Benjamin Johnston's views of the Hampton Institute may have been slightly anomalous in what Du Bois described as an exhibit produced and executed exclusively by African Americans. Indeed, in his review of the exhibit, Du Bois praises Johnston's work, which won a gold medal at the exposition, but as he evaluates the images, he completely effaces Johnston herself as photographer. Du Bois states: "From Hampton there is an especially excellent series of photographs illustrating the Hampton ideas of 'teaching by doing.' "[28] In Du Bois's account, Johnston's images are important because they "illustrate" Hampton ideas, and the photographs

themselves come "from Hampton," not from Johnston. Du Bois emphasizes the discursive formulation of Johnston's subject matter, the pedagogi-
cal philosophy of the Hampton Institute, but he fails to comment on the
codified construction of the photographs themselves. In his review, Du
Bois draws upon discourses of documentary and scientific photography
that erase the ideological underpinnings that inform photographic images
and styles. Putting Johnston back into a reading of the Hampton photographs, one can begin to tease out her ambiguous position as photographer,
if only, finally, to heighten the conundrum of her role as white woman
photographer for an African American exhibit. It is important to underscore the ways in which the American Negro exhibit was implicitly tied to
a complexly gendered and racialized system of white social surveillance at
the turn of the century, in order to explain some of the tensions and conflicting racial ideologies apparent in Johnston's photographs themselves.

The Hampton Institute was an industrial arts and teachers' training
school founded in 1868 by Colonel Samuel Chapman Armstrong and originally designed to educate former slaves after the Civil War. Toward the
latter part of the nineteenth century, the institute began to admit Native
American as well as African American students. In 1899, the second president of Hampton, Hollis Burke Frissell, invited Frances Benjamin Johnston to photograph the school specifically for the Paris Exposition of
1900.[29] Johnston produced dozens of images at Hampton, including landscapes, group portraits of bands, teams, and graduating classes, and a couple of family portraits taken in homes. By far her most common views,
however, were those made in classrooms, depicting students "in action"
working on a project or paying exaggerated attention to the day's lesson.
All of Johnston's classroom images are marked by a certain stiffness, the
result of long camera exposures combined with a staginess aimed at illustrating a particular skill, idea, or theme for later viewers. Messages written
on the board and visual spaces constructed to privilege the camera's point
of view mark the intended presence of a later viewing audience. However,
this future audience (and, indeed, the photographer herself) is not acknowl-
edged directly by the student subjects in Johnston's images. In Johnston's
photographs, Hampton students never meet the camera with curious, approving, or challenging eyes; instead they are depicted as the objects of a
scrutinizing gaze, one that has been invited to evaluate their "progress and
present conditions." The omission of any recorded interaction between
Hampton students and Johnston, photographer standing in for later viewers, the absence of even a documented glance in the direction of the camera, poses Hampton students as the willing objects of an outside investigation, the test subjects of an external study.

Johnston's unquestioned role as observer, as practitioner of a domi-
nating, unreturned gaze at the Hampton Institute, may at first surprise

contemporary viewers schooled in a tradition of psychoanalytic feminist film theory. After Laura Mulvey's groundbreaking analysis of the "male gaze" posed and propelled by the film industry, how can one explain a white woman's visual mastery over African American and Native American students at the turn of the century?[30] Does Johnston adopt a masculine position from which to represent her subjects as the feminine objects of a "male gaze"? Must Johnston perform a kind of "transvestism" in order to visually represent her desire in these images?[31] And what is the nature of the desire Johnston's photographs project? The answers to these questions are not readily available within a field that poses the visual representation of desire as strictly sexual, hegemonically heterosexual, and invisibly white. Scholars such as bell hooks, Jacqueline Bobo, Jane Gaines, Richard Dyer, Manthia Diawara, Isaac Julien, Kobena Mercer, and Mary Ann Doane, who are revising Mulvey's influential work, addressing "race" and "ethnicity" as discourses central to the development of modern visual culture, have problematized understandings of desire and of the gaze that have been dominated by gender categories, reading the history of visual culture (and specifically the history of Hollywood film) as a trajectory bound by white Western ethnocentrism.[32] In addition, artists and scholars such as Coco Fusco and Trinh T. Minh-ha, and cultural critics such as Timothy Mitchell, Deborah Poole, Mary Louise Pratt, Fatimah Tobing Rony, and Deborah Willis are beginning to identify what bell hooks has called a "white supremacist gaze"[33] as a key constituent of Western colonial and imperial power.[34] Bound to a mythology of scientific "objectivity" and a system of increasing social surveillance, an invisible "white gaze" functioned as the arbiter of biological and cultural difference in Jim Crow U.S.A. While one cannot discard the terms of gender in assessing Johnston's gaze, it is important to rearticulate Johnston's visual practice according to the *racialized* discourses of gender and sexuality dominant at the turn of the century.[35]

In the post-Reconstruction South, "the gaze" functioned as a powerful threat within the racist discourse of sexual assault. According to one cultural historian who assesses the spread of lynching at the turn of the century, "If a black man so much as looked a white woman in the eye he risked being accused of lechery or insolence, and in some cases this was as good as committing an actual assault."[36] Given this racist dynamic, Johnston's inability to photograph students looking at the camera, looking at her, takes on profoundly disturbing connotations. Photographing the Hampton Institute during the height of racial terrorism in the South, at a time when African American men were lynched in the name of protecting the sexual (and racial) purity of white womanhood, Frances Benjamin Johnston herself may have posed a dangerous threat to her Hampton subjects.[37] Indeed, while Johnston was pursuing another photographic project six years later, one of her African American male hosts was attacked for his audacity in accompanying a white woman alone at night. In this cultural context, eyes buried in tasks in Johnston's photographs signify doubly the charged power dynamics out of which her images were produced. As a white woman, Johnston represented both a threat and a potentially powerful advocate for young African Americans. African American feminist scholars and activists, like Ida B. Wells and Anna Julia Cooper, recognized the white woman's singular power to dismantle the mythology of rape that fueled post-Reconstruction lynching.[38] However, Johnston's photographs do not forward the radical defense of African American virtue heralded by Wells but instead ambiguously skirt the "challenging" gaze, thereby subtly reproducing a legacy of racial hierarchy in the turn-of-the-century South.

Johnston's position as photographer was embedded within a particularly troubling sexual discourse, a cultural logic sexualized primarily according to a paradigm of white supremacism. As a white woman, Johnston was able to scrutinize African American bodies because, according to white supremacist lynching logics, a white woman's sexual desire for a black man (or woman) was posed as unimaginable. While the white woman's sexual desire itself was marked as a disruptive perversion of "natural" white womanhood in turn-of-the-century U.S. culture, her willing alliance with an African American man could be attributed only to the perversity and moral depravity of her doubly "unnatural" white womanhood. Indeed, as we have seen, a patriarchal white discourse of lynching erased this potential "anomaly" by representing a white woman's alliance with an African American man as the result of a single destructive force, namely, black male aggression.[39] Given these racist mythologies specific to the turn-of-the-century United States, the potentially gendered or sexualized nature of Johnston's gaze cannot be separated from her racialized position as a white woman in an increasingly white supremacist nation. Johnston's role as subject, gazing upon nameless African American bodies, is not, first and foremost, a position privileged in terms of gender but in those of race. As an Anglo-Saxon woman, Johnston represented the very lifeblood, the potential reproduction, not only of the Anglo-Saxon race but also of the "American character" delineated by white supremacists and eugenicists in the United States. Her inability to represent an exchange of looks or glances between herself and Hampton students not only construes her images as the "natural" documents of an unobtrusive assessment but also points to the social distance maintained between Johnston and her photographic subjects. As photographer, and as white woman, Johnston has not "mixed" with her subjects; her photographs remain "objective," and her (white, female) person remains "pure."[40]

Frances Benjamin Johnston's Hampton photographs attest to the social progress of African Americans in several different registers. A set of six family portraits comprise a "before and after" series that demonstrates the upward class mobility of Hampton graduates. Run-down shacks turn into sparkling white mansions through the Hampton metamorphosis depicted by Johnston. Representing the middle-class "success" of Hampton's graduates, these photographs ideologically frame Johnston's images of classroom activities, setting the terms—modern, mechanical, and economic—in which the achievements of the Hampton Institute's program of rigorous discipline and manual training are to be measured. Inside this frame of upward economic mobility, photographs of classroom activities, by far the most numerous in Johnston's portfolio of Hampton images, depict students' rapt attention and willing participation in the day's lesson. The students in Johnston's photographs are shown mastering geography, arithmetic, sewing, welding, agriculture, and a remarkable focus and self-discipline, as well as the explicit codes of an American identity. I am particularly interested here in the images that illustrate Hampton students engaging in American rituals because these images begin to formulate one version of the "American Negro" at the turn of the century. Taken as a whole, Johnston's photographs for the American Negro exhibit would seem to propose that much of the progress made by African Americans after the Civil War was rooted in the process of Americanization itself.

Unlike Mathew Brady's portraits of "Illustrious Americans," Frances Benjamin Johnston's photographs of African American Hampton students do not single out famous individuals but instead depict anonymous groups of schoolchildren and young adult students simply *as* Americans.[41] Further, Johnston does not necessarily assume the American identity of her subjects, as Brady does, and she is at pains to *demonstrate* the American character of Hampton students to the later viewers of her photographs. While Brady may have been eager to specify the exemplary characteristics of his model Americans, Johnston worked hard simply to delineate the American character of Hampton students. In a political climate increasingly dominated by eugenicist white nationalists, Johnston had to establish the American identity of her African American subjects for the resistant portion of her white audience.

In several of her most salient photographs, Johnston represents African American students, even the very young, as preeminently patriotic. The image entitled *Saluting the Flag at the Whittier Primary School* is almost impossible to read as anything other than a performance of national pride.[42] In this photograph the young students are packed so tightly into a square formation that it is very difficult to distinguish their individual characteristics—they are presented as one entity, performing one act—and thus, the image appears to be less about Whittier students than it is about the act they are performing, namely, "saluting the flag." A guiding adult presence is difficult to discern in the photograph, making the image read as the documentation of a self-compelled performance on the part of these

Frances Benjamin Johnston, *The old-time cabin*, 1899. Reproduced from the Collections of the Library of Congress.

African American children. With its visual emphasis on a patriotic performance that appears to be self-directed, this photograph subtly forwards a vision of assimilation that contests scientific definitions of racial difference and national character at the turn of the century. If eugenicists believed in biologically distinct races, and in national characteristics specific, and exclusive, to each race, then Johnston's image of Whittier students saluting the flag presents American patriotism as one of the natural dispositions of young African American students. In other words, Johnston's image naturalizes the *performance* of national identity. It highlights performance in order to demonstrate the "nature" of an essentialized *national character*, if not of an essentialized racial identity.[43] With this image Johnston would seem to cleave American national character from an essentialized Anglo-Saxon identity, countering eugenicists' coterminous delineation of nation and race with a potentially multiracial nation.

In another image taken at the primary school, *Thanksgiving Day lesson at the Whittier*, several young students construct a miniature log cabin as their classmates watch conscientiously. Despite the rather exaggerated attention of the seated classmates, it is clear that the set for this photograph has been constructed to privilege exclusively the gaze of the viewer of this image. The ring of students around the table opens up on the side closest to the

Frances Benjamin Johnston, *A Hampton Graduate's home*, 1899. Reproduced from the Collections of the Library of Congress.

photographic plane, allowing the photographer and later viewers to observe the activity with ease. The view of the children on the far side of the room (farthest away from the camera) is almost surely blocked by this group of students and teachers. The center stage has been shifted away from the students for the benefit of outside viewers. Nevertheless, most of the seated students pretend to watch the scheduled activity with great attention. Their poses are utterly rigid; they sit with hands folded on top of their desks, disciplined into postures of gratitude, as in prayer. The obedient manner of these students in the background, not watched by the teachers in the room, is, perhaps, a "reassuring" performance conducted for the (white) viewer of the photograph. The official, explicit classroom activity is contextualized by words written on the blackboard: "The Landing of the Pilgrim Fathers." These words literally frame the young builders; further, they point to the ideological framework that is being formulated around the performers. These young black children are taught new American histories, and they are given (symbolically) new "fathers." Whittier students become heirs to a patriarchal national lineage, learning where to anchor an official American identity. Their *national heredity*, if not their *racial origin*, is reinvented as they are taught to forget the boats that brought

Frances Benjamin Johnston, *Saluting the Flag at the Whittier Primary School*, 1899. Reproduced from the Collections of the Library of Congress.

many of their forebears to North America in chains, and to relocate their roots on the Pilgrim ships.[44] They are being symbolically reborn, as it were, as Americans of an Anglo-Saxon tradition.

One of the most profoundly disturbing and revealing of Johnston's Hampton photographs is her image entitled *Class in American History*. In this photograph, an American Indian, in fully codified ethnic regalia, including feather headdress, beaded leather, and braided hair, joins the stuffed American bald eagle behind him as a symbol of the American nation. The photograph functions as a "before meets after" image, in which Native and African American Hampton students observe a Native American from the past. The Native American most explicitly on display is studied as part of American history—as an object, an ancient relic, but not as a subject of that history. The other Native Americans, also on display for the viewer in Johnston's image, are to look on him as part of their American, but not their ancestral, past; they are to substitute a national narrative, one now shared with their African American colleagues, for a racialized hereditary bloodline. The Native American students in this image bear no apparent relation to the historic display; like their African American colleagues, they stand in military uniforms and Victorian dresses, with hair worn short or pulled back in a single knot. In this photograph, racially

Frances Benjamin Johnston, *Thanksgiving Day lesson at the Whittier*, 1899. Reproduced from the Collections of the Library of Congress.

specific ethnic identities have been erased in a narrative of national belonging. The image constructs a lesson in which "Americans" learn about the past of "Indians."[45]

Circulating in a period of vast immigration in the United States, Johnston's assimilationist images do not anchor national identity in the land of one's ancestors, but instead in a specific set of cultural codes. Indeed, if the photographs did root American identity in ancestral land, there would be no need to Americanize Hampton students, whose ancestors had resided in the territories of the twentieth-century United States for hundreds (in the case of African Americans) and thousands (in the case of Native Americans) of years. If land occupation were the measure of national inclusion in Johnston's photographs, Johnston's own American identity might prove more tenuous than that of her subjects. Instead, Johnston's Hampton photographs forward a narrative of assimilation in which national identity is first untangled from and then reintegrated into the visual codes of racial identity.[46] Johnston's Hampton photographs show students actively engaged in the process of learning national histories and performing national rites. The photographs would seem to separate national character from a

Frances Benjamin Johnston, *Class in American History*, 1899. Reproduced from the Collections of the Library of Congress.

racially encoded discourse of blood, marking American identity as a set of performative rituals. However, despite this seeming rupture between an essential and a performative national identity, the rituals of turn-of-the-century Americanness posed in Johnston's photographs are rooted, ultimately, in a history delineated by Anglo-Saxon bloodlines—the blood of the "founding" "Pilgrim fathers." Thus, while Johnston's photographs first de-essentialize the markers of American identity, they then re-essentialize those performances by anchoring them in a distinctly Anglo-Saxon lineage. Johnston's images forward the beginnings of Anglo-Saxon heritage on North American soil, celebrating the ethnically specific national identity that was founded with the "landing of the Pilgrim fathers." The unmarked signs of whiteness are visualized through patriotic performances in Johnston's images; Anglo-Saxon identity is consolidated in a specific discourse of national American identity. In Johnston's photographs the "American character" of African American students is measured by the success with which those students can adopt and perform Anglo-Saxon-inspired national rituals. At "best," then, this seeming erasure of racial identity in favor of a common national character is tenuous and readily recuperated in the terms of racial essentialism. Johnston's Americans are easily reinterpreted in the "separate but equal" terms of turn-of-the-century segregation.

CONSERVING RACE IN THE NATION

While Frances Benjamin Johnston's photographs of the Hampton Institute forward a narrative of assimilation, tenuously erasing racial difference under the signs of a national identity, W. E. B. Du Bois's photograph albums recuperate a sense of racial autonomy and self-determination. The three photograph albums (four volumes) that I discuss here constitute one of three displays supervised by W. E. B. Du Bois for the American Negro exhibit at the Paris Exposition of 1900. In addition to the albums, other exhibits included a series of charts and graphs documenting the social and economic progress of African Americans, and a three-volume set containing the complete legal history of African Americans in Georgia.[47] As the photographers who produced the images for Du Bois's albums remain unidentified, the focus of authorship is transferred to Du Bois himself, the person most conspicuously associated with the albums, as collector, organizer, and presenter of the images. Thus, while Du Bois may not have produced the photographs for his albums, I pose Du Bois as the archivist who framed the images both materially and ideologically.

Du Bois's photograph albums, entitled *Types of American Negroes, Georgia, U.S.A.* (volumes 1–3) and *Negro Life in Georgia, U.S.A.*, include formal studio portraits of African Americans, as well as informal snapshots of groups outdoors, children playing, and people working, images of homes and business establishments, and interior views of elaborately decorated middle-class parlors. Unlike Johnston's formal photographs of students at the Hampton Institute, Du Bois's snapshots convey a sense of spontaneity and immediacy. The subjects and scenes of these images are diverse, and many of the photographs suggest an interaction between unnamed photographers and subjects, through the variously questioning, surprised, laughing and smiling faces that greet later viewers. Signifying in the context of Johnston's professional group portraits, the snapshots collected in Du Bois's albums may have functioned in ways similar to those images preserved in African American family archives throughout the twentieth century, as described by bell hooks. According to hooks:

> Photographs taken in everyday life, snapshots in particular, rebelled against all of those photographic practices that reinscribed colonial ways of looking and capturing the images of the black "other." Shot spontaneously, without any notion of remaking black bodies in the image of whiteness, snapshots posed a challenge to black viewers. Unlike photographs constructed so that black im-

ages would appear as the embodiment of colonizing fantasies, these snapshots gave us a way to see ourselves, a sense of how we looked when we were not "wearing the mask," when we were not attempting to perfect the image for a white supremacist gaze.[48]

hooks's sense of snapshots "rebelling" against institutionalized racist representations is important to bring to a reading of the images collected in Du Bois's albums, as Du Bois himself proposed that many of his images of "typical Negro faces . . . hardly square with conventional American ideas."[49] However, while the spontaneity of the snapshot may have enabled a form of African American self-imaging outside the dominant domain of racist representation, it is also important to remember that Du Bois's snapshots were viewed not only privately but also publicly, by a racially and ethnically mixed international audience. Read against Johnston's photographs, and in the context of the American Negro exhibit, Du Bois's images pose a challenge to both black and white viewers. They are offered up explicitly and self-consciously as images that contest racist "American ideas" and representations, as photographs that ask white viewers to rethink dominant American "conventions."

While the presumed spontaneity and informality of the snapshots Du Bois gathered for his albums may have posed them somehow at odds with dominant racist imagery, the more profoundly contestatory images in Du Bois's albums are those that both adopt and subvert turn-of-the-century imaging conventions. The photographs that most powerfully differentiate Du Bois's collection from Johnston's work are the formal, individual portraits that introduce each volume of *Types of American Negroes*. The portrait series presents individuals posed for two photographs each, one a frontal image, the other a profile or semiprofile image. Each pair of photographs is presented on a separate page, and the first two volumes of *Types of American Negroes* consist almost entirely of such portraits (there are well over two hundred). Unlike Johnston's group photographs, constructed uncannily around the "unnoticed" presence of the camera, these images mark their subjects' intentional interaction with the camera, and as the viewer progresses through the albums, she is met with the gaze and the likeness of one individual after another. The subjects of these formal portraits engage the gaze of photographer and later viewer, forcing white viewers to recognize what bell hooks has called a resistant, "oppositional gaze,"[50] a gaze that confronts and challenges the privileged position of the white viewer, a gaze that makes that position apparent.

While Johnston's Hampton photographs, framed by "before and after" images, mark the Hampton Institute's notion of advancement, Du Bois's series of portraits does not produce a narrative of teleological development. In Du Bois's albums there is no explicit activity performed to demonstrate a particular ideology of race progress for later viewers. Further, signs of Americanness, such as those performed in Johnston's photographs, are utterly absent from Du Bois's albums. Du Bois assumes the Americanness of his subjects and indicates no need to demonstrate the "American character" of the "Negroes" of "Georgia, U.S.A." Articulating such a position in "The Conservation of Races," Du Bois delineates the collateral boundaries of "Negro" and "American" identity as follows: "We are Americans, not only by birth and by citizenship, but by our political ideals, our language, our religion. Farther than that, our Americanism does not go. At that point, we are Negroes, members of a vast historic race."[51] The African Americans in Du Bois's albums need not prove their right to be included in an American Negro exhibit; because they are Americans by birth, they need not assimilate. Further, while Du Bois defines the national ties of Americanism in the cultural terms of "political ideals," "language," and "religion," he also defines racial identity primarily in cultural terms that transcend theories of physical difference founded in blood. Rejecting "the grosser physical differences of color, hair and bone" as the definitive determinants of racial identity, Du Bois identifies "subtle, delicate and elusive" forces as the foundation on which distinct races develop. According to Du Bois, "While these subtle forces have generally followed the natural cleavage of common blood, descent and physical peculiarities, they have at other times swept across and ignored these."[52] In other words, for Du Bois, "race," like "national character," is not an essential property, and it does not always follow the reproduction of a single bloodline.

Given Du Bois's assertions regarding the inessential "nature" of racial identity, it is disturbing how the title of his albums—"*Types*" *of American Negroes*—echoes the terms of turn-of-the-century scientific "race" taxonomies.[53] Even the repetition of poses and props evident in Du Bois's collection of portraits marks a consistency in formal representation roughly congruent with the mathematical evenness of scientific photographic archives that sought to map codified bodies of racial "others." Further, the very style in which Du Bois's portraits are made and presented, the combination of frontal and semiprofile poses, marks a striking formal parallel to the photographs Galton hoped parents would collect of their children in *The Life History Album*—"An exact full-face and a profile should be obtained" (5). As noted previously, Galton's *Life History Album* was designed to document the maturation of a single child by creating a standardized archive of images of the child. The archive allowed a reader to compare later documents to earlier documents, and to measure change, valued in terms of "growth" or "progress," via apparent physical alteration over time. While Galton's albums set up a comparison of various representations of a single individual, Du Bois's albums structurally invite a comparison of one individual to another. Like Galton, Du Bois keeps the terms of his

From *Types of American Negroes, Georgia, U.S.A.*, compiled by W. E. B. Du Bois, 1900. Reproduced from the Daniel Murray Collection of the Library of Congress.

archive consistent—Du Bois's images adhere to a singular format that limits the factors of difference to the individuals photographed. Assembled as they are, individuals posed in parallel, Du Bois's photographic portraits encourage viewers to read one image against the next, comparing the aspect of one individual to another. What one finds after a comparative scrutiny of the individuals represented in Du Bois's albums is a vast diversity in the physical characteristics generally held to determine racial identity at the turn of the century. In Du Bois's albums, blond and blue-eyed "Negroes" take their place beside brunette and brown-eyed "Negroes."

Reproducing the variations of "color, hair and bone" that were legally encompassed by "one drop" of blood identity laws at the turn of the century,[54] Du Bois's albums confront white America's obsession with the color

From *Types of American Negroes, Georgia, U.S.A.*, compiled by W. E. B. Du Bois, 1900. Reproduced from the Daniel Murray Collection of the Library of Congress.

line in two ways. First, they dismantle the stereotyped and caricatured images of African Americans reproduced in American popular culture. To that end, Du Bois's portraits construct a kind of composite image in reverse. Instead of blending individual portraits or likenesses into a single, abstract "type," Du Bois's albums dismantle the notion of a unifying image, filtering difference back into the picture, decomposing the singular "American Negro" into diverse, multiple "Negro *Types*."[55] Second, the albums point toward the dual nature of "colonial desire," the white supremacist's simultaneous repulsion from and fascination with interracial reproduction.[56] Du Bois's albums of "types" represent the biracial subjects of the unions so powerfully repressed by lynching at the turn of the century, challenging the very social dictates that forbade Frances Benjamin Johnston's

From *Types of American Negroes, Georgia, U.S.A.*, compiled by W. E. B. Du Bois, 1900. Reproduced from the Daniel Murray Collection of the Library of Congress.

black male subjects to return her gaze.[57] The portraits dispute the notion of racial purity upheld by eugenicists and white supremacists, and the anti-miscegenation laws that prohibited legal, mutually desired unions between whites and blacks, but not the rape of African American women by white men.[58] Looking back at the images of African American men, women, and children procured by Du Bois at the turn of the century, I hope to participate in Du Bois's antiracist project by transforming the trajectory laid out for the white woman scholar, namely, the position culturally delimited for Frances Benjamin Johnston at the turn of the century. To that end, I suggest that Du Bois's images do not purport to represent "real" blackness, to invite white (or black) viewers of the early or late twentieth century to gaze upon blackness "revealed." Du Bois's images do not lift "the Veil" that distorts images of African Americans by projecting them through a lens of

From *Types of American Negroes, Georgia, U.S.A.*, compiled by W. E. B. Du Bois, 1900. Reproduced from the Daniel Murray Collection of the Library of Congress.

colonial desire.[59] Instead, the photographs begin to enable white viewers to see the Veil itself, to see the cultural logics and privileged practices that reproduce racism. Consequently, it is toward an investigation of the visual structures of white supremacy, and of resistance to those forms, that I have directed my reading of Du Bois's images, situating the photographs in the context of the visual legacies produced by the converging discourses of eugenics and white supremacist nationalism at the turn of the century.

Du Bois's photographs signify somewhere between the images collected in scientific archives of "race" at the turn of the century and Mathew Brady's earlier portraits of "Illustrious Americans." Formally similar to Galton's frontal and profile portraits standardized to meet the needs of scientists, Du Bois's albums of "types" present a kind of evidence, but not proof of the essential, physical racial identity sought by eugenicists and

Francis Galton's "Standard Photograph" of himself to illustrate the profile and full-face portraits which are desirable in the case of Family Records and Life-History Albums and are suitable for composite photography.

Francis Galton's "Standard Photograph" of himself to illustrate the profile and full-face portraits, which are desirable in the case of Family Records and Life-History Albums and are suitable for composite photography. Reproduced from Karl Pearson, *The Life, Letters and Labours of Francis Galton*, vol. 2, *Researches of Middle Life* (Cambridge: Cambridge University Press, 1924).

white supremacists.[60] If in style and even title Du Bois's albums evoke a history of racist photographic documentation, they do so only to undercut that scientific register of dehumanized bodies with formal portraits of African Americans elegantly dressed in middle-class trappings. Further, Du Bois's profile and semiprofile portraits formally approximate not only Galton's scientific photographs but also Brady's "illustrious" images. Many of Du Bois's near-profile portraits represent individuals posed not at exact right angles, but instead positioned like Brady's "Illustrious Americans," in a three-quarter turn, with eyes directed slightly upward, out of the photographic frame, perhaps focused on political ideals. Unlike Brady's "model" portraits, however, Du Bois's pairs of portraits enact both the visual tropes of "illustriousness" and those of engagement and recognition. Within the codes of late-nineteenth-century U.S. visual culture, Du Bois's portraits represent African Americans both as "Illustrious Americans" contemplating shared ideals and as distinct individuals. Du Bois's frontal portraits meet and engage the eyes of later viewers, individualizing and particularizing American identity, placing a lofty American character squarely back on the terrain of negotiation, conflict, and "race."[61]

From *Types of American Negroes, Georgia, U.S.A.*, compiled by W. E. B. Du Bois, 1900. Reproduced from the Daniel Murray Collection of the Library of Congress.

While Du Bois's "American Negroes" are Americans both legally and philosophically, their fundamental identity remains racial within the nation. Du Bois's photograph albums contest a program of assimilation by portraying not the "American Negro" but instead the "Negroes" of "America." In his albums, Du Bois subtly challenges the exclusive authority of white Americans, assimilationists and eugenicists alike, to represent and to signify, to embody, the boundaries of national identity. Unlike Galton's racially essentialized notion of American character, Du Bois's sense of national identity is cultural, philosophical, and legal. However, while Du Bois's version of American character corresponds to a set of ideals, his vision of national identity, unlike Brady's, does not erase or conceal racial identity. Unlike Johnston's assimilationist images, Du Bois's photographs do not harness patriotic performance to a single racialized bloodline. In the power-laden struggles to define "nation," "race," and "American" at the turn of the century, W. E. B. Du Bois envisions a nation of multiracial Americans.

CHAPTER SEVEN

Looking Back: Pauline Hopkins's
Challenge to Eugenics

THE RACIALIZING of American character, which I have examined in preceding chapters, had profound effects on African American articulations of national and racial identities at the turn of the century. Indeed, W. E. B. Du Bois was not the only one asking "Am I an American or am I Negro?" Such questions provided both an implicit and an explicit political frame for much African American cultural work at the turn of the century, particularly as evidenced by the very title of one of the most prominent venues for African American cultural debate in the early twentieth century, namely, the *Colored American Magazine*. Initiated in 1901 and running until 1909, the *Colored American Magazine* was the first national magazine written, published, and cooperatively owned by an African American community, and addressed to a national African American audience. In the statement that inaugurated the magazine, the editors proclaimed their desire "to develop and intensify the bonds of that racial brotherhood, which alone can enable a people, to assert their racial rights as men, and demand their privileges as citizens."[1] To the end of "developing and intensifying the bonds of racial brotherhood," the magazine offered a forum through which African Americans could "demonstrate their ability and tastes, in fiction, poetry, and art, as well as in the arena of historical, social and economic literature."[2] The editors thereby located literary production at the center of a racial brotherhood, a racial community strengthened and identified by the bonds of a common culture, a brotherhood finally motivated to claim national rights as citizens through the strength of their culturally mediated racial identifications. The *Colored American Magazine* thus sought to create, through literary forms, an imagined community of African Americans who might contest the rules and regulations of the larger imagined community in which African Americans were denied the full rights of citizenship.

In this chapter I discuss two of the three novels Pauline Hopkins published serially from 1901 to 1904 in the *Colored American Magazine*, noting especially how her fictions posed national and racial identifications that both implicitly and explicitly challenged dominant definitions of racial difference in turn-of-the-century U.S. culture.[3] Hopkins utilized her fiction to create an imagined community of African American readers consolidated around contestatory self-identifications, and the discourses of racial identity she most consistently challenged were those of eugenics. Readers are by now familiar with some of the ways in which eugenics took hold of the dominant cultural imagination in the United States at the turn of the century. In order to understand the subtleties of Hopkins's fictions, it is important to remember that eugenicists, following Francis Galton, considered "race" a biological condition that determined one's innate moral, intellectual, and national character. Once again, eugenicists situated racial characters along a sliding scale, positing the Anglo-Saxon as the modern-day superior race. Posing bloodlines and heredity as central to the reproduction of racial character, eugenicists, committed to a notion of Anglo-Saxon superiority, adamantly opposed racial mixing as a threat to the progress (and dominance) of the Anglo-Saxon race. Hopkins's fiction works to problematize the visual evidence on which Galton supported his categorization of racial "types" and, further, to dismantle the convergence of blood, race, and character so fundamental to Galton's definitions of racial difference. In Hopkins's work, the notion of national character is posed as a human feature corrupted not by interracial mixing but by the standard of white male privilege that leads to rape, adultery, and the rejection of children of mixed racial ancestry. Centered around "white" characters who are legally coded African American, Hopkins's novels provide complicated examinations of character and of racial mixing that challenge the fundamental tenets of eugenics.

While Nancy Leys Stepan and Sander L. Gilman have studied the ways in which African American and Jewish American intellectuals challenged scientific racism with their own scientific treatises at the turn of the century,[4] it is also important to underscore the ways in which literature was utilized both to reinforce and to challenge scientific theories of racial difference. Literature sustained cultural beliefs in racial hierarchy and utter difference, even as science wavered and failed in its own proofs.[5] For example, because the test of sterility, generally used to prove hybridity, or the joining of two distinct species, obviously could not be used to demonstrate that the races were distinct species, the literary figure of the weak, "tragic mulatto" suggested a failure on the part of biracial individuals to survive and to reproduce. If literature reinforced faulty scientific theories of absolute racial difference, it is plausible to imagine that Hopkins saw literature as an important domain in which to challenge the "truths" of scientific racism. As my discussion will elaborate, Hopkins's literary challenge to the "science of race" is particularly evident in her final magazine novel, *Of One Blood*, in which the main character, Reuel Briggs, is himself a scientist of biracial ancestry.

ENVISIONING RACE:
BODIES ON DISPLAY IN *HAGAR'S DAUGHTER*

Pauline Hopkins centered her first and last novels for the *Colored American Magazine* on "white" characters of biracial ancestry who both wittingly and unwittingly pass, at least for a time, as Anglo-Saxons. While Hopkins's focus on such characters has troubled those scholars who believe "white" African American figures reinscribe white-dominated notions of beauty, I follow Hazel Carby, Ann duCille, Mary Ann Doane, and others in claiming that these characters can work to subvert racist taxonomies.[6] By highlighting individuals of biracial ancestry in her fiction, Pauline Hopkins emphasizes precisely the figures at the center of white supremacist hysteria at the turn of the century. Over the course of the late nineteenth century, stemming from Josiah Nott's 1843 proclamations about the congenitally weak nature of the "unnatural mulatto," and culminating in Francis Galton's warnings about the dangers posed by racial mixing for the longevity of the Anglo-Saxon race, white supremacists became increasingly focused on the individuals who challenged their attachment to blood purity. According to Robert Young, "The ideology of race . . . from the 1840s onwards necessarily worked according to a doubled logic, according to which it both enforced and policed the differences between the whites and the non-whites, but at the same time focussed fetishistically upon the product of the contacts between them."[7] By reinscribing the focus of white obsessions as a potentially subversive site in definitions of racial difference, Hopkins utilizes her biracial heroines to undermine dominant ideologies of race.

Hopkins's biracial characters problematize the assumptions on which Francis Galton's "evidence" of racial difference was recorded in composite photographs of various "types." Once again, Galton claimed to be able to delineate physiognomic types,[8] and he believed that physical signs provided indices to the distinct moral and intellectual characters by which he distinguished races from one another. Thus, Galton relied on a visual paradigm to differentiate his theoretically distinct groups. In *Hagar's Daughter*, Hopkins dismantles this scientific categorization of racial difference by highlighting the contradictions in an ontological system in which "race" is defined according to a visual epistemology that literally, and ironically, "fails to see" what it attempts to delineate. The very narrow color line drawn by "one drop" of blood laws, which legally marked individuals with one-thirty-second part African American ancestry as "black," created objects of racial knowledge that could not be discerned by an epistemological paradigm rooted in visual evidence. As Mary Ann Doane has stated, "The mulatta always signifies a potential confusion of racial categories and the epistemological impotency of vision."[9] Indeed, "The mulatta, whose looks and ontology do not coincide, poses a threat to . . . the very idea of racial categorization."[10] With her biracial characters who successfully pass for white, Hopkins problematizes the supposed correspondence between physical attributes and a narrowly defined racial "essence." In *Hagar's Daughter*, the biracial individual's very body challenges the racial epistemology on which the privilege of whiteness, identified as distinct from a knowable, because *visible*, blackness, depends.

In Hopkins's first magazine novel, the biracial woman challenges the *disembodied* nature of a surveillant white masculine gaze, which generally reinscribes its position of authority by practicing unseen seeing and un-named naming. Hopkins begins to problematize the prerogative of that gaze in the troubling scene in which Aurelia Madison, who has been passing for white among the nation's social elite, confronts Cuthbert Sumner, an elite white former suitor who, unbeknownst to Aurelia, has discovered her African ancestry. The scene takes place as Madison enters the prison in which Sumner is incarcerated. Hopkins narrates the scene of their meeting from Cuthbert, the prisoner's, point of view:

> Suddenly the key grated in the lock and the door swung open to admit a visitor. He recoiled as from a blow when he met the gaze of Aurelia Madison who stood staring at him with a glance in which curiosity, fear and love were mingled. She stood in the center of the gloomy cell like a statue, her dazzling beauty as marvelous as ever, the red-gold hair still shining in sunny radiance, the velvet eyes resting upon the man before her with a hidden caress in their liquid depths. Sumner shuddered as he gazed and remembered the dead girl's story. When alone with this woman, she had always possessed an irresistible attraction for him, and in spite of the past the old sensation returned in full force at this unexpected encounter, mingled with fear and repulsion. (235–236)

Hopkins represents the conflicted nature of Cuthbert's desire for Aurelia in the terms, down to the very words, Robert Young has used to describe the dynamic of white Western colonial desire: that of simultaneous "attraction" to and "repulsion" from a racialized other.[11] Again, Aurelia continues to hold "an irresistible attraction" for Cuthbert, even as she now "repulses" him. Further, my reading of this scene suggests that Hopkins's text ultimately aims to dismantle the power of the white male practitioner of colonial desire by undermining the authority of a disembodied gaze, upon which Cuthbert's privileged position depends. As Richard Dyer has argued in his important analysis of representations of whiteness in Hollywood film, the "property of whiteness, to be everything and nothing, is the source of its representational power."[12] As Cuthbert Sumner is forced to recognize his embodied position in the dynamic of colonial desire, he loses, in the particularity of his individual body, the ability to harness the "everything and nothing" power of whiteness. In Hopkins's revision of colonial desire, the white male body cannot remain unspecified in the racial taxonomy that reinscribes its generally invisible power.

Aurelia undermines Cuthbert's disembodied power as she looks back at him from her own ontologically shifting body, challenging the power of a one-way gaze to objectify and to classify her. Even as Aurelia, standing "like a statue," is reified as the captivating object of Cuthbert's white male gaze, her own gaze meets Cuthbert's with a force that causes him to "recoil," "as from a blow." The erasure of the white male viewer's body typically secured by the privilege of a masculine white gaze is doubly denied Cuthbert in this scene. First, as he remembers that Aurelia is no longer his social equal, he "shudders," inhabiting an uncontrollable body even as he gazes upon Aurelia and objectifies her "dazzling beauty." Second, as Aurelia, the object of Cuthbert's desiring gaze, returns that gaze, Cuthbert recoils, thrown back into an undeniable physical embodiment.

In Aurelia, Cuthbert must recognize his own inability both to discern and to enforce the stratified racial codes on which his privileged identity as a white man depends. In the very process of Cuthbert's attempt to objectify Aurelia, the distance maintained between his viewing position and the object of his view threatens to break down as his desire-inspiring gaze leads him toward physical union with the other. In this way, the mulatta figure effects a destabilization of the subject and object positions of a colonial gaze in Hopkins's text. Further, Hopkins's biracial characters disrupt a eugenicist taxonomy first by emphasizing the amalgamation that white men have forcefully produced, and second by demonstrating the subsequent difficulties of establishing and maintaining white supremacist definitions of racial difference.

Aurelia herself is not able to maintain the destabilization of power which she initially effects. Finally, in a court scene reminiscent of that which ends Mark Twain's *Puddn'head Wilson*, Aurelia is placed under the scrutinizing gaze of both the judicial system and the social elite among whom she has been circulating, and condemned for the transgression of passing: "Nothing criminal was charged against Aurelia; in fact, no one desired to inflict more punishment on the unfortunate woman, and when she left the court room that day she vanished forever from public view" (272). As Aurelia "vanishes" from "public view," the ontological and epistemological threat she posed to a visual taxonomy seems to fade out with her. Indeed, after Aurelia disappears, Washington's social elite can congratulate itself on extricating an impure infiltrator in its ranks. Consequently, it appears, at first, that Hopkins is repeating the trope of the "tragic mulatta" who must disappear from a social world that literally has no place for her.

Following this narrative pattern, Jewel, another pale-skinned biracial woman passing (even unbeknownst to her) in Washington's elite white circles, also dies after her own African American ancestry is discovered. Jewel's case is, perhaps, even more perplexing than Aurelia's, because secretly she marries Cuthbert Sumner only days before her African American heritage is disclosed. Thus, the anxiety that Cuthbert voices in regard to Aurelia's passing, namely, the "threat" that the biracial woman poses socially to a white man as his wife, is realized through his union with Jewel. However, after Jewel's African American heritage is discovered, Cuthbert never again meets his wife face-to-face, and therefore never repeats the scene of recognition that he performs with Aurelia. Thus, while the narrative protects Jewel from her husband's repulsion, it also seems to erase neatly her ability, as Cuthbert's wife, to disrupt even more powerfully than Aurelia the discourses that consolidate Cuthbert's privileged white male identity.

While Aurelia and Jewel effectively are erased from Hopkins's text, one woman of mixed racial heritage remains at the close of the narrative, namely Hagar, the namesake of Hopkins's novel. Hagar is Jewel's mother, and the wife of first one, and then another, wealthy white man. Finally, it is Hagar who begins to define a new subject and social position for the white males in Hopkins's text, namely, for those who can no longer posit their own identities in distinction to the objects of their colonial desire. As I will discuss in the following section, it is through Hagar that Hopkins redeems one of her Southern white male aristocrats, namely, Ellis Enson, a.k.a. Detective Henson, from the crime of racism.

While Hagar becomes the vehicle for the racial reeducation of Ellis Enson, it is significantly *not* Hagar's body that is displayed in the final vignettes of Hopkins's novel, but instead the bodies of two white males—those of Cuthbert Sumner and a young orphan boy. By leaving Hagar present, but just off-screen, as it were, Hopkins refuses to repeat the objectification of the biracial woman, the fetish of colonial desire. Instead, Hopkins displays the white male body, suggesting that readers should direct their gazes toward that shifting ontological position in her reinscribed racial taxonomy. As Cuthbert stands in front of his wife's grave, he recognizes "a lesson of the degradation of slavery" embodied in the orphan boy whom he watches chase butterflies across an adjoining field. Once again Cuthbert gazes at a body upon which he reads profound social meaning, but this time the body at which he stares is that of a symbolic white heir. The child is the illegitimate son of Elise Bradford, the white secretary who has been seduced and then murdered by St. Claire Enson, a white American senator and formerly a Southern slaveholding aristocrat. He is the same child who was brought in as an exhibit, as was Aurelia Madison, of the cruel immorality of St. Claire Enson in Hopkins's dramatic court scene. Returning briefly to that earlier moment, one sees how "the motherless and worse than fatherless child—a beautiful fair-haired boy, was led forward and stood upon a chair in the witness-box, to give emphasis to the point made by counsel that the dead woman had a pressing claim upon some man who wished to rid himself of her as encumbrance. Some of the women spectators wept, and many men felt uncomfortable about the eyes" (253). The white boy is made a spectacle at the trial, and his body serves to mark white patriarchal transgression in much the same way as Aurelia Madison's body. The child is yet another product of unsanctified white male desire fed by unfettered social power, and it is through him that Sumner begins to recognize the "sin of the nation" (283).

While Hopkins's parting focus on the body of a young white orphan seems, at first, a rather odd place to conclude a complicated narrative detailing the tangled fate of three white women of biracial ancestry, it remains an important strategical move because it leaves her readers looking at the body of the white male and trying to understand his changing ontological position. The reader is left to ponder this final scene looking through Cuthbert Sumner's "*different eyes* and thoughts" (284; emphasis added). What those "different eyes" begin to see are the sins of a white patriarchy, a social body that cannot be recuperated in Hopkins's narrative until white men learn to take responsibility for the problematics of colonial desire. Leading the way for Cuthbert is Ellis Enson, the uncle of the fair-haired boy, who begins to make recompense for the white supremacist ancestral pride that once divided him from Hagar, by remarrying her at the end of the narrative. In so doing, Ellis also creates a familial structure for his brother's illegitimate son. As the nephew of Ellis and Hagar Enson, the child is placed genealogically as "the last representative of the Enson family" (284) and, by the end of the novel, as the heir of a recognized interracial family.

Shifting focus away from the body of the biracial woman, the ontologically ambiguous fetish of a white supremacist ideology of race, Hopkins relocates the problem of racial ontology and visual epistemology in the bodies of white men. Ultimately, by situating the white male body as the *object* of a discerning gaze, Hopkins brings to the foreground, and thereby dismantles, the disembodied abstraction of whiteness that consolidates the position of the white male in the visual dynamics of colonial desire. By collapsing whiteness into embodiment, Hopkins refuses the normative absence of that signifier. Finally, by giving Cuthbert Sumner "different eyes," Hopkins imagines a white patriarchy whose invisible power is undermined as its constituents begin to direct their gazes onto themselves.

"SONS OF ONE FATHER"

By dismantling both the disembodied privilege of a white male gaze and the authority of that gaze to determine another's ontological position in a racist typology, Hopkins undermines the claims of biological racialists and others to discern racial "types." Indeed, even Detective Henson, trained to read scenes and bodies for signs and clues, does not discover the "blackness" hidden behind Jewel Bowen's unwitting disguise of whiteness.[13] To all eyes, Jewel Bowen remains a beauty of the "Saxon type" (82). Once again, through Jewel, as through Aurelia, Hopkins challenges "one drop" of blood racial identity laws by demonstrating their artificiality and even impracticality.

Hopkins further troubles the authority of a white gaze by closing the distance upon which the authorized observer's visual scrutiny and objectification of the other depend. As Hazel Carby notes, following J. Randolph Cox, the "objectivity" of the detective typical of turn-of-the-century dime-novel fictions was secured by the absence of his family background. " 'He is the only one who can read the riddle because he is never personally involved.' "[14] Through Detective Henson, a.k.a. Ellis Enson, Hopkins negates the separation of the professional observer from the realm of family, history, and the heart. In order to solve the mystery, Detective Enson must realize his part in the historical play and must reclaim his position as Hagar's long-lost husband. He must renounce his position as a disembodied eye and act from the very embodied position of a man with a heart.

In Hopkins's narrative, Ellis Enson must also disavow the distance upon which his privileged whiteness, his ancestral family name, depends. Enson must honor his familial ties to those of biracial ancestry, weighing the bonds of heart, which found a new, mixed bloodstream, over the pride of ancestral heredity. As Claudia Tate has argued, Hopkins's magazine novels transform "the polemic on racial equality and civil justice into tests of true love."[15] Ellis Enson passes the test of true love in *Hagar's Daughter*, a test that requires him to disown his racial pride, which is firmly rooted in an aristocratic ancestral tradition. Thus, as Enson passes the test of true love, he fails the eugenicist test of blood purity by sanctifying both his marriage and his paternal relation to women of biracial ancestry.

Hopkins's reworking of the importance of heredity through the character Ellis Enson is central to her critique of eugenicist racial logics. As visual indices became less clear with ever more closely drawn color lines at the turn of the century, racial identity often became a matter of legal tests of heredity. If the eyes could not be relied upon to gather evidence of racial identity, heredity increasingly was seized as the key to defining one's legal social position. For eugenicists, heredity provided the very foundation of racial identity, as the genealogy that passed along the congenital "character" of any given race. After demonstrating the inability of white patriarchs to determine racial identities according to the subtleties of their own statutes, Hopkins then takes her critique of racial typing one step further, by dismantling the supposed convergence of heredity and character central to eugenicist delineations of racial hierarchies.

Hopkins's critique of white supremacist accounts of African American character are most explicit in the discussions Cuthbert Sumner has with Jewel Bowen and Ellis Enson after discovering the African ancestry of Hagar, Jewel's supposed stepmother (who is actually Jewel's birth mother). Deeming the sweet virtues of Hagar Bowen "an accident of environment," and "not the true nature of her parent stock" (269), Sumner confuses the boundaries between the environmental and biological camps of racial determinism. Sumner attempts to denigrate a "naturally low" African American character, proclaiming, " 'I have always heard that the Negro race excelled in low cunning,' " but his previous comments suggest that "accidents" of environment and training can indeed shape one's comportment. *Hagar's Daughter* as a whole seems to reject both sides of the debate over character determinism. Hopkins's novel is peopled with good and bad African Americans and good and bad Anglo-Saxon Americans, and neither blood nor training can be depended on consistently to shape one's individuality. Isaac is duplicitous, but his daughter Venus is as honest and virtuous as a young woman can be; in short, Venus appears not to have inherited any of her father's negative traits.[16] Similarly, there could not be two men more different than the brothers Ellis and St. Clair Enson, two men of the same racial, aristocratic, and even parental stock. Certainly the two were raised in the same environment, and certainly they share the same blood. Hopkins highlights the ancestral link between the two brothers, even as she draws an irreparable divide between them. In the final moments of the courtroom scenes that reveal so many of the hidden identities at play in the novel, the narrator describes the ultimate confrontation between the two Enson brothers: "So for a moment of dead silence, of untold pain to one, those two men, sons of one father, but with a bridgeless gulf between them, stood face to face after many years" (272). Ellis and St. Clair Enson, "sons of one father," share the same ancestral blood and should, therefore, according to eugenicist logics, share the same character traits. And yet, while St. Clair is wicked through and through, Ellis is honest and honorable. Hopkins's text asks: How can the two men behave so differently? By depicting two men who claim an identical blood source as polar opposites in moral and intellectual characteristics, Hopkins undermines the genealogical delineation of heredity and racial hierarchy upon which Francis Galton founded his theory of eugenics.

Hopkins takes her challenge to eugenicist conceptions of character even further than her depiction of family lines divided by good and evil individuals. In *Hagar's Daughter*, Hopkins demonstrates that immorality can indeed be reproduced, not biologically but socially. The "lesson of the degradation of slavery" (284) that Cuthbert Sumner sees embodied in Elise Bradford's illegitimate son is the evidence of the weakened moral character of Southern white aristocratic men. Hopkins's novel suggests that the system of slavery, which sanctioned the uncontrolled power of white patriarchs over the bodies of their slaves, strained and corrupted the character of aristocratic men, transforming them into rapists and adulterers, men with no respect for sacred family ties. By focusing on the *social* reproduction of character, Hopkins turns eugenicist logics back upon themselves, proposing that the caste system itself threatens to corrupt Anglo-Saxon blood and weaken Anglo-Saxon character by training white men in the crimes of lust. Indeed, in her attack on the social reproduction of immorality, Hopkins come very near to repeating the theory of hereditary corruption offered in Nathaniel Hawthorne's *House of the Seven Gables*. Hopkins's text seems to hint, as does Hawthorne's, that "the act of the passing generation is the germ which may and must produce good or evil fruit in a far-distant time; . . . together with the seed of the merely temporary crop, which mortals term expediency, they inevitably sow the acorns of a more enduring growth, which may darkly overshadow their posterity."[17] Once again Hopkins suggests that white supremacists have only themselves to fear.

While Hopkins troubles both sides of the debate over character determinism, suggesting that training may become so ingrained as to become almost hereditary, she chooses to naturalize only one human force, namely, love. In a wonderful reversal of white supremacist ideology, Ellis Enson explains to a confused Cuthbert Sumner that " 'race prejudice is all right in theory, but when a man tries to practice it against the laws which govern human life and action, there's a weary journey ahead of him, and he's not got to die to realize the tortures of the damned' " (270). Enson proclaims that, for him, " 'nature was stronger than prejudice' " (270). In Hopkins's novel, it is only racism that is unnatural, the effect of training and tradition. Indeed, Hopkins's narrator does not condemn Sumner for his racism, explaining that "Cuthbert Sumner was born with a noble nature; his faults were those caused by environment and tradition" (265). Sumner's faulty character is the result of unnatural cultivation, a bending of the heart away from its true justice. This very problem, the "tradition" of racial caste that dominates U.S. culture, is, for Hopkins, the problem of the nation itself.

In *Hagar's Daughter* Hopkins renames the so-called Negro problem the problem of racism and white supremacism, and situates that problem in the heart of the nation's capital. She demonstrates that everywhere, even among the nation's most elite, " 'amalgamation has taken place; it will continue, and no finite power can stop it' " (270). To remove the African American portion of the population would be to dismember the national body itself. Thus, Hopkins poses racism not only as a problem for African Americans but also as a threat to the stability of the nation. Once again, after his trials, Cuthbert Sumner recognizes that the abuses of power enabled by a caste system founded in white supremacy and unquestioned patriarchal privilege are the "sins of the nation." Sumner envisions "the wrath of a righteous God" (284) come to wash out the nation's "idolatry of the Moloch of Slavery" (283). Finally, in order to make the threat to the nation enacted through caste even more literal, Hopkins links the two white men most explicitly demonized for manipulating the codes of caste and race to the most dramatic of all national crimes, an assassination attempt on the president.

Hopkins introduces her tale with a story of the nation divided in the years just preceding and during the Civil War. She then situates the bulk of her story twenty years later, in the post-Reconstruction era, and depicts a nation still divided, struggling with the racism of its ruling class. In *Hagar's Daughter*, the supposedly reunified nation is torn asunder by a rigid caste system that severs the "natural" ties of love.[18] Indeed, if Harriet Beecher Stowe critiqued the system of slavery for its abuses upon the family, Pauline Hopkins similarly condemns the postemancipation caste system for *its* abuses upon the family. *Hagar's Daughter* critiques anti-interracial marriage laws and prejudice by naturalizing love as the tie that binds according to a higher law. As Ellis Enson states, "The sum total of what Puritan New England philanthropy will allow" is "every privilege but the vital one of deciding a question of the commonest personal liberty which is the fundamental principle of the holy family tie" (271). Hopkins depicts a world in which interracial relations are socially sanctioned only when illicit or brutally forced, demonstrating how the stigma against interracial unions works to victimize women of color, like Aurelia Madison, and to underscore the patriarchal "privileges" of white men, like St. Clair Enson. Hopkins plays out in fiction the realities documented by Ida B. Wells and other African American political activists who demonstrated how antimiscegenation laws worked only to forbid legitimate interracial unions sanctified by love.[19]

In making a case for the naturalness of interracial family bonds, Hopkins reconfigures the family lines central to eugenicist delineations of the color line. As Cuthbert Sumner voices eugenicist hysteria over the purity of "the fountain head" of the Anglo-Saxon "racial stream" (271), Ellis Enson, momentarily bathed in "holy light," proclaims "a higher law than that enacted by any earthly tribunal" (271). In short, Enson suggests that the power of love is stronger than the power of prejudice.[20] Further, he challenges the evolutionary hierarchy Sumner evokes with images of Anglo-Saxon "refinement and intelligence" contrasted to "black bestiality," by deeming prejudice the truly "beastly" social force (270). In this way, Enson subtly reverses the scale of evolutionary progress upheld by eugenicists, marking white supremacist Anglo-Saxons as those uncivilized in light of destiny's plan.[21] Through this extensive interchange, Hopkins models a process of intraracial retraining, in which white elders teach misguided young men to heed the holy flame of love. In *Hagar's Daughter*, Pauline Hopkins attempts to envision a reunified, biracial national family bound by love.

EXCAVATING THE HIDDEN SELF

Reading across Pauline Hopkins's *Hagar's Daughter* and *Of One Blood*, one finds a very complicated vision of political critique and racial liberation at work.[22] While in *Hagar's Daughter* Hopkins seems intent on destabilizing the correspondence of physical features to racial identity, she partially reinvests physical signs with the weight of hereditary evidence in *Of One Blood* by linking relatives through the ancestral birthmark of the lotus-lily. Further, while Hopkins rejects the convergence of character, race, and blood in *Hagar's Daughter*, she revives the importance of blood and heredity in *Of One Blood* by centering her novel around three siblings of royal African heritage ("of one blood").[23] According to Susan Gillman, Hopkins "deliberately entangled herself" with "the language of blood, especially the concepts of 'pure blood' and 'pure race' so deeply associated with the nineteenth-century quasi-scientific study of race."[24] By using siblings to muse upon the convergence of racial and ancestral inheritance, Hopkins once again problematizes the convergence of those factors central to Francis Galton's white supremacism. In *Of One Blood* we see that training, privilege, and (the abuse of) power, not blood, contribute most forcibly to the formation of one's moral character.

As Pauline Hopkins challenges contemporary scientific norms, she shifts the terms for defining racial identity, as does W. E. B. Du Bois in "The Conservation of Races." As I have discussed in the previous chapter, in this early essay Du Bois rejects "the grosser physical differences of color, hair and bone" as the definitive determinants of racial identity, and outlines "subtle, delicate and elusive" forces as the foundations on which distinct races develop.[25] Once again, Du Bois suggests that "while these subtle forces have generally followed the natural cleavage of common blood, descent and physical peculiarities, they have at other times swept across and ignored these."[26] In other words, according to Du Bois, racial alliance and affiliation do not always follow the reproduction of a single bloodline. "What, then, is a race?" asks Du Bois. "It is a vast *family* of human beings, generally of common blood and language, always of common history, traditions and impulses, who are both voluntarily and involuntarily striving together for the accomplishment of certain more or less vividly conceived ideals of life."[27] Du Bois reenvisions the family, the center of hereditary reproduction in eugenics, as a community bound not exclusively by blood but also by more ephemeral "impulses" and "ideals."[28] Du Bois invokes tradition and history to free "race" from the rigid determinants of biology and blood, thereby challenging Francis Galton's method of delineating racial character. One's intellectual and moral character is not determined by one's biological (racial) body but is itself the seat of a cultural racial identification.

In *Of One Blood*, Pauline Hopkins similarly locates racial bonds in subtle impulses and elusive ideals. Even as she holds on to a physical marker as the sign of ancestral lineage, she problematizes that tenuous physical link by tying characters more forcibly together through mystical visions and supernatural powers. Hopkins's central character, Reuel Briggs, is a medical student, a scientist who presumably studies and tends to the body, and yet, Reuel's most dramatic scientific successes are predicted by supernatural visions, and they defy physical signs (such as Dianthe's seeming death), to rely upon the pseudospiritual forces of animal magnetism. Through Reuel, Hopkins uses the figure of a brilliant scientist to challenge the physical, embodied nature of scientific "truths" forwarded by biological racialists and eugenicists at the turn of the century. Further, *Of One Blood* suggests that one's racial "fate" is determined not by physical characteristics but by metaphysical forces. Reuel's destiny as an African leader is mapped by a spiritual guide. Indeed, Hopkins's narrative combines the spiritual world and racial ancestry as constituents of the same order. If for Francis Galton destiny is equivalent to biology, for Pauline Hopkins destiny is a spiritual domain that influences and directs the material world.

Of One Blood tells the story of three siblings mysteriously and tragically linked to one another and to an ancient Ethiopian royal family, to which they are heirs. The three siblings, Reuel, Dianthe, and Aubrey, are of biracial ancestry, and all three pass for white, at least for a time, one knowingly and the other two unwittingly. As siblings, the three characters are connected intimately to one another through blood, and this connection ultimately provides the tragic link of incestuous desire between them. Further, Reuel and Dianthe are joined by visions, by Reuel's healing magnetism, and eventually by love and marriage. In turn, Reuel and Dianthe are linked to Aubrey by the secret of their African ancestry and by his deception, manipulation, and lust. While Aubrey, living as the heir of his white father's patriarchal family, does not seem to possess (or to pay attention to) the highly developed mystical powers of Mira, his (unacknowledged) mother, both Dianthe and Reuel are able to tap into an otherworldly arena "veiled" to the eyes of their white cohorts, the realm of their mother, of the spirit, and of the African race.[29] By joining these three characters with identical ancestral blood, but demonstrating how they are divided culturally, spiritually, and racially from one another by white patriarchal structures, Hopkins once again demonstrates that "race" is not a mere matter of bloodlines but an alliance based on institutions, inclinations, and power.

In her engagement with the tangled knot of bloodlines, Hopkins develops an explicit Pan-Africanism in *Of One Blood*. She introduces her hero, Reuel, by outlining some of his mystical and magnetic powers (by which he recognizes and heals Dianthe), and then links those powers to ancient Ethiopian traditions. "The nature of the mystic within him was, then, but a dreamlike devotion to the spirit that had swayed his ancestors; it was the shadow of Ethiopia's power."[30] Reuel's African ancestry, the self that he keeps hidden as he passes for white at Harvard, is the fount of his supernatural powers, and it is that self which a suicidal Reuel must excavate if he and his fellow Africans and Americans are going to survive. Hopkins literalizes this search for the "Africa within" by sending Reuel on an archaeological excavation led by a researcher who hopes to prove the Ethiopian roots of Egyptian, and therefore also Athenian, culture. It is on this trip, protected and guided by mystical visions and forebodings, that Reuel literally stumbles onto the ancient, hidden city of Telassar, where he not only finds evidence of former and present Ethiopian greatness (in the direct descendants of the inhabitants of Meroe) but also discovers his own responsibility, as King Ergamenes, to "restore to the Ethiopian race its ancient glory."[31]

Although tragedy brought about by Aubrey's duplicitousness does not permit Dianthe to claim her own position as a royal Ethiopian leader, Hopkins also grants her the supernatural powers that tap into an African spiritual heritage. While Dianthe is recovering from her mesmeric trance, having been healed by Reuel's magnetic forces, she stuns a small audience gathered at the Vance home with the eery quality of her restored singing voice. Listeners shocked by the doubled nature of her voice hear "a weird contralto, veiled as it were, rising and falling upon every wave of the great soprano, and reaching the ear as from some strange distance" (502). The doubled nature of Dianthe's voice recalls W. E. B. Du Bois's articulation of double consciousness in *The Souls of Black Folk*—Dianthe seems to give voice to the "twoness" of "two unreconciled strivings," "two warring ideals" in the hearts of African Americans living in a white-dominated America.[32] Like her mother, Mira, born with a "veil," a gift of second-sight, as Du Bois describes it,[33] Dianthe seems able to tap into a consciousness larger than her own. As Thomas J. Otten has explained, that larger consciousness is in fact "the hidden self" of Dianthe's psychology, a part of her that remembers the collective history of Africa. "The hidden self is thus that part of the personality that preserves the memory of ancient African civilization."[34] It is this ancient African civilization that Dianthe's brother, Reuel, literally rediscovers in the latter portions of Hopkins's novel.

The words Dianthe sings with her doubled voice—" 'Go down, Moses, way down in Egypt's land, Tell ol' Pharaoh, let my people go' " (502)—are significant because they point toward a biblical tradition linked to Egypt and to Ethiopia, the lands where Hopkins situates an ancient African kingdom. According to Thomas J. Otten, the biblical Moses was directly connected to the Ethiopians through his wife, Zipporah, whose father was an Ethiopian. Further, as Otten explains, Hopkins makes such connections explicit by naming Dianthe's brother, Reuel, after the Ethiopian father of Zipporah.[35] In this way, Hopkins demonstrates that Ethiopian blood permeates Judeo-Christian Western traditions, reinforcing the biblical refrain with which she concludes her novel: "His promises stand, and He will prove His words, 'Of one blood have I made all races of men' " (621).

Hopkins's emphasis on "one blood" cuts against turn-of-the-century race prejudice and biological racialism in several ways. First, Hopkins suggests that the white elite's concern over "blood purity" is rather ludicrous, even sacrilegious, because it would seem to fall outside of God's plan. By drawing upon biblical accounts of the creation of "all races of men" from "one blood," Hopkins rejects the claims of polygenesists, including Josiah Nott, who argued that the races were made separately, in distinct moments. Second, Hopkins plays upon the notion voiced by Ellis Enson in *Hagar's Daughter* that "amalgamation has taken place" and will continue, in order to question the arbitrary divisions of a color line founded in blood percentages and (invisible) visual differences. As the narrator of *Of One Blood* states, "The slogan of the hour is 'Keep the Negro down!' but who is clear enough in vision to decide who hath black blood and who hath it not? Can any one tell? No, not one" (607). According to Hopkins, visual differences between the races are effaced as racial mixing continues, and that very mixing appears to have been part of God's plan to reunite the races now literally "of one [mixed] blood": "In His own mysterious way He has united the white race and the black race in this new continent. By the transgression of the law He proves His own infallibility: 'Of one blood have I made all nations of men to dwell upon the whole face of the earth,' is as true today as when given to the inspired writers to be recorded. No man can draw the dividing line between the two races, for they are both of one blood!" (607). While Hopkins proposes that amalgamation is the vehicle of a restored biblical order, she explains the origins of the divisions now being rectified through Ai, the high priest of Telassar. With a story closely resembling the biblical tale of the Tower of Babel, Ai explains that the enslavement of the Ethiopian people was a punishment for their pride (555). According to Ai, "Great were the sins of our fathers, and the white stranger was to Ethiopia but a scourge in the hands of an offended God" (555). While Ai proclaims that Ethiopia's punishment is now over, he is a bit more ambiguous about the future fate of the "white strangers" who served as the vehicles of a divinely ordained destruction.

Hopkins exemplifies the horrors of the white "scourge" in her ultimate, and perhaps most disturbing, foray into the tangle of bloodlines. Through the revelations of Aunt Hannah, Hopkins links Aubrey, Reuel, and Dianthe in an incestuous love triangle (" 'all of one blood!' ").[36] In this way, she demonstrates yet another "lesson of the degradation of slavery" and its toll on the fount of Anglo-Saxon character. For if slavery bred licentiousness and indifference in white patriarchs, that same institution perpetuated not only rape but also incest, as white heirs raped the half sisters begotten by their own fathers.[37] Thus, Hopkins demonstrates that slavery not only broke family ties but also knit them together too closely in the "unnatural" bonds of incest. As Elizabeth Ammons has stated, "With dramatic force, this double incest exposes the literal horror of slavery."[38] Hopkins's focus on incest also recalls turn-of-the-century white hysteria over blood mixing and reinvests that discourse with the monstrous implications of its own solipsistic logics. As Susan Gillman notes, "though narrative order is restored" by the end of Hopkins's novel, "once we learn all about the characters' mysterious and intertwined pasts under slavery, this knowledge offers no possibility of restoring the American social and moral order."[39] Indeed, Hopkins shows how the sins of the father literally have been visited upon the sons. In order to avoid the tragic traps of an immoral American order, Hopkins also seems to suggest, as Elizabeth Ammons has noted, that African Americans must somehow reject the American racial hierarchy in which they are socially inscribed.[40] It is to that end that Hopkins directs her writing of pre-American African history.

One of the most subversive aspects of Hopkins's narrative in *Of One Blood* is the way in which it resituates the origins of white European culture in Ethiopia. Readers will remember that the ancient Athenian race served as the exemplary race, the height of all racial genius throughout history, in Francis Galton's study of "hereditary genius."[41] Modeling the future success or failure of the modern Anglo-Saxon race on ancient Athenian fate, Galton traced a trajectory of European Western history with continuous lines extending from ancient Greece to modern Anglo-Saxon culture. While a cultural inheritance stemming from ancient Greece was called upon to reinforce the supremacy of "whites" throughout history, Egypt's place in this trajectory, as the possible origin of ancient Greek culture, proved ambiguous for white supremacists, as the racial components of ancient Egyptian culture seemed less clearly "white" than inscriptions of Athenian racial attributes. According to Robert Young, "Egypt, as the earliest civilization, developed in Africa, clearly represented the major potential stumbling-block to the claim for the permanent inferiority of the black race which, it was alleged, had never created or produced anything whatsoever of value."[42] To clarify this point of possible contention, in 1844 the now-familiar American ethnologist Josiah Nott (a prominent polygenesist) proclaimed that the ancient Egyptians had been Caucasians. In this claim Nott followed another American, George R. Gliddon, who had published *Ancient Egypt* just one year earlier, in 1843, a text that also argued for the Caucasian origins of Egyptian culture. The American Egyptologist S. G. Morton sought to prove the hypotheses forwarded by Nott and Gliddon by measuring the skulls of Egyptian mummies, and in his *Crania Aegyptica* of 1844, he concluded that ancient Egyptian culture was in fact the product of a Caucasian high caste. While members of Egypt's servant class may have been African, according to Morton, the elite ruling class was of Caucasian stock.[43]

It is precisely this history of the "whitening of Egypt" that Hopkins and other African American intellectuals contested at the turn of the century.[44] Through Professor Stone, the leader of Reuel's archaeological team, Hopkins outlines a global history that locates the origin and height of Western civilization in Ethiopia. According to Professor Stone, " 'All records of history, sacred and profane, unite in placing the Ethiopian as the primal race' " (521). Reuel challenges Professor Stone with veiled sarcasm: " 'Your theories may be true, Professor, but if so, your discoveries will establish the primal existence of the Negro as the most ancient source of all that you value in modern life, even antedating Egypt. How can the Anglo-Saxon world bear the establishment of such a theory?' " (520). To this query Professor Stone responds with a statement that may veil Hopkins's own sarcasm: " 'You and I, Briggs, know that the theories of prejudice are swept away by the great tide of facts' " (520–521). Hopkins knew only too well how theories of prejudice could be construed and reinforced by the so-called facts of science, and it was against such "facts" that she wrote her fictions, intertwining the fact and fiction of both scientific and literary representations of "race."

VISIONS BEYOND THE COLOR LINE

As Hopkins challenged the "facts" of Egyptology, she also problematized the visual paradigms on which racial taxonomies and hierarchies were founded at the turn of the century. Eugenicists and others sought to generalize and to codify physical characteristics, tying them to essentialized interior essences. As I have demonstrated in previous chapters, photography was used to locate individual bodies within a genealogy of familial hereditary traits and racial characteristics. In this increasingly surveillant culture, in which the body was read ever more carefully for signs of narrowly defined racial markers and documented with the visual technologies of photography, Hopkins imagined a new order of visual identification with her depiction of metaphysical visions. Dissociating knowledge, identity, and racial bonds from the "skin, hair and bone" of the body, Hopkins relocated "truth" in spiritual visions that lie beyond the physical, material world. In *Of One Blood*, those of the highest social caste (royalty) are marked by powers that defy the ordinary terrain of visual scrutiny and codification. Reuel is clairvoyant, and both Reuel and Dianthe are visited by spirits and visions. Indeed, one of the vehicles of knowledge for the two siblings is a disembodied spirit, namely, their mother, Mira. Hopkins's characters challenge the designs of power imposed by the normative influence of surveillance by transcending the terrain of physical view. Their powers are not visual but visionary.

As Thomas J. Otten has argued, Hopkins's use of mesmerism, visions, and clairvoyance challenges the parameters of identity as posed by the sciences of biological racialism.[45] Explaining the radical import of African American tales of clairvoyance and mesmerism at the turn of the century, stories largely misread or ignored as simply "strange," Otten states that such texts make a case for "the potential instability of the boundaries of identity."[46] Tracing some of Hopkins's metaphysical images to an essay written by William James, which shares the subtitle of Hopkins's final novel, namely, "The Hidden Self," Otten explains that William James believed those "facts that established scientific systems cannot explain or accept"—" 'the unclassified residuum' "—are the best arena for challenging accepted scientific systems of knowledge.[47] Otten lays out James's view as follows: "Precisely because they do provide occasion for such rethinking, such anomalies are potentially the richest area for investigation; the best way to 'renovate' a system is to study what it leaves out."[48] By posing technologies of knowledge and power not circumscribed by normative definitions of scientific veracity at the turn of the century, Hopkins imagined new means of establishing identities, communities, family, and "race." Countering eugenicist obsession over the body with a story of phenomena unaccounted for in the field of biological science, Hopkins challenged that discipline's ability to delineate and define "the strange meaning of being black"[49] at the turn of the century.

Hopkins's use of mesmerism, magnetism, and vision in *Of One Blood* is powerful not only in its challenge to the materialist visual paradigms of scientific racialism and eugenics at the turn of the century but also as a comment on Nathaniel Hawthorne's prominent use of some of the same venues over fifty years earlier, in *The House of the Seven Gables*. As readers will recall, a penetrating, mesmerizing masculine gaze is one of the vehicles whereby Hawthorne (and others) established a feminine interiority in need of masculine protection at midcentury. Utilizing a penetrating gaze to project an interiorized essence beyond the pierced body, Hawthorne envisioned a middle-class order in which such essences would be protected and displayed in fortuitous heterosexual unions. Hopkins's *Of One Blood* similarly places a female essence in the hands and under the protection of a male mesmerist. However, Hopkins's narrative cannot repeat the happy ending of Hawthorne's romance. Hopkins depicts an African American woman betrayed by a white patriarchal social structure from which her African American protector cannot save her. Reuel awakens Dianthe from a deathlike mesmeric trance with his magnetic powers, but he cannot protect her from others who will manipulate the "African essence" even Reuel decides to keep hidden. In Hopkins's novel Hawthorne's happy ending is transformed into the horror of rape and incest, which Hopkins suggests is indicative of the brutal reality facing African Americans living on the color line.[50]

Hopkins's final novel also revises Hawthorne's image of white middle-class romance by focusing on the very repression of "race" forwarded by the earlier narrative. If the aristocratic bloodlines that are submerged in "subterranean pipes" (*The House of the Seven Gables*, 408) in Hawthorne's text register a repressed racial logic at midcentury, such bloodlines have emerged as a source of white hysteria by the turn of the century, as Hopkins writes *Of One Blood*. By briefly juxtaposing Hopkins's *Of One Blood* to Hawthorne's *The House of the Seven Gables*, I would like to suggest that Hopkins's challenge to the delineations of race and identity dominant in theories of biological racialism revised not only images of African American identity but also those of Anglo-Saxon identity. As Hopkins's *Of One Blood* relocates the origins of Western civilization in Ethiopian culture, the novel also subtly suggests the African origins of the Anglo-Saxon self. Thomas J. Otten has assessed the intersections between psychological theories of the hidden self and Africa's role in history in *Of One Blood*,[51] and one might expand upon those connections to read Hopkins's novel as an exploration of the African origins of all modern selves. The novel suggests that "the hidden self" is an interiorized essence joined to all other essences by the singular blood of biblical tradition. *Of One Blood* proposes an Afro-centric Western history, and in the context of turn-of-the-century biological racialism, it thus troubles the authority of a stridently enforced color line. Hopkins's novel exposes the dead ends of racialized logics of blood purity to demonstrate that mixed bloodlines cannot remain submerged, for they gurgle in the throats of white supremacists. After demonstrating how blood has been mixed across race lines for hundreds of years, Hopkins also suggests that such mixing may lead races back to the African origins of European and Euro-American civilization. The blood that is hidden in Hawthorne's romance of white middle-class ascendance becomes, in Hopkins's *Of One Blood*, the repressed vehicle of the individual psychology, of an African genealogy, and of a collective Western cultural history. Finally, then, Hopkins's most radical challenge to eugenics lies in her claim that all races are "of one [African] blood."

CHAPTER EIGHT

Reconfiguring a Masculine Gaze

IN AN ALMOST irresistible passage in Theodore Dreiser's *Sister Carrie*, a pair of soft, new leather shoes calls out to the young Caroline Meeber: " 'Ah, such little feet, . . . how effectively I cover them. What a pity they should ever want my aid.' "[1] A lace collar admonishes her: " 'My dear, . . . I fit you beautifully; don't give me up' " (99). The appeal of such commodities is sensual and intoxicating to Carrie, and she hears them with a willing heart, abandoning herself to what Walter Benjamin has deemed the empathetic "soul" of the commodity. As Benjamin explains, "If the soul of the commodity which Marx occasionally mentions in jest existed, it would be the most empathetic ever encountered in the realm of souls, for it would have to see in everyone the buyer in whose hand and house it wants to nestle."[2] Perhaps Carrie is particularly susceptible to the whispers of commodities because she herself is so closely aligned with them in Dreiser's text. As she rises to stardom, Carrie makes a home for the delicate things that invite her, and in so doing, she makes a delicious little commodity of herself. Men yearn for the elegantly dressed Carrie (411), responding to the empathy of her face, which seems "representative of all desire" (448).

Feminist scholars have generally read the course of Carrie's commodification as emblematic of the disempowered position and passive role of the commodified "woman-as-consumer."[3] However, I would like to suggest that Dreiser's *Sister Carrie* also offers an alternative means of understanding both the position and the relative power of woman as commodity in consumer culture, a different way of looking at the links between gender and "conspicuous consumption."[4] By assessing the image of commodified femininity as it appears in relation to a "masculine gaze" in Dreiser's text, I would like to suggest that Caroline Meeber's commodified position becomes the site of an ambiguous agency in *Sister Carrie*. Indeed, that aspect of women's position in consumer culture that has most troubled feminist cultural critics—namely, women's self-conception as image[5]—becomes, for Dreiser's Carrie, the initial condition for a provisional mobility and power.[6]

In Theodore Dreiser's *Sister Carrie*, the white woman sheds her "true" middle-class moorings. Carrie is neither pious nor pure, and, as an unmarried, childless woman, she does not anchor a racialized family structure— her sexuality is not harnessed to racial reproduction. Adrift in a white middle-class patriarchy, Carrie reproduces only herself. She finds and wields

her cultural power as the object of a masculine gaze, and her various successes are measured by her ability to attract that gaze, to entrance—to
mesmerize—a masculine viewer. In *Sister Carrie*, Dreiser presents a white
masculine gaze captivated by an image of white womanhood it no longer
fully controls. Read in relation to Pauline Hopkins's magazine novels,
which undermine the visual paradigms that informed white supremacist
(mis)understandings of "race," Dreiser's novel might be said to register
white middle-class anxiety over such perceived threats to the supremacy of
a white masculine gaze, and a white patriarchy, at the turn of the century.
In *Sister Carrie* a white woman, the anchor to antebellum and postbellum
discourses of middle-class cultural privilege, reproduces herself right out
of the white middle-class family.

VISIONS OF COMMODIFIED IDENTITY
IN CONSUMER CULTURE

The "consumer culture" that Dreiser examines in *Sister Carrie* is a culture
profoundly mediated by a gaze. The new forms of commodified display
that emerged as capitalism was consolidated around urban centers in the
late nineteenth century privileged new visual practices. Emblematizing
these new visual customs, the department store with its glass windows and
electrical lights displayed a vast array of commodities that captivated the
gaze and kindled new desires.[7] Describing Carrie's first foray into The Fair,
one of Chicago's first department stores, Dreiser's narrator explains the
allure of these new commodity showcases:

> Such a flowering out of a modest trade principle the world had never witnessed
> up to that time. They were along the line of the most effective retail organiza-
> tion, with hundreds of stores co-ordinated into one and laid out upon the
> most imposing and economic basis. They were handsome, bustling, successful
> affairs, with a host of clerks and a swarm of patrons. Carrie passed along the
> busy aisles, much affected by the remarkable displays of trinkets, dress goods,
> stationery, and jewelry. Each separate counter was a showplace of dazzling
> interest and attraction. She culd [*sic*] not help feeling the claim of each trinket
> and valuable upon her personally, and yet she did not stop. There was nothing
> there which she could not have used—nothing which she did not long to own.
> The dainty slippers and stockings, the delicately frilled skirts and petticoats,
> the laces, ribbons, haircombs, purses, all touched her with individual desire,
> and she felt keenly the fact that not any of these things were in the range of
> her purchase. (26)

The department store encouraged a new kind of shopping, a mode of consumption based on browsing, on a leisurely perusal of unnecessary items

that called out first to the eyes and then to the heart and finally to the purse of a new kind of shopper.[8] Despite Carrie's initial inability to participate fully in this intoxicating realm, despite her inability to consume, we see here the call of commodities, the fulfillment offered by the little slippers and stockings so carefully displayed. Ultimately, the department store encouraged shoppers to see themselves in the commodities that promised to shed their distinction and allure onto those who would purchase them.[9] In short, the department store announced the reign of what Thorstein Veblen has deemed "conspicuous consumption."

In his *Theory of the Leisure Class*, published in 1899, just one year before Dreiser's *Sister Carrie*, Thorstein Veblen describes "conspicuous consumption" as the means by which class distinctions are both claimed and displayed in the modern city.[10] Veblen defines conspicuous consumption as the practice of buying commodities that do not, strictly speaking, "serve human life" (97). In other words, conspicuous commodities are those that are not necessary for survival but are instead, in Veblen's terms, "wasteful" (96). Veblen explains that conspicuous consumption eclipses leisure as the most effective means of demonstrating one's wealth as the modern city becomes an ever more densely populated and increasingly anonymous space. According to Veblen, leisure functions as an effective demonstration of social and economic privilege only in a community that is necessarily rather small and intimate, in which one's personal habits can be known throughout the community. Conversely, in the turn-of-the-century city, in which one cannot possibly know all of one's neighbors, the practices of private leisure might make one simply invisible. Thus commodities, mobile, visible signs of pecuniary strength, come to serve as more effective markers of class station in the consumer culture of the city (86–89).

While the anonymity of the city encouraged new forms of social surveillance, such as the Rogues' Gallery which incited individuals to study disguises, and the criminal typologies, which impelled individuals to categorize the whirl of faces that rushed by them in the streets, that same anonymity invited new performances of identity and shows of distinction. For if surveillance proposed that one could read the faces and bodies of others, it also reminded viewers that their own bodies were constantly on exhibit for a scrutinizing gaze. Thus surveillance both coincided with and encouraged a culture of display, a culture in which the spectacle of the commodity enabled members of the middle classes to present the "correct" identities. As Theodore Dreiser depicts that culture in *Sister Carrie*, such acts ultimately might usurp the purported power of viewing, capturing and overwhelming an entranced gaze.

The power of the commodity spectacle to unsettle the privilege of a gaze is illuminated by the surprising visual analogy upon which Karl Marx draws to describe the mysterious allure of the commodity:

A commodity is therefore a mysterious thing, simply because in it the social character of men's labour appears to them as an objective character stamped upon the product of that labour; because the relation of the producers to the sum total of their own labour is presented to them as a social relation, existing not between themselves, but between the products of their labour. This is the reason why the products of labour become commodities, social things whose qualities are at the same time perceptible and imperceptible by the senses. *In the same way the light from an object is perceived by us not as the subjective excitation of our optic nerve, but as the objective form of something outside the eye itself.*[11]

The commodity presents itself to the laborer as a mystifying object utterly detached from his or her physical exertion, as an object foreign to production. The commodity reifies labor, presenting congealed labor back to the worker as the commodity's own possession.[12] Similarly, according to Marx, the viewer fails to see his or her own role in the process of visual perception. A viewer perceives only the object seen, not the embodied process of sight itself (the excitation of the optic nerve). In this sense, sight is conceived as emanating from an object under view, not as the act of the subject viewing. Thus, in Marx's analysis, sight is a kind of perpetual process of mystification. Extending Marx's analogy, one might say that in the phantasmagoria[13] of a consumer culture, the commodity is doubly reified: First, as it objectifies labor as a characteristic of its own possession, the commodity presents itself as an object utterly detached from the physical production of the laborer; second, as it is perceived primarily through vision, the commodity is seen as a vision-generating object that creates and controls the gaze that perceives it.

The phantasmagoria of commodity spectacle overwhelms the sense of sight, numbing the viewer who is mesmerized by enchanting objects of view.[14] In a "society of spectacle,"[15] the viewer is entranced by a reified world that seeks the gaze. At the turn of the century, then, we find that Nathaniel Hawthorne's depiction of powerful viewers mesmerizing, penetrating, and controlling the objects of their gaze has been inverted by the specter of commodities and of commodified subjectivity. In Theodore Dreiser's *Sister Carrie*, viewers are mesmerized, seduced, and subtly overpowered by the objects that seek their view.

As Dreiser's *Sister Carrie* unsettles the privilege of the gaze, it also disrupts the gendered power dynamics according to which consumption and viewing have generally been examined. While consumption has been both associated with women and denigrated as a feminine practice that objectifies and commodifies women, the power of the gaze that watches those feminine objects has typically been deemed masculine. Dreiser's text offers a new way of theorizing these relationships, for while *Sister Carrie* partially maintains the gendered logics by which women consume and self-commodify for a masculine gaze, it also shifts the locus of power and privilege from the position of the gazer to that of the gazed upon. Thus, while women are targeted as consumers by a wide range of advertising practices,[16] and while commodified objects of view are frequently feminized, gendered relations of power shift as feminized objects of view are invested with a kind of agency that escapes or supersedes a mesmerized masculine gaze.

CONSPICUOUS CONSUMPTION UNDER A MASCULINE GAZE: RETHINKING GENDER IN *SISTER CARRIE*

The course of Sister Carrie's commodification, and her relative successes and failures in consumer society, are measured via her relation to a masculine gaze in Theodore Dreiser's text. Dreiser's narrator announces Carrie's status as the object of a masculine gaze in the opening pages of the novel. As Carrie rides a train bound for Chicago, she gradually realizes that she has become the object of admiring looks cast by the man sitting behind her (Drouet)—"She felt him observing her mass of hair" (8). While Drouet's flirtatious solicitude at first makes Carrie rather nervous, confusing slightly her sense of appropriate gender protocol, after she has inspected Drouet's clothes, polish, and genial manner, she decides it is rather pleasant to be the object of this man's gaze: "There was something satisfactory in the attention of this individual with his good clothes" (11). While Drouet's style makes Carrie uncomfortably aware of the poverty of her own dress, it also makes him a valuable admirer. Indeed, Drouet's attention seems to Carrie to transpose some of his own apparent "worth" onto Carrie herself.

The pleasure of receiving Drouet's gaze, and the world of entertainment and glamour that Drouet encourages Carrie to imagine, ends rather abruptly as Carrie is met in Chicago by the "cold reality" of labor, embodied in the figure of her sister, Minnie. The "maze, uproar, and novelty" of the "world of light and merriment," "of amusement," that Carrie dreams of disappears in "the grimness of shift and toil" that seems to cling to Minnie (15).

By utilizing Drouet and Minnie as the two figures that introduce Carrie to Chicago, Dreiser suggests the two different life courses the city offers a young white woman—that of consumption and that of labor. Carrie emphatically, and rather unrealistically, prefers the former, and we see her displeasure with a life of labor emblematized by her discomfort under a gaze. As one seeking employment, Carrie feels herself to be powerless both as the merely curious object of an empowered viewer's gaze and as an alienated viewer on the outside looking in. The narrator describes her uneasiness as follows: "As she contemplated the wide windows and imposing signs, she became conscious of being gazed upon and understood for what she was—a wage seeker" (22). Carrie's unemployment, and consequent deficiency in money and clothes, is emphasized as she becomes aware, again and again, that she is being scrutinized by viewers whom she imagines to be in possession of all that she desires. In The Fair, one of Chicago's great department stores, as Carrie encounters "the eye" of the smartly dressed shopgirls, it is "only to recognize in it a keen analysis of her own position— her individual shortcomings of dress" (27). As a wage seeker, Carrie has not yet become a fully fledged participant in consumer culture;[17] her femininity has not yet been "appropriately" commodified.

Carrie finally does secure a position as an underpaid laborer in, of all things, a shoe factory. The shoes she encounters in the factory do not, however, call out to her warmly, sympathetically, affectionately; these shoes are not yet commodities. Indeed, these shoes come at Carrie only in bits and pieces, all too quickly, down the assembly line. Carrie's discomfort in her newfound position as laborer is marked not only by her physical pain but also by her distress as the object of other laborers' curious looks. At the close of her first day as a factory girl, Carrie begins to receive unwanted scrutiny from the bolder of her male coworkers, and one "dusty, toil-stained youth" (43) aims an aggressive leer in Carrie's face. Disturbed by the attention of laboring men, Carrie spurns the gaze of "boys who, beside Drouet, seemed uncouth and ridiculous" (42).

In Carrie's rejection of her fellow workers, we see that Drouet has become, in Carrie's eyes, the ideal of a masculine admirer after just one brief encounter on the train. Indeed, Carrie does not regain a sense of pleasure at finding herself the object of a masculine gaze until she has been initiated into the process of self-commodification by Drouet. Ultimately, it is Drouet who "saves" Carrie from the world of labor, educates her in the role of consumer, aids her in the process of self-commodification, and finally introduces her to the possibilities a sexual relationship might offer as an economic exchange. It is only with Drouet's money, those "soft, green, handsome" bills (62), that Carrie is able to attract the middle-class masculine gaze she seeks, with the appearance she wants to project.

On a dreary Chicago day, even as Carrie is looking for a new job, Drouet sweeps her up off the street and into the luxurious warmth and sparkle of the Windsor dining room. With Drouet, Carrie does not have to stand as an outsider peering in, avoiding the returned gaze of privilege; with Drouet, Carrie can exercise her own powers of observation. Seated with Drouet at a large window facing the street—Drouet "loved the changing panorama of the street," he loved "to see and be seen as he dined" (58)— Carrie feels at first a bit out of place, but she eventually finds herself buoyed up by the splendid "view of the well-dressed throng" (60). Carrie also finds herself heartened by her view of Drouet. As she sits across from him, "the warmth" of Drouet's "spirit," framed in Carrie's eyes by the material accoutrements of "white napery" and the shine of "silver platters," rubs off onto Carrie, until she feels herself quite a "new girl" (60).

Through her subsequent relations with Drouet, Carrie does indeed become a "new girl." With Drouet's money, Carrie is made over, piece by piece. Drouet becomes Carrie's first guide through the "shine and rustle" (70) of the commodity world, and Carrie depends on Drouet to validate her new self, to mark her new being, with his approving gaze. As Carrie finally is persuaded to try on a much-coveted little tan jacket with mother-of-pearl buttons, Drouet's face "lightens" at the sight —"She looked quite smart" (71). Dreiser details the acquisition of Carrie's first outfit, and Drouet's guiding role as both purchaser and evaluator, item by item: After securing the jacket, the two pick out shoes, purse, gloves, stockings, skirt, and shirtwaist (70–76). Finally, with Drouet's money, Carrie buys "the little necessaries of toilet, until at last she looked quite another maiden." And then, "The mirror convinced her of a few things which she had long believed. She was pretty, yes, indeed! How nice her hat set, and weren't her eyes pretty. She caught her little red lip with her teeth and felt her first thrill of power" (76).

As Rachel Bowlby, Philip Fisher, and Thorstein Veblen have argued, clothes were especially important commodities in an emerging U.S. consumer culture at the turn of the century.[18] According to Veblen, dress became an important marker of class standing in the city precisely because it was so easy to display, to see, and to read: "Our apparel is always in evidence and affords an indication of our pecuniary standing to all observers at first glance."[19] Fashionable clothing made one's consumption "conspicuous" in Veblen's terms, demonstrating one's ability to purchase unnecessary items. For example, in *Sister Carrie*, Caroline Meeber might actually need a coat in order to survive an impending Chicago winter, but it is the "peculiar little tan jacket" with the "large mother-of-pearl buttons" that she really must have. Only that little jacket, the one that is "all the rage" (68), can transform her, in Rachel Bowlby's terms, into a "citizen of consumer society."[20]

In her analysis of the fashion industry, Rachel Bowlby demonstrates how women were enticed not only into buying the "proper" commodities but also into commodifying their own appearances to become themselves "all the rage." As I noted in chapter 3, Bowlby describes Fashion as a kind of mirror held up to women, a surface on which women come to see themselves as images. Once again, Fashion presents an image of the unified, perfected self desired but never attained, thereby reproducing a kind of perpetual Lacanian mirror stage. As women are persuaded to recognize their possible selves in ever-changing images, they are also encouraged to self-conceptualize as the object of a gaze.[21] And while in Bowlby's assessment the gaze for which women self-commodify is typically masculine, in *Sister Carrie*, as we shall see, Fashion entices consumers to reproduce themselves for a gaze that is not exclusively gendered.

As Carrie concludes her inspection and admiration of her newly commodified appearance, she reflects—"Drouet was so good" (76)—and as her fate unfolds, as the "strange tie of affection" (62) that binds Carrie to Drouet solidifies into a more permanent relationship, Carrie continues to judge Drouet's value according to how adeptly he embellishes Carrie's appearance. Thus, while Drouet is constantly admiring and evaluating Carrie's self-commodification, Carrie is also esteeming Drouet according to his capacity to aid her in the process of self-production. Indeed, Drouet's "power" is evaluated according to the degree to which he can make Carrie feel "thrills of power" in her own commodified image (76).

Sister Carrie is never only the object of a masculine gaze in Dreiser's text; she is also always the subject of her own gaze, and quit often both subject and object simultaneously. Indeed, Carrie's image of herself is always first and foremost in her mind as a constant afterimage against which the appearance of other women is perceived. Carrie's self-conception as image allows her to make and remake herself in the ever-changing image of another. Observation is always the initial stage of a repeated practice for Carrie; Carrie looks first to evaluate and to admire, and finally, to imitate.[22] Imitation allows Carrie to avoid stasis, a "satisfied" condition that leads only to death in Dreiser's economy, as Walter Benn Michaels has argued.[23] Thus, what has often been regarded as a passive, nonproductive act—namely, imitation—becomes a site of agency and movement in Dreiser's *Sister Carrie*.

With Drouet's financial resources and his initial guidance, Carrie proves herself a very deft student of "fortune's ways" (99). Carrie sets to imitating everything Drouet admires in other women. When Drouet points out a "fine stepper," Carrie turns to look and immediately compares the woman to herself: "If that was so fine, she must look at it more closely. Instinctively, she felt a desire to imitate it. Surely she could do that too" (100). Carrie very quickly masters the full range of Drouet's "taste"; indeed, Carrie's powers of observation and evaluation soon outstretch those of Drouet himself, and she begins to discern a certain amiable laxity in Drouet's general approval. Carrie's own scrutiny of others is more meticulous, and she makes more subtle distinctions. Further, and perhaps more important, Carrie begins her own study of *men's* fashions, and she begins to notice that Drouet's appearance is not always among the most refined.

In a text that is increasingly read by literary scholars as one that details the transformation of a woman, subsumed by her desire for fashion and fame, into a commodity spectacle, we see that men must also consume conspicuously in order to enter the gendered domain of commodity courtship. Men are constantly measured according to their perceived ability to provide. Drouet, the ultimate admirer and consumer of women, must also self-commodify in order to participate in his favorite exchanges. His appearance and manner are crafted precisely "to elicit the admiration of susceptible young women" (9), and "good clothes, of course, were the first essential, the things without which he was nothing" (10). In order to catch the attention of a young woman, Drouet must walk the "indescribably faint line in the matter of man's apparel which somehow divides for her those who are worth glancing at and those who are not" (10).

In *Sister Carrie* it is not only women, but also men, who must parade themselves under evaluating gazes. Men must pay for the privilege of the masculine gaze through their own conspicuous consumption. A dynamic of vision and visibility, centered around commodity display and engaged in by both men and women, is reenacted repeatedly in Dreiser's text, even long after Drouet and Carrie have parted. Dreiser depicts the Broadway of New York City as an arena in which "all the pretty women who love a showy parade," and "the men who love to gaze upon and admire them" (288), gather to pursue one another and to be pursued. While the scene on Broadway appears to be constructed for "the men who love to gaze," those men must nevertheless purchase a pricey entrance into this fabulous throng with their own commodified appearances. In order to participate in this interaction of seeing and being seen—in order to look—men must also demonstrate their ability to buy and to be seen. As women decked out in their very best stroll the avenue, the men parade, "equally," in the "very latest" they can afford (288). As Dreiser's narrator explains: "A tailor might have secured hints on suit measurements, a shoemaker on proper lasts and colors, a hatter on hats. It was literally true that if a lover of fine clothes secured a new suit, it was sure to have its first airing on Broadway. So true and well understood was this fact, that several years later a popular song, detailing this and other facts concerning the afternoon parade on matinee days, and entitled 'What Right Has He on Broadway?' was published, and had quite a vogue" (288). Men must demonstrate their "rights" to be on Broadway, to assume an admiring gaze, with their own ability to draw attention to themselves. Only men with "flawless topcoats, high hats, and silver-headed walking sticks" are welcome to look into "conscious eyes" (289). Hurstwood comments on the restricted nature of the privilege of the masculine gaze after his own economic decline is well under way. Chancing upon the Broadway throng, "he [sees] coquettish glances cast by magnificent girls" and muses to himself, "Ah, the money it required to train with such—how well he knew!" (324).

Theodore Dreiser's *Sister Carrie* offers cultural critics an opportunity to reread, in a more nuanced manner, the *economic* underpinnings of the heterosexual relationship, and the *heterosexual* underpinnings of the economic relationship at the turn of the century, especially as they are described by Thorstein Veblen. In *The Theory of the Leisure Class*, Veblen argues that women serve as auxiliary exhibits for men in a culture of conspicuous consumption, demonstrating men's ability to pay for their fashionable clothing and jewelry.[24] Women's consumption displays the buying power of their husbands. Veblen's equation of women's consumption with men's pecuniary strength is possible, of course, only because he assumes women's economic dependence on men. In other words, Veblen supposes that women shop only with money that belongs to men. And while such gendered economic relationships were still overwhelmingly common at the turn of the century, women could also claim new legal powers of possession by that time. The laws of coverture were gradually rewritten over the course of the nineteenth century, granting women the ability to claim ownership of property and ownership of the self in new ways.[25] Such laws inform Carrie's economic success in *Sister Carrie*,[26] but Dreiser also carefully demonstrates the possible consequences of the dominant gendered economic relationship for men, suggesting that women can be powerful negotiators in such transactions, precisely *as* the commodified objects of a masculine gaze. In Dreiser's world, men can no longer remain stable fixtures in a patriarchal system that circulates commodities and exchanges women as commodities. In Dreiser's consumer culture, men must self-commodify in order to participate in patriarchal exchange.

As Amy Kaplan has explained, Dreiser himself, as author, felt rather keenly the need to self-commodify for a consumer audience composed primarily of white women readers. As Kaplan suggests, Dreiser came to see writing as a process not only of producing but also of marketing.[27] And the commodity to be marketed was not simply the literary text but also the author himself: The author had to "project a personage as an objectified commodity."[28] In this sense, then, we might reinterpret an early editorial Dreiser wrote for *Every Month*, treating "the tendency of wealthy American women to ignore budding young geniuses,"[29] as a comment on Dreiser's gendered relationship to women consumers. For as women become buyers, and authors (of both genders) become sellers, male "geniuses" assume a paradoxical position in the circulation of (destabilized) patriarchal exchange. As consumers, wealthy American women, once ripe for patriarchy's traffic in women, come to control the circulation of commodities produced by men.[30]

Sister Carrie was not actively promoted by Doubleday, Page when it was first published, due to its "unpleasant" subject matter; in fact, the novel very nearly was not published at all.[31] Initial editorial responses alluded to Dreiser's purportedly scandalous depiction of Carrie's sexual behavior and suggested that such a subject might offend women readers.[32] However, I think we might also read in the ambiguous responses to this novel anxiety over Dreiser's representation of a vulnerable white patriarchy. For

Dreiser's tale suggests not only that unvirtuous white *women* might rise, but also that unvirtuous white *men* might fall. In Dreiser's novel, it is not Carrie who goes off and quietly kills herself, as does Stephen Crane's Maggie and a host of other turn-of-the-century "fallen" heroines;[33] instead, it is Carrie's second lover, Hurstwood, who commits suicide. Ultimately, Carrie's sexual purity is not what is really at stake in Dreiser's novel, and what may have been truly "threatening" about *Sister Carrie* is Dreiser's depiction of a patriarchy that is no longer omnipotent in economic and heterosexual relations. In the consumer patriarchy that Dreiser represents, men's economic privilege is maintained only so long as it converges with their sexual relations. While Carrie enters into economic (and sexual) relationships with men, eventually to become economically and sexually *independent* of men, Hurstwood finds himself inextricably bound economically to his wife, on the one hand, and emasculated by his inability to provide for his new mistress, on the other.

Having traced the beginnings of Carrie's self-commodification, a process first enabled by her economic dependence on Drouet, I would like to describe here the beginnings of her perceived independence from men, precisely *as* a commodity, and as the commodified object of a masculine gaze. Carrie's awakening to the sense of freedom that her newly commodified appearance might grant occurs as she enters the world of the theater, as an amateur actress. In her first performance, after a rather dreadful start, Carrie finally makes a hit, and her success sends her suitors into a flurry of excitement, leading each to claim her as his prize. After her small triumph, Hurstwood "felt a keen delight in realizing that she was *his*" (175; emphasis added), and Drouet is "delighted with his *possession*" (176; emphasis added). Both begin to see Carrie, with her talents framed by the stage, and praised by so many, as a commodity "worthy" of their devotions (180–181). Drouet revels: "He would marry her, by George! She was worth it" (180). However, Carrie's rising value as a commodity on display also makes her a "prize" (182) to be competed for, and Hurstwood resolves, "By the Lord, he would have that lovely girl if it took his all. . . . The drummer [Drouet] should not have her" (181).

Carrie's success makes her suitors see what they perceive to be her "true" value, and both seek to claim her, to align themselves with this brilliance. The exchange of money for sexual intimacy no longer satisfies Drouet, and for the first time he hopes to marry Carrie. Drouet seeks to harness this spectacular being to himself by socially acceptable means and, in Veblen's terms, to display Carrie publicly as his dependent, to claim her successes as his own showings. However, after Carrie's success, Drouet finds that his offer of marriage is professed too late. Further, because Drouet has not legally bound Carrie to himself, her current success not only fails to bolster

Drouet's worth but also gives Carrie something with which to negotiate in new economic and heterosexual interactions.

While Carrie's triumph on stage sends her suitors into a frenzy, Carrie's response to their passion is surprisingly calm for a young woman feeling her first success. Carrie smiles, clearly pleased, but her actions bear a note of sweet condescension: "The little actress was in fine feather. She was realizing now what it was to be petted. For once she was the admired, the sought-for. The independence of success now made its first faint showing. With the tables turned, she was looking down, rather than up, to her lover" (181). Carrie's accomplishment makes her suitors feel more strongly tied to her than ever, but for Carrie it signifies the beginnings of her "independence." Even Drouet, with his very limited powers of perception, notes that after her performance Carrie no longer "[studies] him" "with eyes expressive of dependence" (186). Indeed, the day after her first success, Carrie meets with Hurstwood and agrees to leave Drouet (194).

Carrie's initial experience as an amateur actress foreshadows the career she will have later as a professional chorus girl and comic actress in New York. Ultimately, it is Carrie's work on stage that completes the process of her commodification, and also, paradoxically, takes her out of the domain of patriarchal control. One might say that by becoming the ultimate commodity, the most dazzling object of a masculine gaze, Carrie embraces commodification so thoroughly that she bypasses patriarchal exchange.

According to Philip Fisher, the actress sells her "self, her inner emotional being," to a paying audience.[34] However, Fisher maintains that even as she seems to sell her "inner self" to any number of ticket holders, acting allows the actress "to preserve a freedom of the self from its appearance."[35] Shifting Fisher's argument, I would like to suggest that acting, as it is portrayed in *Sister Carrie*, enables not a freedom of self from its appearance but instead a freedom of self from the binding transaction of exchange.[36] Further, I would like to propose that the "essence" that the actress sells is not her own but a kind of *empathy*, an imagined empathetic relationship that she establishes between her audience and herself. Indeed, it is Carrie's ability, as an actress, to project empathy that perhaps most clearly defines her role as commodity, even as she remains a commodity that, ultimately, can be neither bought nor sold.

As we have already seen, Carrie herself hears the empathetic call of commodities quite clearly—leather shoes and lace collars speak "tenderly," pleading their exceptional capacities to meet Carrie's particular needs. Carrie succumbs easily to the call of commodities, but she also learns how to project her own powerful empathy through self-commodification and performative self-display. Seduced by commodities, Carrie transforms herself into a self-commodified seductress. As an actress, Carrie projects empathy to her audience, especially to her masculine viewers; she becomes a "delicious little morsel" (411). "All the gentlemen [yearn] toward her" (411), and all imagine that she wants to nestle in their houses and hands. Even Ames, who would like to change Carrie, recognizes her particular power to be a kind of empathy. Ames discerns Carrie's "disposition," her "nature," to be rather "sympathetic" (445). That "something peculiar" about Carrie's mouth and the "depth" of her eyes (447) is, according to Ames, "a thing the world likes to see, because it's a natural expression of its longing" (448). For Ames, as for other masculine viewers, Carrie's face becomes, once again, the "representative of all desire" (448).[37]

As an actress, Carrie epitomizes the very soul of the commodity, namely, empathy itself. The men who yearn for her as they gaze upon her imagine that Carrie calls out to each of them individually, pleading with them to let her fulfill their specific needs. Carrie's face represents the desires her audience cannot articulate. As Ames explains, "Most people are not capable of voicing their feelings. They depend upon others" (448). Carrie's face acts as a kind of magic mirror, reflecting the emotions of those who pay to watch her. She objectifies and makes visible the thoughts and desires of others, giving them substance through her empathetic performance. Carrie's function as actress is therefore analogous to the "effective demand based on money" that Karl Marx describes. For just as money, according to Marx, can convert "the imagined which exists merely within me [into] the imagined as it is for me outside me as a real object,"[38] Carrie transforms the interiorized imagination and desire of her audience into something external, into something "real." As Carrie's face comes to emblematize her viewers' desire, it affirms the very existence of her audience. Thus, as represented in Dreiser's novel, the paradoxical nature of sight is not only, as Marx suggests in his description of the commodity, that the viewer fails to see him- or herself embodying vision, but also that the viewer begins to see him- or herself materializing in the object viewed. If, as Marx implies, the viewer perceives the object to be the active agent in sight, in Dreiser's text this dynamic is intensified to the point that the viewer begins to see himself represented in the object he views. Entranced by commodified empathy, the viewer finds himself embodied in and by the actress who projects his desire and imagination, thereby making his interiority "real" through her performance and display. In this sense, then, one might say that in Dreiser's *Sister Carrie* the commodified object of view performs a portrait of her viewer, capturing his interior essence in her every gesture.

While Carrie offers her enacted empathy to be consumed by a viewing audience, she does not offer her body as a commodity to be possessed materially. Carrie's male suitors do not always understand the subtlety of this exchange, and as Carrie becomes a popular New York showgirl, she receives countless letters and marriage proposals from men who "love" her and seek to possess her as their own. One suitor demonstrates his love with an explicit offer: "I have a million in my own right. I could give you every luxury" (419). As Carrie now is able to provide her own luxuries, she is no longer taken in by such bids. Carrie masters self-commodification, but she does not enter patriarchal exchange. As the supreme, commodified object of a masculine gaze, Carrie now dominates that gaze. No longer a wage seeker, and no longer economically dependent on men, Carrie no longer assumes that her viewers are empowered, or that they possess anything she might desire.

Carrie's rise to stardom and wealth is depicted against the backdrop of Hurstwood's fall into pauperism and poverty, and, at the end of Dreiser's tale, Drouet makes a cameo appearance, so that readers may perceive that he has not changed at all. If clothes provide a clear indication of one's pecuniary standing, as Veblen suggests, the reader can see, at a glance, in Carrie's gowns, in Hurstwood's rags, and in Drouet's immutable suit, how Dreiser's characters have fared in consumer culture.

Hurstwood is "punished" in Dreiser's novel because he violates the economic and heterosexual mores delineated by the practice of conspicuous consumption as outlined by Veblen. Hurstwood steals money and kidnaps Carrie, in a culture that demands that men "earn" money in order to attract women. If commodities are not paid for, then they cease to function as "true" indicators of one's pecuniary strength. Hurstwood breaks the ties that bind financial power to conspicuous consumption, as well as those that tie women to men, and thereby initiates a series of events that ultimately leads to his own extinction. Hurstwood's first mistake is his failure to keep his economic and sexual interests on the same trajectory; his wife catches him in an affair, divorces him, and sues for alimony. Thus, Hurstwood is faced with having to provide the means for his wife's conspicuous consumption, without being able to claim her displays as the effects of his own buying power. In this sense, Hurstwood's wife becomes a free agent at his expense. At this juncture, Hurstwood steals money, demonstrating the beginnings of his pecuniary weakness, of his failure to provide "properly" for either of the women in his life. Finally, Hurstwood fails to win Carrie, and ends up stealing her as well.

As Dreiser's novel draws to a close, Hurstwood's inability to provide for Carrie is symbolized by his increasingly unkempt appearance. Hurstwood's consumption fails to be conspicuous, and he even begins to begrudge spending money for the necessities of daily sustenance.[39] Hurstwood's utter failure as a male citizen of consumer society is epitomized on the day he sits at home in his shabby clothes, as Carrie goes to work in order to support them both. Given the logic of conspicuous consumption as Dreiser depicts it, this inverted gender relationship cannot last long. Carrie is unable to imagine that she might continue to be the provider for Hurstwood; her sense of appropriate gender protocol allows her to support herself but

requires a man to support her if she is sexually involved with one. Soon Carrie is angered by Hurstwood's expectation that she will follow him on his way down the economic ladder. Upon discovering that Hurstwood never actually married her, that she is not bound to him in any legal way, Carrie decides that she really "needs" whatever money she earns as a show-girl in order to pay for her clothes. Hurstwood is not holding up his end of the gender relationship endemic to this consumer culture, and Carrie feels no need to sacrifice her own conspicuous consumption in order to support him. Leaving Hurstwood with twenty dollars (the exact amount she herself originally received from Drouet), Carrie abandons her lover to become the commodified object of a masculine gaze on the stage.

PARTING GLANCES

The consumer culture of conspicuous consumption that Carrie so success-fully manipulates is a culture founded in and perpetuated by gazing. But the gaze engendered by commodified spectacle is not the empowered gaze of a surveillant system, such as that embraced by Alphonse Bertillon or that theorized by Michel Foucault.[40] For while surveillance typically imagines an observer who exercises control over objects and bodies under view, a society of spectacle poses a viewer controlled by the objects that capture the gaze.[41] The viewer who is captivated by commodities in the world of conspicuous consumption occupies a relatively disempowered position in relation to the subversive agency of the commodity. In this way, then, Dreiser's *Sister Carrie* enables us to imagine a visual relationship that partially undermines the authority of scientific and disciplinary surveillance in turn-of-the-century U.S. culture. Not entirely unlike W. E. B. Du Bois's photographic *Types of American Negroes*, or Pauline Hopkins's biracial hero-ines, Dreiser's depiction of conspicuous consumption suggests that objects of view may be empowered in ways that escape the disciplinary gaze of surveillance.

Theodore Dreiser's fiction entertains the failure of "objective" observa-tion, examining the ways in which lust and anxiety ever threaten to collapse or reconfigure the relationship between viewer and viewed. As June How-ard explains, the naturalist narrator's privileged location and authority is never quite secure because "fear and desire—sexual passion and violence, the fatal spell of the commodity, the fascination of the Other—constantly disrupt the design of safety" posited by narrative distance.[42] While the nat-uralist text purports to demonstrate the higher, more objective knowledge of a narrator situated somewhere beyond the forces of determinism that control the world of blind, powerless characters,[43] the authoritative identity of the narrator always threatens to dissolve into the observed other as desire and fear unsettle the divide posed by surveillance.

In this light, the concluding passage of Dreiser's *Sister Carrie* which has so troubled literary critics, in which the masculine narrator despairs Carrie's fate in moralizing tones—"Oh, Carrie, Carrie!" (464)—might be reexamined as a comment on the narrator's viewing position. For as the narrator admonishes Carrie—"In your rocking chair, by your window dreaming, shall you long, alone. In your rocking chair, by your window, shall you dream such happiness as you may never feel" (465)—he also marks his own position as the entranced observer of this scene.[44] One surmises that if Carrie must remain by her window, the narrator must also remain there with her, observing her, his surveillant masculine gaze mesmerized by a feminine commodity he can never possess.[45]

Dreiser's *Sister Carrie* offers new ways of reading the position and the relative power not only of woman-as-consumer and of woman-as-commodity but also of Woman as the object of a masculine gaze. Dreiser's text proposes that in these very positions women can attain a kind of ambiguous agency, a mobility with which they may stir, if not out of consumer culture, then perhaps out of the confines of patriarchal exchange. Carrie's challenge to patriarchal gender privilege is undermined, of course, by her dogged reinforcement of class privilege—she utterly dismisses the labor that produces the commodities by which she in turn reproduces herself. Further, Carrie's unquestioned whiteness grants her a mobility denied to Pauline Hopkins's Aurelia, Jewel, and Dianthe, who are ruined by the logics of a white supremacist patriarchy. But while these serious limitations make it impossible to celebrate Carrie as a truly feminist heroine, my reading of Carrie's agency might redirect those critiques of commodity capitalism that condemn consumption by deeming it "feminine." If we denigrate Carrie, a commodified woman-consumer, as "merely imitative," and not productive, we may miss her capacity to disrupt the discourses that circumscribe the "productive" role of the white middle-class woman in the home. Certainly Carrie's devotion to her shoes is a little odd, but in heeding their call, she walks away from other middle-class demands.

A Brief Look at American Visual Culture in the 1990s

IN THE FALL of 1993, the editors of *Time* magazine created a new American cover girl, a computer-generated, "multiethnic" "Eve."[1] For a special issue devoted to immigration and national identity, *Time* introduced this "new Eve" as "a symbol of the future, multiethnic face of America." Like her namesake, the new Eve was described as "beguiling," "mysterious," seductive. Of her creation *Time* tells us: "As onlookers watched the image of our new Eve begin to appear on the computer screen, several staff members promptly fell in love." One proclaimed: " 'It really breaks my heart that she doesn't exist' " (2). As *Time* calls attention to Eve's mesmerizing allure, the editors also emphasize the fact that she is unreal, a mere figment of the imagination: "The woman on the cover of this special issue of *Time* does not exist—except metaphysically. Her beguiling if mysterious visage is the product of a computer process called morphing" (2). Despite such proclamations to the contrary, I am interested precisely in how this new Eve *does* exist—as image, as captivating emblem of desire and anxiety, as symbol of a historically codified imagination. How was this "multiethnic face of America" conceived?

Time's "new face" has a very old history, a genealogy stemming from the inaugural moments this book has studied. The image is not simply the product of the new visual technology of morphing but also the result of a long legacy of racial science and visual typology, of the discourses and images that have defined racial inscription in the United States. *Time*'s new Eve suggests that such logics are still powerfully present in contemporary U.S. visual culture, and intimates that one will not understand fully the layered signifying registers of today's racial images without looking to their historical antecedents.

Time's multiethnic Eve is a strange, minutely divided mathematical composite. Her face is described as "15% Anglo-Saxon, 17.5% Middle Eastern, 17.5% African, 7.5% Asian, 35% Southern European and 7.5% Hispanic" (2). One might question how it was possible to settle on the image of a "Hispanic type," and then to visualize a 7.5% portion of it. We have seen the roots of such conceptions developed in the nineteenth-century sciences of phrenology, physiognomy, and biological racialism, and emblematized most dramatically in the photographic experiments of Francis Galton, the founder of eugenics. Indeed, in Galton's work we found a paradigmatic

Time cover, fall special issue 1993, "The New Face of America." Copyright 1993 TIME Inc. Reprinted with permission.

obsession with racial reproduction, the visual codification of racial "types," and statistical fractions of "typical" faces.

One might say that the abstract images of racial types and the narratives of biological reproduction that Galton sought to represent with his composite portraits and his family photograph albums have resurfaced in the computer morphing program that *Time* imaging specialist Kin Wah Lam designed to produce multiethnic Eve. In addition to this striking cover image, Lam also created an interracial reproduction grid that aimed to entertain viewers with visions of biracial progeny (66–67). To make this grid, Lam began with fourteen images of models, seven men and seven women, representing a curious mix of racial, ethnic, national, and regional groups: Middle Eastern, Italian, African, Vietnamese, Anglo-Saxon, Chinese, and Hispanic (66–67). Using his morphing software, Lam then paired these images together in fifty-fifty ratios, producing a pattern that purports to predict the physical features that would be inherited by the offspring of interracial reproductions. While *Time* states that it "makes no claim to scientific accuracy" with its visual chart, and presents Lam's results in the "spirit of fun and experiment" (2), such contemporary play is enabled only by a history of scientific racial production. In a sense, Lam's computer graphics program begins where Galton's composite photographic portraiture ended, by envisioning distinct ethnic types, to then project the representation of "race" in a direction Galton himself did not want to proceed, namely, toward mixture. Thus, Lam's project might seem, at first, to be a radical departure from eugenicist logics; however, a commitment to racial percentages, to images of racial parts, reaffirms a belief in the distinct essences of racial and ethnic types that Galton sought to establish and reinforce.

Time's visual grid works on the assumption that racial "types" can be measured and itemized mathematically, divided into fractions, and combined with other racial components. And, of course, this assumption becomes even more salient in the image of the new Eve. Once again, this "ideal" image is "15% Anglo-Saxon, 17.5% Middle Eastern, 17.5% African, 7.5% Asian, 35% Southern European and 7.5% Hispanic" (2). The new Eve is part this and part that, but she is always the sum of statistically equivalent pieces. Eve's mathematically divided racial and ethnic composition signals a renewed interest in separating racial "types," even as it envisions them mixing, for the racial "type" itself remains (at least ideologically) discrete in this composite.[2] Indeed, why else is it important to know with exactly what parts and in exactly what portions this image was realized? In the percentages that compose *Time*'s new Eve we find the fractions of racial "essence" that constitute Galton's composite portraits—the ghostly one-fourth, one-eighth, one-sixteenth parts. A code of visual distinctions remains intact, if ever more meticulously codified, even as racial mixture is imagined. In short, multicultural identity is figured as the sum of "separate but equal" parts.

Time's new Eve frames articles that demonstrate that the United States is still an ideologically white-dominated nation fascinated, and yet concerned, like nineteenth- and early-twentieth-century eugenicists, by the "coloring" of America. In the editorial that introduces this special issue, entitled "America's Immigrant Challenge," the editors assert that "the U.S. before long will have to redefine just who its minorities are" (3), predicting that African Americans will soon be outnumbered by Latinos in the United States. Further, according to the editors, and "even more startling," "sometime during the second half of the 21st century the descendants of white Europeans, the arbiters of the core national culture for most of its existence, are likely to slip into minority status" (5). Quoting Martha Farnsworth Riche, the director of policy studies at Washington's Population Reference Bureau, the editors note: " 'We have left the time when the nonwhite, non-Western part of our population could be expected to assimilate to the dominant majority. In the future, the white, Western majority will have to do some assimilation of its own' " (5). In *Time*'s multicultural issue, the "origins" of an American nation delineated by an image of Anglo-Saxon whiteness are mourned as Anglo-Saxon identity becomes one racial and ethnic statistic among many.

In thinking about "America's Immigrant Challenge," we might reconsider the inaugural history of the Daughters of the American Revolution. Didn't the Daughters produce an image of "true" Anglo-Saxon American identity during a period of increased immigration, and during a time in which white American fascination with and fear of racial mixing was especially intense, when not only visual typologies but also "one drop" of blood identity laws sought to define and determine racial "essence"? Given the striking similarities between discourses of racial and national identities in the 1890s and 1990s, it is uncertain how the image of multiethnic Eve might function for those white Americans nervous about the prospects of their minority status. Will *Time*'s new Eve serve simply as a prediction, then, or as an image of America's "fall" from a white "paradise"—a representation that incites white middle-class women to reinscribe and literally to reproduce a privileged white American identity?

What *Time*'s new Eve does make clear is that contemporary attempts to envision, to define, and to codify racial and national identities, as well as to determine where and when those constructs intersect, diverge, and can be challenged, are haunted by their explicitly racist nineteenth-century origins.[3] In order to understand American visual culture today, we need to look back to foundational moments in nineteenth-century visual culture and "race" science. Finally, *Time*'s new American cover girl would seem to suggest that the United States remains a nation in which "the ability to read facial types" is considered "a matter of vital importance."[4]

Notes

Introduction
American Archives

1. Walter Benjamin, "A Small History of Photography," in *One Way Street and Other Writings*, trans. Edmund Jephcott and Kingsley Shorter (London: New Left Books, 1979), 252.

2. Allan Sekula, "The Body and the Archive," *October* 39 (Winter 1986): 3–64.

3. Judith Butler, *Gender Trouble: Feminism and the Subversion of Identity* (New York: Routledge, 1990), 136.

4. Benedict Anderson, *Imagined Communities: Reflections on the Origin and Spread of Nationalism* (London: Verso, 1983).

5. Ibid.

6. In her important study of ethnographic film, Fatimah Tobing Rony describes such visual resistance as the work of "the third eye," which recognizes "the process of being visualized as an object, but returns the glance" (213). Fatimah Tobing Rony, *The Third Eye: Race, Cinema, and Ethnographic Spectacle* (Durham, N.C.: Duke University Press, 1996).

7. Michel Foucault, *Discipline and Punish: The Birth of the Prison*, trans. Alan Sheridan (New York: Vintage, 1979).

8. Jonathan Crary, *Techniques of the Observer: On Vision and Modernity in the Nineteenth Century* (Cambridge: MIT Press, 1990), 71.

9. Sekula, "The Body and the Archive."

10. "White supremacist gaze" is bell hooks's useful phrase. bell hooks, "In Our Glory: Photography and Black Life," in *Picturing Us: African American Identity in Photography*, ed. Deborah Willis (New York: New Press, 1994), 50.

11. Walter Benjamin, "The Work of Art in the Age of Mechanical Reproduction," in *Illuminations*, ed. Hannah Arendt, trans. Harry Zohn (New York: Schocken Books, 1969), 217–252.

12. Linda K. Kerber, *Women of the Republic: Intellect and Ideology in Revolutionary America* (Chapel Hill: University of North Carolina Press, 1980).

13. Hazel V. Carby, *Reconstructing Womanhood: The Emergence of the Afro-American Woman Novelist* (New York: Oxford University Press, 1987).

Chapter One
Prying Eyes and Middle-Class Magic in *The House of the Seven Gables*

1. Nathaniel Hawthorne, *The House of the Seven Gables* (1851; New York: Signet, 1981), 328. I will be referring to this edition throughout this chapter. Subsequent citations will be given as parenthetical page numbers within the text.

2. The scholarly model of "separate spheres" that dominated discussions of antebellum middle-class American culture from the early 1970s to the late 1980s proposed that the activities of women and men in the antebellum period were divided

strictly into two distinct, gendered "spheres": a feminine, "private" domestic space, and a masculine, "public," capitalist domain. Influential historical studies of "private and public," "separate" middle-class social structures include Nancy Cott, *The Bonds of Womanhood: "Woman's Sphere" in New England, 1780–1835* (New Haven, Conn.: Yale University Press, 1977); Barbara Leslie Epstein, *The Politics of Domesticity: Women, Evangelism, and Temperance in Nineteenth-Century America* (Middletown, Conn.: Wesleyan University Press, 1981); Mary P. Ryan, *Cradle of the Middle Class: The Family in Oneida County, New York, 1790–1865* (Cambridge: Cambridge University Press, 1981); and Barbara Welter, *Dimity Convictions: The American Woman in the Nineteenth Century* (Athens: Ohio University Press, 1976). For a remarkable overview of shifts in the scholarly use of the construct "separate spheres," see Linda K. Kerber, "Separate Spheres, Female Worlds, Woman's Place: The Rhetoric of Women's History," *Journal of American History* 75 (June 1988): 9–39.

Important literary studies of nineteenth-century women's fiction and the domestic novel influenced by a model of "separate spheres" include Nina Baym, *Woman's Fiction: A Guide to Novels by and about Women in America, 1820–1870* (Ithaca, N.Y.: Cornell University Press, 1978); Mary Kelley, *Private Woman, Public Stage: Literary Domesticity in Nineteenth-Century America* (New York: Oxford University Press, 1984); and Jane Tompkins, *Sensational Designs: The Cultural Work of American Fiction, 1790–1860* (New York: Oxford University Press, 1984). Laura Wexler provides an important overview of the literary and cultural debates that grew out of studies of sentimental and domestic fiction in "Tender Violence: Literary Eavesdropping, Domestic Fiction, and Educational Reform," in *The Culture of Sentiment: Race, Gender, and Sentimentality in Nineteenth-Century America*, ed. Shirley Samuels (New York: Oxford University Press, 1992), 9–38.

The following studies have begun to problematize the formulation of "separate spheres": Richard H. Brodhead, "Veiled Ladies: Toward a History of Antebellum Entertainment," *American Literary History* 1:2 (Summer 1989): 273–294; Lori D. Ginzberg, *Women and the Work of Benevolence: Morality, Politics, and Class in the Nineteenth-Century United States* (New Haven, Conn.: Yale University Press, 1990); Kerber, "Separate Spheres"; Linda K. Kerber, Nancy F. Cott, Robert Gross, Lynn Hunt, Carroll Smith-Rosenberg, and Christine M. Stansell, Forum: "Beyond Roles, Beyond Spheres: Thinking about Gender in the Early Republic," *William and Mary Quarterly* 46 (1989): 565–585.

In her examination of early twentieth-century women social scientists, Rosalind Rosenberg has studied the first women to challenge systematically the notion of innate sexual difference that undergirded the social construct of separate spheres. Rosalind Rosenberg, *Beyond Separate Spheres: Intellectual Roots of Modern Feminism* (New Haven, Conn.: Yale University Press, 1982).

3. Gillian Brown, *Domestic Individualism: Imagining Self in Nineteenth-Century America* (Berkeley: University of California Press, 1990), 1.

4. In her foundational study of gender and domesticity in nineteenth-century middle-class America, Barbara Welter defines the tenets of True Womanhood as those of piety, purity, submissiveness, and domesticity. See especially "The Cult of True Womanhood: 1800–1860," in *Dimity Convictions*, 21–41.

Nancy Armstrong provides a formative reading of the ways in which middle-class identity is formulated in the terms of gender in nineteenth-century British novels in *Desire and Domestic Fiction: A Political History of the Novel* (New York: Oxford University Press, 1987). See especially Armstrong's analysis of Jane Austen's *Pride and Prejudice* in chap. 1, "The Rise of Female Authority in the Novel."

Drawing upon Mary P. Ryan's *Cradle of the Middle Class*, Stuart Blumin also analyzes the role gender played in the articulation of nineteenth-century middle-class identity: "Events on the other side of the retail sales counter, and in the 'separate sphere' of domestic womanhood, were influential, perhaps even crucial, in generating new social identities. To this extent, middle-class formation was woman's work." Stuart M. Blumin, *The Emergence of the Middle Class: Social Experience in the American City, 1760–1900* (Cambridge: Cambridge University Press, 1989), 191.

5. In my analysis of how social constructs are configured around the images of envisioned selves, I follow the important work of Susan M. Griffin and Carolyn Porter, both of whom have examined the self as a visual social construct. In her study of Henry James's late texts, Griffin suggests that James's characters (and even James himself) come to a socially defined self-consciousness through visual perception (58–59). In an earlier study, Porter investigates how seeing and being seen establish one's identity in a social world defined in the economic terms of reification. Susan M. Griffin, *The Historical Eye: The Texture of the Visual in Late James* (Boston: Northeastern University Press, 1991); Carolyn Porter, *Seeing and Being: The Plight of the Participant Observer in Emerson, James, Adams, and Faulkner* (Middletown, Conn.: Wesleyan University Press, 1981).

6. My reading here is informed by Peter Brooks's analysis of "prying eyes" "invading" a "private" domain. Peter Brooks, *Body Work: Objects of Desire in Modern Narrative* (Cambridge: Harvard University Press, 1993), 32, 37. I am most interested in Brooks's suggestion that "privacy is consubstantial with the idea of its violation" (37).

7. My analysis resonates with Karen Halttunen's insightful study of middle-class culture, in which she proposes that the "moral terms" in which middle-class identity were most prominently posed in the nineteenth century were those of sentimental sincerity. In *Confidence Men and Painted Women*, Halttunen suggests that "the sentimental ideal of sincerity that shaped the norms of middle-class conduct in the antebellum period was central to the self-conscious self-definition of middle-class culture during the most critical period of its development." Karen Halttunen, *Confidence Men and Painted Women: A Study of Middle-Class Culture in America, 1830–1870* (New Haven, Conn.: Yale University Press, 1982), xvii.

My reading of Hawthorne's romance shifts the terms of Halttunen's claims slightly, to suggest that the antebellum middle classes identified themselves under a banner of interiorized gender virtue.

8. For histories of the daguerreotype see Beaumont Newhall, *The History of Photography* (New York: Museum of Modern Art, 1982); Naomi Rosenblum, *A World History of Photography* (New York: Abbeville Press, 1989); and Robert Taft, *Photography and the American Scene* (New York: Dover, 1989).

9. Oliver Wendell Holmes, quoted in Newhall, *The History of Photography*, 31, 32.

10. Cathy N. Davidson, "Photographs of the Dead: Sherman, Daguerre, Hawthorne," *South Atlantic Quarterly* 89:4 (Fall 1990): 675.

11. John Tagg, *The Burden of Representation: Essays on Photographies and Histories* (Amherst: University of Massachusetts Press, 1988), 37.

12. Cathy N. Davidson suggests that $1.50 was the average price of a daguerreotype throughout the 1840s. Davidson, "Photographs of the Dead," 678.

13. Davidson similarly notes that with daguerreotypy, middle-class and even working-class people "for the first time in history, could afford to purchase a portrait of themselves, a daguerrean emblem of heritage to pass on to their progeny (dime-store redactions of Colonel Pyncheon's portrait)." Davidson, "Photographs of the Dead," 678.

14. Alan Trachtenberg, "Illustrious Americans," in *Reading American Photographs: Images as History, Mathew Brady to Walker Evans* (New York: Hill and Wang, 1989), 21–70; Trachtenberg, "Likeness as Identity: Reflections on the Daguerrean Mystique," in *The Portrait in Photography*, ed. Graham Clarke (London: Reaktion, 1992), 173–192.

15. T. S. Arthur, "American Characteristics: No. V—The Daguerreotypist," *Godey's Lady's Book*, 1849, 353.

16. For an extended discussion of the link between mesmerism and daguerreotypy, and the sexual undertones of both nineteenth-century practices, see Eric J. Sundquist's chapter " 'The Home of the Dead': Representation and Speculation in Hawthorne and *The House of the Seven Gables*," in *Home as Found: Authority and Genealogy in Nineteenth-Century American Literature* (Baltimore, Md.: Johns Hopkins University Press, 1979), esp. 125–138.

17. "The Magnetic Daguerreotypes," *Photographic Art-Journal*, June 1852, 353–359.

My discussion of various "gazes" throughout this chapter is informed by the work of feminist film theorists, such as Mary Ann Doane and Janet Bergstrom, who have challenged Laura Mulvey's foundational essay "Visual Pleasure and Narrative Cinema" by seeking to historicize spectators and spectatorship. Drawing upon this theoretical work, I read specific practices and representations of disparate gazes to assess the ways in which gender and class identities are enacted, challenged, and reconfigured through control of vision and visibility in the mid–nineteenth century. I am interested in the ways in which gazes are gendered within specific historical contexts predating the invention of narrative cinema. While I focus primarily on gender and class in this discussion of the gaze, I take up configurations of racial identity in relation to the gaze in subsequent chapters. Laura Mulvey, "Visual Pleasure and Narrative Cinema," in *Art after Modernism*, ed. Brian Wallis (New York: Museum of Contemporary Art, 1984), 360–374; Mulvey, "Afterthoughts on 'Visual Pleasure and Narrative Cinema' Inspired by *Duel in the Sun*," in *Feminism and Film Theory*, ed. Constance Penley (New York: Routledge, 1988), 69–79; Mary Ann Doane, "Film and the Masquerade: Theorizing the Female Spectator," *Screen* 23:3–4 (September–October 1982): 74–87; Doane, "The Shadow of Her Gaze," in *The Desire to Desire: The Woman's Film of the 1940s* (Bloomington: Indiana University Press, 1987), 176–183; Janet Bergstrom and Mary Ann Doane, "The Female Spectator: Contexts and Directions," *Camera Obscura* 20–21 (May–September 1989): 5–27.

18. For another discussion of the gaze in Hawthorne's work, see Edgar A. Dryden, *Nathaniel Hawthorne: The Poetics of Enchantment* (Ithaca, N.Y.: Cornell Univer-

sity Press, 1977), 68–78. According to Dryden, "Hawthorne's characters find themselves in a threatening world where the primary danger comes from the gaze of other people" (68).

19. Nancy Armstrong describes the aristocratic body on display in her discussion of the British aristocracy in the sixteenth, seventeenth, and eighteenth centuries. According to Armstrong, the aristocratic woman's body "was an ornamental body representing the family's place in an intricately precise set of kinship relations determined by the metaphysics of blood" (*Desire and Domestic Fiction*, 70). While the landed aristocracy of nobility in England may never have existed as such in the United States, Hawthorne's Pyncheons, especially his eighteenth-century Pyncheons, are clearly seeking to land their family name.

20. Alice's aristocratic class status permits her to assume an erotic gaze of mastery, what Laura Mulvey has deemed a "masculine gaze" ("Visual Pleasure and Narrative Cinema").

21. According to Edgar Dryden, "Alice seals her own fate when she cast [*sic*] an 'admiring glance' at Matthew Maule, for he recognizes the threat which her gaze poses to his own subjectivity." Edgar A. Dryden, "Hawthorne's Castle in the Air: Form and Theme in *The House of the Seven Gables*," *English Literary History* 38:2 (1972): 305–306. This scene also demonstrates the extent to which both Alice's and Matthew's subjectivities are positioned at the intersection of class and gender axes.

22. Maule, with his wonderfully phallic, protruding pocket ruler, is clearly sexualized in Alice's objectifying gaze.

23. Nineteenth-century practitioners of mesmerism believed the brain to be divided into two parts: the cerebrum, the domain of voluntary nerves and actions, and the cerebellum, the seat of involuntary nerves and actions. When a subject was mesmerized, his or her cerebrum supposedly was coaxed into an inactive state and effectively replaced by the active cerebrum of the operator; thus, the subject's and the operator's consciousness became one, namely, that of the operator.

Gillian Brown provides a fascinating explanation and analysis of mesmerism in *Domestic Individualism*, 86–90. For histories and further studies of mesmerism, see Robert Darnton, *Mesmerism and the End of the Enlightenment in France* (Cambridge: Harvard University Press, 1968); George Frederick Drinka, *The Birth of Neurosis: Myth, Malady, and the Victorians* (New York: Simon and Schuster, 1984); F. A. Mesmer, *Mesmerism*, trans. George Bloch (Los Altos, Calif.: William Kauffman, 1980); and Maria M. Tartar, *Spellbound: Studies on Mesmerism and Literature* (Princeton, N.J.: Princeton University Press, 1978).

24. Brown, *Domestic Individualism*, 87.

25. Ibid.

26. Utilizing Gayle Rubin's conception of the "traffic in women," namely, the exchange of women in patriarchal culture, Teresa Goddu argues: "Since she is traded as a commodity instead of being exchanged as a gift, Alice serves as a disruptive force instead of as an agent of communal cohesion and stability" (123). See Teresa Goddu, "The Circulation of Women in *The House of the Seven Gables*," *Studies in the Novel* 23:1 (Spring 1991): 119–127, esp. 122–124; and Gayle Rubin, "The Traffic in Women: Notes on the 'Political Economy of Sex,' " in *Toward an*

Anthropology of Women, ed. Rayna Reiter (New York: Monthly Review Press, 1975), 157–210.

27. Gordon Hutner, *Secrets and Sympathy: Forms of Disclosure in Hawthorne's Novels* (Athens: University of Georgia Press, 1988), 88. As Hutner has stated, Holgrave learns from his own story and its effects the secret of "the respect for the fundamental mystery of another person and the subsequent necessity for the 'rare and high quality of reverence for another's individuality' " (86–87).

28. Hepzibah's perpetual scowl may be an ancestral curse, the remnant of Alice Pyncheon's once-haughty gaze.

29. Hawthorne's text suggests that Phoebe's purifying effect on the Pyncheons' ancestral house may also initiate a transformation in the aristocratic system of patriarchal exchange. As Phoebe establishes herself as mistress of her own domestic sphere, her home may also become her legal property, an heirloom she can pass on to her children, property that will follow matriarchal bloodlines. Hawthorne wrote *The House of the Seven Gables* only a few years after the enactment of the first New York Married Women's Property Act (1848), a law that permitted women to maintain control over the property they brought into or accrued during marriage. Gillian Brown provides a suggestive analysis of women's property rights and familial inheritance in *The House of the Seven Gables* in "Hawthorne, Inheritance, and Women's Property," *Studies in the Novel* 23:1 (Spring 1991): 107–118.

30. See especially Lori Ginzberg's study of middle-class women's benevolence work in the nineteenth century. Ginzberg analyzes the extension of women's "moral suasion" out of the home and into the realm of business organization. She demonstrates that "true" women entered the public domain of charity collection, organization, and distribution under the banner of women's moral superiority in the early nineteenth century. Ginzberg, *Women and the Work of Benevolence*.

31. As Hepzibah opens her little shop, she can no longer even pretend to play the role her forebear Alice once performed, that of aristocratic body on display for an elite gaze.

32. In her chapter on *The House of the Seven Gables*, entitled "Women's Work and Bodies in *The House of the Seven Gables*" (63–95), Gillian Brown also discusses this scene as Hepzibah's "subjection to sight." Brown, *Domestic Individualism*, 85.

33. Blumin, *The Emergence of the Middle Class*, 10.

34. Gordon Hutner has noted that as Hawthorne's romance concludes, "male and female live together without the oppressive weight of class and gender prejudices" (*Secrets and Sympathy*, 100). In my reading, it is precisely the union of complementary hetero-normal gender positions that masks the "oppressive weight" of middle-class dominance in Hawthorne's romance.

35. Through this union, Holgrave, once the radical spokesman for "self-reliance" and social reform, becomes partial heir to the Pyncheon property with an ease and rapidity that has long puzzled and disappointed twentieth-century Hawthorne scholars. Michael Gilmore has read Hawthorne's ending as representative of the conflict Hawthorne faced both as a writer of private, even dark, truths and as an author called upon to please a reading audience with the sunshine of happy endings. Michael T. Gilmore, "The Artist and the Marketplace in *The House of the Seven Gables*," *English Literary History* 48:1 (Spring 1981): 182, 184, 187.

Nina Baym suggests, in accord with Hawthorne's own account of his attempt " 'to pour some setting-sunshine' " over a text that " 'darkens damnably towards the close,' " that the ending of *The House of the Seven Gables* reflects the conflict that emerges for Hawthorne "between the writer Hawthorne wants to be and the writer he has discovered himself to be." Nina Baym, *The Shape of Hawthorne's Career* (Ithaca, N.Y.: Cornell University Press, 1976), 153. In another particularly suggestive analysis of the close of *The House of the Seven Gables*, Baym demonstrates how Holgrave's ultimate transformation identifies the "hero" of what I have deemed a romance of middle-class ascendance as an inherently conservative "solid social citizen." Nina Baym, "Hawthorne's Holgrave: The Failure of the Artist-Hero," *Journal of English and Germanic Philology* 69 (1970): 598.

Similarly, Gordon Hutner proposes that "the secret that the novel demonstrates but cannot say is the disharmony underlying its sentimental vision of union and progress" (*Secrets and Sympathy*, 100). Hutner also suggests that the discord of Hawthorne's sunny ending is the result of his unsuccessful attempt to ease the tensions of a complex plot by disclosing secrets whose effects have outreached their seeming cause (65, 66, 69). According to Hutner, "Such secrets as Holgrave's genealogy or the Pyncheon's congenital susceptibilities do not warrant the effects their concealment produces" (69).

While many scholars have critiqued the end of *The House of the Seven Gables*, others (including some who have also read the close of the romance as a failure) have attempted to explain the ending as an inherent part of the text's design. Focusing on the tension between realism and romance in *The House of the Seven Gables*, Richard Brodhead and Brook Thomas have noted how the unresolved ending of this text successfully involves the reader in the construction of narrative conclusions, an activity in which, for Thomas, "authority becomes intersubjective" and "the basis for a community is established" (207). Richard H. Brodhead, *Hawthorne, Melville, and the Novel* (Chicago: University of Chicago Press, 1976); Brook Thomas, "*The House of the Seven Gables*: Reading the Romance of America," *PMLA* 97:2 (March 1982): 195–211.

While Nina Baym describes the end of *The House of the Seven Gables* as problematic, she also notes that the "disjunction" between the surface romance and the gothic undertones found in *The House of the Seven Gables* need not necessarily be read as a failure because this tension "corresponds to the meaning" of the text: "The romance assumes that behind or beneath the actual world is an unseen world of motive and meaning, which actually controls the shape of the visible." Baym, *The Shape of Hawthorne's Career*, 154.

Charles Campbell also provides an interesting counterreading of Holgrave's transformation, arguing that the novel need not adhere to a single, coherent image of any of its characters because it is actually about "the process of representation" itself. Charles Campbell, "Representing Representation: Body as Figure, Frame, and Text in *The House of the Seven Gables*," *Arizona Quarterly* 47:4 (Winter 1991): 5.

Similarly, John Carlos Rowe has described *The House of the Seven Gables* as a "metaliterary" work, which "employs its dramatic action to comment on how and why one writes." John Carlos Rowe, *Through the Custom-House: Nineteenth-Century American Fiction and Modern Theory* (Baltimore, Md.: Johns Hopkins University Press, 1982), 58.

Susan Van Zanten Gallagher also suggests an alternative interpretation of this ending, arguing that the engagement of Holgrave and Phoebe is a logical close to a domestic novel. Susan Van Zanten Gallagher, "A Domestic Reading of *The House of the Seven Gables*," *Studies in the Novel* 21:1 (Spring 1989): 1–13.

Reading across Baym's and Hutner's critiques and Gallagher's reevaluation of the ending of *The House of the Seven Gables*, I would like to suggest that Hawthorne's closing image is ultimately "successful" in forwarding a romance of middle-class ascendance, providing an image of "natural" class dominance that is inherently conservative.

Chapter Two
The Properties of Blood

1. Once again, throughout this chapter I will be citing Nathaniel Hawthorne, *The House of the Seven Gables* (1851; New York: Signet, 1981).

2. Hepzibah's pseudo-incestuous relationship with Clifford stands as an example of aristocratic "perversion" in Hawthorne's romance and connects the Pyncheons' obsession with blood purity to their inability to reproduce. Cathy N. Davidson provides a fascinating analysis of "reproduction" (both biological and mechanical) in *The House of the Seven Gables* in "Photographs of the Dead," 667–701.

See also Teresa Goddu's interesting examination of capitalist and sexual reproduction in "The Circulation of Women." According to Goddu, Hepzibah "symbolizes a static, sterile order that adds nothing to the functioning of society. Opposing this barren aristocratic order, the novel posits an emerging productive capitalist order that is associated with an excessive sexuality" (122).

3. Kwame Anthony Appiah, "Race," in *Critical Terms for Literary Study*, ed. Frank Lentricchia and Thomas McLaughlin (Chicago: University of Chicago Press, 1990), 274–287.

Other important studies of the sciences of biological racialism include George M. Fredrickson, *The Black Image in the White Mind: The Debate on Afro-American Character and Destiny, 1817–1914* (New York: Harper and Row, 1971); Reginald Horsman, *Race and Manifest Destiny: The Origins of American Racial Anglo-Saxonism* (Cambridge: Harvard University Press, 1981); William H. Tucker, *The Science and Politics of Racial Research* (Urbana: University of Illinois Press, 1994); and Robert J. C. Young, *Colonial Desire: Hybridity in Theory, Culture, and Race* (New York: Routledge, 1995).

4. Horsman, *Race and Manifest Destiny*, 134. According to Horsman, "The idea of distinct races with innately different capabilities was firmly ingrained in American scientific thinking by the middle of the century. Polygenesis remained controversial, though the most important American ethnologists accepted it; but the idea of a hierarchy of races, with the Caucasians clearly and permanently at the top, was generally accepted. American science provided Americans with a confident explanation of why blacks were enslaved, why Indians were exterminated, and why white Americans were expanding their settlements rapidly over adjacent lands" (37).

5. Ibid., 138.

6. Fredrickson, *The Black Image in the White Mind*, 73. See also Horsman, *Race and Manifest Destiny* and Young, *Colonial Desire*.

7. Although Dr. Charles Caldwell had theorized polygenesis as early as 1830, this new doctrine was not accepted in scientific and intellectual circles until the 1840s and 1850s, when, according to George Fredrickson, "the 'American school of ethnology' emerged and affirmed on the basis of new data that the races of mankind had been separately created as distinct and unequal species" (*The Black Image in the White Mind*, 74). For another discussion of Caldwell and the later work of the American school of ethnology, see Horsman, "Superior and Inferior Races," in *Race and Manifest Destiny*, 116–138.

8. Josiah Nott's most influential work is *Types of Mankind*, coauthored with George R. Gliddon (Philadelphia: Lippincott, Grambo and Company, 1854). Important studies of Nott and his work can be found in Fredrickson, *The Black Image in the White Mind*; Reginald Horsman, *Josiah Nott of Mobile: Southerner, Physician, and Racial Theorist* (Baton Rouge: Louisiana State University Press, 1987); Horsman, *Race and Manifest Destiny*; and Young, *Colonial Desire*.

Hortense J. Spillers provides an insightful critique of the ways in which the categories "mulatto/a" tell us "little or nothing about the subject buried beneath them, but quite a great deal more concerning the psychic and cultural reflexes that invent and invoke them," in "Notes on an Alternative Model—Neither/Nor," in *The Difference Within: Feminism and Critical Theory*, ed. Elizabeth Meese and Alice Parker (Philadelphia: John Benjamin, 1989), 166.

9. Nott, *Types of Mankind*, 375.

10. Ibid., 397–398.

11. Ibid., 376.

12. Ibid., 375. For an insightful discussion of Nott's move from a theory of racial species to a theory of racial types, see Young, *Colonial Desire*, 129–133.

13. Nott, *Types of Mankind*, 407.

14. Ibid., 405.

15. Ibid.

16. Ibid., 52.

17. Ibid., 409.

18. See Fredrickson, *The Black Image in the White Mind*, 78–82; Horsman, *Josiah Nott of Mobile*, esp. chap. 5, "A National Figure."

19. Fredrickson, *The Black Image in the White Mind*, 86–87.

20. Ibid., 85.

21. Ibid., 171–172.

22. L. Seaman, *What Miscegenation Is! And What We Are to Expect Now That Mr. Lincoln is Re-elected* (New York: Waller and Willetts, 1864), 4.

23. Ibid., 5–6.

24. Nott, *Types of Mankind*, 404.

25. Carby, *Reconstructing Womanhood*, 24–25.

26. Nott, *Types of Mankind*, 401.

27. Ibid., 401–402.

28. In attempting to explain his failure to obtain satisfactory statistics concerning the prolificacy of biracial women, Nott proclaims, "The difficulty arises solely from the want of chastity among mulatto women, which is so notorious as to be proverbial." Nott, *Types of Mankind*, 398.

29. Carby, *Reconstructing Womanhood*, 24–25.

30. Karen Sanchez-Eppler, "Bodily Bonds: The Intersecting Rhetorics of Feminism and Abolition," *Representations* 24 (Fall 1988): 28–59.

31. In the introduction to *Bordering on the Body*, Laura Doyle asserts that the "interdependence of racial and patriarchal practices compels me to speak of 'racial patriarchy.' " Laura Doyle, *Bordering on the Body: The Racial Matrix of Modern Fiction and Culture* (New York: Oxford University Press, 1994), 6. According to Doyle, her "theory of racial patriarchy focuses attention primarily on women's reproductive roles in kinship structures" (23).

32. Because Hawthorne seems to suggest that the Pyncheon line has been effected by a single act, he seems to support a negative kind of Lamarckian view of acquired characteristics. Jean-Baptiste Lamarck believed that one could pass along acquired improvements (in knowledge or physical strength) to one's progeny. In the late nineteenth and early twentieth centuries, Lamarck's views were overtaken by eugenicist notions of innate (as opposed to acquired) hereditary characteristics.

For brief discussions of Lamarckianism, see Fredrickson, *The Black Image in the White Mind*, 55, 314–315; Marouf Arif Hasian, Jr., *The Rhetoric of Eugenics in Anglo-American Thought* (Athens: University of Georgia Press, 1996), 18, 20, 22; Richard Hofstadter, *Social Darwinism in American Thought*, rev. ed. (Boston: Beacon Press, 1944), 77; and Daniel J. Kevles, *In the Name of Eugenics: Genetics and the Uses of Human Heredity* (New York: Knopf, 1985), 66.

33. Francis Galton's studies include *Hereditary Genius: An Inquiry into Its Laws and Consequences* (London: Macmillan, 1892); *Inquiries into Human Faculty and Its Development*, 2d ed. (London: J. M. Dent and Sons, 1907); and *Natural Inheritance* (London: Macmillan, 1889).

Works that discuss the impact of eugenics on late-nineteenth- and early-twentieth-century U.S. culture include Mark Haller, *Eugenics: Hereditarian Attitudes in American Thought* (New Brunswick, N.J.: Rutgers University Press, 1963); Hasian, *The Rhetoric of Eugenics*; Hofstadter, *Social Darwinism in American Thought*, esp. 161–167; Kevles, *In the Name of Eugenics*; Kenneth M. Ludmerer, *Genetics and American Society: A Historical Appraisal* (Baltimore, Md.: Johns Hopkins University Press, 1972); Donald K. Pickens, *Eugenics and the Progressives* (Nashville, Tenn.: Vanderbilt University Press, 1968); Philip R. Reilly, *The Surgical Solution: A History of Involuntary Sterilization in the United States* (Baltimore, Md.: Johns Hopkins University Press, 1991); and Nicole Hahn Rafter, ed. and intro., *White Trash: The Eugenic Family Studies 1877–1919* (Boston: Northeastern University Press, 1988).

34. Galton, *Hereditary Genius*, 1. *Hereditary Genius* was originally published in 1869, and was reprinted and revised in 1892.

35. According to Donna Haraway, "Eugenic sterilization laws are passed by 30 state legislatures in the United States from 1907–31." Donna J. Haraway, *Modest_Witness@Second_Millennium.FemaleMan_Meets_OncoMouse: Feminism and Technoscience* (New York: Routledge, 1997), 224. See also Pickens, *Eugenics and the Progressives*, esp. chap. 6, "Sterilization: The Search for Purity in Mind and Body"; and Reilly, *The Surgical Solution*, esp. chap. 4, "Sterilization Laws."

36. Nott, *Types of Mankind*, 50.

37. It would appear that Hawthorne modeled Holgrave after Ralph Waldo Emerson's "self-reliant" man. "Self-dependent while yet a boy" (*The House of the Seven Gables*, 400), Holgrave fits the exterior description of Emerson's ideal man with

surprising precision. Holgrave has pursued the various trades of Emerson's "sturdy lad" from New England, a young man "who in turn tries all the professions, who *teams it, farms it, peddles,* keeps a school, preaches, edits a newspaper" ("Self-Reliance," 145). At one time a traveling peddler, Holgrave also has been "first, a country schoolmaster; next, a salesman in a country store; and either at the same time or afterwards, the political editor of a country newspaper" (*The House of the Seven Gables,* 401). Worth much more than the "city dolls" ("Self-Reliance," 145) who lose heart upon encountering first obstacles, according to Emerson, "sturdy," "self-reliant" young men, like Holgrave, maintain not only their manhood but also their masculinity. In addition to a masculinized rigor and independence, Holgrave possesses the more important interior qualities that define Emerson's self-reliant man. Holgrave respects the sacred integrity of his own mind: "The true value of his character lay in that deep consciousness of inward strength, which made all his past vicissitudes seem merely an exchange of garments" (*The House of the Seven Gables,* 404). Ralph Waldo Emerson, "Self-Reliance," in *Ralph Waldo Emerson,* ed. Richard Poirier (New York: Oxford University Press, 1990), 131–151.

I am particularly interested in the implicitly racialized nature of this Emersonian character.

38. Through Holgrave, Hawthorne might be said to herald a "positive eugenics" bent upon encouraging the reproduction of the mentally and morally "fit" (as opposed to a program of "negative eugenics," which promoted the sterilization of the "unfit"). For a discussion of negative and positive eugenics, see Doyle, *Bordering on the Body,* 16–20.

Walter Benn Michaels argues that by celebrating Holgrave's character, Hawthorne's romance actually forwards an aristocratic claim to entitlement through inalienable possession. Michaels asserts that Holgrave's character is analogous to the nobility of a titled aristocracy, and suggests that Hawthorne employs this aristocratic ideal to counter the money aristocracy emblematized by Judge Jaffrey Pyncheon. Walter Benn Michaels, "Romance and Real Estate," in *The American Renaissance Reconsidered,* ed. Walter Benn Michaels and Donald E. Pease (Baltimore, Md.: Johns Hopkins University Press, 1985), 158–166.

I am interested in the ways in which Holgrave's character is celebrated precisely as a middle-class construct in its gendered and racialized manifestations in *The House of the Seven Gables.*

39. Nott, *Types of Mankind,* 407–408.

40. Josiah C. Nott, "Physical History of Man," in *Two Lectures on the Connection between the Biblical and Physical History of Man* (1849; reprint, New York: Negro Universities Press, 1969), 45.

41. Galton, *Hereditary Genius,* 348.

42. David Green, "Veins of Resemblance: Photography and Eugenics," in *Photography/Politics Two,* ed. Patricia Holland, Jo Spence, and Simon Watney (London: Comedia Publishing Group, 1986), 19.

Laura Doyle similarly argues: "The eugenicists' privileging of intelligence of course serves the self-interest of middle-class professionals, whose claim to power rests partly on their 'higher' education and 'higher' intelligence." Doyle, *Bordering on the Body,* 28.

43. Green, "Veins of Resemblance," 19.

44. Harriet Beecher Stowe, *Uncle Tom's Cabin* (1852), ed. Ann Douglas (New York: Penguin, 1981). For a reading of domesticity and racial and gender politics in *Uncle Tom's Cabin*, see Brown, *Domestic Individualism*.

45. Hazel Carby and bell hooks provide important analyses of these racialized sexual relationships and representations of womanhood. See Carby, *Reconstructing Womanhood*; bell hooks, *Ain't I a Woman: Black Women and Feminism* (Boston: South End Press, 1981).

46. Elizabeth Alexander, " 'Can you be BLACK and look at this?' Reading the Rodney King Video(s)," in *Black Male: Representations of Masculinity in Contemporary American Art*, ed. Thelma Golden (New York: Whitney Museum of American Art, 1994), 90–110.

47. Ibid., 96.

48. Ibid.

49. According to Cathy N. Davidson, "The invention of the daguerreotype fueled the nineteenth century's fascination with physiognomy, the decoding of the face's moral and intellectual sign system." Davidson, "Photographs of the Dead," 682.

50. Horsman, *Race and Manifest Destiny*, 54–55.

51. Horsman discusses phrenology in relation to theories of racial superiority and inferiority in *Race and Manifest Destiny*, 120–121. For Horsman's discussion of Caldwell, whom he claims was "the best-known American phrenologist" by the end of the 1830s, see *Race and Manifest Destiny*, 117–118.

For more on the racial inflection of phrenology in America, see Joan Burbick's insightful work, *Healing the Republic: The Language of Health and the Culture of Nationalism in Nineteenth-Century America* (New York: Cambridge University Press, 1994), esp. 137–144.

52. For a fascinating discussion of the "whitening" of Egypt, see Young, *Colonial Desire*, chap. 5, "Egypt in America, the Confederacy in London."

53. Nott, *Types of Mankind*, 50.

54. Ibid., 412.

55. According to Cathy N. Davidson, "Holgrave's sundrawn picture 'fixes' the Judge's identification with his brutal aristocratic ancestor—exploiting both the evidential and surveillant potentialities of photography that would not be fully utilized for another 20 years." Davidson, "Photographs of the Dead," 688.

Chapter Three
Superficial Depths

1. Newhall, *The History of Photography*; Rosenblum, *A World History of Photography*.

2. In "The Work of Art in the Age of Mechanical Reproduction," Benjamin defines "aura" as the remnants of ritual that surround the art object, once valued as a religious, not secular, object. In "A Small History of Photography," he defines "aura" as "a strange weave of space and time: the unique appearance or semblance of distance, no matter how close the object may be" (250).

3. Benjamin, "The Work of Art in the Age of Mechanical Reproduction," 225–226.

4. R.H.E., "My Photograph," *Godey's Lady's Book*, April 1867, 342.

5. Ibid., 343.

6. Ibid., 342.

7. Benjamin, "The Work of Art in the Age of Mechanical Reproduction," 226.

8. I am borrowing from Judith Butler's discussion of how the boundaries of the body are policed and inscribed. Butler, *Gender Trouble*, 136.

9. Fanny Fern, "How I Don't Like Pictures," *New York Ledger*, June 11, 1859. Many thanks to Nicole Tonkovich for presenting me with several Fanny Fern columns on photography.

10. Ibid.

11. Fanny Fern, "Taking Portraits," *New York Ledger*, September 22, 1860.

12. Arthur Hoeber, "A Portrait and a Likeness," *Camera Notes* 2:3 (January 1899): 74.

13. "Inner Likeness" is Dallett Fuguet's term. See Dallett Fuguet, "Portraiture as Art," *Camera Notes* 5:2 (October 1901): 81.

14. See Trachtenberg, "Illustrious Americans," in *Reading American Photographs*, 21–70, esp. 27, 36, 40. See also Barbara McCandless, "The Portrait Studio and the Celebrity: Promoting the Art," in *Photography in Nineteenth-Century America*, ed. Martha A. Sandweiss (Fort Worth, Tex.: Amon Carter Museum, 1991), 48–75, esp. 55. According to McCandless, "By the early 1850s, the standard for a *truly* accurate likeness [a portrait] had become not merely to reproduce the subject's physical characteristics but to express the inner character as well" (55; emphasis added).

15. The journal included this tag as part of its title.

16. Hoeber, "A Portrait and a Likeness," 76.

17. Ibid., 75.

18. Ibid.

19. In an essay describing a lecture given by W. M. Hollinger, William M. Murray states: "Mr. Hollinger gave the audience many valuable thoughts and hints, and especially drew attention to the psychological truth, that every human being, young or old, has a beauty peculiar to himself—a soul—and that it is the mission of the portrait painter and the portrait photographer to find that soul and express its beauty in his picture." William M. Murray, "Mr. W. M. Hollinger on Photographic Portraiture," *Camera Notes* 2:4 (April 1899): 161.

20. Trachtenberg, "Likeness as Identity," 189–190. See also Inderpal Grewal's discussion of physiognomy and the discourses of transparency and beauty in *Home and Harem: Nation, Gender, Empire, and the Cultures of Travel* (Durham: Duke University Press, 1996), esp. chap. 1; and Joan Burbick's examination of phrenology and physiognomy in *Healing the Republic*.

According to Walter Benjamin, in the first few decades of photography "the photographer was confronted, in every client, with a member of a rising class equipped with an aura that had seeped into the very folds of the man's frock coat or floppy cravat." Benjamin, "A Small History of Photography," 248.

21. Murray, "Mr. W. M. Hollinger on Photographic Portraiture," 161.

22. Fuguet, "Portraiture as Art," 81.

23. Sadakichi Hartmann, "Portrait Painting and Portrait Photography," *Camera Notes* 3:1 (July 1899): 10.

24. Ibid.

25. Jane M. Gaines, "Photography 'Surprises' the Law: The Portrait of Oscar Wilde," in *Contested Culture: The Image, the Voice, and the Law* (Chapel Hill: University of North Carolina Press, 1991), 42–83.

26. William M. Murray, "Too Well Done!" *Camera Notes* 2:2 (October 1898): 92.

27. Hoeber, "A Portrait and a Likeness," 376.

28. Henry James, "The Real Thing," in *Daisy Miller and Other Stories*, ed. Michael Swan (New York: Penguin, 1983), 43–69.

For critical assessments of this short story, see Martha Banta, "Artists, Models, Real Things, and Recognizable Types," *Studies in the Literary Imagination* 16:2 (Fall 1983): 7–34; Miles Orvell, "Reproduction and 'The Real Thing': The Anxiety of Realism in the Age of Photography," in *The Technological Imagination: Theories and Fictions*, ed. Teresa de Lauretis, Andreas Huyssen, and Kathleen Woodward (Madison, Wis.: Coda, 1980), 49–64; Miles Orvell, *The Real Thing: Imitation and Authenticity in American Culture, 1880–1940* (Chapel Hill: University of North Carolina Press, 1989), 122–123; Catherine Vieilledent, "Representation and Reproduction: A Reading of Henry James's 'The Real Thing,' " in *Interface: Essays on History, Myth, and Art in American Literature*, ed. Daniel Royot (Montpellier: Publications de la Recherche, Université Paul Valéry, 1985), 31–49.

29. Although James's artist is a painter and a sketch artist, not a photographer, photographic portraiture plays a prominent role in the story as counterexample to the artist's aims.

30. Barbara McCandless describes this marketing technique, utilized extensively by Mathew Brady, in her essay "The Portrait Studio and the Celebrity," 56. According to McCandless, the strategy escalated significantly by the late nineteenth century, when celebrity cartes-de-visite and cabinet cards were popular. By the late 1860s, celebrities could demand a fee for a sitting, and it is reported that Napoleon Sarony paid Sarah Bernhardt $1,500 and Lillie Langtry $5,000 for their sittings. McCandless, "The Portrait Studio and Celebrity," 67.

31. According to Martha Banta, "Faces are the focus of a person's particular identity, whereas outlines of the figure provide generalizations that, even if 'sold,' preserve the privacy of an inner life." Banta, "Artists, Models, Real Things, and Recognizable Types," 11. I am most interested in how the Monarchs protect their *class* identity in this negotiation of face and figure.

32. The narrator of James's story responds to Mrs. Monarch's disapproval of Miss Churm by stating, " 'Oh, you think she's shabby, but you must allow for the alchemy of art.' " James, "The Real Thing," 53.

33. According to Catherine Vieilledent, "The upper-class models incarnate a consummate social artistry, a perfect mastery of forms and manners which they offer up whole because they have and are nothing else." Vieilledent, "Representation and Reproduction," 41.

34. Murray, "Too Well Done!" 92.

35. Ibid.

36. In their first meeting, Major Monarch tells the artist, " 'We thought that if you ever have to do people like us, we might be something like it' " (46). The problem for the artist is that the Monarchs are precisely not *like*—they are. As Martha Banta explains in her discussion of "The Real Thing," Mrs. Monarch is

"unable to hire herself out as a projectionist of imagined identities"; unlike Miss Churm, who can subtly sublimate the self "in order to approximate the type," Mrs. Monarch is always, only her (aristocratic) self. See Banta, "Artists, Models, Real Things, and Recognizable Types," 12.

37. Armstrong, *Desire and Domestic Fiction*, 70.

38. Cultural critics also note the ways in which a dwindling aristocracy began to take on bourgeois self-representational strategies in the nineteenth century. See Rosalind H. Williams, *Dream Worlds: Mass Consumption in Late Nineteenth-Century France* (Berkeley: University of California Press, 1982).

39. For a discussion of exteriors and interiors in the construction of class identities through fashion in the nineteenth century, see Halttunen, *Confidence Men and Painted Women*.

40. It is extremely ironic that the New York Edition, the collected volumes of Henry James's work (a tribute to him as author), was illustrated by the "artistic" photographer Alvin Langdon Coburn. See Leon Edel, *Henry James, The Master, 1901–1916* (Philadelphia: Lippincott, 1972), 333–339.

41. Trachtenberg, "Illustrious Americans," 27.

42. R.H.E., "My Photograph," 344.

43. Sekula, "The Body and the Archive," 7.

44. Once again, for an excellent analysis of Bertillonage, see ibid.

45. Ibid., 28.

46. The preciseness and relative subtlety of the other measurements made them impractical for popular use.

47. This statement from an 1847 edition of the *American Journal of Photography* is quoted in Trachtenberg, "Illustrious Americans," 28–29.

48. Thomas Byrnes, *Professional Criminals of America* (New York: Cassell, 1886). See also Sekula, "The Body and the Archive," 37.

49. In Michel Foucault's formulation of the workings of a surveillant society, he describes how normative behavior is established through the assumption of an ever-present, all-pervasive gaze, a regulator imagined to be outside the body, perceiving one's every move. The panopticon, a cylindrical prison architecture centered around an invisible optical monitor, exemplifies, for Foucault, the function of a more general, colloquial state power of surveillance that establishes a normative social image against the deviance of the criminal body. Just as Foucault's prisoner begins to discipline his or her own behavior, self-regulating in relation to an always potentially monitoring gaze, the subjects of a surveillant state curb their behavior against imagined images of normative and deviant action. See Foucault, *Discipline and Punish*.

50. Sekula, "The Body and the Archive."

51. Ibid., 34.

52. Cesare Lombroso's *Criminal Man*, originally published in 1876, was summarized, revised, and translated into English by his daughter Gina Lombroso-Ferrero in 1911. In *Criminal Man*, Lombroso outlines a positivist methodology for identifying the congenital or "born" criminal.

In his introduction to the 1911 edition of *Criminal Man* compiled by his daughter, Lombroso explains that the volume is written in English for an American audience because America was the first nation to put the ideas of the Modern School into practice (xxix–xxx). Cesare Lombroso and Gina Lombroso-Ferrero, *Criminal Man* (1876; trans. Gina Lombroso-Ferrero, intro. Cesare Lombroso, 1911; reprint, intro. Leonard Savitz, Montclair: Paterson Smith, 1972). For a description of shifts in criminological inquiry, see Lombroso's introduction, xxii.

53. According to Cynthia Eagle Russett, Darwin's theory of evolution infused the natural and social sciences with a notion of hierarchy and "progress" hitherto unknown. Cynthia Eagle Russett, *Sexual Science: The Victorian Construction of Womanhood* (Cambridge: Harvard University Press, 1989), 4–5.

Joan Burbick assesses earlier attempts to read the body for signs of interior essence in her analysis of phrenology. See Burbick, "Managing Mental Labor," in *Healing the Republic*, 137–155.

54. This statement is made by Leonard Savitz in his introduction to the reprint edition of Cesare Lombroso and Gina Lombroso-Ferrero's *Criminal Man*, xi, which is also introduced by Cesare Lombroso, as noted previously.

55. Savitz, introduction to *Criminal Man* (1972), ix.

56. See Cesare Lombroso and William Ferrero, *The Female Offender* (New York: D. Appleton, 1899).

57. Savitz, introduction to *Criminal Man* (1972), x.

58. According to Leonard Savitz, by the time Lombroso wrote the introduction to the English edition of *Criminal Man* in 1911, he had revised his theories (of 1876) and claimed that the born criminal type represented only one-third of all criminals (xv). While in the 1876 version of *Criminal Man* Lombroso had traced criminal behavior directly to biological, hereditary origins, by 1911 he also admitted social causes for crime, including population density, education, immigration, economic conditions, age, sex, and meteoric and atmospheric conditions (xvi). At the end of his life Lombroso also conceded that physical anomalies did not have absolute predictive value for identifying the born criminal (xvi). See the introduction by Leonard Savitz to the reprint edition of Cesare Lombroso and Gina Lombroso-Ferrero's *Criminal Man*.

59. Savitz, introduction to *Criminal Man* (1972), x.

60. Ibid. According to Savitz, in his first studies of criminal skulls, Lombroso compared them with the skulls of Hottentots and Bushmen. Ibid., xii.

61. Lombroso and Lombroso-Ferrero, *Criminal Man*, 147.

62. According to Walter Benjamin, in 1841 seventy-six new physiologies were written, presumably describing seventy-six different social types. Walter Benjamin, "The Flaneur," in *Charles Baudelaire: A Lyric Poet in the Era of High Capitalism*, trans. Harry Zohn (London: New Left Books, 1973), 35.

63. Ibid., 39. According to Benjamin: "The soothing little remedies which the physiologist offered for sale were soon passe" ("The Flaneur," 40). The literature of types was soon replaced by detective fiction, a genre less focused on mapping social space in general than on identifying individual agents. I think a similar shift can be marked in uses of photography, from Galton's composites in the 1870s to Bertillon's photographs of individual physical anomalies in the 1890s.

64. Walter Benjamin describes August Sander's photographs of social types in the 1930s as a "physiognomic gallery": "Sander's work is more than a picture book. It is a training manual." Benjamin, "A Small History of Photography," 252.

65. Francis Galton, Appendix A: "Composite Portraiture," in *Inquiries into Human Faculty and Its Development*, 221–241.

66. Galton, "Composite Portraiture," 230, 233, 239.

67. Ibid., 222.

68. Francis Galton himself claimed that the artist's genius is his or her ability to record "blended" images: "They [artists] are of all men the most capable of producing forms that are not copies of any individual, but represent the characteristic features of classes." Galton, "Composite Portraiture," 230.

69. Galton, *Inquiries*, 10.

70. Galton's treatise on fingerprinting in 1892 marks an important shift in his methodology. Francis Galton, *Finger Prints* (1892; reprint, New York: Da Capo, 1965).

71. Galton, "Composite Portraiture," 240.

72. Ibid., 230.

73. Ibid., 224.

74. Ibid., 233.

75. Galton, *Inquiries*, 8.

76. Fanny Fern, "Then and Now," *New York Ledger*, April 5, 1862.

77. Ibid.

78. Ibid.

79. Ibid.

80. As I discussed in chapter 1, the relationship between women and other nineteenth-century technologies of vision, such as mesmerism, was also sexualized.

81. Arthur, "American Characteristics: No. V—The Daguerreotypist," 353.

82. Rachel Bowlby, *Just Looking: Consumer Culture in Dreiser, Gissing, and Zola* (New York: Methuen, 1985); Bowlby "Modes of Modern Shopping: Mallarmé at the *Bon Marche*," in *The Ideology of Conduct: Essays on Literature and the History of Sexuality*, ed. Nancy Armstrong and Leonard Tennenhouse (New York: Methuen, 1987), 185–205; Williams, *Dream Worlds*; Jean Baudrillard, *For a Critique of the Political Economy of the Sign*, trans. Charles Levin (St. Louis: Telos, 1981); Baudrillard, *Selected Writings*, ed. Mark Poster (Stanford, Calif.: Stanford University Press, 1988); Benjamin, *Charles Baudelaire*; Benjamin, "Paris, Capital of the Nineteenth Century," in *Reflections*, ed. Peter Demetz (New York: Schocken Books, 1986), 146–162; and Susan Buck-Morss, "The Flaneur, the Sandwichman and the Whore: The Politics of Loitering," *New German Critique* 39 (Fall 1986): 99–140.

83. Bowlby, *Just Looking*, 28. According to French sociologist Pierre Bourdieu, the objects one chooses to consume demonstrate one's "taste," an effect of one's class station. Pierre Bourdieu, *Distinction: A Social Critique of the Judgement of Taste*, trans. Richard Nice (Cambridge: Harvard University Press, 1984).

84. Bowlby, *Just Looking*, 28.

85. Gaines, *Contested Culture*, 42–83.

86. Bowlby, *Just Looking*, 28.

87. Trachtenberg, "Likeness as Identity," 190.

88. Bowlby, *Just Looking*, 32.

89. Bowlby, "Modes of Modern Shopping." Alan Trachtenberg also discusses the ways in which photography allowed people to see themselves as others saw

them, as images, but he does not explicitly theorize this new mode of self-conception in terms of gender. See Trachtenberg, "Illustrious Americans," 29.

90. Jacques Lacan, "The Mirror Stage as Formative of the Function of the I," in *Ecrits: A Selection*, trans. Alan Sheridan (New York: Norton, 1977), 1–7.

91. Doane, *The Desire to Desire*, 30.

92. My thinking here has been heavily influenced by Luce Irigaray, *This Sex Which Is Not One*, trans. Catherine Porter (Ithaca, N.Y.: Cornell University Press, 1985), esp. 196, 198.

93. Gaines, *Contested Culture*, 83.

94. Abigail Solomon-Godeau, "The Legs of the Countess," *October* 39 (Winter 1986): 65–105.

95. Ibid., 67.

96. Ibid., 105.

97. Butler, *Gender Trouble*, 139.

98. Ibid., 137.

99. See also ibid., 145.

100. Solomon-Godeau, "The Legs of the Countess," 67.

101. Chantal Mouffe, "Citizenship and Political Identity," *October* 61 (Summer 1992): 28.

102. Judith Butler, "Discussion," *October* 61 (Summer 1992): 110.

103. Mary Ann Doane, "The Shadow of Her Gaze," in *The Desire to Desire*, 182–183.

104. Solomon-Godeau, "The Legs of the Countess," 78.

105. Doane, "The Shadow of Her Gaze"; Doane, "Film and the Masquerade," 74–87; Doane, "Woman's Stake: Filming the Female Body," in *Feminism and Film Theory*, ed. Constance Penley (New York: Routledge, 1988), 216–228.

106. Again, see Irigaray, *This Sex Which Is Not One*.

107. Lacan, "The Mirror Stage"; Martin Jay, "Lacan, Althusser, and the Specular Subject of Ideology," in *Downcast Eyes: The Denigration of Vision in Twentieth-Century French Thought* (Berkeley: University of California Press, 1993), 329–380.

108. Butler, *Gender Trouble*, 136.

Chapter Four
"Baby's Picture Is Always Treasured": Eugenics and the Reproduction of Whiteness in the Family Photograph Album

1. The author of this article is identified by initials only, as "R.H.E." R.H.E., "My Photograph," 343.

2. Barbara Welter, "The Cult of True Womanhood: 1800–1860," in *Dimity Convictions*, 21–41. For more on True Womanhood and middle-class domesticity, see chapter 1.

3. Advertisement, "Baby's Picture Is Always Treasured," *Ladies' Home Journal*, July 1898. The *Ladies' Home Journal* and *Godey's Lady's Book* were both aimed at a middle-class and upper-middle-class white female readership. In her profile on Sarah Josepha Hale, the literary editor of *Godey's Lady's Book*, Nicole Tonkovich Hoffman proposes that "women across the American continent . . . acclaimed *Godey's* as their connection to New England values and mores, whether those values

were connected to fashion, homemaking skills, language, literature, intellectual trends, or current events." Nicole Tonkovich Hoffman, "Legacy Profile: Sarah Josepha Hale (1788–1874)," *Legacy: A Journal of American Women Writers* 7:2 (Fall 1990): 47.

4. As noted in chapter 2, Francis Galton's influential studies include *Hereditary Genius, Inquiries into Human Faculty and Its Development*, and *Natural Inheritance*. Galton also wrote the following autobiography: *Memories of My Life* (London: Methuen, 1908).

Once again, for studies of the impact of eugenics on late-nineteenth- and early-twentieth-century U.S. culture, see Haller, *Eugenics*; Hasian, *The Rhetoric of Eugenics*; Hofstadter, *Social Darwinism in American Thought*, esp. 161–167; Kevles, *In the Name of Eugenics*; Ludmerer, *Genetics and American Society*; Pickens, *Eugenics and the Progressives*; Reilly, *The Surgical Solution*; and Rafter, *White Trash*. For further discussion of the sciences of biological racialism, see chapter 2.

5. I will discuss at length two family albums designed by Francis Galton that utilized the photograph as evidence of heritable characteristics. For other analyses of the role photography played in eugenics, see Green, "Veins of Resemblance," 9–21; Sekula, "The Body and the Archive," 3–64.

For further analyses of how "race" is constructed through photographic representation in the nineteenth century, see James Guimond, "Frances Johnston's *Hampton Album*: A White Dream for Black People," in *American Photography and the American Dream* (Chapel Hill: University of North Carolina Press, 1991), 21–53; Deborah Poole, *Vision, Race, and Modernity: A Visual Economy of the Andean Image World* (Princeton, N.J.: Princeton University Press, 1997); Vicente L. Rafael, "Nationalism, Imagery, and the Filipino Intelligentsia in the Nineteenth Century," *Critical Inquiry* 16:3 (Spring 1990): 591–611; Rafael, "White Love: Surveillance and Nationalist Resistance in the U.S. Colonization of the Philippines," in *Cultures of United States Imperialism*, ed. Amy Kaplan and Donald Pease (Durham, N.C.: Duke University Press, 1993), 185–218; Laura Wexler, "Black and White and Color: American Photographs at the Turn of the Century," *Prospects* 13 (Winter 1988): 341–390; Wexler, "Seeing Sentiment: Photography, Race, and the Innocent Eye," in *Female Subjects in Black and White: Race, Psychoanalysis, Feminism*, ed. Elizabeth Abel, Barbara Christian, and Helene Moglen (Berkeley: University of California Press, 1997), 159–186; and Wexler, "Tender Violence," 9–38.

Eugenicist desires to represent race fed a larger white nation-building enterprise in the United States at the turn of the century. Indeed, Francis Galton, the founder of eugenics, often conflated the terms "nation" and "race," and many patriotic societies attempted to do the same. As we will see in chapter 5, the Daughters of the American Revolution, founded in the 1890s, used intricate genealogical charts to map a national history confined by "white" Anglo-Saxon bloodlines. In a period of increased immigration, and African American social and economic mobilization, white supremacist nationalists evoked the eugenicist categories of Anglo-Saxon superiority in order to privilege an imagined white American identity.

6. For critical discussions of the African American family photograph album, see Deborah Willis, "Introduction: Picturing Us" (3–26), bell hooks, "In Our Glory: Photography and Black Life" (42–53), and Christian Walker, "Gazing Colored: A

Family Album" (64–70), all in *Picturing Us: African American Identity in Photography*, ed. Deborah Willis (New York: New Press, 1994).

7. See Julie Dash's film *Daughters of the Dust*, in which family photography becomes a vehicle for musing upon family relationships and ancestral history, and Clarissa Sligh's book project *Reading Dick and Jane with Me*, in which Sligh challenges the white, middle-class norms forwarded by the Dick and Jane reading primers by juxtaposing images of white Dick and Jane to photographs of Sligh and her brother as children. See also Deborah Willis's multimedia quilt and photograph pieces in *African American Extended Family* (1994), an exhibit presented at the Center for Creative Photography in Tucson, Arizona, September 18 to November 6, 1994 (brochure copyright 1994, Center for Creative Photography and Arizona Board of Regents); and Carrie Mae Weems's documentary photographs of her family members (1978–1984), in *Carrie Mae Weems*, catalogue (Washington, D.C.: National Museum of Women in the Arts, 1993). Again, see the essays collected by Deborah Willis in *Picturing Us: African American Identity in Photography*.

8. hooks, "In Our Glory," 48.

9. Once again, for histories of the daguerreotype see Newhall, *The History of Photography*; Rosenblum, *A World History of Photography*; and Taft, *Photography and the American Scene*.

10. Tagg, *The Burden of Representation*, 37.

11. See Davidson, "Photographs of the Dead," 678.

12. Francis Galton conceptualized his early work on racial classification as a study of "hereditary genius." See Galton, *Hereditary Genius*.

13. Arthur, "American Characteristics: No. V—The Daguerreotypist," 352.

14. For discussions of Mathew Brady's Daguerrean Gallery, see McCandless, "The Portrait Studio and the Celebrity," 48–75; and Trachtenberg, "Illustrious Americans," in *Reading American Photographs*, 21–70.

15. See Davidson, "Photographs of the Dead," 678.

16. Marouf Arif Hasian, Jr., Kenneth M. Ludmerer, Donald K. Pickens, and Philip R. Reilly all note Theodore Roosevelt's rhetoric of "race suicide." Hasian, *The Rhetoric of Eugenics*, 48; Ludmerer, *Genetics and American Society*, 25; Pickens, *Eugenics and the Progressives*, 28; Reilly, *The Surgical Solution*, 43.

17. I am indebted to Laura Wexler for helping me to develop this portion of my argument.

18. See Newhall, *The History of Photography*; Rosenblum, *A World History of Photography*.

19. McCandless, "The Portrait Studio and the Celebrity," 62.

20. In "A Small History of Photography," Walter Benjamin describes the family photograph album as the place where "foolishly draped or corseted figures were displayed: Uncle Alex and Aunt Riecken, little Trudi when she was still a baby, Papa in his first term at university . . . and finally, to make our shame complete, we ourselves." Benjamin, "A Small History of Photography," 246.

21. Philip Stokes, "The Family Photograph Album: So Great a Cloud of Witnesses," in *The Portrait in Photography*, ed. Graham Clarke (London: Reaktion, 1992), 194.

22. "Kodaks," *Ladies' Home Journal*, December 1897, 21.

23. Ibid.

24. E. B. Core, "Getting Good Pictures of Children," *Ladies' Home Journal*, February 1898, 13.

25. Although printed several months after "Getting Good Pictures of Children," Isaac Porter, Jr.'s, "Photographing Children at Home" serves as a companion to the earlier article, and refers to E. B. Core's article directly. Isaac Porter, Jr., "Photographing Children at Home," *Ladies' Home Journal*, December 1898, 35.

26. Ibid.

27. Ibid.

28. Contemporary feminist photographers and theorists Jo Spence and Rosy Martin investigate the ways in which family photographs document parents' (not children's) investment in the (projected) life of the child. Rosy Martin, "Dirty Linen: Photo Therapy, Memory and Identity," *Ten 8* 2:1 (Spring 1991): 34–49; Jo Spence, *Putting Myself in the Picture: A Political, Personal and Photographic Autobiography* (Seattle: Real Comet Press, 1988); Rosy Martin and Jo Spence, "Photo-therapy: Psychic Realism as a Healing Art?" *Ten 8* 30 (Autumn 1988): 2–17.

29. Stokes, "The Family Photograph Album," 200.

30. According to Carroll Smith-Rosenberg, New Women of the Anglo-Saxon middle and upper-middle classes often rejected marriage and motherhood in favor of education, careers, and homosocial bonds at the turn of the century. In the New Woman's turn from domesticity, marriage, and motherhood, eugenicists and others saw a threat to the literal reproduction of the white middle classes. Carroll Smith-Rosenberg, "The New Woman as Androgyne: Social Disorder and Gender Crisis, 1870–1936," in *Disorderly Conduct: Visions of Gender in Victorian America* (New York: Oxford University Press, 1985), 245.

31. In her discussion of W. E. Castle's *Genetics and Eugenics*, Laura Doyle summarizes eugenicist ideology as follows: "In other words, by deciding to delay marriage or to use birth control, some middle-class women were threatening the economic dominance of the ruling races." Doyle, *Bordering on the Body*, 18–19.

32. According to Laura Doyle, eugenicists "honored—or burdened—the procreative woman of the 'higher races' with a special responsibility: reproduction for the race and, in turn, for the nation." Doyle, *Bordering on the Body*, 11.

The white woman also emerged as the explicit fount of racial reproduction in the more violent context of lynching, as we will see in chapter 5.

33. Albert Edward Wiggam, *The Fruit of the Family Tree* (London: T. Werner Laurie, 1924), 280.

34. Ibid.

35. Ibid.

36. Hasian, *The Rhetoric of Eugenics*, 82. For information on Davenport and Goddard, see Elazar Barkan, *The Retreat of Scientific Racism: Changing Concepts of Race in Britain and the United States between the World Wars* (New York: Cambridge University Press, 1992), esp. 66–76; Kevles, *In the Name of Eugenics*, esp. 41–56, 77–82, 92–93; Pickens, *Eugenics and the Progressives*, 51–53, 89; and Rafter, *White Trash*.

37. Rafter, *White Trash*, 66.

38. In *The Fruit of the Family Tree*, Albert Edward Wiggam exclaims, "Investigation proves that an enormous proportion of its [America's] undesirable citizens are descended from undesirable blood overseas. America's immigration problem is

mainly a problem of blood" (6–7). See also Ludmerer, *Genetics and American Society*, and Hasian, *The Rhetoric of Eugenics*, 43–44.

39. R.H.E., "My Photograph," 343.

40. Ibid.

41. For examinations of the use of photography in eugenics, again see Green, "Veins of Resemblance," and Sekula, "The Body and the Archive." As we saw in chapter 3, photography was also utilized by criminologists in the nineteenth century as they attempted to link physiognomic features to a congenital criminal character. Lombroso and Ferrero, *The Female Offender*.

42. Galton, *The Life History Album* (London: Macmillan, 1884), and *Record of Family Faculties* (London: Macmillan, 1884).

43. Galton, *Record of Family Faculties*, 1.

44. Ibid., 5.

45. This announcement was included as an insert in ibid.

46. Hasian, *The Rhetoric of Eugenics*, 43–44.

47. Galton, *Record of Family Faculties*, 9.

48. Ibid., 8.

49. Galton, *The Life History Album*, 5.

50. Galton, *Hereditary Genius*, 23.

51. Ibid., xxvi–xxvii.

52. Galton first used the term "eugenics" to describe his "science of heredity," or "science of race," in 1884, in *Inquiries into Human Faculty and Its Development*.

53. Francis Galton, "The Comparative Worth of Different Races," in *Hereditary Genius*, 392–404.

54. Francis Galton, "Influences That Affect the Natural Ability of Nations," in *Hereditary Genius*, 405–415. See also Doyle, *Bordering on the Body*, 11.

55. Among other factors, Galton identified "miscegenation" as one of the causes of the fall of the Athenian race. Galton, "The Comparative Worth of Different Races," 398.

Josiah Nott argued that " 'the superior [Anglo-Saxon] race must inevitably become deteriorated by any intermixture with the inferior.' " Nott quoted in Fredrickson, *The Black Image in the White Mind*, 80.

56. Once again, for studies of the extended impact of eugenics on late-nineteenth- and early-twentieth-century U.S. culture, see Hofstadter, *Social Darwinism in American Thought*, esp. 161–167; Kevles, *In the Name of Eugenics*; and Pickens, *Eugenics and the Progressives*.

57. For discussions of the sciences of biological racialism in the United States, see chapter 2.

58. Hasian, *The Rhetoric of Eugenics*, 30.

59. Ibid., 37.

60. Fredrickson, *The Black Image in the White Mind*, 73; Appiah, "Race," 276; and Young, *Colonial Desire*, esp. chap. 5, "Egypt in America, the Confederacy in London," and chap. 6, "White Power, White Desire."

61. Ludmerer, *Genetics and American Society* 89, 95–113.

62. Ibid., 90–95. See also Reilly, *The Surgical Solution*. Once again, according to Donna Haraway, "Eugenic sterilization laws are passed by 30 state legisla-

tures in the United States from 1907–31." Haraway, *Modest_Witness@ Second_Millenium.FemaleMan_ Meets_OncoMouse*, 224.

63. For a brief example of Galton's delineation of "natural" social hierarchies, see the preface to the 1892 edition of *Hereditary Genius*. Francis Galton, "Prefatory Chapter to the Edition of 1892," *Hereditary Genius*, 25–41.

64. Contrary to other historical images of the family, which define the family as an inclusive structure indifferent to racial difference, Galton's eugenics posed the family as what Walter Benn Michaels has called an exclusive institution marking "the unequivocal source of racial difference." Walter Benn Michaels, "Race into Culture: A Critical Genealogy of Cultural Identity," *Critical Inquiry* 18:4 (Summer 1992): 664.

65. As we saw in chapter 3, Galton also devised a system of composite portraiture through which he claimed to be able to capture the central physiognomic characteristics of any given biological "type" of individuals. Galton, Appendix A: "Composite Portraiture," in *Inquiries into Human Faculty and Its Development*, 221–241.

66. Hasian, *The Rhetoric of Eugenics*, 31.

67. Ibid., 37–38. See also Daniel Kevles, "Annals of Eugenics, A Secular Faith—II," *New Yorker*, October 15, 1984, 52.

68. Hasian, *The Rhetoric of Eugenics*, 43–44.

69. For a description and the actual text of many of these documents, see Rafter, *White Trash*. Rafter discusses the photographs reproduced in these texts in her preface, pp. ix, x.

70. John E. Anderson and Florence L. Goodenough, *The Modern Baby Book and Child Development Record* (New York: Norton and *The Parents' Magazine*, 1929), ix.

71. Ibid., v.

72. Ibid., x.

73. In the following discussion of "aura" and "evidence," I will be working closely with Walter Benjamin's influential essay "The Work of Art in the Age of Mechanical Reproduction," 217–252. I regard distinctions between the "auratic" and the "evidential" photograph as primarily the result of the discursive contexts in which images are viewed and consumed. The supposed "objectivity" of the evidential photograph has been thoroughly critiqued by photography scholars. For a review of these critiques, see Victor Burgin, ed., *Thinking Photography* (London: Macmillan, 1982), especially Allan Sekula's essay "On the Invention of Photographic Meaning" (84–109), and John Tagg's essay "The Currency of the Photograph" (110–141). See also Richard Bolton, ed., *The Contest of Meaning: Critical Histories of Photography* (Cambridge: MIT Press, 1989); Martha Rosler, "in, around, and afterthoughts (on documentary photography)," in *Martha Rosler, 3 works* (Halifax: Nova Scotia College of Art and Design, 1981); Allan Sekula, *Photography against the Grain: Essays and Photo Works, 1973–1983* (Halifax: Nova Scotia College of Art and Design, 1984); Tagg, *The Burden of Representation*.

74. Benjamin, "The Work of Art in the Age of Mechanical Reproduction," 224.

75. Ibid., 225–226.

76. Ibid., 226.

77. R.H.E., "My Photograph," 343.

78. Benjamin heralds Atget as the first photographer to make photographs that signify according to exhibition or evidential value. Benjamin, "The Work of Art in the Age of Mechanical Reproduction," 226.

79. Ibid.

80. Benjamin states: "What we require of the photographer is the ability to give his picture the caption that wrenches it from modish commerce and gives it a revolutionary useful value." Walter Benjamin, "The Author as Producer," in *Reflections*, ed. Peter Demetz (New York: Schocken Books, 1968), 230.

81. Foucault, *Discipline and Punish*; Michel Foucault, *The History of Sexuality*, Vol. 1, trans. Robert Hurley (New York: Vintage, 1980).

82. Richard Dyer, "White," *Screen* 29:4 (Autumn 1988): 44–46.

Chapter Five
America Coursing through Her Veins

1. Miss Eugenia Washington, "History of the Organization of the Society of the Daughters of the American Revolution," Atlanta Exposition (October 18, 1895), 5.

2. Ibid., 10.

3. Ibid., 2.

4. Marion van Riper Palmer, "The Women's Patriotic Societies," *Ladies' Home Journal*, July 1897, 10. According to Donald K. Pickens, by 1900 there were seventy hereditary organizations in the United States, thirty-five of them inaugurated in the 1890s. Pickens, *Eugenics and the Progressives*, 16.

5. According to Linda Kerber, "In the years of the early Republic a consensus developed around the idea that a mother, committed to the service of her family and to the state, might serve a political purpose. Those who opposed women in politics had to meet the proposal that women could—and should—play a political role through the raising of a patriotic child. The Republican Mother was to encourage in her sons civic interest and participation. She was to educate her children and guide them in the paths of morality and virtue. But she was not to tell her male relatives for whom to vote. She was a citizen but not really a constituent." Kerber, *Women of the Republic*, 283.

6. According to Laura Doyle, in "positive eugenics" we find "what amounts to a cult of racialized motherhood following on the heels of the nineteenth-century cult of true womanhood." Doyle, *Bordering on the Body*, 19.

7. Mary Swart Hoes Burhans, "Eligibility," *American Monthly Magazine* 3:4 (October 1893): 426. The *American Monthly Magazine* was the official magazine of the National Society of the Daughters of the American Revolution.

8. *American Monthly Magazine* 4:4 (1894): 404. I have not been able to determine exactly when American women of color were admitted to the Daughters of the American Revolution. According to one member of the staff at the national headquarters of the DAR in Washington, D.C., the first woman of color was admitted to the society sometime in the 1960s or 1970s.

9. National Society of the Daughters of the American Revolution, *Proceedings of the Second Continental Congress*, 1893, 81.

10. Ibid.

11. In the first volume of the *American Monthly Magazine* (1892), an editor describes the "Principle of Organization" of the Society as follows: "The main motive of the Society of the Daughters of the American Revolution is love of country, and the leading object of its effort is to perpetuate a spirit of true Americanism" (8).

12. J. Collins Pumpelly, "Eligibility," *American Monthly Magazine* 2:2 (February 1893): 236.

13. Laura Doyle has argued similarly: "Eugenics fostered a widespread public discourse on the race mother which conceived of her as instrumental to achieving a high 'national intelligence' and adequate 'national strength' in a competitive and imperialistic political world." Doyle, *Bordering on the Body*, 7. See also 10–12.

14. Pumpelly, "Eligibility," 236.

15. Burhans, "Eligibility," 426.

16. Mary Isabella Forsyth, "The Eligibility Question," *American Monthly Magazine* 3:5 (November 1893): 563.

17. Mary Isabella Forsyth, "The Eligibility Question," *American Monthly Magazine* 3:6 (December 1893): 677.

18. Washington, "History," 2.

19. Anna Julia Cooper, *A Voice from the South* (1892), intro. Mary Helen Washington (New York: Oxford University Press, 1988), 103–104.

20. According to Hazel Carby, "Cooper saw that the manipulative power of the South was embodied in the southern patriarch, but she describes its concern with 'blood,' inheritance, and heritage in entirely female terms and as a preoccupation that was transmitted from the South to the North and perpetuated by white women." Hazel V. Carby, " 'On the Threshold of Woman's Era': Lynching, Empire, and Sexuality in Black Feminist Theory," in *"Race," Writing, and Difference*, ed. Henry Louis Gates, Jr. (Chicago: University of Chicago Press, 1986), 306.

21. See Stephanie McCurry, "The Two Faces of Republicanism: Gender and Proslavery Politics in Antebellum South Carolina," *Journal of American History* 78:4 (March 1992): 1245–1264.

22. See Martha Strayer, *The D.A.R.: An Informal History* (Washington, D.C.: Public Affairs, 1958), 57–67.

23. Cooper, *A Voice from the South*, 163.

24. Ibid. Cooper's text has a confusing typo: "The Mayflower, a pretty venerable institution, landed in the year of Grace 1620, and the first delegation from Africa just one year ahead of that,—in 1819 [*sic*]" (163). I assume "1819" should read "1619."

25. See Carby, " 'On the Threshold of Woman's Era"; Carby, *Reconstructing Womanhood*, esp. 96–108 and 114–117; Nancie Caraway, *Segregated Sisterhood: Racism and the Politics of American Feminism* (Knoxville: University of Tennessee Press, 1991), 123, 128–129.

26. Such arguments on the part of some white Southern women divided the turn-of-the-century women's suffrage movement and led to Elizabeth Cady Stanton and Susan B. Anthony's racist "compromise," which united white women by excluding black women. Angela Y. Davis, "Woman Suffrage of the Turn of the Century: The Rising Influence of Racism," in *Women, Race, and Class* (New York: Vintage, 1983), 110–126; Bettina Aptheker, *Woman's Legacy: Essays on Race, Sex, and Class in American History* (Amherst: University of Massachusetts Press, 1982), 50–

51. Cooper also points directly to the suffrage movement in *A Voice from the South*, 108.

27. Cooper, *A Voice from the South*, 111. Cooper also asserts that a caste system, stemming from slavery and based on a division of the black and white races, is ludicrous because "the black race constitutes one-seventh the known population of the globe; and there are representatives of it here as elsewhere who were never in bondage at any time to any man,—whose blood is as blue and lineage as noble as any, even that of the white lady of the South." Cooper, *A Voice from the South*, 109.

28. See also Carby, "On the Threshold of Woman's Era," 305–306.

29. Cooper, *A Voice from the South*.

30. Adrian Piper quoted in Maurice Berger, "The Critique of Pure Racism: An Interview with Adrian Piper," *Afterimage*, October 1990, 5–9. According to Piper, "The fact is that there are no genetically distinguishable white people in this country anymore, which is about what you'd expect after four hundred years of intermarrying. And the longer a person's family has been in this country, the higher the likely proportion of African ancestry" (5).

31. Frederick Douglass, "Why Is the Negro Lynched?" in *The Lesson of the Hour*, pamphlet, (1894), reprinted in Philip S. Foner, *The Life and Writings of Frederick Douglass*, vol. 4 (New York: International Publishers, 1955), 513.

32. Posited as an heirloom rooted in the very cells of the body, "Americanness" at the turn of the century was imagined increasingly to be an attribute of biology and blood, rather than one of comportment and culture. Walter Benn Michaels has studied this phenomenon in the 1920s. Michaels, "Race into Culture," 655–685.

33. Paula Giddings, *When and Where I Enter: The Impact of Black Women on Race and Sex in America* (New York: William Morrow, 1984), 18; Fredrickson, *The Black Image in the White Mind*, 272–273.

34. For cultural analyses of lynching and antilynching campaigns, see Jane Addams and Ida B. Wells, *Lynching and Rape: An Exchange of Views*, Occasional Paper No. 25, ed. Bettina Aptheker (New York: American Institute for Marxist Studies, 1977); Aptheker, *Woman's Legacy*; Gail Bederman, " 'Civilization,' the Decline of Middle-Class Manliness, and Ida B. Wells's Antilynching Campaign (1892–94)," *Radical History Review* 52 (1992): 5–30; Carby, " 'On the Threshold of Woman's Era' " and *Reconstructing Womanhood*; Giddings, *When and Where I Enter*; Jacquelyn Dowd Hall, *Revolt against Chivalry: Jessie Daniel Ames and the Women's Campaign against Lynching*, rev. ed. (New York: Columbia University Press, 1993); Trudier Harris, *Exorcising Blackness: Historical and Literary Lynching and Burning Rituals* (Bloomington: Indiana University Press, 1984); Vron Ware, *Beyond the Pale: White Women, Racism, and History* (London: Verso, 1992); Robyn Wiegman, *American Anatomies: Theorizing Race and Gender* (Durham, N.C.: Duke University Press, 1995), esp. 81–113.

35. Works by Ida B. Wells include *Crusade for Justice: The Autobiography of Ida B. Wells*, ed. Alfreda M. Duster (Chicago: University of Chicago Press, 1970); and *Selected Works of Ida B. Wells-Barnett*, compiled with an introduction by Trudier Harris (New York: Oxford University Press, 1991), which includes *Southern Horrors: Lynch Law in All Its Phases* (1892), *The Reason Why the Colored American Is Not in the World's Columbian Exposition* (1893), and *A Red Record* (1895).

36. Aptheker, *Woman's Legacy*; Carby, *Reconstructing Womanhood*, 115; Giddings, *When and Where I Enter*, 26; Ware, *Beyond the Pale*, 179.

37. Wells, *Southern Horrors*, 19.

38. McCurry, "The Two Faces of Republicanism."

39. Carby, *Reconstructing Womanhood*, 112.

40. Wiegman, *American Anatomies*, 90.

41. For an examination of the uses of "civilization" in lynching and antilynching rhetoric, see Bederman, " 'Civilization,' the Decline of Middle-Class Manliness, and Ida B. Wells's Antilynching Campaign (1892–94)."

42. "The Negro Problem and the New Negro Crime," *Harper's Weekly*, June 20, 1903, 1050.

W. E. B. Du Bois critiqued turn-of-the-century depictions of so-called Negro criminality in *Notes on Negro Crime, Particularly in Georgia* (A Social Study made under the direction of Atlanta University by the Ninth Atlanta Conference), Atlanta University Publications, No. 9, ed. W. E. Burghardt Du Bois (Atlanta: Atlanta University Press, 1904).

43. This was also true in antebellum representations of white womanhood. See Sanchez-Eppler, "Bodily Bonds," 28–59.

44. Lombroso and Ferrero, *The Female Offender*.

45. Wells, *Crusade for Justice*, 65, 66.

46. According to Karen Sanchez-Eppler, the white wife's or white daughter's desire for a black man must become the unimaginable in order to ensure the perpetuation of the white patriarch's cultural privilege. Sanchez-Eppler, "Bodily Bonds."

47. Alexander, " 'Can you be BLACK and look at this?' " 105–106.

48. Wells, *Southern Horrors*.

49. As bell hooks has suggested, "White women and men justified the sexual exploitation of enslaved black women by arguing that they were the initiators of sexual relations with men." bell hooks, *Ain't I a Woman: Black Women and Feminism* (Boston: South End Press, 1981), 52. See also Aptheker, *Woman's Legacy*; Caraway, *Segregated Sisterhood*; Carby, *Reconstructing Womanhood*; Davis, *Women, Race, and Class*; and Giddings, *When and Where I Enter*.

50. Cooper, *A Voice from the South*, 31. See Hazel Carby's important work on Anna Julia Cooper in *Reconstructing Womanhood*, esp. 95–120.

51. I draw the concept of the race mother from Laura Doyle's *Bordering on the Body*. According to Doyle, "ideologies of slavery prefigure and prepare the way for the cult of racialized motherhood typical of modern eugenics" (28). Frances Ellen Watkins Harper also celebrates maternal inheritance as a sign of racial identity and race pride in *Iola Leroy*. Frances Ellen Watkins Harper, *Iola Leroy, or Shadows Uplifted*, 2d ed., 1893; reprint, with intro. by Frances Smith Foster (New York: Oxford University Press, 1988).

52. Harriet Ann Jacobs provides one of the most explicit critiques of the African American slave woman's role in maintaining the "pure" white woman's domestic sphere in *Incidents in the Life of a Slave Girl* (1861), ed. Jean Fagan Yellin (Cambridge: Harvard University Press, 1987).

Once again, see Hazel V. Carby on Harriet Jacobs in *Reconstructing Womanhood*, 40–61. For further background see hooks, *Ain't I a Woman*.

53. Cooper, *A Voice from the South*, 29.

54. In *Friendly Counsels for Freedmen*, a tract published for newly freed African American men and women, Reverend J. B. Waterbury suggests the details that a stranger should notice upon entering an African American home, conflating taste with political and social power: "As he glances around, it would be pleasant if he could see a little picture here and there hanging on the wall, or a flower-pot with a pretty pink or rose blooming in it, showing that you have a liking for such things. He would say, 'Well, this looks like freedom. I think you must be quite a happy family.' " Reverend J. B. Waterbury, D.D., *Friendly Counsels for Freedmen* (New York: Published by the American Tract Society, 1864), 26–27. I am indebted to Nicole Tonkovich for this source.

55. For other analyses of the ways in which African American women writers have utilized sentimental rhetoric and the marriage plot toward political ends, see Ann duCille, *The Coupling Convention: Sex, Text, and Tradition in Black Women's Fiction* (New York: Oxford University Press, 1993); Claudia Tate, *Domestic Allegories of Political Desire: The Black Heroine's Text at the Turn of the Century* (New York: Oxford University Press, 1992).

56. Frances Ellen Watkins Harper, "Woman's Political Future" (1894), collected in *The Heath Anthology of American Literature*, vol. 2, 2d ed., ed. Paul Lauter et al. (Lexington, Mass.: D. C. Heath, 1994), 1941–1944.

57. Cooper, *A Voice from the South*, 143.

58. Ibid., 142.

59. Ibid., 142–143.

60. Ibid., 144.

61. Ibid.

62. Ibid.

63. Ibid., 145.

64. Hawthorne, *The House of the Seven Gables*, 249.

65. Cooper, *A Voice from the South*, 145.

Chapter Six
Photographing the "American Negro"

1. W. E. B. Du Bois, "The Conservation of Races" (1897), in *A W. E. B. Du Bois Reader*, ed. Andrew G. Paschal, intro. Arna Bontemps (New York: Macmillan, 1971), 25.

2. In *The Souls of Black Folk*, published in 1903, Du Bois asserts that "double consciousness," the "twoness" of living as both a "Negro" and an "American" (8), is central to "the strange meaning of being black" (3) in the United States at the dawn of the twentieth century. W. E. B. Du Bois, *The Souls of Black Folk* (1903; New York: Vintage, 1990).

3. Studies of the "nation" that focus on the printed word generally follow the influential work of Benedict Anderson. See Anderson, *Imagined Communities*.

4. Deborah Poole and Vicente Rafael have begun the important task of investigating the role photography played in nation-building. See Poole, *Vision, Race, and Modernity*; Rafael, "Nationalism, Imagery and the Filipino Intelligentsia," 591–611; and Rafael, "White Love," 185–218.

5. See the section entitled "The Negro Building" in the *Report of the Board of Commissioners Representing the State of New York at the Cotton States and International Exposition Held at Atlanta, Georgia, 1895* (Albany, N.Y.: Wynkoop Hallenbeck Crawford, 1896), 197–199. This text also reproduces Booker T. Washington's famous "Atlanta Compromise" speech delivered at the opening ceremonies of the Cotton States and International Exposition in Atlanta, 1895.

6. For discussions of racism at the Chicago World's Columbian Exposition of 1893, see Hazel V. Carby, " 'Woman's Era': Rethinking Black Feminist Theory," in *Reconstructing Womanhood*, 3–19; and Robert W. Rydell, "The Chicago World's Columbian Exposition of 1893: 'And Was Jerusalem Builded Here?' " in *All the World's a Fair: Visions of Empire at American International Expositions, 1876–1916* (Chicago: University of Chicago Press, 1984), 38–71.

The exclusion of African Americans from official participation in the Chicago World's Columbian Exposition was protested by both Ida B. Wells and Frederick Douglass. See Wells, *The Reason Why: The Colored American Is Not in the World's Columbian Exposition*, 46–137.

7. W. E. B. Du Bois, "The American Negro at Paris," *American Monthly Review of Reviews* 22:5 (November 1900): 576.

8. The success of the exhibit is reported by Morris Lewis in "Paris and the International Exposition," *Colored American Magazine* 1:5 (October 1900): 295.

9. Du Bois, "The American Negro at Paris," 575.

10. For further discussion of the extended impact of eugenics on late-nineteenth- and early-twentieth-century U.S. culture, see chapter 4. See also Hofstadter, *Social Darwinism in American Thought*, esp. 161–167; Kevles, *In the Name of Eugenics*; and Pickens, *Eugenics and the Progressives*.

11. Anderson, *Imagined Communities*.

12. Galton, *Hereditary Genius*; Galton, *Inquiries into Human Faculty and Its Development*; Galton, *Memories of My Life*; Galton, *Natural Inheritance*.

13. Fatimah Tobing Rony describes such exhibits in her fascinating essay on anthropology and early ethnographic film, entitled "Those Who Squat and Those Who Sit: The Iconography of Race in the 1895 Films of Felix-Louis Regnault," *Camera Obscura* 28 (January 1992): 262–289.

Robert W. Rydell uses the image of a "sliding scale of humanity" to describe the racialized spatial logics that organized "ethnic" displays at the World's Columbian Exposition of 1893. See "The Chicago World's Columbian Exposition of 1893," esp. 64 and 65.

14. Thomas J. Schlereth, "The Material Universe of the American World Expositions, 1876–1915," in *Cultural History and Material Culture: Everyday Life, Landscapes, Museums* (Ann Arbor: University of Michigan Press, 1990), 284–285. See also Rydell, "The Chicago World's Columbian Exposition of 1893."

15. Alan Trachtenberg, "Illustrious Americans," in *Reading American Photographs*, 38.

16. See my discussions of Walter Benjamin's theory of "aura" in chapters 3 and 4. Benjamin, "The Work of Art in the Age of Mechanical Reproduction," 217–252. I do not mean to claim that Johnston's or Du Bois's images were more "objective" than any others, but simply to underscore that these images were imbedded in new

discursive contexts, new institutional paradigms that sought to claim the photograph as objective evidence for social science.

17. For an analysis of the ways in which Lewis Hine and Jacob Riis were posed as the "fathers" of documentary photography in the United States by photography historians working in the 1940s, see Sally Stein's essay "Making Connections with the Camera: Photography and Social Mobility in the Career of Jacob Riis," *Afterimage* 10:10 (May 1983): 9–16. After first outlining how many historians have conflated the work of Hine and Riis, Stein goes on to analyze important political and aesthetic differences in the work of these two men. For more on the invention of "documentary" photography, see Alan Trachtenberg, "Camera Work/Social Work," in *Reading American Photographs*, 164–230. For more on the work of Lewis Hine and Jacob Riis see Verna Posever Curtis and Stanley Mallach, *Photography and Reform: Lewis Hine and the National Child Labor Committee* (Milwaukee, Wis.: Milwaukee Art Museum, 1984); Judith Mara Gutman, *Lewis W. Hine and the American Social Conscience* (New York: Walker, 1967); and Jacob Riis, *How the Other Half Lives* (1890; reprint, New York: Dover, 1971).

18. Booker T. Washington, Hampton's most famous graduate and founder of the Tuskegee Institute, has come to be regarded as one of the most important advocates of manual training for African Americans at the turn of the century. Washington argued that manual training and strict self-discipline would provide economic independence for African Americans, a resource Washington viewed as more immediately important than political power. Washington advocated slow, gradual economic and social advancement for African Americans, arguing that manual, as opposed to professional, white-collar labor, was a necessary first stage in "the natural law of evolution" for any race. Washington claimed: "In a word, we have got to pay the price for everything we get, the price that every civilized race or nation has paid for its position, that of beginning naturally, gradually, at the bottom and working up towards the highest civilization." See Booker T. Washington, "The Storm before the Calm," *Colored American Magazine* 1:4 (September 1900): 202. See also the following works by Washington: "Industrial Education: Will It Solve the Negro Problem?" *Colored American Magazine* 7:2 (February 1904): 87–92; *The Successful Training of the Negro* (New York: Doubleday, 1903); and *Up from Slavery* (1901; reprint, New York: Penguin, 1986).

For counterarguments to an educational system focused exclusively on manual labor, see W. E. B. Du Bois, *The Souls of Black Folk*, and "The Training of Negroes for Social Power," *Colored American Magazine* 7:5 (May 1904): 333–339.

19. Du Bois, "The American Negro at Paris," 577.

20. This is how James Guimond describes Frances Benjamin Johnston's photographs of the Hampton Institute, displayed at the Paris Exposition of 1900. I am suggesting that the entire American Negro exhibit may have communicated this sense of moral and political reprieve or reconciliation to white viewers. James Guimond, "Frances Johnston's *Hampton Album*: A White Dream for Black People," in *American Photography and the American Dream*, 39.

21. See Allan Sekula's fascinating study of the body as constituted by its imagined place within (or outside of) the photographic archive in "The Body and the Archive," 3–64.

22. Galton, *Record of Family Faculties*, and *The Life History Album*.

23. Galton, *The Life History Album*, 5.

24. For more on Brady's "Illustrious Americans," as well as a history of the "celebrity" photographic portrait in nineteenth-century U.S. culture, see McCandless, "The Portrait Studio and the Celebrity," 48–75.

25. Alan Trachtenberg describes the formal style of Brady's daguerreotype portraits in relation to a tradition of Roman sculpture in "Illustrious Americans," in *Reading American Photographs*, 46.

26. Ibid., 50–51.

27. Ibid., 50.

28. Du Bois, "The American Negro at Paris," 577.

29. Frances Benjamin Johnston, *The Hampton Album*, ed. Lincoln Kirstein (New York: Museum of Modern Art, 1966). For more background information see also Guimond, "Frances Johnston's *Hampton Album*"; and Wexler, "Black and White and Color," 341–390.

30. Laura Mulvey, "Visual Pleasure and Narrative Cinema," in *Art after Modernism*, ed. Brian Wallis (New York: Museum of Contemporary Art, 1984), 360–374.

31. In a piece entitled "Afterthoughts on 'Visual Pleasure and Narrative Cinema' Inspired by *Duel in the Sun*," Laura Mulvey explains a woman's pleasure in the scopophilic process of film viewing as the result of a kind of "transvestism" through which the female viewer adopts a masculine viewing position. The film Mulvey reads in order to come to this conclusion, namely *Duel in the Sun*, follows the life course of a "mixed-blood" female protagonist who is exoticized, feared, and desired primarily in terms of her racialized identity. Mulvey's analysis of "transvestism" does not account for the power of racialized identities and racialized identifications in this film, and it is into this interpretive space that my own reading of Frances Benjamin Johnston's photographs enters a history of visual theory. I read Johnston's work, and her position as photographer, not only through the terms of gender but also through the terms of race posed at the turn of the century in the United States. Mulvey, "Afterthoughts on 'Visual Pleasure and Narrative Cinema' Inspired by *Duel in the Sun*," 69–79.

32. bell hooks, "The Oppositional Gaze: Black Female Spectators," in *Black Looks: Race and Representation* (Boston: South End Press, 1992), 115–131; Jacqueline Bobo, *Black Women as Cultural Readers* (New York: Columbia University Press, 1995); Jane M. Gaines, "White Privilege and Looking Relations: Race and Gender in Feminist Film Theory," *Screen* 29:4 (Autumn 1988): 12–27; Dyer, "White," 44–64; Manthia Diawara, "Black Spectatorship: Problems of Identification and Resistance," in *Black American Cinema*, ed. Manthia Diawara (New York: Routledge, 1993), 211–220; Isaac Julien and Kobena Mercer, "Introduction: De Margin and De Centre," *Screen* 29:4 (Autumn 1988): 2–10; Mary Ann Doane, "Dark Continents: Epistemologies of Racial and Sexual Difference in Psychoanalysis and the Cinema," in *Femmes Fatales: Feminism, Film Theory, Psychoanalysis* (New York: Routledge, 1991), 209–248.

Discussing the "characteristic aesthetic and political problems of postmodernism," Isaac Julien and Kobena Mercer note: "It is ironic that while some of the loudest voices offering commentary have announced nothing less than the 'end of representation' or the 'end of history,' the political possibility of the *end of ethnocentrism* has not been seized upon as a suitably exciting topic for description or inquiry"

(2). Julien and Mercer call for critical theorists of visual culture to "recognize and reckon with the kinds of complexity inherent in the culturally constructed nature of ethnic identities," and to assess the "implications" such complexity "has for the analysis of representational practices" (3). Julien and Mercer, "Introduction: De Margin and De Centre."

33. hooks, "In Our Glory," 50.

34. Coco Fusco, *English Is Broken Here: Notes on Cultural Fusion in the Americas* (New York: New Press, 1995); Trinh T. Minh-ha, *Woman, Native, Other: Writing Postcoloniality and Feminism* (Bloomington: Indiana University Press, 1989); Timothy Mitchell, *Colonizing Egypt* (Berkeley: University of California Press, 1988); Poole, *Vision, Race, and Modernity*; Mary Louise Pratt, *Imperial Eyes: Travel Writing and Transculturation* (New York: Routledge, 1992); Rony, *The Third Eye*; Willis, "Introduction: Picturing Us," 3–26.

I find hooks's "white supremacist gaze" useful as a means of making explicit the ways in which the cultural privilege of looking has been racially coded in the United States. Playing upon Richard Dyer's notion that "white" generally functions as an invisible cultural category, while, as Julien and Mercer note, the "colored" is made all too visible, I would suggest that "white" is rarely the object of the Western gaze because it is almost always behind (not in front of) that gaze, imbedded in the viewing position, structuring the reception and the evaluation of Other bodies represented. hooks, "In Our Glory," 50; Dyer, "White"; Julien and Mercer, "Introduction: De Margin and De Centre," 6.

35. In my analysis of Frances Benjamin Johnston's racially encoded viewing privilege, I have tried to follow the lines of analysis suggested by Mary Ann Doane in her individual response for the "Spectatrix" special issue of *Camera Obscura*. According to Doane, "Consideration of race ought to transform the entire framework of the questions posed to the media rather than simply initiating an extension of existing feminist categories (such as the female spectator) to include other, neglected differences. Racial difference and sexual difference are not parallel modes of differentiation that are equally accessible to the same theoretical apparatus. Neither are they totally unrelated: there is a densely intricate history of relations between the two which requires analysis. What is needed is a theorization of the relation between racial and sexual differences, particularly with respect to questions of visibility and invisibility, power and sexuality." Mary Ann Doane, "Introduction," *Camera Obscura* 20–21 (May–September 1989): 146.

According to bell hooks, such a space is opened up by the critical black female spectator. "Black female spectators, who refused to identify with white womanhood, who would not take on the phallocentric gaze of desire and possession, created a critical space where the binary opposition Mulvey posits of 'woman as image, man as bearer of the look' was continually deconstructed." hooks, "The Oppositional Gaze," 122–123.

In my reading of Johnston's position as photographer/viewer I am trying to tease out the "densely intricate" relations posed between "race" and "gender" at the turn of the century in the United States. I am trying to read Johnston's position as one inscribed not only by a heterosexual, binary gender hierarchy but also by a racial hierarchy of access to the gaze.

36. Ware, *Beyond the Pale*, 182. bell hooks also discusses this powerful cultural prohibition against the African American gaze in her analysis of an "oppositional gaze," specifically the critical gaze of the African American female spectator who interrogates filmic representation in order to protest the negation of African American women in Hollywood films ("The Oppositional Gaze"). Jane Gaines also notes that there is a need for work that analyzes "the social prohibitions against the black man's sexual glance" (21), in order to demonstrate the ways in which "racial difference structures a hierarchy of access to the female image" ("White Privilege and Looking Relations," 17).

37. Lynching, legally defined as murder committed by a mob of three or more persons, increased dramatically in the 1890s. See Fredrickson, *The Black Image in the White Mind*, and Giddings, *When and Where I Enter*, 18. For further analysis of the racialized and sexualized nature of lynching at the turn of the century, see chapter 5.

38. Wells, *Southern Horrors*, 14–45; Cooper, *A Voice from the South*.

39. See Sanchez-Eppler, "Bodily Bonds," 28–59.

40. My discussion of Johnston's relative social privilege in relation to African American students at Hampton is not meant to suggest that Johnston's own visual mastery of African American bodies was not itself subject to a more comprehensive white male social prerogative. Indeed, the discourse and the practice of lynching worked to protect the interests of the white male body and the reproduction of a patriarchal white bloodline. See especially Sanchez-Eppler, "Bodily Bonds," and Ware, *Beyond the Pale*.

41. I wish to distinguish both the aim and the signifying context of Johnston's Hampton photographs from Brady's earlier portraits of "Illustrious Americans." However, the terms of these distinctions might become much more subtle if one were to compare Johnston's own presidential portraits to those of Brady's. In addition to her extensive work photographing Hampton and Tuskegee Institutes, Johnston ran a successful portrait business, and she established herself as a kind of court photographer for several presidents, including Theodore Roosevelt.

For biographical information on Johnston, see Pete Daniel and Raymond Smock, *A Talent for Detail: The Photographs of Miss Frances Benjamin Johnston, 1889–1910* (New York: Harmony, 1974); Olaf Hansen, "Frances Benjamin Johnston" in *Notable American Women: A Biographical Dictionary*, vol. 4, ed. Barbara Sicherman and Carol Hurd Green (Cambridge: Belknap Press, of Harvard University Press, 1980), 381–383.

42. Whittier was the primary school affiliated with the Hampton Institute. According to Eric Hobsbawm, "The educational system was transformed into a machine for political socialization by such devices as the worship of the American flag, which as a daily ritual in the country's schools, spread from the 1880s onward." Eric Hobsbawm, "Mass-Producing Traditions: Europe, 1870–1914," in *The Invention of Tradition*, ed. Eric Hobsbawm and Terence Ranger (Cambridge: Cambridge University Press, 1983), 280.

43. My reading of the way patriotic performance establishes an essentialized "Americanism" for Hampton students in Johnston's images is informed by Judith Butler's innovative work on gender. Butler reads gender as an endlessly repeated performance that fabricates an interiorized, "essentialized," sexual identity. Butler,

Gender Trouble, esp. "Subversive Bodily Acts" (79–141), and "Conclusion: From Parody to Politics" (142–149).

While I find Butler's work particularly useful because her analysis denaturalizes the notion of "essence," I do not mean to suggest that gender identities and national identities (or racial identities) are culturally coextensive, or even parallel. I am chiefly interested here in noting the ways in which "essences" of various kinds are inscribed on the body through ritualized and repeated performances.

44. According to Laura Wexler, "The students she [Johnston] photographs are the sons and daughters of 'freedom's first generation,' but nothing about their appearance reveals this fact. Instead, the invisibility of the marks of slavery seems to be part of the point." Wexler, "Black and White and Color," 369.

45. My reading of this image is inspired by Laura Wexler's insightful interpretation of this image and other of Johnston's Hampton photographs in "Black and White and Color," esp. 381–383. For another important reading of this image, see Guimond, "Frances Johnston's *Hampton Album*," 35.

46. In a lecture he delivered at the University of California, San Diego, on March 4, 1992, entitled "Nationalism and Ethnicity," Benedict Anderson argued that ethnic identities were maintained in the modern age of international migrations through the family photograph album. According to Anderson, before modern mass migrations, ethnic and national identities were considered almost coextensive, subsumed under the single category "nationality." In premodern days, one "knew who [and what] one was" because his or her ancestors were buried in the local graveyard, in the earth, where one would someday join them. Families and identities were tied to the local, to the land of one's "patria." After the mass migrations of the nineteenth and twentieth centuries, ethnic identities ceased to be isomorphic with national identities. In the new social context of the late twentieth century, Anderson claims that the photograph album replaces the graveyard as the site of ethnic identifications. Grandmother and grandfather are no longer buried in one's local graveyard—they are buried in the family photo album. Thus, the photograph album enables one to formulate and maintain an ethnic identity distinct from one's national identity.

In this chapter, I examine the intersection of racial (Anglo-Saxon) and national identifications in the construction of "American" identities at the turn of the century, and explore photographs as sites of racially inflected *national* identities.

47. This collection of Du Bois's papers is housed in the Prints and Photographs Division of the Library of Congress.

48. hooks, "In Our Glory," 50.

49. Du Bois, "The American Negro at Paris," 577.

50. hooks, "The Oppositional Gaze."

51. Du Bois, "The Conservation of Races," 26.

52. Ibid., 21.

53. For a detailed analysis of how nineteenth-century white supremacists came to use the category of "type" to describe what they considered permanent racial differences, see Young, *Colonial Desire*, esp. 13–18 and 129–133.

54. In her fascinating study of how the law was employed to perpetuate a "broadreaching ideology of white supremacy" at the turn of the century, Susan Gillman demonstrates how "for purposes of racial identification, the color line was more

stringently and narrowly defined" in legal terms in the early twentieth century. Gillman also notes that "the legal fraction defining blackness was still one thirty-second 'Negro blood' " in Louisiana, as late as 1970. Susan Gillman, " 'Sure Identifiers': Race, Science, and the Law in Twain's *Puddn'head Wilson*," *South Atlantic Quarterly* 87:2 (Spring 1988): 205.

55. In his reading of the latter portion of *The Souls of Black Folk*, Paul Gilroy suggests that W. E. B. Du Bois makes "a bid to escape not just from the South or even from America but from the closed codes of *any* constricting or absolutist understanding of ethnicity." Paul Gilroy, *The Black Atlantic: Modernity and Double Consciousness* (Cambridge: Harvard University Press, 1993), 138.

56. See Young, *Colonial Desire*, chapter 6, "White Power, White Desire: The Political Economy of Miscegenation."

57. Du Bois's biracial "types" problematize the notion that "race" is visible in physical characteristics by demonstrating that "Negroes," legally defined as such by "one drop" of African American blood, may nevertheless bear the stereotypical features of "whiteness" (blond hair, blue eyes, and pale skin). Du Bois's photographs of "types of Negroes" thus function in ways similar to the typecasting of white actresses to play mulatta characters in mid-twentieth-century Hollywood films that Mary Ann Doane describes in "Dark Continents." According to Doane, the practice of employing white actresses to represent mulatta characters "tends to demonstrate inadvertently the quiescent discordance between ideologies of racial identity (defined by blood) and cinematic ideologies of the real (as defined by the visible)" (235).

58. Ida B. Wells makes this critique in *Southern Horrors*, 26–28.

59. I am drawing on Du Bois's well-known image of "the Veil," which he employs to introduce *The Souls of Black Folk*. Du Bois, *The Souls of Black Folk*, 3. I am also borrowing the notion of "colonial desire" from Young's *Colonial Desire*.

60. Adapting Henry Louis Gates, Jr.'s, theory of Signifyin(g) to the domain of visual culture, we might say that Du Bois's photographs of "Types of American Negroes" Signify upon Francis Galton's eugenicist photographs and albums, reproducing those images with a difference. Henry Louis Gates, Jr., *The Signifying Monkey: A Theory of African-American Literary Criticism* (New York: Oxford University Press, 1988). Coco Fusco has utilized Gates's theory of Signifyin(g) in her analysis of Lorna Simpson's photographic art. Fusco, *English Is Broken Here*, esp. 100.

61. Fatimah Tobing Rony describes the Other's resistant "look back" as a "third eye" in her fascinating study of ethnographic film, *The Third Eye*.

Chapter Seven
Looking Back: Pauline Hopkins's Challenge to Eugenics

1. Quoted in Carby, *Reconstructing Womanhood*, 123.

2. Ibid.

3. Throughout this chapter I will be making reference to Pauline Hopkins, *Hagar's Daughter: A Story of Southern Caste Prejudice* (1901–1902), in *The Magazine Novels of Pauline Hopkins*, intro. Hazel V. Carby (New York: Oxford University Press, 1988), 1–284; and Hopkins, *Of One Blood: Or, the Hidden Self* (1902–1903), in *The*

Magazine Novels of Pauline Hopkins, intro. Hazel V. Carby (New York: Oxford University Press, 1988), 439–621.

4. Nancy Leys Stepan and Sander L. Gilman, "Appropriating the Idioms of Science: The Rejection of Scientific Racism," in *The Bounds of Race: Perspectives on Hegemony and Resistance*, ed. and intro. Dominick LaCapra (Ithaca, N.Y.: Cornell University Press, 1991), 72–103.

5. According to Robert Young, "The most consistent arguments regarding race have always been cultural and aesthetic ones." Young, *Colonial Desire*, 94.

6. Ann duCille particularly critiques the claims of scholars Houston Baker and Barbara Christian, arguing that the mulatta figure functions as "both a rhetorical device and a political strategy." duCille, *The Coupling Convention*, 7.

As Hazel Carby suggests, by the turn of the century, "the mulatto figure in literature became a more frequently used literary convention for an exploration and expression of what was increasingly socially proscribed," namely, social and sexual contact between the races. Carby, *Reconstructing Womanhood*, 89.

Similarly, Kristina Brooks proposes that Hopkins's biracial heroines confront "turn-of-the-century racism with visible proof that racial barriers were indeed artificially constructed and imposed." Kristina Brooks, "Mammies, Bucks, and Wenches: Minstrelsy, Racial Pornography, and Racial Politics in Pauline Hopkins's *Hagar's Daughter*," in *The Unruly Voice: Rediscovering Pauline Elizabeth Hopkins*, ed. John Cullen Gruesser (Urbana: University of Illinois Press, 1996), 124. See also Doane, "Dark Continents," 209–248.

7. Young, *Colonial Desire*, 180–181.

8. Galton, *Inquiries into Human Faculty and Its Development*, 10.

9. Doane, "Dark Continents," 234.

10. Ibid., 235.

11. In describing a Tennyson poem, Robert Young states: "In this characteristic ambivalent movement of attraction and repulsion, we encounter the sexual economy of desire in fantasies of race, and of race in fantasies of desire." Young, *Colonial Desire*, 90.

12. Dyer, "White," 45.

13. For an analysis of whiteness as a disguise in Hopkins's fiction, see Hazel V. Carby, " 'All the Fire and Romance': The Magazine Fiction of Pauline Hopkins," in *Reconstructing Womanhood*, esp. 147, 148.

14. J. Randolph Cox, "The Detective Hero in the American Dime Novel," *Dime Novel Roundup* 50 (February 1981): 7–8; quoted in Carby, *Reconstructing Womanhood*, 150.

15. Tate, *Domestic Allegories of Political Desire*, 196.

16. For an important reading of Isaac and other "minstrel-like" characters in Pauline Hopkins's *Hagar's Daughter*, see Brooks, "Mammies, Bucks, and Wenches."

17. Hawthorne, *The House of the Seven Gables*, 254.

18. Once again, according to Claudia Tate, "the most distinctive feature" of Hopkins's magazine novels is the way they transform struggles for racial equality and civil justice into "tests of true love," tests which in turn repudiate racism. Tate, *Domestic Allegories of Political Desire*, 196.

19. Ida B. Wells, *Southern Horrors: Lynch Law in All Its Phases* (1892), in *Selected Works of Ida B. Wells-Barnett*, intro. Trudier Harris (New York: Oxford University Press, 1991), 19.

20. As Dickson D. Bruce, Jr., has argued, "Hopkins' 'Hagar's Daughter' held out the possibility of a real inter-racial love that triumphed over prejudice." Dickson D. Bruce, Jr., *Black American Writing from the Nadir: The Evolution of a Literary Tradition, 1877–1915* (Baton Rouge: Louisiana State University Press, 1989), 150–151. See also Tate, *Domestic Allegories of Political Desire*, esp. 194–200.

21. According to Gail Bederman, Ida B. Wells used a similar tactic in her anti-lynching campaign, turning white conceit over "civilization" against those whites who implicitly condoned lynching. Bederman, " 'Civilization,' " 5–30.

22. According to Dickson D. Bruce, Jr., while Hopkins supported "wholehearted assimilationism" in *Hagar's Daughter*, she moved "toward an appreciation of black distinctiveness" in *Of One Blood*. Bruce, *Black American Writing from the Nadir*, 155.

23. Cynthia D. Schrager has similarly proposed that "*Of One Blood* turns increasingly away from representations of mulatto characters and their deployment as figures of racial indeterminacy and increasingly toward a discourse of blood that reconstructs family and community based on an essential notion of race" (321). According to Schrager, the dueling subtitles of the novel, namely, "Of One Blood" and "The Hidden Self," "name the very doubleness of the text's representation of racial identity, a split that is never satisfactorily reconciled, so that the critic is continually forced to confront its contradictions" (322). Cynthia D. Schrager, "Pauline Hopkins and William James: The New Psychology and the Politics of Race," in *Female Subjects in Black and White: Race, Psychoanalysis, Feminism*, ed. Elizabeth Abel, Barbara Christian, and Helene Moglen (Berkeley: University of California Press, 1997), 307–329.

24. Susan Gillman, "The Mulatto, Tragic or Triumphant? The Nineteenth-Century American Race Melodrama," in *The Culture of Sentiment: Race, Gender, and Sentimentality in Nineteenth-Century America*, ed. Shirley Samuels (New York: Oxford University Press, 1992), 234.

Jennie A. Kassanoff also suggests that "blood functioned as a crucial signifier in the emerging struggle to represent the twentieth-century African American" (165). Specifically, Kassanoff argues that the "semiotics of blood" in Hopkins's novel "manifests four competing discourses subsumed in the palimpsest of the New Negro" (165). Kassanoff proposes that Hopkins's *Of One Blood* deconstructs "the monolith of the New Negro" (160) and critiques "the New Negro's appropriation of the female body" (176). Jennie A. Kassanoff, " 'Fate Has Linked Us Together': Blood, Gender, and the Politics of Representation in Pauline Hopkins's *Of One Blood*," in *The Unruly Voice: Rediscovering Pauline Elizabeth Hopkins*, ed. John Cullen Gruesser (Urbana: University of Illinois Press, 1996), 158–181.

25. Du Bois, "The Conservation of Races," 21. Once again, Kwame Anthony Appiah provides an insightful interpretation of this piece in "The Uncompleted Argument: Du Bois and the Illusion of Race," in *"Race," Writing, and Difference*, ed. Henry Louis Gates, Jr. (Chicago: University of Chicago Press, 1986), 21–37.

26. Du Bois, "The Conservation of Races," 21.

27. Ibid.; emphasis added.

28. Susan Gillman provides an interesting analysis of Du Bois's conceptions of "race" in relation to the family over the course of his career. See Gillman, "The Mulatto, Tragic or Triumphant?" esp. 236–241.

29. According to Susan Gillman, "*Of One Blood* establishes a narrative of origins traced through the maternal line—in profound mockery of slavery's law that the

condition of the child follow that of the mother." Gillman, "The Mulatto, Tragic or Triumphant?" 235.

30. Hopkins, *Of One Blood*, 558.

31. Ibid., 547. In his study of African American "uplift" ideology at the turn of the century, Kevin Gaines suggests that Reuel's ascension to an Ethiopian throne, as King Ergamenes, replicates "the assimilationist assumptions of Western cultural superiority," demonstrating the extent to which uplift ideology was tied to civilizationist logics founded in the hierarchies of evolutionism. According to Gaines, many African American intellectuals reinforced evolutionary notions of "civilized" versus "savage" in their attempts to fight biological racialism in turn-of-the-century U.S. culture. Kevin Gaines, "Black Americans' Racial Uplift Ideology as 'Civilizing Mission': Pauline E. Hopkins on Race and Imperialism," in *Cultures of United States Imperialism*, ed. Amy Kaplan and Donald E. Pease (Durham, N.C.: Duke University Press, 1993), 445.

Paul Gilroy argues similarly that Martin Delany's mid-nineteenth-century Pan-Africanist work was both contradictory and ambivalent. According to Gilroy, in Delany's work "the proposed mission to elevate the black American racial self was inseparable from a second mission to elevate and enlighten the uncultured Africans by offering them the benefits of civilized life." Gilroy, *The Black Atlantic*, 24.

32. Du Bois, *The Souls of Black Folk*, 8–9.

33. Ibid., 8.

34. Thomas J. Otten, "Pauline Hopkins and the Hidden Self of Race," *English Literary History* 59:1 (Spring 1992): 244. As Cynthia D. Schrager has argued, "In mobilizing the trope of the hidden self in relation to Reuel and Dianthe, Hopkins uses the figure of the mulatto to dramatically represent the split consciousness of the African American subject." See Schrager, "Pauline Hopkins and William James," 319.

35. Otten, "Pauline Hopkins and the Hidden Self of Race," 250.

36. Hopkins, *Of One Blood*, 607.

37. As Cynthia D. Schrager suggests, in *Of One Blood* "incest is recognized as the condition of the slave institution." See Schrager, "Pauline Hopkins and William James," 314.

38. Elizabeth Ammons, *Conflicting Stories: American Women Writers at the Turn into the Twentieth Century* (New York: Oxford University Press, 1991), 83.

39. Gillman, "The Mulatto, Tragic or Triumphant?" 232.

40. Ammons, *Conflicting Stories*, 82. Jennie A. Kassanoff argues that Hopkins's novel makes a case for "black eugenics," for an African American investment in racial blood purity as a means of protesting a history of interracial rape in slavery. See Kassanoff, " 'Fate Has Linked Us Together,' " esp. 168.

41. Galton, *Hereditary Genius*.

42. Young, *Colonial Desire*, 127. Pauline Hopkins was not alone in her endeavors to reinscribe the Ethiopian origins of Egyptian culture. Frederick Douglass, among others, traveled to Egypt in the late 1880s in order to prove his long-standing ethnological claims of ancient African greatness. According to Paul Gilroy, "It is obvious that the appeal of Egypt as evidence of the greatness of pre-slave African cultures, like the enduring symbol that Egypt supplies for black creativity and civili-

zation, has had a special significance within black Atlantic responses to modernity." Gilroy, *The Black Atlantic*, 59–60.

In the early twentieth century, Du Bois also "began to retell the narrative of western civilization in systematic ways that emphasized its African origins." Gilroy, *The Black Atlantic*, 113.

43. For an important discussion of these texts and what he has called "the whitening of Egypt," see Young, "Egypt in America," in *Colonial Desire*, 126–133, esp. 127–129. According to Young, American Egyptologists were intent on establishing the permanent supremacy of the Caucasian race throughout time, in order to legitimize the "natural" order of American slavery.

Josiah Nott blamed the fall of ancient "Caucasian" Egyptian culture on interracial reproduction (Young, *Colonial Desire*, 129), a scenario that I would argue is remarkably close to that used by Francis Galton to describe the fall of ancient Athenian culture.

44. Once again, in *The Black Atlantic* Paul Gilroy provides a compelling analysis of the ways in which African American intellectuals evoked ancient Egyptian civilization to contest the dominance of a Eurocentric history of modernity. See Gilroy, *The Black Atlantic*, esp. 59–60.

45. Otten, "Pauline Hopkins and the Hidden Self of Race."

46. Ibid., 235.

47. Cynthia D. Schrager and Eric J. Sundquist also link Pauline Hopkins's *Of One Blood* to William James's early psychological works. See Schrager, "Pauline Hopkins and William James"; and Eric J. Sundquist, *To Wake the Nations: Race in the Making of American Literature* (Cambridge: Belknap Press of Harvard University Press, 1993), esp. 569–574.

48. Otten, "Pauline Hopkins and the Hidden Self of Race," 241, discussing William James's, "The Hidden Self," in *Essays in Psychology*, ed. Frederick H. Burkhardt (Cambridge: Harvard University Press, 1983), 248.

49. Du Bois, *The Souls of Black Folk*, 3.

50. In *Domestic Allegories of Political Desire*, Claudia Tate suggests that Hopkins's magazine novels "undermine the conventional happy ending of the domestic genre, thereby emphasizing the failure of the U.S. civil sphere of Hopkins's epoch to sustain the ideal ending" (195–196). Once again, see also Elizabeth Ammons, *Conflicting Stories*, 83.

51. Otten, "Pauline Hopkins and the Hidden Self of Race," 244. As Eric Sundquist suggests, "for both Hopkins and Du Bois, James provided the key to a theory of diasporic consciousness." See Sundquist, *To Wake the Nations*, 571.

Chapter Eight
Reconfiguring a Masculine Gaze

1. Throughout this chapter I will be referring to the Signet Classic version of *Sister Carrie*, which follows the original Doubleday, Page edition published in 1900. Theodore Dreiser, *Sister Carrie* (1900; New York: New American Library, 1961).

2. Benjamin, "Paris, Capital of the Nineteenth Century," 55.

3. Rachel Bowlby's work perhaps best emblematizes this influential position. See Bowlby, *Just Looking*.

Miles Orvell critiques a culture of imitation in *The Real Thing*. Clare Virginia Eby suggests, conversely, that Dreiser poses Carrie's imitation (which she describes in terms of invidious comparison and emulation) as an imaginative method of self-construction and self-transformation. Clare Virginia Eby, "The Psychology of Desire: Veblen's 'Pecuniary Emulation' and 'Invidious Comparison' in *Sister Carrie* and *An American Tragedy*," *Studies in American Fiction* 21:2 (Autumn 1993): 191–208, esp. 194–195.

In a recent essay, Blanche H. Gelfant describes the woman-as-consumer as a kind of Medusa figure within "a deterministic structure of desire" (179): "The woman herself is a static figure, arrested in a pattern of desire, but she generates a vortex of forces that flow inexorably toward consumption and death. Men should fear this woman, for a man who gazes upon her may be doomed, as may be those upon whom she gazes" (192). Blanche H. Gelfant, "What More Can Carrie Want? Naturalistic Ways of Consuming Women," in *The Cambridge Companion to American Realism and Naturalism, Howells to London*, ed. Donald Pizer (New York: Cambridge University Press, 1995), 178–210.

I am interested in the *subversive* power of the woman-as-consumer to "doom" the men who gaze upon her commodified body. In my reading, the woman-as-consumer acquires a limited mobility and agency as the object of a masculine gaze.

4. As I will explain later, Thorstein Veblen describes "conspicuous consumption" as the means whereby class distinctions are displayed in the turn-of-the-century industrial city. Thorstein Veblen, *The Theory of the Leisure Class: An Economic Study of Institutions* (1899; reprint, New York: Modern Library, 1931).

5. According to Rachel Bowlby, "It was above all to women that the new commerce made its appeal, urging and inviting them to procure its luxurious benefits and purchase sexually attractive images for themselves. They were to become in a sense like prostitutes in their active, commodified self-display." Bowlby, *Just Looking*, 11. See also Bowlby's chapter entitled "Commerce and Femininity" in *Just Looking*.

6. Contrary to Amy Kaplan and others who propose that "the consumption of commodities in *Sister Carrie* functions in the novel to compensate for social powerlessness," I would like to suggest that the consumption of commodities opens up a new kind of gendered social power (albeit a limited one) for women in Dreiser's *Sister Carrie*. Amy Kaplan, *The Social Construction of American Realism* (Chicago: University of Chicago Press, 1988), 147.

7. For analyses of the department store and nineteenth-century consumer culture, see Gunther Barth, *City People: The Rise of Modern City Culture in Nineteenth-Century America* (New York: Oxford University Press, 1980); Bill Lancaster, *The Department Store: A Social History* (New York: Leicester University Press, 1995); William Leach, *Land of Desire: Merchants, Power, and the Rise of a New American Culture* (New York: Pantheon, 1993); Michael B. Miller, *The Bon Marche: Bourgeois Culture and the Department Store, 1869–1920* (Princeton, N.J.: Princeton University Press, 1981); and Williams, *Dream Worlds*.

On gender and shopping see Elaine S. Abelson, *When Ladies Go A-Thieving: Middle-Class Shoplifters in the Victorian Department Store* (New York: Oxford University Press, 1989); Bowlby, *Just Looking*; Bowlby, "Modes of Modern Shopping,"

185–205; and Meaghan Morris, "Things to Do with Shopping Centres," in *Grafts: Feminist Cultural Criticism*, ed. Susan Sheridan (New York: Verso, 1988), 193–225.

For more general theoretical analyses of consumerism and commodity capitalism, see Baudrillard, *For a Critique of the Political Economy of the Sign*; Baudrillard, *Selected Writings*; Benjamin, *Charles Baudelaire*; Benjamin, "Paris, Capital of the Nineteenth Century," 146–162; and Buck-Morss, "The Flaneur, the Sandwichman and the Whore," 99–140.

Stanley Corkin offers a concise description of the economic and social shifts engendered by industrialization and urbanization in late-nineteenth-century America in "*Sister Carrie* and Industrial Life: Objects and the New American Self," *Modern Fiction Studies* 33:4 (Winter 1987): 605–619, esp. 606–607.

8. See Bowlby's *Just Looking*. According to Mariana Valverde, the department store was also associated with moral dangers in turn-of-the-century reform literature. Mariana Valverde, "The Love of Finery: Fashion and the Fallen Woman in Nineteenth-Century Social Discourse," *Victorian Studies* 32:2 (Winter 1989): 169–188, esp. 173.

9. Philip Fisher has suggested that "for a man inside the city his self is not inside his body but around him, outside the body." Philip Fisher, *Hard Facts: Setting and Form in the American Novel* (New York: Oxford University Press, 1987), 134.

Similarly, Stanley Corkin suggests that in the turn-of-the-century city "commodities served as vital components of self-definition, seemingly filling a void created by the alienation of industrial life." According to Corkin, Dreiser's *Sister Carrie* "reflects this world view, while arguing for its correctness and promoting its acceptance." Corkin, "*Sister Carrie* and Industrial Life," 607.

Clare Virginia Eby also proposes that *Sister Carrie* is "crammed with consumer goods not just to enhance the setting, to document economic history, or to facilitate social commentary, but to bring together economic and psychological concerns into a new theory of the self." Eby, "The Psychology of Desire," 191.

10. Veblen, *The Theory of the Leisure Class*, esp. chap. 4, "Conspicuous Consumption."

11. Karl Marx, *Capital*, vol. 1, in *The Marx-Engels Reader*, 2d ed., ed. Robert C. Tucker (New York: Norton, 1978), 320–321; emphasis added.

12. For an examination of reification see George Lukacs, *History and Class Consciousness: Studies in Marxist Dialectics*, trans. Rodney Livingstone (Cambridge: MIT Press, 1971).

13. Walter Benjamin describes the "phantasmagoria" of commodified life as a display that overwhelms the senses in "Paris, Capital of the Nineteenth Century," 152. Susan Buck-Morss further explains Benjamin's and Marx's use of the term "phantasmagoria" in *The Dialectics of Seeing: Walter Benjamin and the Arcades Project* (Cambridge: MIT Press, 1989).

14. Again see Benjamin, "Paris, Capital of the Nineteenth Century," 152; and Buck-Morss, *The Dialectics of Seeing*, 81.

15. This phrase is most directly associated with Guy Debord's work *Society of the Spectacle* (Detroit: Black and Red, 1983). According to Debord, "The spectacle, as a tendency *to make one see* the world by means of various specialized mediations (it can no longer be grasped directly), naturally finds vision to be the privileged human sense which the sense of touch was for other epochs; the most abstract, the

most mystifiable sense corresponds to the generalized abstraction of present-day society" (paragraph 18). I am also interested in the ways Frankfurt school scholars such as Walter Benjamin have placed vision at the center of commodity capitalism. Benjamin poses the flaneur, a loitering *observer*, as the figure who embodies, even as he critiques, the logics of early commodity capitalism. See Benjamin, "The Flaneur," in *Charles Baudelaire*, 35–66; Benjamin, "Paris, Capital of the Nineteenth Century." See also Buck-Morss, *The Dialectics of Seeing*, and "The Flaneur, the Sandwichman and the Whore." Janet Wolff has theorized the "invisible flaneuse" as the female flaneur, the subject that nineteenth-century culture failed to accommodate. See the chapter entitled "The Invisible *Flaneuse*: Women and the Literature of Modernity," in Janet Wolff, *Feminine Sentences: Essays on Women and Culture* (Cambridge: Polity, 1990), 34–50.

16. Once again, see Bowlby, *Just Looking*, 11.

17. Once again, according to Rachel Bowlby, the citizen of consumer society is identifiable by the consumption of "appropriate" commodities.

18. Bowlby, *Just Looking*; Fisher, *Hard Facts*; Veblen, *The Theory of the Leisure Class*.

19. Veblen, *The Theory of the Leisure Class*, 167.

20. Mariana Valverde notes that working-class women's conspicuous consumption of "finery" was often met with moral judgment on the part of middle-class reformers. See Valverde, "The Love of Finery," 172.

21. Bowlby, "Modes of Modern Shopping."

22. Clare Virginia Eby provides a fascinating analysis of imitation in "The Psychology of Desire," focusing her analysis on Thorstein Veblen's theories of "pecuniary emulation" and "invidious comparison." According to Eby, "What is 'innate' to the mind of modern man and woman, according to Dreiser, is first to compare one's self and its objects to others, then to improve the self by emulation" (191). Eby proposes that "Carrie's psychology conforms to the prime tenets of invidious comparison: observation, contrast, emulation, and consecutive change" (193). Eby, "The Psychology of Desire."

According to Blanche H. Gelfant, a "sequence of seeing, wanting, and buying constitutes a deterministic structure of desire underlying naturalistic novels, like *Sister Carrie*, and advertisements psychologically programmed to motivate the modern consumer." Gelfant, "What More Can Carrie Want?" 179–180.

23. Walter Benn Michaels, "Sister Carrie's Popular Economy," in *The Gold Standard and the Logic of Naturalism: American Literature at the Turn of the Century* (Berkeley: University of California Press, 1987), 29–58. Stanley Corkin also suggests that "Carrie finally succeeds because she is able to assimilate the knowledge that in this world self is at best a transient quality. It is not a stable center from which one approaches the world but a shifting appearance that one adapts expediently." Corkin, *"Sister Carrie* and Industrial Life," 616.

24. Veblen, *The Theory of the Leisure Class*, chap. 4, "Conspicuous Consumption," esp. 81–83, and chap. 7, "Dress as an Expression of the Pecuniary Culture," esp. 180–182.

25. As noted in chapter 1, Gillian Brown discusses nineteenth-century women's property laws, particularly the first New York Married Women's Property Act of 1848, in "Hawthorne, Inheritance, and Women's Property," 107–118, esp. 109.

26. An interesting reading of Hurstwood's wife might also be made along these lines.

27. See Kaplan, *The Social Construction of American Realism*, chap. 5, "Theodore Dreiser's Promotion of Authorship."

28. Ibid., 110.

29. Ibid., 121.

30. *Sister Carrie* was rejected by the first publishing house Dreiser pursued, the prestigious Harper and Brothers, because an editor felt that the text would fail to hold the attention and interest of "the feminine readers who control the destinies of so many novels." Quoted in the historical commentary by James W. West III, John C. Berkeley, and Alice M. Winters to the Pennsylvania edition of Theodore Dreiser's *Sister Carrie* (Philadelphia: University of Pennsylvania Press, 1981), 519.

31. Once again, see the historical commentary published in the Pennsylvania edition of *Sister Carrie*, esp. 519–529.

32. Doubleday, Page did not promote *Sister Carrie* after the firm finally published the novel, and many critics attribute the initial commercial failure of the novel to this lack of marketing. Stanley Corkin provides another reading, suggesting that the novel initially failed to gain a wide readership because "American readers were not yet used to making the intellectual leaps the book required of them: that is, knowing the meanings of various common objects and being able to apply those meanings immediately to objectified humans" (618). In other words, readers did not yet fully understand "the world of commodities" (607). Corkin, "*Sister Carrie* and Industrial Life."

33. Lawrence Hussman compares Stephen Crane's *Maggie: A Girl of the Streets* to Dreiser's *Sister Carrie* in "The Fate of the Fallen Woman in *Maggie* and *Sister Carrie*." According to Hussman, *Sister Carrie* is the more "radical" novel of the two because it proposes that "the transgressions by which we define a fallen woman may in fact lead to a fortunate fall." Lawrence E. Hussman, Jr., "The Fate of the Fallen Woman in *Maggie* and *Sister Carrie*," in *The Image of the Prostitute in Modern Literature*, ed. Pierre L. Horn and Mary Beth Pringle (New York: Frederick Ungar, 1984), 99.

34. Fisher, *Hard Facts*, 163.

35. Fisher, *Hard Facts*, 167.

36. Barbara Hochman similarly suggests that "the organization of the theater enforces that separation between audience and actress that allows Carrie unabashedly to display her desire-full self, without risking its being appropriated." Barbara Hochman, "A Portrait of the Artist as a Young Actress: The Rewards of Representation in *Sister Carrie*," in *New Essays on Sister Carrie*, ed. Donald Pizer (New York: Cambridge University Press, 1991), 52.

Amy Kaplan also proposes that "the theater allows Carrie to translate the threats of city life into a form of art that can be instantly consumed by an audience, without consuming her." Kaplan, *The Social Construction of American Realism*, 158.

37. Clare Virginia Eby suggests: "The 'burden of duty' (p. 448) that Ames wants Carrie to bear is the burden of encouraging others to desire." Eby, "The Psychology of Desire," 196.

38. Marx, *The Marx-Engels Reader*, 104.

39. As Stanley Corkin notes, "When his [Hurstwood's] goal becomes mere subsistence, he is doomed to poverty, for the consumption of objects is as fundamental to this world as nutrition." Corkin, "*Sister Carrie* and Industrial Life," 615.

40. Michel Foucault's most influential discussion of surveillance and discipline is found in his *Discipline and Punish*.

41. Guy Debord theorizes this passive spectator in *Society of the Spectacle*.

42. June Howard, *Form and History in American Literary Naturalism* (Chapel Hill: University of North Carolina Press, 1985), x.

43. See especially chap. 4, "Slumming in Determinism: Naturalism and the Spectator," in June Howard's *Form and History in American Literary Naturalism*.

44. Clare Virginia Eby provides a useful reading of this conclusion, arguing, contrary to many literary critics, that Carrie's perpetual desire is not an indication of an "empty or failed self." According to Eby, "given the terms of invidious comparison, the ending, however rhetorically overblown, is thematically consistent with Carrie's continuing self-creation." Eby, "The Psychology of Desire," 195.

45. In drawing upon this ending I am privileging the version of *Sister Carrie* first published in 1900 by Doubleday, Page. A long debate among Dreiser scholars has ensued since the 1981 publication of the Pennsylvania edition of this novel, which claims to restore the text to Dreiser's pre-edited "original" form. In opting for the edited, first-printed version of the novel, I follow Donald Pizer in preferring "to read the novel that emerged out of the personal tensions, conflicting motives, and cultural complexities of that moment and that in the eighty years since its publication has accrued a rich public responsiveness and role." Donald Pizer, "Self-Censorship and Textual Editing," in *Textual Criticism and Literary Interpretation*, ed. Jerome J. McGann (Chicago: University of Chicago Press, 1985), 160.

Afterimages
A Brief Look at American Visual Culture in the 1990s

1. *Time* 142:21 (special issue, Fall 1993), 2. Since my initial interest in *Time*'s "new Eve," several intriguing and important examinations of this image have been published. See Lauren Berlant, *The Queen of America Goes to Washington City: Essays on Sex and Citizenship* (Durham, N.C.: Duke University Press, 1997), 200–209; Victor Burgin, *In/Different Spaces: Place and Memory in Visual Culture* (Berkeley: University of California Press, 1996), 258–264; and Haraway, *Modest_Witness@ Second_Millennium.FemaleMan_Meets_OncoMouse*, 259–265.

2. In his discussion of nineteenth-century notions of hybridity, Robert Young states, "The idea of race here shows itself to be profoundly dialectical: it only works when defined against potential intermixture, which also threatens to undo its calculations altogether." Young, *Colonial Desire*, 19.

3. In their recent, very popular book, Richard Herrnstein and Charles Murray make a case for the innate intellectual capabilities of different races, an argument disturbingly reminiscent of Francis Galton's nineteenth-century studies of "hereditary genius" and eugenics. Richard J. Herrnstein and Charles A. Murray, *The Bell Curve: Intelligence and Class Structure in American Life* (New York: Free Press, 1994).

4. Benjamin, "A Small History of Photography," 252.

Bibliography

Abelson, Elaine S. *When Ladies Go A-Thieving: Middle-Class Shoplifters in the Victorian Department Store*. New York: Oxford University Press, 1989.

Alexander, Elizabeth. " 'Can you be BLACK and look at this?': Reading the Rodney King Video(s)." In *Black Male: Representations of Masculinity in Contemporary American Art*. Ed. Thelma Golden. New York: Whitney Museum of American Art, 1994, 90–110.

Ammons, Elizabeth. *Conflicting Stories: American Women Writers at the Turn into the Twentieth Century*. New York: Oxford University Press, 1991.

Anderson, Benedict. *Imagined Communities: Reflections on the Origin and Spread of Nationalism*. London: Verso, 1983.

———. "Nationalism and Ethnicity." Lecture delivered at the University of California, San Diego, March 4, 1992.

Anderson, John E., and Florence L. Goodenough. *The Modern Baby Book and Child Development Record*. New York: Norton and *The Parents' Magazine*, 1929.

Appelbaum, Stanley. *The Chicago World's Fair of 1893*. New York: Dover, 1980.

Appiah, Kwame Anthony. "Race." In *Critical Terms for Literary Study*. Ed. Frank Lentricchia and Thomas McLaughlin. Chicago: University of Chicago Press, 1990, 274–287.

———. "The Uncompleted Argument: Du Bois and the Illusion of Race." In *"Race," Writing, and Difference*. Ed. Henry Louis Gates, Jr. Chicago: University of Chicago Press, 1986, 21–37.

Aptheker, Bettina. *Woman's Legacy: Essays on Race, Sex, and Class in American History*. Amherst: University of Massachusetts Press, 1982.

———, ed. *Lynching and Rape: An Exchange of Views*. Occasional Paper No. 25. New York: American Institute for Marxist Studies, 1977.

Armstrong, Nancy. *Desire and Domestic Fiction: A Political History of the Novel*. New York: Oxford University Press, 1987.

Arthur, T. S. "American Characteristics: No. V—The Daguerreotypist." *Godey's Lady's Book*, 1849, 352–355.

"Baby's Picture Is Always Treasured." *Ladies' Home Journal*, July 1898.

Banta, Martha. "Artists, Models, Real Things, and Recognizable Types." *Studies in the Literary Imagination* 16:2 (Fall 1983): 7–34.

Barkan, Elazar. *The Retreat of Scientific Racism: Changing Concepts of Race in Britain and the United States between the World Wars*. New York: Cambridge University Press, 1992.

Barth, Gunther. *City People: The Rise of Modern City Culture in Nineteenth-Century America*. New York: Oxford University Press, 1980.

Baudrillard, Jean. *For a Critique of the Political Economy of the Sign*. Trans. Charles Levin. St. Louis: Telos, 1981.

———. *Selected Writings*. Ed. Mark Poster. Stanford, Calif.: Stanford University Press, 1988.

Baudrillard, Jean. *Simulations*. Trans. Paul Foss, Paul Patton, and Philip Beitchman. New York: Semiotext(e), 1983.

Baym, Nina. "Hawthorne's Holgrave: The Failure of the Artist-Hero." *Journal of English and Germanic Philology* 69 (1970): 584–598.

———. *The Shape of Hawthorne's Career*. Ithaca, N.Y.: Cornell University Press, 1976.

———. *Woman's Fiction: A Guide to Novels by and about Women in America, 1820–1870*. Ithaca, N.Y.: Cornell University Press, 1978.

Beasley, Maurine, and Sheila Silver. "*The Journalist*: Black Writers—'The Newspaper Woman.'" In *Women in Media: A Documentary Source Book*. Washington, D.C.: Women's Institute for Freedom of the Press, 1977.

Bederman, Gail. "'Civilization,' the Decline of Middle-Class Manliness, and Ida B. Wells's Antilynching Campaign (1892–94)." *Radical History Review* 52 (1992): 5–30.

Beecher, Catherine. *Treatise on Domestic Economy*. Boston: Marsh, Capen, Lyon and Webb, 1841.

Benjamin, Jessica. *The Bonds of Love: Psychoanalysis, Feminism, and the Problem of Domination*. New York: Pantheon, 1988.

Benjamin, Walter. "The Author as Producer." In *Reflections*. Ed. Peter Demetz. New York: Schocken Books, 1968, 220–238.

———. *Charles Baudelaire: A Lyric Poet in the Era of High Capitalism*. Trans. Harry Zohn. London: New Left Books, 1973.

———. "Paris, Capital of the Nineteenth Century." In *Reflections*. Ed. Peter Demetz. New York: Schocken Books, 1986, 146–162.

———. "A Small History of Photography." In *One Way Street and Other Writings*. Trans. Edmund Jephcott and Kingsley Shorter. London: New Left Books, 1979, 240–257.

———. "The Work of Art in the Age of Mechanical Reproduction." In *Illuminations*. Ed. Hannah Arendt. Trans. Harry Zohn. New York: Schocken Books, 1969, 217–252.

Berger, Maurice. "The Critique of Pure Racism: An Interview with Adrian Piper." *Afterimage*, October 1990, 5–9.

Bergstrom, Janet, and Mary Ann Doane. "The Female Spectator: Contexts and Directions." *Camera Obscura* 20–21 (May–September 1989): 5–27.

Berlant, Lauren. "The Female Woman: Fanny Fern and the Form of Sentiment." *American Literary History* 3:3 (Fall 1991): 429–454.

———. *The Queen of America Goes to Washington City: Essays on Sex and Citizenship*. Durham, N.C.: Duke University Press, 1997.

Bertillon, Alphonse. *Identification Anthropométrique, Instructions Signalétiques*. Nouvelle Édition. Melun: Imprimerie Administrative, 1893.

"Bicycle Kodaks." *Ladies' Home Journal*, April 1897, 19.

Black, Alexander. "How to Give a Picture-Play." *Ladies' Home Journal*, October 1898, 25.

Blumin, Stuart M. *The Emergence of the Middle Class: Social Experience in the American City, 1760–1900*. Cambridge: Cambridge University Press, 1989.

Bobo, Jacqueline. *Black Women as Cultural Readers*. New York: Columbia University Press, 1995.

Bolton, Richard, ed. *The Contest of Meaning: Critical Histories of Photography*. Cambridge: MIT Press, 1989.

Bourdieu, Pierre. *Distinction: A Social Critique of the Judgement of Taste*. Trans. Richard Nice. Cambridge: Harvard University Press, 1984.

Bowlby, Rachel. *Just Looking: Consumer Culture in Dreiser, Gissing, and Zola*. New York: Methuen, 1985.

———. "Modes of Modern Shopping: Mallarmé at the *Bon Marche*." In *The Ideology of Conduct: Essays on Literature and the History of Sexuality*. Ed. Nancy Armstrong and Leonard Tennenhouse. New York: Methuen, 1987, 185–205.

Brodhead, Richard H. *Hawthorne, Melville, and the Novel*. Chicago: University of Chicago Press, 1976.

———. "Sparing the Rod: Discipline and Fiction in Antebellum America." *Representations* 21 (Winter 1988): 67–96.

———. "Veiled Ladies: Toward a History of Antebellum Entertainment." *American Literary History* 1:2 (Summer 1989): 273–294.

Brooks, Kristina. "Mammies, Bucks, and Wenches: Minstrelsy, Racial Pornography, and Racial Politics in Pauline Hopkins's *Hagar's Daughter*." In *The Unruly Voice: Rediscovering Pauline Elizabeth Hopkins*. Ed. John Cullen Gruesser. Urbana: University of Illinois Press, 1996, 119–157.

Brooks, Peter. *Body Work: Objects of Desire in Modern Narrative*. Cambridge: Harvard University Press, 1993.

Brown, Gillian. *Domestic Individualism: Imagining Self in Nineteenth-Century America*. Berkeley: University of California Press, 1990.

———. "Hawthorne, Inheritance, and Women's Property." *Studies in the Novel* 23:1 (Spring 1991): 107–118.

Bruce, Dickson D., Jr. *Black American Writing from the Nadir: The Evolution of a Literary Tradition, 1877–1915*. Baton Rouge: Louisiana State University Press, 1989.

Buck-Morss, Susan. "Aesthetics and Anaesthetics: Walter Benjamin's Artwork Essay Reconsidered." *October* 62 (Fall 1992): 3–41.

———. *The Dialectics of Seeing: Walter Benjamin and the Arcades Project*. Cambridge: MIT Press, 1989.

———. "The Flaneur, the Sandwichman and the Whore: The Politics of Loitering." *New German Critique* 39 (Fall 1986): 99–140.

Burbick, Joan. *Healing the Republic: The Language of Health and the Culture of Nationalism in Nineteenth-Century America*. New York: Cambridge University Press, 1994.

Burger, Peter. *Theory of the Avant-Garde*. Trans. Michael Shaw. Minneapolis: University of Minnesota Press, 1984.

Burgin, Victor. *In/Different Spaces: Place and Memory in Visual Culture*. Berkeley: University of California Press, 1996.

———, ed. *Thinking Photography*. London: Macmillan, 1982.

Burhans, Mary Swart Hoes. "Eligibility." *American Monthly Magazine* 3:4 (October 1893): 420–433.

Butler, Judith. "Discussion." *October* 61 (Summer 1992): 108–120.

———. *Gender Trouble: Feminism and the Subversion of Identity*. New York: Routledge, 1990.

Byrnes, Thomas. *Professional Criminals of America*. New York: Cassell, 1886.

" 'Camera Tea Party.' " *Ladies' Home Journal*, June 1898, 33.

Cameron, Sharon. *The Corporeal Self: Allegories of the Body in Melville and Hawthorne*. Baltimore, Md.: Johns Hopkins University Press, 1981.

Campbell, Charles. "Representing Representation: Body as Figure, Frame, and Text in *The House of the Seven Gables*." *Arizona Quarterly* 47:4 (Winter 1991): 1–26.

Caraway, Nancie. *Segregated Sisterhood: Racism and the Politics of American Feminism*. Knoxville: University of Tennessee Press, 1991.

Carby, Hazel V. " 'On the Threshold of Woman's Era': Lynching, Empire, and Sexuality in Black Feminist Theory." In *"Race," Writing, and Difference*. Ed. Henry Louis Gates, Jr. Chicago: University of Chicago Press, 1986, 301–316.

———. *Reconstructing Womanhood: The Emergence of the Afro-American Woman Novelist*. New York: Oxford University Press, 1987.

Carey, James. "Culture, Geography and Communications: The Work of Harold Innis in an American Context." In *Culture, Communication, and Dependency: The Tradition of H. A. Innis*. Ed. William Melody. Norwood, N.J.: A BLEX, 1981, 73–91.

———. "The Press and the Public Discourse." *The Center Magazine*, (March/April 1987), 4–16.

———. "Technology and Ideology: The Case of the Telegraph." In *Prospects: An Annual of American Cultural Studies*. Ed. Jack Salzman. Cambridge: Cambridge University Press, 1983, 303–324.

Chopin, Kate. *The Awakening and Selected Short Stories by Kate Chopin*. Intro. Marilynne Robinson. New York: Bantam, 1989.

———. "Desiree's Baby." In *The Awakening and Selected Short Stories by Kate Chopin*. Intro. Marilynne Robinson. New York: Bantam, 1989, 175–181.

Cooper, Anna Julia. *A Voice from the South*. 1892. Intro. Mary Helen Washington. New York: Oxford University Press, 1988.

Core, E. B. "Getting Good Pictures of Children." *Ladies' Home Journal*, February 1898, 13.

Corkin, Stanley. "*Sister Carrie* and Industrial Life: Objects and the New American Self." *Modern Fiction Studies* 33:4 (Winter 1987): 605–619.

Cott, Nancy. *The Bonds of Womanhood: "Woman's Sphere" in New England, 1780–1835*. New Haven, Conn.: Yale University Press, 1977.

Cox, J. Randolph. "The Detective Hero in the American Dime Novel." *Dime Novel Roundup* 50 (February 1981): 2–18.

Crane, Stephen. *Maggie: A Girl of the Streets*. 1893. New York: Fawcett, 1960.

Crary, Jonathan. *Techniques of the Observer: On Vision and Modernity in the Nineteenth Century*. Cambridge, Mass.: MIT Press, 1990.

Curtis, Verna Posever, and Stanley Mallach. *Photography and Reform: Lewis Hine and the National Child Labor Committee*. Milwaukee, Wis.: Milwaukee Art Museum, 1984.

Daniel, Pete, and Raymond Smock. *A Talent for Detail: The Photographs of Miss Frances Benjamin Johnston, 1889–1910*. New York: Harmony, 1974.

Darnton, Robert. *Mesmerism and the End of the Enlightenment in France*. Cambridge: Harvard University Press, 1968.

Darwin, Charles. *The Origin of Species*. New York: P. F. Collier, 1909.

Davidson, Cathy N. "Photographs of the Dead: Sherman, Daguerre, Hawthorne." *South Atlantic Quarterly* 89:4 (Fall 1990): 667–701.

Davis, Angela Y. *Women, Race, and Class*. New York: Vintage, 1983.

Debord, Guy. *Society of the Spectacle*. Detroit: Black and Red, 1983.

de Lauretis, Teresa. "Eccentric Subjects: Feminist Theory and Historical Consciousness." *Feminist Studies* 16:1 (Spring 1990): 115–150.

———. "The Essence of the Triangle or, Taking the Risk of Essentialism Seriously: Feminist Theory in Italy, the U.S., and Britain." *differences* 1:2 (Summer 1989): 3–37.

———. *Technologies of Gender: Essays on Theory, Film, and Fiction*. Bloomington: Indiana University Press, 1987.

Diawara, Manthia. "Black Spectatorship: Problems of Identification and Resistance." In *Black American Cinema*. Ed. Manthia Diawara. New York: Routledge, 1993, 211–220.

Doane, Mary Ann. "Dark Continents: Epistemologies of Racial and Sexual Difference in Psychoanalysis and the Cinema." In *Femmes Fatales: Feminism, Film Theory, Psychoanalysis*. New York: Routledge, 1991, 209–248.

———. *The Desire to Desire: The Woman's Film of the 1940s*. Bloomington: Indiana University Press, 1987.

———. "Film and the Masquerade: Theorising the Female Spectator." *Screen* 23:3–4 (September–October 1982): 74–87.

———. "Introduction." *Camera Obscura* 20–21 (May–September 1989): 142–146.

———. "Technology's Body: Cinematic Vision in Modernity." *differences* 5:2 (1993): 1–23.

———. "Woman's Stake: Filming the Female Body." In *Feminism and Film Theory*. Ed. Constance Penley. New York: Routledge, 1988, 216–228.

Doriani, Beth Maclay. "Black Womanhood in Nineteenth-Century America: Subversion and Self-Construction in Two Women's Autobiographies." *American Quarterly* 43:2 (June 1991): 199–222.

Douglas, Ann. *The Feminization of American Culture*. New York: Knopf, 1977.

Douglass, Frederick. *Narrative of the Life of Frederick Douglass*. 1845. *The Classic Slave Narratives*. Ed. and intro. Henry Louis Gates, Jr. New York: New American Library, 1987.

———. "Why Is the Negro Lynched?" In *The Lesson of the Hour*, pamphlet, 1894. Reprint, Philip S. Foner, *The Life and Writings of Frederick Douglass*. Vol. 4. New York: International Publishers, 1955, 491–523.

Dow, Arthur W. "Mrs. Gertrude Kasebier's Portrait Photographs." *Camera Notes* 3:1 (July 1899): 22–23.

Doyle, Laura. *Bordering on the Body: The Racial Matrix of Modern Fiction and Culture*. New York: Oxford University Press, 1994.

Dreiser, Theodore. *Newspaper Days*. Ed. T. D. Nostwich. Philadelphia: University of Pennsylvania Press, 1991.

———. "Nigger Jeff." In *Free and Other Stories*. New York: Boni and Liveright, 1918, 76–111.

———. *Sister Carrie*. 1900. New York: New American Library, 1961.

Dreiser, Theodore. *Sister Carrie*. Ed. James W. West III, John C. Berkeley, and
    Alice M. Winters. Philadelphia: University of Pennsylvania Press, 1981.
Drinka, George Frederick. *The Birth of Neurosis: Myth, Malady, and the Victorians*.
    New York: Simon and Schuster, 1984.
Dryden, Edgar A. "Hawthorne's Castle in the Air: Form and Theme in *The House
    of the Seven Gables*." *English Literary History* 38:2 (1972): 294–317.
———. *Nathaniel Hawthorne: The Poetics of Enchantment*. Ithaca, N.Y.: Cornell Uni-
    versity Press, 1977.
Du Bois, W. E. B. "The American Negro at Paris." *American Monthly Review of
    Reviews* 22:5 (November 1900): 575–577.
———. "The Conservation of Races." 1897. In *A W. E. B. Du Bois Reader*. Ed.
    Andrew G. Paschal. Intro. Arna Bontemps. New York: Macmillan, 1971, 19–31.
———. *The Souls of Black Folk*. 1903. New York: Vintage, 1990.
———. "The Training of Negroes for Social Power." *Colored American Magazine*
    7:5 (May 1904): 333–339.
———, ed. *Notes on Negro Crime, Particularly in Georgia*. Atlanta University Publi-
    cations, No. 9. Atlanta: Atlanta University Press, 1904.
———, comp. *Types of American Negroes, Georgia, U.S.A.* Vols. 1–3. 1900. Daniel
    Murray Collection, Library of Congress.
———, comp. *Negro Life in Georgia, U.S.A.* 1900. Daniel Murray Collection, Li-
    brary of Congress.
duCille, Ann. *The Coupling Convention: Sex, Text, and Tradition in Black Women's
    Fiction*. New York: Oxford University Press, 1993.
Dyer, Richard. "White." *Screen* 29:4 (Autumn 1988): 44–64.
Earle, Edward W., ed. *Points of View: The Stereograph in America—A Cultural History*.
    New York: Visual Studies Workshop, 1979.
Eby, Clare Virginia. "The Psychology of Desire: Veblen's 'Pecuniary Emulation'
    and 'Invidious Comparison' in *Sister Carrie* and *An American Tragedy*." *Studies in
    American Fiction* 21:2 (Autumn 1993): 191–208.
Edel, Leon. *Henry James, The Master, 1901–1916*. Philadelphia: Lippincott, 1972.
Eisenstein, Elizabeth L. *The Printing Press as an Agent of Change*. Cambridge: Cam-
    bridge University Press, 1979.
Emerson, Ralph Waldo. "Self-Reliance." In *Ralph Waldo Emerson*. Ed. Richard
    Poirier. New York: Oxford University Press, 1990, 131–151.
Epstein, Barbara Leslie. *The Politics of Domesticity: Women, Evangelism, and Temper-
    ance in Nineteenth-Century America*. Middletown, Conn.: Wesleyan University
    Press, 1981.
Fern, Fanny. *Caper-Sauce*. New York: G. W. Carleton, 1872.
———. *Fern Leaves from Fanny's Portfolio*. 2d series. Auburn: Miller, Orton, and
    Mulligan, 1854.
———. *Folly as It Flies*. New York: G. W. Carleton, 1868.
———. *Ginger-Snaps*. New York: G. W. Carleton, 1870.
———. "How I Don't Like Pictures." *New York Ledger*, June 11, 1859.
———. *Ruth Hall and Other Writings*. Ed. Joyce W. Warren. New Brunswick, N.J.:
    Rutgers University Press, 1986.
———. "Taking Portraits." *New York Ledger*, September 22, 1860.
———. "Then and Now." *New York Ledger*, April 5, 1862.

Fields, Barbara J. "Ideology and Race in American History." In *Region, Race, and Reconstruction*. Ed. J. Morgan Kousser and James M. McPherson. New York: Oxford University Press, 1982, 143–178.

Fisher, Philip. *Hard Facts: Setting and Form in the American Novel*. New York: Oxford University Press, 1987.

Forrest, D. W. *Francis Galton: The Life and Work of a Victorian Genius*. New York: Taplinger, 1974.

Forsyth, Mary Isabella. "The Eligibility Question." *American Monthly Magazine* 3:5 (November 1893): 561–566.

———. "The Eligibility Question." *American Monthly Magazine* 3:6 (December 1893): 676–679.

Foster, Hal. *Recodings: Art, Spectacle, Cultural Politics*. Seattle: Bay Press, 1985.

Foucault, Michel. *Discipline and Punish: The Birth of the Prison*. Trans. Alan Sheridan. New York: Vintage, 1979.

———. *Foucault Live (Interviews, 1966–84)*. Trans. John Johnston. Ed. Sylvere Lotringer. New York: Semiotext(e), 1989.

———. *The History of Sexuality*. Vol. 1. Trans. Robert Hurley. New York: Vintage, 1980.

———. *Power/Knowledge: Selected Interviews and Other Writings, 1972–1977*. Ed. Colin Gordon. New York: Pantheon, 1980.

Fredrickson, George M. *The Black Image in the White Mind: The Debate on Afro-American Character and Destiny, 1817–1914*. New York: Harper and Row, 1971.

Fuguet, Dallett. "Portraiture as Art." *Camera Notes* 5:2 (October 1901): 3, 80–82.

Fuller, Margaret. *"These Sad but Glorious Days": Dispatches from Europe, 1846–1850*. Ed. Larry Reynolds and Susan Belasco Smith. New Haven, Conn.: Yale University Press, 1991.

Fusco, Coco. *English Is Broken Here: Notes on Cultural Fusion in the Americas*. New York: New Press, 1995.

Fuss, Diana. *Essentially Speaking: Feminism, Nature and Difference*. New York: Routledge, 1989.

Gaines, Jane M. *Contested Culture: The Image, the Voice, and the Law*. Chapel Hill: University of North Carolina Press, 1991.

———. "White Privilege and Looking Relations: Race and Gender in Feminist Film Theory." *Screen* 29:4 (Autumn 1988): 12–27.

Gaines, Kevin. "Black Americans' Racial Uplift Ideology as 'Civilizing Mission': Pauline E. Hopkins on Race and Imperialism." In *Cultures of United States Imperialism*. Ed. Amy Kaplan and Donald E. Pease. Durham, N.C.: Duke University Press, 1993, 433–455.

Gallagher, Susan Van Zanten. "A Domestic Reading of *The House of the Seven Gables*." *Studies in the Novel* 21:1 (Spring 1989): 1–13.

Galton, Francis. *Finger Prints*. 1892. Reprint, New York: Da Capo, 1965.

———. *Hereditary Genius: An Inquiry into Its Laws and Consequences*. London: Macmillan, 1892.

———. *Inquiries into Human Faculty and Its Development*. 2d ed. London: J. M. Dent and Sons, 1907.

———. *The Life History Album*. London: Macmillan, 1884.

———. *Memories of My Life*. London: Methuen, 1908.

Galton, Francis. *Natural Inheritance*. London: Macmillan, 1889.

———. *Record of Family Faculties*. London: Macmillan, 1884.

Gates, Henry Louis, Jr. *The Signifying Monkey: A Theory of African-American Literary Criticism*. New York: Oxford University Press, 1988.

———. "The Trope of a New Negro and the Reconstruction of the Image of the Black." *Representations* 24 (Fall 1988): 129–155.

Gelfant, Blanche H. "What More Can Carrie Want? Naturalistic Ways of Consuming Women." In *The Cambridge Companion to American Realism and Naturalism, Howells to London*. Ed. Donald Pizer. New York: Cambridge University Press, 1995, 178–210.

Giddings, Paula. *When and Where I Enter: The Impact of Black Women on Race and Sex in America*. New York: William Morrow, 1984.

Gillman, Susan. "The Mulatto, Tragic or Triumphant? The Nineteenth-Century American Race Melodrama." In *The Culture of Sentiment: Race, Gender, and Sentimentality in Nineteenth-Century America*. Ed. Shirley Samuels. New York: Oxford University Press, 1992, 221–243.

———. " 'Sure Identifiers': Race, Science, and the Law in Twain's *Puddn'head Wilson*." *South Atlantic Quarterly* 87:2 (Spring 1988): 195–218.

Gilman, Charlotte Perkins. "The Yellow Wall-Paper." 1892. In *The Heath Anthology of American Literature*. Vol. 2. 2d ed. Ed. Paul Lauter et al. Lexington, Mass.: D. C. Heath, 1994, 800–812.

Gilmore, Michael T. "The Artist and the Marketplace in *The House of the Seven Gables*." *English Literary History* 48:1 (Spring 1981): 172–189.

Gilroy, Paul. *The Black Atlantic: Modernity and Double Consciousness*. Cambridge: Harvard University Press, 1993.

Ginzberg, Lori D. " 'Moral Suasion Is Moral Balderdash': Women, Politics, and Social Activism in the 1850s." *Journal of American History* 73:3 (December 1986): 601–622.

———. *Women and the Work of Benevolence: Morality, Politics, and Class in the Nineteenth-Century United States*. New Haven, Conn.: Yale University Press, 1990.

Goddu, Teresa. "The Circulation of Women in *The House of the Seven Gables*." *Studies in the Novel* 23:1 (Spring 1991): 119–127.

Gover, C. Jane. *The Positive Image: Women Photographers in Turn of the Century America*. Albany: State University of New York Press, 1988.

Green, David. "Veins of Resemblance: Photography and Eugenics." In *Photography/Politics Two*. Ed. Patricia Holland, Jo Spence, and Simon Watney. London: Comedia Publishing Group, 1986, 9–21.

Green, Rayna. "The Pocahontas Perplex: The Image of Indian Women in American Culture." In *Unequal Sisters: A Multicultural Reader in U.S. Women's History*. Ed. Ellen Carol DuBois and Vicki L. Ruiz. New York: Routledge, 1990, 15–21.

Grewal, Inderpal. *Home and Harem: Nation, Gender, Empire, and the Cultures of Travel*. Durham, N.C.: Duke University Press, 1996.

Griffin, Susan M. *The Historical Eye: The Texture of the Visual in Late James*. Boston: Northeastern University Press, 1991.

Grimke, Angelina Emily. "Appeal to the Christian Women of the South." In *The Public Years of Sarah and Angelina Grimke*. Ed. Larry Ceplair. New York: Columbia University Press, 1989, 36–79.

Grover, Jan Zita. "AIDS: Keywords." In *AIDS: Cultural Analysis, Cultural Activism*. Ed. Douglas Crimp and Leo Bersani. 1st MIT Press ed. Cambridge: MIT Press, 1988, 17–30.

———. "Dykes in Context: Some Problems in Minority Representation." In *The Contest of Meaning: Critical Histories of Photography*. Ed. Richard Bolton. Cambridge: MIT Press, 1989, 145–161.

Guimond, James. *American Photography and the American Dream*. Chapel Hill: University of North Carolina Press, 1991.

Gutman, Judith Mara. *Lewis W. Hine and the American Social Conscience*. New York: Walker, 1967.

Hall, Jacquelyn Dowd. *Revolt against Chivalry: Jessie Daniel Ames and the Women's Campaign against Lynching*. Rev. ed. New York: Columbia University Press, 1993.

Haller, Mark. *Eugenics: Hereditarian Attitudes in American Thought*. New Brunswick, N.J.: Rutgers University Press, 1963.

Halttunen, Karen. *Confidence Men and Painted Women: A Study of Middle-Class Culture in America, 1830–1870*. New Haven, Conn.: Yale University Press, 1982.

Hansen, Olaf. "Frances Benjamin Johnston." In *Notable American Women: A Biographical Dictionary*. Vol. 4. Ed. Barbara Sicherman and Carol Hurd Green. Cambridge: Belknap Press of Harvard University Press, 1980, 381–383.

Haraway, Donna J. "A Manifesto for Cyborgs: Science, Technology, and Socialist Feminism in the 1980s." *Socialist Review* 80 (March/April 1985): 64–107.

———. *Modest_Witness@Second_Millennium.FemaleMan_Meets_OncoMouse: Feminism and Technoscience*. New York: Routledge, 1997.

———. *Primate Visions: Gender, Race, and Nature in the World of Modern Science*. New York: Routledge, 1989.

———. *Simians, Cyborgs, and Women: The Reinvention of Nature*. New York: Routledge, 1991.

Harper, Frances Ellen Watkins. *Iola Leroy, or Shadows Uplifted*. 2d ed. 1893. Reprint, with intro. by Frances Smith Foster, New York: Oxford University Press, 1988.

———. "Woman's Political Future." 1894. In *The Heath Anthology of American Literature*. Vol. 2. 2d ed. Ed. Paul Lauter et al. Lexington, Mass.: D. C. Heath, 1994, 1941–1944.

Harris, Susan K. "Inscribing and Defining: The Many Voices of Fanny Fern's *Ruth Hall*." *Style* 22:4 (Winter 1988): 613–627.

Harris, Trudier. *Exorcising Blackness: Historical and Literary Lynching and Burning Rituals*. Bloomington: Indiana University Press, 1984.

Hartmann, Sadakichi. "Portrait Painting and Portrait Photography." *Camera Notes* 3:1 (July 1899): 3–21.

Hasian, Marouf Arif, Jr. *The Rhetoric of Eugenics in Anglo-American Thought*. Athens: University of Georgia Press, 1996.

Hawthorne, Nathaniel. *The Blithedale Romance*. 1852. New York: Penguin, 1983.

———. *The House of the Seven Gables*. 1851. New York: Signet, 1981.

———. *The Scarlet Letter*. 1850. New York: Signet, 1981.

Herrnstein, Richard J., and Charles A. Murray. *The Bell Curve: Intelligence and Class Structure in American Life*. New York: Free Press, 1994.

Hobart, George. *Mathew Brady*. London: Macdonald, 1984.

Hobsbawm, Eric. "Mass-Producing Traditions: Europe, 1870–1914." In *The Invention of Tradition*. Ed. Eric Hobsbawm and Terence Ranger. Cambridge: Cambridge University Press, 1983, 263–307.

Hochman, Barbara. "A Portrait of the Artist as a Young Actress: The Rewards of Representation in *Sister Carrie*." In *New Essays on Sister Carrie*. Ed. Donald Pizer. New York: Cambridge University Press, 1991, 43–64.

Hoeber, Arthur. "A Portrait and a Likeness." *Camera Notes* 2:3 (January 1899): 74–76.

Hoff, Joan. *Law, Gender, and Injustice: A Legal History of U.S. Women*. New York: New York University Press, 1991.

Hoffman, Nicole Tonkovich. "Legacy Profile: Sarah Josepha Hale (1788–1874)." *Legacy: A Journal of American Women Writers* 7:2 (Fall 1990): 47–55.

Hofstadter, Richard. *Social Darwinism in American Thought*. Rev. ed. Boston: Beacon Press, 1944.

Holland, W. W. "Photography for Our Young People." *Colored American Magazine* 5:1 (May 1902): 5–9.

hooks, bell. *Ain't I a Woman: Black Women and Feminism*. Boston: South End Press, 1981.

———. "In Our Glory: Photography and Black Life." In *Picturing Us: African American Identity in Photography*. Ed. Deborah Willis. New York: New Press, 1994, 42–53.

———. "The Oppositional Gaze: Black Female Spectators." In *Black Looks: Race and Representation*. Boston: South End Press, 1992, 115–131.

———. "Representations of Whiteness in the Black Imagination." In *Black Looks: Race and Representation*. Boston: South End Press, 1992, 165–178.

Hopkins, Pauline. "Famous Men of the Negro Race: Booker T. Washington." *Colored American Magazine* 3:6 (October 1901): 436–441.

———. *Hagar's Daughter: A Story of Southern Caste Prejudice*. 1901–1902. In *The Magazine Novels of Pauline Hopkins*. Intro. Hazel V. Carby. New York: Oxford University Press, 1988, 1–284.

———. *Of One Blood: Or, the Hidden Self*. 1902–1903. In *The Magazine Novels of Pauline Hopkins*. Intro. Hazel V. Carby. New York: Oxford University Press, 1988, 439–621.

Horan, James D. *Mathew Brady: Historian with a Camera*. New York: Crown, 1955.

Horsman, Reginald. *Josiah Nott of Mobile: Southerner, Physician, and Racial Theorist*. Baton Rouge: Louisiana State University Press, 1987.

———. *Race and Manifest Destiny: The Origins of American Racial Anglo-Saxonism*. Cambridge: Harvard University Press, 1981.

Howard, June. *Form and History in American Literary Naturalism*. Chapel Hill: University of North Carolina Press, 1985.

Howe, Daniel Walker. "American Victorianism as a Culture." *American Quarterly* 27:5 (December 1975): 507–532.

Hunter, M. F. "The Alabama Conference." *Colored American Magazine* 1:2 (June 1900): 104–108.

Hussman, Lawrence E., Jr. "The Fate of the Fallen Woman in *Maggie* and *Sister Carrie*." In *The Image of the Prostitute in Modern Literature*. Ed. Pierre L. Horn and Mary Beth Pringle. New York: Frederick Ungar, 1984, 91–100.

Hutner, Gordon. *Secrets and Sympathy: Forms of Disclosure in Hawthorne's Novels.* Athens: University of Georgia Press, 1988.

Irigaray, Luce. *This Sex Which Is Not One.* Trans. Catherine Porter. Ithaca, N.Y.: Cornell University Press, 1985.

Jacobs, Harriet Ann. *Incidents in the Life of a Slave Girl.* 1861. Ed. Jean Fagan Yellin. Cambridge: Harvard University Press, 1987.

James, Henry. "The Real Thing." In *Daisy Miller and Other Stories.* Ed. Michael Swan. New York: Penguin, 1983, 43–69.

James, William. "The Hidden Self." In *Essays in Psychology.* Ed. Frederick H. Burkhardt. Cambridge: Harvard University Press, 1983, 247–268.

Jay, Martin. *Downcast Eyes: The Denigration of Vision in Twentieth-Century French Thought.* Berkeley: University of California Press, 1993.

———. "Scopic Regimes of Modernity." In *Vision and Visuality.* Ed. Hal Foster. Seattle: Bay Press, 1988.

Johnson, Abby Arthur, and Ronald Mayberry Johnson. *Propaganda and Aesthetics: The Literary Politics of Afro-American Magazines in the Twentieth Century.* Amherst: University of Massachusetts Press, 1979.

Johnston, Frances Benjamin. *The Hampton Album.* Ed. Lincoln Kirstein. New York: Museum of Modern Art, 1966.

———. "The New Tenants of the White House." *Ladies' Home Journal*, October 1897, 3.

———. "What a Woman Can Do with a Camera." *Ladies' Home Journal*, September 1897 6–7.

Julien, Isaac, and Kobena Mercer. "Introduction: De Margin and De Centre." *Screen* 29:4 (Autumn 1988): 2–10.

Kamuf, Peggy. *Signature Pieces: On the Institution of Authorship.* Ithaca, N.Y.: Cornell University Press, 1988.

Kaplan, Amy. *The Social Construction of American Realism.* Chicago: University of Chicago Press, 1988.

Kassanoff, Jennie A. " 'Fate Has Linked Us Together': Blood, Gender, and the Politics of Representation in Pauline Hopkins's *Of One Blood.*" In *The Unruly Voice: Rediscovering Pauline Elizabeth Hopkins.* Ed. John Cullen Gruesser. Urbana: University of Illinois Press, 1996, 158–181.

Kelley, Mary. *Private Woman, Public Stage: Literary Domesticity in Nineteenth-Century America.* New York: Oxford University Press, 1984.

Kerber, Linda K. "Separate Spheres, Female Worlds, Woman's Place: The Rhetoric of Women's History." *Journal of American History* 75 (June 1988): 9–39.

———. *Women of the Republic: Intellect and Ideology in Revolutionary America.* Chapel Hill: University of North Carolina Press, 1980.

Kerber, Linda K., and Nancy F. Cott, Robert Gross, Lynn Hunt, Carroll Smith-Rosenberg, and Christine M. Stansell. Forum: "Beyond Roles, beyond Spheres: Thinking about Gender in the Early Republic." *William and Mary Quarterly* 46 (1989): 565–585.

Kevles, Daniel J. "Annals of Eugenics, A Secular Faith—II." *New Yorker*, October 15, 1984, 52–125.

———. *In the Name of Eugenics: Genetics and the Uses of Human Heredity.* New York: Knopf, 1985.

Kirstein, Lincoln, ed. *The Hampton Album.* By Frances Benjamin Johnston. New York: Museum of Modern Art, 1966.

"Kodaks." *Ladies' Home Journal*, December 1897, 21.

Krasner, James. *The Entangled Eye: Visual Perception and the Representation of Nature in Post-Darwinian Narrative.* New York: Oxford University Press, 1992.

Krauss, Rosalind E. *The Originality of the Avant-Garde and Other Modernist Myths.* Cambridge: MIT Press, 1985.

Lacan, Jacques. "The Mirror Stage as Formative of the Function of the I." In *Ecrits: A Selection.* Trans. Alan Sheridan. New York: Norton, 1977, 1–7.

Lancaster, Bill. *The Department Store: A Social History.* New York: Leicester University Press, 1995.

Leach, William. *Land of Desire: Merchants, Power, and the Rise of a New American Culture.* New York: Pantheon, 1993.

Lehan, Richard. "*Sister Carrie*: The City, the Self, and the Modes of Narrative Discourse." In *New Essays on Sister Carrie.* Ed. Donald Pizer. Cambridge: Cambridge University Press, 199, 65–86.

Lewis, Morris. "Paris and the International Exposition." *Colored American Magazine* 1:5 (October 1900): 295.

Lingwood, James. "Self-Portraits Staging-Posts." In *Identity: Documents 6.* London: Institute of Contemporary Arts, 1987, 20–22.

Lombroso, Cesare, and William Ferrero. *The Female Offender.* New York: D. Appleton, 1899.

Lombroso, Cesare, and Gina Lombroso-Ferrero. *Criminal Man.* 1876. Trans. Gina Lombroso-Ferrero. Intro. Cesare Lombroso, 1911. Reprint, intro. Leonard Savitz. Montclair, N.J.: Paterson Smith, 1972.

Lott, Eric. *Love and Theft: Blackface Minstrelsy and the American Working Class.* New York: Oxford University Press, 1993.

———. "Love and Theft: The Racial Unconscious of Blackface Minstrelsy." *Representations* 39 (Summer 1992): 23–50.

Ludmerer, Kenneth M. *Genetics and American Society: A Historical Appraisal.* Baltimore, Md.: Johns Hopkins University Press, 1972.

Lukacs, George. *History and Class Consciousness: Studies in Marxist Dialectics.* Trans. Rodney Livingstone. Cambridge: MIT Press, 1971.

Macpherson, C. B. *The Political Theory of Possessive Individualism, Hobbes to Locke.* London: Oxford University Press, 1962.

"The Magnetic Daguerreotypes." *Photographic Art-Journal*, June 1852, 353–359.

Martin, Rosy. "Dirty Linen: Photo Therapy, Memory and Identity." *Ten 8* 2:1 (Spring 1991): 34–49.

Martin, Rosy, and Jo Spence. "Photo-therapy: Psychic Realism as a Healing Art?" *Ten 8* 30 (Autumn 1988): 2–17.

Marx, Karl. *The Marx-Engels Reader.* 2d ed. Ed. Robert C. Tucker. New York: Norton, 1978.

Marzolf, Marion. *Up from the Footnote: A History of Women Journalists.* New York: Hastings House, 1977.

Mavor, Carol. *Pleasures Taken: Performances of Sexuality and Loss in Victorian Photographs.* Durham, N.C.: Duke University Press, 1995.

McCall, Laura. " 'The Reign of Brute Force Is Now Over': A Content Analysis of *Godey's Lady's Book*, 1830–1860." *Journal of the Early Republic* 9 (Summer 1989): 217–236.

McCandless, Barbara. "The Portrait Studio and the Celebrity: Promoting the Art." In *Photography in Nineteenth-Century America*. Ed. Martha A. Sandweiss. Fort Worth, Tex.: Amon Carter Museum, 1991, 48–75.

McCurry, Stephanie. "The Two Faces of Republicanism: Gender and Proslavery Politics in Antebellum South Carolina." *Journal of American History* 78:4 (March 1992): 1245–1264.

McNamara, Kevin R. "The Ames of the Good Society: *Sister Carrie* and Social Engineering." *Criticism* 34:2 (Spring 1992): 217–235.

Merck, Mandy. " 'Transforming the Suit': A Century of Lesbian Self-Portraits." In *Stolen Glances: Lesbians Take Photographs*. Ed. Tessa Boffin and Jean Fraser. London: Pandora, 1991, 22–29.

Meredith, Roy. *Mr. Lincoln's Camera Man, Mathew Brady*. New York: Charles Scribner's Sons, 1946.

———. *The World of Mathew Brady: Portraits of the Civil War Period*. Los Angeles: Brooke House, 1976.

Mesmer, F. A. *Mesmerism*. Trans. George Bloch. Los Altos, Calif.: William Kauffman, 1980.

Michaels, Walter Benn. *The Gold Standard and the Logic of Naturalism: American Literature at the Turn of the Century*. Berkeley: University of California Press, 1987.

———. "Race into Culture: A Critical Genealogy of Cultural Identity." *Critical Inquiry* 18:4 (Summer 1992): 655–685.

———. "Romance and Real Estate." In *The American Renaissance Reconsidered*. Ed. Walter Benn Michaels and Donald E. Pease. Baltimore, Md.: Johns Hopkins University Press, 1985, 156–182.

Miller, D. A. *The Novel and the Police*. Berkeley: University of California Press, 1988.

Miller, Michael B. *The Bon Marche: Bourgeois Culture and the Department Store, 1869–1920*. Princeton, N.J.: Princeton University Press, 1981.

Minh-ha, Trinh T. *Woman, Native, Other: Writing Postcoloniality and Feminism*. Bloomington: Indiana University Press, 1989.

Mitchell, Timothy. *Colonizing Egypt*. Berkeley: University of California Press, 1988.

Mizruchi, Susan L. *The Power of Historical Knowledge: Narrating the Past in Hawthorne, James, and Dreiser*. Princeton, N.J.: Princeton University Press, 1988.

Morris, Meaghan. "Things to Do with Shopping Centres." In *Grafts: Feminist Cultural Criticism*. Ed. Susan Sheridan. New York: Verso, 1988, 193–225.

Mouffe, Chantal. "Citizenship and Political Identity." *October* 61 (Summer 1992): 28–32.

Moutoussamy-Ashe, Jeanne. *Viewfinders: Black Women Photographers*. New York: Dodd, Mead, 1986.

Mulvey, Laura. "Afterthoughts on 'Visual Pleasure and Narrative Cinema' Inspired by *Duel in the Sun*." In *Feminism and Film Theory*. Ed. Constance Penley. New York: Routledge, 1988, 69–79.

———. "Visual Pleasure and Narrative Cinema." In *Art after Modernism*. Ed. Brian Wallis. New York: Museum of Contemporary Art, 1984, 360–374.

Murray, William M. "Mr. W. M. Hollinger on Photographic Portraiture." *Camera Notes* 2:4 (April 1899): 160–161.

———. "Too Well Done!" *Camera Notes* 2:2 (October 1898): 92–94.

National Child Welfare Association. *The Baby Book*. New York: National Child Welfare Association, 1916.

National Society of the Daughters of the American Revolution. *Proceedings of the Second Continental Congress*. February 1893.

———. *Proceedings of the Third Continental Congress*. 1894.

"The Negro Problem and the New Negro Crime." *Harper's Weekly*, June 20, 1903, 1050–1051.

Newhall, Beaumont. *The History of Photography*. New York: Museum of Modern Art, 1982.

Nicholson, Linda J., ed. *Feminism/Postmodernism*. New York: Routledge, 1990.

Nott, Josiah C. *Two Lectures on the Connection between the Biblical and Physical History of Man*. 1849. Reprint, New York: Negro Universities Press, 1969.

Nott, Josiah C., and George R. Gliddon. *Types of Mankind*. Philadelphia: Lippincott, Grambo and Company, 1854.

Ohmann, Richard. "Reading and Writing, Work and Leisure." In *Only Connect: Uniting Reading and Writing*. Upper Montclair, N.J.: Boynton-Cook, 1986, 11–26.

Orvell, Miles. *The Real Thing: Imitation and Authenticity in American Culture, 1880–1940*. Chapel Hill: University of North Carolina Press, 1989.

———. "Reproduction and 'The Real Thing': The Anxiety of Realism in the Age of Photography." In *The Technological Imagination: Theories and Fictions*. Ed. Teresa de Lauretis, Andreas Huyssen, and Kathleen Woodward. Madison, Wis.: Coda, 1980, 49–64.

Otten, Thomas J. "Pauline Hopkins and the Hidden Self of Race." *English Literary History* 59:1 (Spring 1992): 227–256.

Owens, Craig. "The Discourse of Others: Feminists and Postmodernism." In *The Anti-Aesthetic: Essays on Postmodern Culture*. Ed. Hal Foster. Port Townsend, Wash.: Bay Press, 1983, 57–82.

Palmer, Marion van Riper. "The Women's Patriotic Societies." *Ladies' Home Journal*, July 1897, 10.

Palmquist, Peter E., ed. *Camera Fiends and Kodak Girls: Fifty Selections by and about Women in Photography, 1840–1930*. New York: Midmarch, 1989.

———. *Directory of California Women Photographers before 1910*. Arcata, Calif.: Palmquist, 1990.

Pearson, Karl. *The Life, Letters, and Labours of Francis Galton*. Cambridge: Cambridge University Press, 1924.

Pease, Donald E. *Visionary Compacts: American Renaissance Writings in Cultural Context*. Madison: University of Wisconsin Press, 1987.

Peiss, Kathy. " 'Charity Girls' and City Pleasures: Historical Notes on Working-Class Sexuality, 1880–1920." In *Unequal Sisters: A Multicultural Reader in U.S. Women's History*. Ed. Ellen Carol DuBois and Vicki L. Ruiz. New York: Routledge, 1990, 157–166.

Peiss, Kathy. *Cheap Amusements: Working Women and Leisure in Turn-of-the-Century New York*. Philadelphia: Temple University Press, 1986.

Pickens, Donald K. *Eugenics and the Progressives*. Nashville, Tenn.: Vanderbilt University Press, 1968.

Pizer, Donald. *The Novels of Theodore Dreiser: A Critical Study*. Minneapolis: University of Minnesota Press, 1976.

———. *Realism and Naturalism in Nineteenth-Century American Literature*. Rev. ed. Carbondale: Southern Illinois University Press, 1984.

———. "Self-Censorship and Textual Editing." In *Textual Criticism and Literary Interpretation*. Ed. Jerome J. McGann. Chicago: University of Chicago Press, 1985.

Poole, Deborah. *Vision, Race, and Modernity: A Visual Economy of the Andean Image World*. Princeton, N.J.: Princeton University Press, 1997.

Porter, Carolyn. *Seeing and Being: The Plight of the Participant Observer in Emerson, James, Adams, and Faulkner*. Middletown, Conn.: Wesleyan University Press, 1981.

Porter, Isaac, Jr. "Photographing Children at Home." *Ladies' Home Journal*, December 1898, 35.

Pratt, Mary Louise. *Imperial Eyes: Travel Writing and Transculturation*. New York: Routledge, 1992.

Pumpelly, J. Collins. "Eligibility." *American Monthly Magazine* 2:2 (February 1893): 234–236.

Rabinovitz, Lauren. "Temptations of Pleasure: Nickelodeons, Amusement Parks, and the Sights of Female Sexuality." *Camera Obscura* 23 (May 1990): 70–89.

Rafael, Vicente L. "Nationalism, Imagery and the Filipino Intelligentsia in the Nineteenth Century." *Critical Inquiry* 16:3 (Spring 1990): 591–611.

———. "White Love: Surveillance and Nationalist Resistance in the U.S. Colonization of the Philippines." In *Cultures of United States Imperialism*. Ed. Amy Kaplan and Donald Pease. Durham, N.C.: Duke University Press, 1993, 185–218.

Rafter, Nicole Hahn, ed. and intro. *White Trash: The Eugenic Family Studies, 1877–1919*. Boston: Northeastern University Press, 1988.

Reilly, Philip R. *The Surgical Solution: A History of Involuntary Sterilization in the United States*. Baltimore, Md.: Johns Hopkins University Press, 1991.

Report of the Board of Commissioners Representing the State of New York at the Cotton States and International Exposition Held at Atlanta, Georgia, 1895. Albany, N.Y.: Wynkoop Hallenbeck Crawford, 1896.

R.H.E. "My Photograph." *Godey's Lady's Book*, April 1867, 341–345.

Riis, Jacob. *How the Other Half Lives*. 1890. Reprint, New York: Dover, 1971.

Rogin, Michael. *Blackface, White Noise: Jewish Immigrants in the Hollywood Melting Pot*. Berkeley: University of California Press, 1996.

Rollins, Judith. *Between Women: Domestics and Their Employers*. Philadelphia: Temple University Press, 1985.

Rony, Fatimah Tobing. *The Third Eye: Race, Cinema, and Ethnographic Spectacle*. Durham, N.C.: Duke University Press, 1996.

———. "Those Who Squat and Those Who Sit: The Iconography of Race in the 1895 Films of Felix-Louis Regnault." *Camera Obscura* 28 (January 1992): 262–289.

Rosenberg, Rosalind. *Beyond Separate Spheres: Intellectual Roots of Modern Feminism.* New Haven, Conn.: Yale University Press, 1982.

Rosenblum, Naomi. "Women in Photography: An Historical Overview." *Exposure* 24:4 (Winter 1986): 6–26.

———. *A World History of Photography.* New York: Abbeville Press, 1989.

Rosler, Martha. "in, around, and afterthoughts (on documentary photography)." In *Martha Rosler, 3 works.* Halifax: Nova Scotia College of Art and Design, 1981.

———. "Lookers, Buyers, Dealers, and Makers: Thoughts on Audience." In *Art after Modernism.* Ed. Brian Wallis. New York: New Museum of Contemporary Art, 1984, 311–339.

Ross, Ishbel. *Ladies of the Press: The Story of Women in Journalism by an Insider.* New York: Harper and Brothers, 1936.

Rowe, John Carlos. *Through the Custom-House: Nineteenth-Century American Fiction and Modern Theory.* Baltimore, Md.: Johns Hopkins University Press, 1982.

Rubin, Gayle. "The Traffic in Women: Notes on the 'Political Economy of Sex.' " In *Toward an Anthropology of Women.* Ed. Rayna Reiter. New York: Monthly Review Press, 1975, 157–210.

Russett, Cynthia Eagle. *Sexual Science: The Victorian Construction of Womanhood.* Cambridge: Harvard University Press, 1989.

Ryan, Mary P. *Cradle of the Middle Class: The Family in Oneida County, New York, 1790–1865.* Cambridge: Cambridge University Press, 1981.

Rydell, Robert W. *All the World's a Fair: Visions of Empire at American International Expositions, 1876–1916.* Chicago: University of Chicago Press, 1984.

Sanchez-Eppler, Karen. "Bodily Bonds: The Intersecting Rhetorics of Feminism and Abolition." *Representations* 24 (Fall 1988): 28–59.

Saxton, Alexander. *The Rise and Fall of the White Republic: Class Politics and Mass Culture in Nineteenth-Century America.* London: Verso, 1990.

Schlereth, Thomas J. "The Material Universe of the American World Expositions, 1876–1915." In *Cultural History and Material Culture: Everyday Life, Landscapes, Museums.* Ann Arbor: University of Michigan Press, 1990, 264–299.

Schor, Naomi. "*Cartes Postales*: Representing Paris 1900." *Critical Inquiry* 18:2 (Winter 1992): 188–244.

Schrager, Cynthia D. "Pauline Hopkins and William James: The New Psychology and the Politics of Race." In *Female Subjects in Black and White: Race, Psychoanalysis, Feminism.* Ed. Elizabeth Abel, Barbara Christian, and Helene Moglen. Berkeley: University of California Press, 1997, 307–329.

Schudson, Michael. *Discovering the News: A Social History of American Newspapers.* New York: Basic Books, 1978.

Scott, Joan. *Gender and the Politics of History.* New York: Columbia University Press, 1988.

———. "Multiculturalism and the Politics of Identity." *October* 61 (Summer 1992): 12–19.

Seaman, L. *What Miscegenation Is! And What We Are to Expect Now That Mr. Lincoln Is Re-elected.* New York: Waller and Willetts, 1864.

Sekula, Allan. "The Body and the Archive." *October* 39 (Winter 1986): 3–64.

———. "On the Invention of Photographic Meaning." In *Thinking Photography.* Ed. Victor Burgin. London: Macmillan, 1982, 84–109.

———. *Photography against the Grain: Essays and Photo Works, 1973–1983*. Halifax: Nova Scotia College of Art and Design, 1984.

Selzer, Mark. *Bodies and Machines*. New York: Routledge, 1992.

Shevelow, Kathryn. *Women and Print Culture: The Construction of Femininity in the Early Periodical*. New York: Routledge, 1989.

Silverman, Kaja. *The Threshold of the Visible World*. New York: Routledge, 1996.

Sklar, Kathryn Kish. *Catherine Beecher: A Study in American Domesticity*. New York: Norton, 1976.

Smith-Rosenberg, Carroll. *Disorderly Conduct: Visions of Gender in Victorian America*. New York: Oxford University Press, 1985.

Sobchack, Vivian. *The Address of the Eye: A Phenomenology of Film Experience*. Princeton, N.J.: Princeton University Press, 1992.

Sollors, Werner. "Ethnicity." In *Critical Terms for Literary Study*. Ed. Frank Lentricchia and Thomas McLaughlin. Chicago: University of Chicago Press, 1990, 288–305.

Solomon-Godeau, Abigail. "The Legs of the Countess." *October* 39 (Winter 1986): 65–105.

———. "Photography after Art Photography." In *Art after Modernism*. Ed. Brian Wallis. New York: New Museum of Contemporary Art, 1984, 75–85.

Spence, Jo. *Putting Myself in the Picture: A Political, Personal and Photographic Autobiography*. Seattle: Real Comet, 1988.

Spillers, Hortense J. "Notes on an Alternative Model—Neither/Nor." In *The Difference Within: Feminism and Critical Theory*. Ed. Elizabeth Meese and Alice Parker. Philadelphia: John Benjamin, 1989, 165–187.

Stansell, Christine. *City of Women: Sex and Class in New York, 1789–1860*. Urbana: University of Illinois Press, 1987.

Stanton, Elizabeth Cady, Susan B. Anthony, and Matilda Joslyn Gage, eds. *History of Woman Suffrage*. Vol. 1. 2d ed. 1889. New York: Source Book, 1970.

Stein, Sally. "The Graphic Ordering of Desire: Modernization of a Middle-Class Women's Magazine, 1919–1939." In *The Contest of Meaning: Critical Histories of Photography*. Ed. Richard Bolton. Cambridge: MIT Press, 1989, 145–161.

———. "Making Connections with the Camera: Photography and Social Mobility in the Career of Jacob Riis." *Afterimage* 10:10 (May 1983): 9–16.

Stepan, Nancy Leys, and Sander L. Gilman. "Appropriating the Idioms of Science: The Rejection of Scientific Racism." In *The Bounds of Race: Perspectives on Hegemony and Resistance*. Ed. and intro. Dominick LaCapra. Ithaca, N.Y.: Cornell University Press, 1991, 72–103.

Stokes, Philip. "The Family Photograph Album: So Great a Cloud of Witnesses." In *The Portrait in Photography*. Ed. Graham Clarke. London: Reaktion, 1992, 193–205.

Stowe, Harriet Beecher. *Uncle Tom's Cabin*. 1852. Ed. Ann Douglas. New York: Penguin, 1981.

Strayer, Martha. *The D.A.R.: An Informal History*. Washington, D.C.: Public Affairs Press, 1958.

Sundquist, Eric J. *Home as Found: Authority and Genealogy in Nineteenth-Century American Literature*. Baltimore, Md.: Johns Hopkins University Press, 1979.

Sundquist, Eric J. *To Wake the Nations: Race in the Making of American Literature*. Cambridge: Belknap Press of Harvard University Press, 1993.

Taft, Robert. *Photography and the American Scene*. New York: Dover, 1989.

Tagg, John. *The Burden of Representation: Essays on Photographies and Histories*. Amherst: University of Massachusetts Press, 1988.

———. "The Currency of the Photograph." In *Thinking Photography*. Ed. Victor Burgin. London: Macmillan, 1982, 110–141.

Tartar, Maria M. *Spellbound: Studies on Mesmerism and Literature*. Princeton, N.J.: Princeton University Press, 1978.

Tate, Claudia. *Domestic Allegories of Political Desire: The Black Heroine's Text at the Turn of the Century*. New York: Oxford University Press, 1992.

Terrell, Mary Church. *A Colored Woman in a White World*. Washington, D.C.: Ransdell, 1940.

Thomas, Brook. "*The House of the Seven Gables*: Reading the Romance of America." *PMLA* 97:2 (March 1982): 195–211.

Thoreau, Henry David. "Civil Disobedience." In *Walden and Civil Disobedience*. Ed. Owen Thomas. New York: Norton, 1966.

Time 142:21. Special Issue, Fall 1993.

Tompkins, Jane. *Sensational Designs: The Cultural Work of American Fiction, 1790–1860*. New York: Oxford University Press, 1984.

Trachtenberg, Alan. *The Incorporation of America: Culture and Society in the Gilded Age*. New York: Hill and Wang, 1982.

———. "Likeness as Identity: Reflections on the Daguerrean Mystique." In *The Portrait in Photography*. Ed. Graham Clarke. London: Reaktion, 1992, 173–192.

———. *Reading American Photographs: Images as History, Mathew Brady to Walker Evans*. New York: Hill and Wang, 1989.

———. "Who Narrates? Dreiser's Presence in *Sister Carrie*." In *New Essays on Sister Carrie*. Ed. Donald Pizer. Cambridge: Cambridge University Press, 1991, 87–122.

Trennert, Robert A. "Educating Indian Girls at Nonreservation Boarding Schools, 1878–1920." In *Unequal Sisters: A Multicultural Reader in U.S. Women's History*. Ed. Ellen Carol DuBois and Vicki L. Ruiz. New York: Routledge, 1990, 224–237.

Troth, Henry. "Amateur Photography at Its Best"—"First Article." *Ladies' Home Journal*, January 1897, 17.

———. "Fourth Article." *Ladies' Home Journal*, April 1897, 19.

———. "Second Article." *Ladies' Home Journal*, February 1897, 17.

———. "Third Article." *Ladies' Home Journal*, March 1897, 17.

Tucker, William H. *The Science and Politics of Racial Research*. Urbana: University of Illinois Press, 1994.

Twain, Mark. *Puddn'head Wilson*. 1894. New York: Bantam Classics, 1984.

Valverde, Mariana. "The Love of Finery: Fashion and the Fallen Woman in Nineteenth-Century Social Discourse." *Victorian Studies* 32:2 (Winter 1989): 169–188.

Veblen, Thorstein. *The Theory of the Leisure Class: An Economic Study of Institutions*. 1899. Reprint, New York: Modern Library, 1931.

Vieilledent, Catherine. "Representation and Reproduction: A Reading of Henry James's 'The Real Thing.' " In *Interface: Essays on History, Myth, and Art in American Literature*. Ed. Daniel Royot. Montpellier: Publications de la Recherche, Université Paul Valéry, 1985, 31–49.

Wald, Priscilla. *Constituting Americans: Cultural Anxiety and Narrative Form*. Durham, N.C.: Duke University Press, 1995.

Walker, Christian. "Gazing Colored: A Family Album." In *Picturing Us: African American Identity in Photography*. Ed. Deborah Willis. New York: New Press, 1994, 64–70.

Ware, Vron. *Beyond the Pale: White Women, Racism, and History*. London: Verso, 1992.

Washburne, Marion Foster. "A New Profession for Women: Photography and the Success Which Follows Earnest Endeavor and Diligent Work." *Godey's Lady's Book*, February 1897, 123–128.

Washington, Booker T. "Industrial Education: Will It Solve the Negro Problem?" *Colored American Magazine* 7:2 (February 1904): 87–92.

———. "The Storm before the Calm." *Colored American Magazine* 1:4 (September 1900): 3, 200–213.

———. *The Successful Training of the Negro*. New York: Doubleday, 1903.

———. *Up from Slavery*. 1901. Reprint, with intro. and notes by Louis Harlan. New York: Penguin, 1986.

Washington, Miss Eugenia. "History of the Organization of the Society of the Daughters of the American Revolution." Atlanta Exposition. October 18, 1895.

Waterbury, Reverend J. B., D.D. *Friendly Counsels for Freedmen*. New York: American Tract Society, 1864.

Weems, Carrie Mae. *Carrie Mae Weems*. Catalogue. Washington, D.C.: National Museum of Women in Arts, 1993.

Wells, Ida B. *Crusade for Justice: The Autobiography of Ida B. Wells*. Ed. Alfreda M. Duster. Chicago: University of Chicago Press, 1970.

———. *The Reason Why the Colored American Is Not in the World's Columbian Exposition*. 1893. In *Selected Works of Ida B. Wells-Barnett*. Intro. Trudier Harris. New York: Oxford, University Press, 1991, 46–137.

———. *A Red Record*. 1895. In *Selected Works of Ida B. Wells-Barnett*. Intro. Trudier Harris. New York: Oxford University Press, 1991, 138–252.

———. *Southern Horrors: Lynch Law in All Its Phases*. 1892. In *Selected Works of Ida B. Wells-Barnett*. Intro. Trudier Harris. New York: Oxford University Press, 1991, 14–45.

Welter, Barbara. *Dimity Convictions: The American Woman in the Nineteenth Century*. Athens: Ohio University Press, 1976.

Wexler, Laura. "Black and White and Color: American Photographs at the Turn of the Century." *Prospects* 13 (Winter 1988): 341–390.

———. "Seeing Sentiment: Photography, Race, and the Innocent Eye." In *Female Subjects in Black and White: Race, Psychoanalysis, Feminism*. Ed. Elizabeth Abel, Barbara Christian, and Helene Moglen. Berkeley: University of California Press, 1997, 159–186.

———. "Tender Violence: Literary Eavesdropping, Domestic Fiction, and Educational Reform." In *The Culture of Sentiment: Race, Gender, and Sentimentality in*

Nineteenth-Century America. Ed. Shirley Samuels. New York: Oxford University Press, 1992, 9–38.

Wiegman, Robyn. *American Anatomies: Theorizing Race and Gender*. Durham, N.C.: Duke University Press, 1995.

Wiggam, Albert Edward. *The Fruit of the Family Tree*. London: T. Werner Laurie, 1924.

Williams, Raymond. "Individual." In *Keywords: A Vocabulary of Culture and Society*. New York: Oxford University Press, 1983, 161–165.

Williams, Rosalind H. *Dream Worlds: Mass Consumption in Late Nineteenth-Century France*. Berkeley: University of California Press, 1982.

Willis, Deborah. "Introduction: Picturing Us." *Picturing Us: African American Identity in Photography*. Ed. Deborah Willis. New York: New Press, 1994, 3–26.

Wolff, Janet. *Feminine Sentences: Essays on Women and Culture*. Cambridge: Polity, 1990.

Wood, Ann D. " 'The Scribbling Women' and Fanny Fern: Why Women Wrote." *American Quarterly* 23 (1971): 3–14.

"Working with the Hands." *Colored American Magazine* 7:6 (June 1904).

Young, Robert J. C. *Colonial Desire: Hybridity in Theory, Culture, and Race*. New York: Routledge, 1995.